**2 Litchfield Road
Londonderry, NH 03053**
Meetinghouseofnhdems@gmail.com

THE CHALLENGE OF RESTRUCTURING

In the series LABOR AND SOCIAL CHANGE

edited by Paula Rayman and Carmen Sirianni

The Challenge of Restructuring

NORTH AMERICAN LABOR MOVEMENTS RESPOND

Edited by

Jane Jenson and Rianne Mahon

Temple University Press

 Philadelphia

Temple University Press, Philadelphia 19122
Copyright © 1993 by Temple University. All rights reserved
Published 1993
Printed in the United States of America

LIBRARY OF CONGRESS CATALOGING-IN-PUBLICATION DATA
The Challenge of restructuring : North American labor movements
    respond / edited by Jane Jenson and Rianne Mahon.
        p.   cm. — (Labor and social change)
    Includes bibliographical references.
    ISBN 0-87722-981-3 (cloth : alk. paper)
    1. Trade-unions—United States.   2. Trade-unions—Canada.
3. Industrial relations—United States.   4. Industrial relations—
Canada.   5. Corporate reorganizations—United States.   6. Corporate
reorganizations—Canada.   I. Jenson, Jane.   II. Mahon, Rianne,
1948–   .   III. Series.
HD6508.C39   1993
331.88'0973—dc20   92-20464

Contents

Acknowledgments

This book began at a conference called "North American Labour Movements into the 1990s: Similarities or Differences," which took place at the Center for International Affairs (CFIA), Harvard University, in February 1989. Support for the conference was generously provided by a grant from the Canadian Embassy in Washington as part of its Canadian Studies Program. Funds and other support also came from the CFIA and the William Lyon Mackenzie King Chair in Canadian Studies. Jean Shildneck worked on the details of conference organisation in her well-known professional fashion.

We want to take this opportunity to express our thanks to the Canadian Embassy and the CFIA for making the original project possible and to Jean for making it happen. We also thank all the conference participants for the knowledge and help they contributed to the final volume.

The production of the book manuscript was supported by the Department of Political Science, Carleton University. We wish especially to thank Valerie Pereboom for her efforts in getting the chapters into shape.

Introduction

JANE JENSON AND RIANNE MAHON

North American Labour:
Divergent Trajectories

For more than a decade, the labour movements in all Western countries have been forced to grapple with the challenges posed by economic restructuring. In the United States the issues raised by the secular decline of the goods-producing sector (long a union stronghold), the changing composition of the workforce, and management's pursuit of antiunion strategies confront a labour movement that can claim to speak for less than one-fifth of the nonagricultural workforce. In this context, defence of the status quo is clearly not an option: the unions must improve their position if they are to survive.

The search for a strategy to revitalize U.S. unions has led to a renewed interest in comparative analysis. People have begun to seek lessons for the U.S. labour movement in those countries whose unions appear to have confronted the challenges of economic restructuring with greater effect. While some have looked to traditional labour strongholds in the social democratic countries of Western Europe, others have discovered in Canada an example nearer to hand. How have Canadian unions, many of which belong to the same internationals and face the same corporations across the bargaining table, managed to retain their presence in the workplace and society at large? Is it because they enjoy certain legislative advantages, or is the difference political in a broader sense, being one of political culture?

Looked at from Canada, however, the situation appears rather different. Although the Canadian labour movement has managed overall to maintain the level of organizational density reached in the 1950s and 1960s, no one is complacent. Unions have experienced a decline in bargaining effectiveness as employer pressure for concessions in the private sector has been reinforced by government willingness to impose wage controls and back-to-work legislation on its own workers.

Two "national questions," however, form the centre of the Canadian debate. For the labour movement in anglophone Canada, the Free Trade Agreement (FTA) with the United States, now being extended to include Mexico, threatens to erode social and collective-bargaining rights and deprives the Canadian state of the policy instruments it needs to pursue an effective industrial strategy.[1] For labour in Quebec, too, the national question is critical. There, however, the national space to be defended is not Canadian, but Québécois. Mastery of the restructuring process requires political control over Quebec's economic destiny. Increasingly the labour movement argues that this power will be available only when Quebec becomes an independent state within the North American economy (Lipsig-Mummé 1991).

This introductory chapter develops these and the other themes that the book explores, by providing a comparative overview of three historically connected yet increasingly distinct labour movements' responses to the challenges of restructuring. The reach of this volume extends, however, beyond the usual concerns of comparative analysis. While lessons may indeed be learned from critical examination of the experiences of others, in this case the learning is also taking place in a context that is throwing these three labour movements together in new ways. As business and governments press for the construction of a North American regional economic power capable of facing up to other regional blocs, the labour movements too are forced to contemplate their common future.

Breakdown of the Postwar Accords

If we are now undergoing "restructuring," this process needs to be situated in relation to the earlier system of political and economic arrangements now being altered. The postwar accord, for most advanced capitalist countries, can be described as Fordist, a term that designates a system based on mass production (Taylorism plus the assembly line) and its corollary, mass consumption. Collective bargaining, Keynesian demand management, and the welfare state provided the means by which workers could consume the goods they produced, while also ensuring that those who, for "legitimate" reasons, were unable to work were not left out. This institutional complex and the matching arrangements that secured a degree of international coordination—Bretton Woods, GATT, and the like—helped to sustain the long boom that came to an end at the beginning of the 1970s.[2]

Of course, not all Fordist accords featured precisely the same terms, and these differences have affected the form and intensity of their breakdowns. The U.S. brand of Fordism differed from many of its Western European counterparts to the extent that it was based on a system of decentralized collective bargaining, tolerated a higher level of unemployment, and offered a less-developed set of social rights. These features meant that the accord was largely confined to the primary labour market, centred in the older transport and communications services, construction, and the steel, transport equipment, food, and textiles industries, as Joel Rogers argues. Canada's Fordism differed from the U.S. model in certain significant ways, as Ian Robinson, Jenson and Mahon, and Donald Swartz point out. During the boom years, however, these differences were easily overlooked. After all, Canadian workers were usually represented by the same international unions, were often employed by the same U.S.-based multinational corporations, and operated under similar legislation.

The differences among the labour movements became more apparent in the turbulent 1960s. To be sure, in both countries there were new social and labour-market policy initiatives and the unionization of public-sector employees took off. Yet, in Canada, both these developments went somewhat further, as provincial and federal governments instituted more far-reaching social programs, expanded their public-sector employment, and granted more comprehensive collective-bargaining rights to their employees. The significance of these differences would become clearer as the crisis hit.

For example, the relatively larger size and greater strength of public-sector unionism fed into and found support within a left nationalist movement in anglophone Canada that sought greater autonomy from the U.S. economy. In Quebec, too, public-sector workers joined other nationalists seeking dramatic changes in that province's relationship to the rest of Canada, although they never committed themselves to leading it, as Carla Lipsig-Mummé demonstrates. In the United States, in contrast, no such common political agenda united the unions and the social movements that constituted the New Left.

The sixties also gave differences between the labour movements of Quebec and the rest of Canada a new meaning. What had been long-standing organizational separateness became in these years profound disagreement over strategies for securing the futures of the two parts of Canada. After 1960 the "Quiet Revolution" began the "catch-up" modernization of Quebec. It also spawned an *indépendantiste* movement, eventually led by the Parti Québécois. That party, under the leadership of Réné Lévesque, offered a potent blend of nationalism and social democracy and attracted much support from an increasingly militant and innovative trade-union movement. As Lipsig-Mummé, Brian Tanguay, and Gérard Hébert argue, the effects of the new Quebec unionism that blossomed in that decade are felt to this day.

The divergent trajectories of the three union movements, however, would only become fully apparent in the 1970s and 1980s when the Fordist accords were first stretched, and then broken. Chapters 6 through 9 consider the labour movements' respective capacities to weather the crisis. Here, however, we focus on the common aspects of the onslaught they faced as companies and states sought to identify possible routes out of the economic crisis.

One dramatic development of the early 1970s was the Nixon administration's reaction to the economic consequences of the "war on two fronts"—the Vietnam War and the War on Poverty—whose difficulties were compounded by the OPEC-induced oil shocks and a mounting international trade challenge led by, but not confined to, Japan. All three elements eventually undermined confidence in the institutional arrangements that had sustained the postwar boom, thereby prompting states and corporations to jettison some of the terms of the Fordist accord.

Underlying these new circumstances was a crisis at the heart of Fordist mass production. This system was based on the systematic denial of shop-floor knowledge and a sharp division between conception and execution. As such, productivity gains could be achieved only with expensive technical innovations. This form of innovation, however, increased the rigidity of a system geared to the mass production of standardized goods in a period when mass markets were rapidly being eroded. At the same time shop-floor rebellions against this labour process rocked the fragile labour peace achieved through the Fordist accord.

The first phase of corporate restructuring was marked by plant closures and the shift to offshore (usually low-wage) production sites. In the United States, a wave of corporate mergers led to the formation of ever-larger conglomerates dedicated to the pursuit of financial strategies that stressed short-term profit at the expense of productive investment.[3] This does not mean that potential embedded in technological innovation was completely ignored, but in the first years of the crisis it was looked at through Fordist eyes, that is, as a route to the "workerless factory." It was only as the reasons for Japan's phenomenal success came to be more closely scrutinized that interest in the flexible potential of micro-electronics—and related organizational innovations—grew.

In certain Western European countries, the new "flexible specialization" is being pursued in a manner more consistent with maintaining the high wages and institutional framework characteristic of the Fordist years (Mahon 1987; Sorge and Streeck 1988). In North America, however, the interest in flexibility has been closely associated with a drive to lower labour costs. Technical flexibility is joined with three forms of labour flexibility: numerical flexibility, functional flexibility, and flexible forms of remuneration. In combination, they threaten to yield a new form of segregated development, as Stephen Herzenberg argues, as well as to encourage a sustained assault on trade unions.

Numerical flexibility applies to the secondary labour market whose growth is being fuelled by employers' increasing recourse to contracting out and part-time and casual work. Use of "just-in-time" workers allows employers to lower costs by paring down the core workforce to which they have to pay higher wages and fringe benefits. The pattern of work organization here resembles the authoritarian relations of pre-Fordist production. Functional flexibility applies to the shrinking core of the labour market and involves an attack on certain workplace rights expressed in the seniority system and the finely articulated set of job ladders to which it is linked. The streamlining of job classifications is supposed to pave the way for the creation of a multiskilled workforce, capable of performing all of the tasks allocated to work teams. Quality circles and other forms of employee-involvement (EI) schemes are designed to enable employers to overcome barriers to incremental innovation posed by postwar production relations. This form of work organization involves the integration of "involved" workers into the corporate culture.

While measures aimed at securing functional flexibility destroy certain forms of job security enjoyed by core workers, new systems of remuneration threaten to reduce their income security. Employers attempt to extract concessions in the form of two-tier systems. These are now being followed by a concerted effort to institutionalize new forms of remuneration. As part of this, employers press to alter collective-bargaining arrangements centred on formulas linking wage increases to productivity gains and the rate of inflation. New payment systems seek to jettison cost-of-living adjustments, replacing these with various forms of lump-sum payments that reflect the firm's—or more frequently, a particular plant's—annual or quarterly performance. Standardized patterns of wage increases are also being replaced by increments associated with individual achievement such as the "pay for knowledge" systems. Frequently such changes involve the institutionalization of de facto enterprise unionism.

Taken together, these employer strategies constitute an all-out assault on Fordist industrial relations systems. They threaten to deepen the old division between the primary and secondary segments of the labour market, while leaving a reduced core in a more vulnerable and subordinate position to employers. Nor has restructuring left untouched those components of the postwar accord secured via public policy. Macroeconomic policies geared to sustaining high employment, and social policies supplementing or substituting for privately negotiated wages, have all fallen from favour with politicians and corporate officials. The "Keynesian welfare state" may not have been demolished, but it has been subjected to a reorganization along neo-liberal lines. The restructuring of the state, in turn, has involved an attack on public-sector workers: wage restraint, privatization, contracting out, new forms of work organization, as well as outright union busting have all become the order of the day.

The Unions' Response:
A Comparative Assessment

The employers' assault has proven particularly successful in the United States, where union density has fallen to less than one-fifth of the non-agricultural labour force. This decline cannot be attributed solely to the shift of employment toward the harder-to-organize service sector. As Rogers argues, density in sectors that were former union strongholds began to decline precipitously under the crisis conditions of the seventies, and deunionization accelerated in the eighties.

This pattern contrasts with the situation north of the forty-ninth parallel. The unions in Canada and Quebec have more or less been able to hold their own. The density differential holds across the board. Therefore, as Noah Meltz demonstrates, even if none of the labour movements has been able to make substantial inroads into the growing private-service sectors, unions in Canada have done better than those in the United States.

Ian Robinson and Ruth Milkman point to the accommodationist stance of the old-line unions to account for the U.S. unions' inability to resist the employers' onslaught. For Robinson, in particular, the current path is deeply rooted in the past. The U.S. unions' present willingness to compromise with demands of employers reflects their historic attachment to "economistic unionism." This orientation is in marked contrast to the "social unionism" that has predominated in the Canadian labour movement and has made the latter more willing both to resist and to innovate.

The potential effects of social unionism are reflected in a willingness to incorporate the kind of bargaining issues that appeal to an increasingly feminized workforce, as Julie White's case study of the Canadian Union of Postal Workers (CUPW) suggests. The CUPW's solidaristic bargaining strategy did much to improve the position of women postal workers well before feminism had become a force within the labour movement. The CUPW may be somewhat exceptional in this regard, however. Céline Saint-Pierre's analysis of the Quebec labour movement suggests that it has taken a feminist presence within the unions to bring these issues to the fore. Unions are forced to take such issues on board now, however. In the post-Fordist economy the "typical" worker is no longer the male industrial worker supporting a dependent family. As the labour force feminizes, it is increasingly the case that the female service-sector worker, whether as one part of a two-income family or as a single parent, is now the norm (Hagen and Jenson 1988: 3–4).

The greater relative strength of social unionism north of the forty-ninth parallel is also reflected in divergent experiences with political parties. In the United States, the unions have been but one of many interests associated with the Democratic party, whereas Canadian unions, along with party activists and intellectuals, undertook to remake social democracy by founding the New Democratic Party (NDP) in 1961. As one of the main organizational supports of the NDP since then, this privileged position with the party has been sustained. Although the party has never won a national election, it has been able to influence the federal policy agenda, especially when minority governments have been in power. It has also formed the governments in several provinces where it has introduced legislation favourable to unions and collective bargaining rights. Although the NDP has never been able to make a breakthrough in Quebec, the Parti Québécois, with its blend of nationalism and social democratic themes, can be seen as a functional equivalent, as Tanguay argues.

The presence of a social democratic party helps to explain what some observers see as the more supportive legislative environment enjoyed by Canadian unions. Peter Bruce, however, attributes the relative strength of Canadian unions more specifically to a favourable set of administrative practices that reflect, in part, historical differences in the role of the judiciary. The relatively autonomous federal and provincial labour boards, composed of representatives of labour and management, have developed procedures that make it more difficult for Canadian employers to get away with unfair labour practices.

The contrast between the U.S. and Canadian labour movements—and, within Canada, between Quebec and the rest—can, however, be overdrawn. It overlooks pockets of new strength in the U.S. labour movement, especially in the public and health-care unions. The latter, Milkman argues, have been gaining ground because they have been more responsive to the concerns of women and other "new" workers than have the traditional unions. While Herzenberg's assessment of developments in the U.S. autoworkers' union (UAW) is more pessimistic than that offered by Charlotte Yates for the breakaway Canadian Auto Workers (CAW), he does see signs of hope in the stance taken by certain locals.

A number of the Canadian contributors also provide a critical picture of the labour movement in Quebec and the rest of Canada. Swartz takes issue with favourable depictions of the application of Canadian labour law. He argues that the unions' legal rights are more honoured in the breach than in practice, as federal and provincial governments (even social democratic ones) have shown an increasing willingness to impose wage controls and back-to-work legislation. Bargaining effectiveness has also declined as Canadian workers have been forced to make concessions on wages, fringe benefits, and job security. Certainly, real wages fell throughout most of the 1980s and unions have found it hard to counter the spread of "nonstandard" work as employers turn to part-time and casual workers or contract out services formerly produced in-house.

Faced with such pressures, Canadian unions have tended to be more resistant to management's attempts to reorganize work than many of their American counterparts. Nevertheless, Donald Wells argues that even relatively strong unions like the Canadian Auto Workers have had to accept new, potentially divisive forms of work. Yates's assessment of the CAW's capacity to continue to pursue a more militant strategy than the UAW contains similar grains of pessimism. The CAW has found it very difficult to organize in the Japanese "transplant" plants, and the 1990s recession has turned its struggle to hold the line in traditional strongholds into an uphill battle.

A comparison of the three analyses of union-party relations also suggests that the three labour movements face problems that are more similar than different. Elaine Bernard's analysis of the factors behind the disappointing stance taken by the NDP in the 1988 Canadian election highlights a problem—the NDP's unwillingness to take a proactive stance on economic policy issues. Richard Valelly argues that a similar problem bedevilled the Democrats in the 1984 election. Thus, neither labour movement could convince the supposed "party of labour" to follow its lead in economic matters. Tanguay's analysis of the Parti Québécois government in the late 1970s and early 1980s suggests that the Quebec unions have been no more successful than their counterparts in the rest of Canada or the United States.

If the first two decades of restructuring have had a visibly devastating impact on the U.S. unions, the contrast to their counterparts north of the forty-ninth parallel ought not to be overplayed. Caution is more appropriate. In Canada, as in the United States, the unions have lost ground to private- and public-sector employers, and the extension of the Canadian-U.S. free trade arrangements to include Mexico threatens to tilt the balance even more sharply against labour in all the countries involved. Nevertheless, the crisis has *also* provoked an effort to rethink union strategy from the ground up, and elements within all three labour movements have shown a capacity for innovation. This should not be underplayed either.

Union Strategies for the Future

The challenge the unions face can be put quite simply: They must avoid both the Scylla of accommodation to the polarized growth model favoured by many employers and the Charybdis of defensive militancy, a valiant but doomed attempt to maintain the arrangements of the Fordist accord. The tentative outlines of a strategy that might allow the unions to steer a course between these two perils can be gleaned from various contributors' reflections on directions already being explored within the unions.

The first element of such a strategy pertains to workplace reorganization. The dominant tendency among U.S. unions has been to accommodate the employers' demands for wage and functional flexibility, whereas Canadian unions have tried to guard the rights already won. For Herzenberg and Wells, neither strategy is adequate. The unions should instead press for a high-quality, high-skill system of production in which teamwork has its part to play. The teams, however, need to be integrated into an ongoing process of collective bargaining, with elected stewards from each team forming part of a larger network of shop stewards capable of negotiating on issues like the composition and role of problem-solving committees, staffing levels, and training.

The unions' capacity to advance a workers' version of post-Fordist production may be strengthened by the kind of "works council" legislation Richard Freeman recommends. Nevertheless, emphasis on workplace unionism cannot come at the expense of involvement in struggles within the wider labour market. As Jenson and Mahon argue, unions have a role to play in supporting workplace initiatives through research and education as well as by forging the kind of cross-plant and cross-firm links necessary to avoid the dangers of enterprise unionism.

More broadly, if polarized growth is to be halted and reversed, the unions need to devise strategies for organizing the just-in-time workers who have been made to bear the heaviest costs. Many of these workers are women who are more likely to join a union that has demonstrated its willingness to fight sexual harassment and to press for pay equity. Yet such workers are also sometimes critical of the way that the world of work fits with the rest of life. Issues like parental leave, dependent care, and even the attractiveness of part-time work and homework highlight the need for a new conception of working time. Unions need to counterpose a different notion of time from that of the employers, who seek flexibility in their operations (and payrolls) while ignoring the rest of life, inside and outside the workplace.

New workplace strategies and strategies that recognize the issues of concern particularly to women workers also entail a restructuring of the unions themselves. Some analysts, Meltz and Freeman in particular, call for the creation of trade-union centrals like the Swedish TCO (Tjänstemannens Centralorganisation), a federation of white-collar unions. As the latter are finding, however, economic restructuring is blurring the blue-collar/white-collar divide and forcing unions to find new ways to work together (Mahon 1991). In this context, it might be more useful to focus on the development of the kind of democratic internal structures identified by Wells, Herzenberg, Milkman, and Saint-Pierre than to dissipate energy trying to create new institutions.

While these strategic and organizational changes are important, the unions cannot combat polarized growth on their own. They need to work with allies like the women's movement, antiracist groups, environmentalists, and peace activists. In Canada, the struggle against the FTA did bring such a coalition together, but the Pro-Canada Network largely remained an alliance of the leaders of such groups, and its lack of depth showed in the network's inability to present a viable alternative to the neo-liberalism of their opponents. For Bernard, a progressive post-Fordist accord can only be developed through involvement in a party that is capable of putting pressure on the unions and other social movements to find positive-sum solutions to their differences. None of the "pro-labour" parties has yet demonstrated a capacity to do this.

Finally, the three labour movements have to rethink the spatial horizons of action. Ironically, at the very moment that continental economic integration is taking place, the three labour movements have grown further apart. During the Fordist era, U.S. and Canadian workers often belonged to the same international unions, and the latter also represented the majority of private-sector workers in Quebec. Since the late sixties, however, nationalism in both Quebec and the rest of Canada has eroded the internationals' position. Moreover, Québécois nationalism has led to further divisions between the two labour movements in Canada. In June 1992, for example, the Fédération des travailleurs et des travailleuses du Québec, the provincial federation of unions affiliated with the Canadian Labour Congress, broke away from the CLC in a dispute over the organizational "distinctiveness" of Quebec unions. The heart of the matter was the "national question." This decision means that in the future there will be no major union peak organization that can claim to speak for unionists in Quebec and the rest of Canada.

These divisions bring dangers. As both Tanguay and Saint-Pierre warn, there is a risk that class and gender interests might be sacrificed in the name of the nation. There is a very real chance that the three labour movements will be rallied to the cause of "their" corporations in a zero-sum battle for competitive position. This need not, however, be the case. Both Valelly and Herzenberg hold out the possibility of an alternative economic strategy based on managed trade, coordinated expansion, regulation of financial markets, and respect for labour rights.

Labour movements across the world have been forced to begin grappling with the challenges posed by a restructuring process that is global in scope. While each movement's response is coloured by its own past experience (and ways of understanding this), there is much to be gained from comparative analyses. Such analyses, however, are unlikely to reveal *the* way forward. Circumstances do differ and "learning" has to take these differences into account. At the same time, nations are even more permeable to global forces than they were before. "Globalization" and "continentalization" are real forces pressing national labour movements to find new ways to work together. It is our hope that the essays in this volume contribute to the development of the kind of mutual understanding from which such cooperation must arise.

Notes

1. For a description of the Canadian labour movement's concerns about the FTA, see Bradford and Jenson (1992). While most political actors in Quebec demonstrated a greater enthusiasm for the 1988 agreement than did their counterparts in the rest of Canada, the unions were an exception. They made common cause with the Canadian Labour Congress's campaign in opposition to the FTA.

2. The literature on post-1945 Fordism and its characteristics is immense. See, for example, Piore and Sabel (1984), Lipietz (1983), Ross and Jenson (1985).

3. See Thompson (1987) for a good review of the literature produced in the early eighties to explain America's competitive decline. Thompson concurs with those political economists and business school experts who focus on "abstract" and shortsighted managerial strategies at the expense of the "manufacturing function."

References

Bradford, Neil, and Jane Jenson. 1992. The Roots of Social Democratic Populism in Canada. In Frances Fox Piven, ed., *Labor Parties in Postindustrial Societies*, New York: Oxford.

Lipietz, Alain. 1983. *L'Audace et l'enlisement*, Paris: La Découverte.

Lipsig-Mummé, Carla. 1991. Future Conditional: Fragmentation and Realism in the Quebec Labour Movement. *Studies in Political Economy* 36.

Mahon, Rianne. 1987. From Fordism to ?: New Technology, Labour Markets, and Unions. *Economic and Industrial Democracy* 8:1.

———. 1991. From Solidaristic Wages to Solidaristic Work: A Post-Fordist Historic Compromise for Sweden? *Economic and Industrial Democracy* 12:3.

Piore, Michael, and Charles Sabel. 1984. *The Second Industrial Divide: Possibilities for Prosperity*, New York: Basic.

Ross, George, and Jane Jenson. 1985. Postwar Class Struggle and the Crisis of Left Politics. In R. Miliband and J. Saville, eds., *The Socialist Register* 1985/86, London: Merlin.

Sorge, Arndt, and Wolfgang Streeck. 1988. Industrial Relations and Technical Change: The Case for an Extended Perspective. In R. Hyman and W. Streeck, eds., *New Technology and Industrial Relations*, Oxford: Basil Blackwell.

Thompson, G. 1987. The American Industrial Policy Debate: Any Lessons for the U.K.? *Economy and Society* 16:1.

Two Decades of Restructuring and Political Change

2   IAN ROBINSON

Economistic Unionism in Crisis: The Origins, Consequences, and Prospects of Divergence in Labour-Movement Characteristics

The Great Depression and World War II dramatically changed the character of the labour movements in both Canada and the United States, fixing the parameters in which they would operate up to the 1980s.[1] Yet these years of crisis and transformation set the two labour movements moving in very different directions. By 1955, a form of mass "economistic" unionism had emerged as the central tendency of organized labour in the United States. In Canada, "social" unionism prevailed, though it was underpinned by quite different moral economies in the English- and French-speaking wings of the labour movement.

Why did the character of the labour movements of these two countries diverge at that juncture? Did the next major wave of unionization—the public-sector expansion of the 1960s and 1970s—alter or reinforce these tendencies? What difference did this divergence in labour-movement character make to the power of these labour movements and, with it, the industrial relations and politics of the two countries? Given what is known about the factors that have shaped union and labour-movement character in the past, what can be said about the likely prospects of these labour movements over the next decade?

This chapter seeks to answer these questions by developing a "moral-economy" approach to the analysis of union character and strategic choice. The first section sketches the moral-economy account. The next section applies this approach to an analysis of the union character shaping events of the 1930s and 1940s. The third section extends it to the public-sector union expansion of the 1960s and 1970s. The next section identifies some of the most important consequences of labour-movement character divergence. The final section considers the prospects of the labour movements in Canada and the United States in light of the events and experiences of the late 1970s and the 1980s.

The Moral Economy of
Labour-Movement Character

As a going concern, unions are strategic collective actors, seeking to realize their goals under the constraints imposed by their external environment: the behaviour of other strategic actors, such as governments and employers, and larger trends beyond the control of any single actor, such as global economic restructuring. Analysis of the logic of external constraints shaping union strategic choices can be understood as the macro dimension of labour-movement analysis. Here I would locate "political-exchange" accounts of variations in strike levels, labour relations, and economic performance (e.g., Pizzorno 1978; Cameron 1984; Regini 1984), as well as Sabel's (1981) perceptive analysis of the antinomies of accommodation versus militance as union strategies in power struggles with employers.

Yet the existence of unions, federations, and labour movements as going concerns cannot be taken for granted, and neither can their "character"—that is, the goals they pursue and the means that they typically choose to realize them.[2] Unions must be able to attract, retain, and mobilize members, and to do these things, they must overcome the "free-rider" problems that attend any form of collective action. There are a limited number of ways in which this can be done, each constituting a distinct organizational maintenance strategy (Wilson 1973: Golden 1988). The requirements of each strategy constitute a second, internal set of constraints with profound implications for union and labour-movement ends and means. Good theoretical work on this micro dimension of union collective action exists (e.g., Olson 1965; Wilson 1973; Lange, Ross, and Vannicelli 1982), but it has seldom been systematically applied to the comparative study of the formation and evolution of labour-movement character and behaviour.

The analysis of labour-movement divergence presented in this paper is grounded in a particular account of the microfoundations of collective action, applied to the case of unions and labour movements. I call it the "moral-economy" account (Thompson 1966, 1971; Scott 1976) because it stresses the importance of the moral commitments of labour-movement members, leaders, and supporters qua vital power resources, and the requirements of maintaining those commitments (Sen 1979/1990; Jenkins 1985; Hirschman 1986). This approach contrasts with conventional accounts, which stress the importance of appeals to selective incentives grounded in rational economic self-interest (e.g., Olson 1965) or, in their more sociological restatements, to individual preferences as shaped by social conditioning (e.g., Wilson 1973).

Union recourse to coercion to solve collective-action problems is highly constrained, for a variety of reasons.[3] There are three basic union "organizational-maintenance" strategies that rely on noncoercive means: primary reliance on selective incentives, primary reliance on moral commitments, and an effective synthesis of the two. There are, accordingly, three basic types of unionism: economistic, sectarian, and synergistic.

Social unionism is the inclusive version—as opposed to the exclusive craft version—of synergistic unionism.[4] It is "social" in the scope of its ambitions and sense of obligation: It seeks to change the entire society and to advance the interests of many who are not union members. It is also social in its capacity to articulate a moral critique of the existing order, a critique that resonates with the values and experiences of most working people rather than smaller groups committed to full-blown sectarian ideologies. Social unionism can be supported by different types of moral economy. The "ethical" socialism of social critics such as R. H. Tawney and George Orwell has been the most powerful moral culture in the labour movements of the United Kingdom and anglophone Canada (Dennis and Halsey 1988; Horowitz 1968); social Catholicism has been important in the French, Italian, and Québécois labour movements (Lange, Ross, and Vannicelli 1982; Rouillard 1989).

The alternatives to social unionism involve heavy reliance on one of the two types of motivation. "Economistic" unionism relies primarily on selective incentives, and "sectarian" unionism on moral commitments.[5]

Neither of these relatively pure union types yields an organization as strong or as resilient as does an effective synthesis of the two.

Economistic unionism is highly vulnerable to government and employer coercion because it is relatively easy for either of these actors to threaten penalties that more than outweigh the small economic benefits that the union can offer with its selective incentives. It is also vulnerable to corruption, because if union leaders and members are accustomed by the union's own moral economy to think primarily in terms of advancing their personal preferences, they are more likely to respond to external threats and inducements as self-interested individuals.

Sectarian unionism is also vulnerable, albeit to a different set of ailments: to schism among those who continue to see their lives in highly moralistic terms but cannot agree on who or what is morally correct; to disillusion on the part of those who no longer believe in the morality of the cause or the leadership; and to burnout on the part of those who still believe and still cooperate but cannot continue to live day after day as a moral crusade. Few manage to avoid all of these shoals year after year.

Why, then, does every union not rely extensively upon both types of motive? Most do try. Even the most conservative and narrowly self-interested unions routinely invoke the language of social justice when advancing their claims, while maintaining a steady supply of selective incentives if they can. But only some unions and leaders are credible claimants to such moral authority. Precisely because such authority really does matter, most people and organizations will try to frame their demands in moral terms, whatever their real motives. Knowing this, most people are quite reasonably skeptical of such claims. Only when unions and their leaders prove that they stand behind their principles, even when they work to their disadvantage, are people inclined to take such appeals seriously. Here, as in many areas involving difficult questions of motivation, most people rely on the adage that "actions speak louder than words" (Goodin 1982). One hallmark of genuine social unionism, then, is that moral and political arguments and appeals really matter to the organization and its members, in contrast to economistic unionism, but they are not framed in such a narrow, sectarian fashion that no real debate can be tolerated within the organization.

The political environment in which unions are formed critically affects the viability of the different organizational maintenance strategies and, hence, the type of unionism and labour movement that prevails. If the state protects the more conservative elements of the labour movement, cooperative unions may receive sufficient material resources to generate a lot of positive selective incentives and face only limited negative incentives from employers. Economistic unionism, whether it calls itself revolutionary and anticapitalist (as in the party unions of Mexico or the Soviet Union) or antirevolutionary and pro-capitalist (as in the United States), will predominate in such circumstances, other things being equal.

If the state is more reactionary, however, seeking to exclude or even destroy all forms of unionism, this will make it impossible for economistic unionism to flourish (Fishman 1990: 47–54). The only question then is whether synergistic or sectarian unionism will prevail. Perhaps the most important determinant here is the level of coercion that the state uses—or permits private employers to use—against workers and their organizations. The more severe the coercion, the fewer material incentives are available to unions, and so the further toward pure sectarian unionism the labour movement will be driven. Conversely, where states exclude and isolate all unions from political power and exchange but do not engage in or permit large-scale physical repression, social unionism is more likely to emerge as the dominant form.[6]

Historical Origins of Divergence

Golden argues that "critical decisions" concerning organization-maintenance strategy, taken at critical junctures in the development of an organization,

> fix the assumptions of policy-making as to the nature of the enterprise—its distinctive aims, methods, and role in the community. Once its character has been stabilized, the organization tends to make subsequent decisions as matters of routine, working within the assumptions laid down initially and behaving in ways consistent with its established mission and set role. . . . Officials, rather than recalculate their policies from the top at every opportunity, deliberately avoid questioning the established routines and integrity of their organization, in a perfectly (if bounded) rational allocation of intellectual and organizational resources. Only catastrophic organizational failure or suddenly successful innovation makes it likely that the or-

ganization will reconsider the parameters of its established identity.
(1988: 8)

The moment of near catastrophic organizational failure that redefined the
character of the labour movements in Canada and the United States was
the Great Depression. By 1929, union density had fallen to 12 percent in
the United States and 13 percent in Canada. As the two economies
plunged into the most profound depression of the twentieth century,
most observers predicted that union membership and density would decline even further, as they always had during past recessions (Goldfield
1987: 245). Yet 1930 was the beginning of the biggest upsurge in the
history of either labour movement, an upsurge that would continue until
the early 1950s. By that time, both labour movements had far surpassed
their previous high-water marks with about one-third of all organizable
workers organized in each country. The same large international unions,
located in the private sector, were at the core of this resurgence in both
countries. Yet social unionism emerged dominant in Canada, while economistic unionism prevailed in the United States. This difference can be
traced to the very different political environments in which the unions
made their critical choices during the 1930s and the 1940s.

In the United States, Roosevelt's New Deal administration was perceived as friendly to labour, encouraging a wave of union organizing.
The Wagner Act—passed in 1935 and enforced from 1937 (when the U.S.
Supreme Court upheld its constitutionality)—significantly reduced the
levels of employer coercion that unions had previously had to endure.[7]
This deprived social unionism, then concentrated in the new industrial
unions of the Congress of Industrial Organizations (CIO), of the comparative advantage that it had enjoyed in hostile environments over the
economistic unionism that predominated within the American Federation of Labor (AFL). Once this advantage was eliminated, the AFL
unions had a number of advantages in the competition to organize new
members: AFL unions were more widely dispersed geographically, and
generally took on smaller employers. They could also portray themselves
to employers as the lesser of evils when compared with the CIO (Milton
1982: 118; Griffith 1988: 157; Wallace, Rubin, and Smith 1988; Robinson
1990: 312–17).

In both Quebec and the rest of Canada, however, conservative, antiunion governments remained in power at both the federal and the pro-

vincial levels until the last years of World War II (and beyond in some cases).[8] There was no equivalent to the New Deal or the Wagner Act in Canada until 1944, when the King government introduced several new social programs, together with a new labour law, PC 1003 (Easterbrook and Aitken 1958: 506–13; Robinson 1990: 338–45; Simeon and Robinson 1990: 61–98).[9] In this more hostile environment, social and sectarian unionisms retained their comparative advantage. Had levels of coercion been severe, sectarian unionism might have prevailed. But while the Canadian labour movement was rigorously excluded from political power, and economic coercion was widely employed, there were no death squads. Consequently, social unionism prevailed.

The statistics support this story. While the CIO unions grew by leaps and bounds between 1935 and 1937, as soon as the Wagner Act began to be enforced, AFL membership growth rates pulled ahead of the CIO's in the United States. Between 1937 and 1944, AFL membership increased by 208 percent, as compared to 198 percent for the CIO; from 1944 to 1955, it was 115 percent for the CIO and 148 percent for the AFL. These trends meant that by 1955, when the two federations merged, the AFL unions had more than twice the membership of the CIO (Robinson 1990: 323). They were thus able to dominate the AFL-CIO, putting their man, George Meany, into the presidency and keeping him there until he retired in 1979 (Zeiger 1987).

In Canada, the Canadian Congress of Labour (CCL), affiliated with the CIO, increased its membership by 292 percent between 1937 and 1944, as compared to 149 percent for the Trades and Labour Congress (TLC) unions affiliated with the AFL. Following the introduction of PC 1003, however, the CCL membership growth rate fell to half its previous level (i.e., to 147 percent), while TLC membership growth rose to 191 percent (Robinson 1990: 319–20). By the time of the merger of 1956, total TLC membership was 165 percent that of the CCL. Yet the consequences of this imbalance were not to prove as grave as in the United States, for even the TLC leadership had been pushed toward social unionism by the political exclusion of the formative depression and war years (Robinson 1990: 321–23).

The different experiences of the two labour movements during the Second World War also directed CIO unions in the United States toward economistic unionism and Canadian TLC unions toward social unionism. What pulled the CIO unions in this direction more than any-

thing else was their decision to sign the No-Strike Pledge. All major
labour leaders—except John L. Lewis and his United Mine Workers
(Milton 1982: 148–51)—enforced this pledge on their membership from
1941 to the end of the war. They did so out of mixed motives: to support
the war effort; to affirm their loyalty to President Roosevelt, by 1940
under attack from a revitalized right wing; and to secure greater government protection of unions (Milton 1982: 121–38; Lichtenstein 1982: 44–
53, 78–81).

With the strike weapon no longer available to bring pressure to bear
on the many antiunion employers who remained, American organizing
performance fell from its 1942 peak of about 100 workers organized per
thousand union members to about 59 by 1945, bottoming out at 18 in
1948, and then stabilizing in the middle 20s from the early 1950s (Robinson 1992). Moreover, enforcing the No-Strike Pledge pitted national
union leaders against many rank-and-file members and shop-floor activists, as inflation eroded real wages and wildcat strikes grew in the defence
industries beginning in 1941 (Milton 1982: 133–53; Lichtenstein 1982). This
substantially reduced the moral authority of union leaders vis-à-vis the
rank and file, forcing them to rely more and more heavily on selective
incentives, government coercion, or both to control their membership
and maintain labour peace. At the same time, it disillusioned many activists and rank-and-file members, so that they could no longer be mobilized except by recourse to selective incentives.

The Liberal government of Canada also sought a No-Strike Pledge
from labour leaders, but the CCL unions demanded Wagner-type labour
legislation and participation in the federal government's economic planning councils in exchange for abandoning their most powerful weapon in
a rare period of full employment. Prime Minister Mackenzie King refused. The more conservative TLC unions agreed to King's no-strike request, perhaps hoping for his help in their struggle to outpace the CCL,
as did the Communists within both federations after Hitler invaded the
Soviet Union in June 1941. But the leaders of most of the CCL unions—
often members of the Cooperative Commonwealth Federation (CCF)—
stuck to their position: no government concessions, no pledge (Abella
1973; MacDowell 1983; Bruce 1988: 226; Robinson 1990: 356–59). As a
result, organizing momentum was not broken, and membership grew
more rapidly than at any other period in Canadian history. Organizing
performance levels were still over 60 new members per thousand existing
members in 1951 (Robinson 1990: 56).

Bitter recognition strikes were often necessary to convince recalcitrant employers. As a result, by 1943, strikes in Canada had reached levels without parallel since the strike wave of 1919: One in every three workers was on strike at some point during that year (Jamieson 1968: 280). Such militance required strong community support if it was to succeed, pushing the CCL into closer alliance with the intellectuals and farmers who had dominated the CCF up to this point. By 1943, the CCL and most of its affiliates had endorsed the CCF's platform for a socialist Canada. The alliance worked well. When pollsters in late 1944 asked if Canadians would "prefer to see business or labour exert a dominant influence over public policy, Canadians favoured labour by a two-to-one margin, while Americans favoured business by the same margin" (Bruce 1988: 243). The CCF went from one victory to the next, coming only a few seats shy of forming the government of Ontario in 1943 and capturing the Saskatchewan government in 1944 (Horowitz 1968: 54–57; Young 1969).

The combination of unprecedented strike levels and major political gains by an avowedly socialist party was enough to move Mackenzie King's Liberals to introduce new labour and social legislation in 1944. King's belated "New Deal"—combined with a lot of antisocialist propaganda—proved sufficient to shift public support (which had showed the CCF leading the other two parties late in 1943) back to the Liberal party in time to win the federal election of 1945. But CCL and CCF leaders and activists claimed that nothing but the combination of political and economic *force majeure* that they had generated through popular mobilization had brought about this eleventh-hour Liberal conversion to "social-market" economic principles.

In contrast, the leaders of the CIO unions in the United States were unwilling to devote the resources and make the sacrifices necessary to support a third party. When surveyed by C. Wright Mills (1948) in 1946, only 23 percent of CIO officials and 13 percent of AFL officials favoured the creation of a new labour party in the next two to three years (though positive responses jumped to 52 and 23 percent, respectively, when they were asked if they would favour such a party ten years hence). The short-run costs of forming a third party seemed too high, given how easy it seemed to be to make real progress with pragmatic, reform Democrats. So, rather than support such a development, the American CIO devoted considerable resources to stopping its affiliates in states such as Michigan from creating third parties inspired by the CCF's gains in Ontario and Saskatchewan (Brody 1980: 221).

The demobilization of the wartime organizing drive, however, left the American labour movement without the organizational and social base to mount a serious challenge to conservative Southern Democrats. The survival of this antiunion wing of the Democratic party was critical to the failure of the postwar effort to organize the South (Operation Dixie) and to the passage of the antiunion Taft-Hartley Act (Griffith 1988; Goldfield 1987: 235–41). The authors of that act focussed on dramatically curtailing traditional forms of member mobilization, particularly its more solidaristic forms, and on making it easier for employers to resist union organizing efforts (Yates 1987: 26–32; Tomlins 1985: 247–316; Rogers 1984).

When Canada finally got its New Deal, it was a New Deal from below rather than from above. The ten extra years that it took to generate a movement from below strong enough to produce parallel reforms in Canada had a profound impact on the character of the Canadian labour movement. It strengthened leadership legitimacy with members, since the former were not required to suppress rank-and-file strikes, making mobilization in later years easier and more effective.[10] The economic and political successes that this helped to make possible raised to the status of conviction the heavy reliance on member mobilization and social alliances, a strategy originally born of necessity. It became the conventional wisdom of that generation of labour leaders that unions and their social allies must have their own party, even if it did not succeed in winning national power, in order to keep the other parties on the road to reform.

Social unionism thus emerged from World War II considerably stronger in Canada than in the United States. Yet if the moral economy underpinning Canadian social unionism had been a form of Communism rather than the ethical socialism of the CCF, Canadian social unionism would not have survived the Cold War. Thus an adequate account of union-density divergence must include an explanation for social democracy's relative success against Communism in the 1930s and 1940s.

In brief, the story is that in Canada organized agriculture was excluded from the governing coalition and radicalized by that exclusion just as organized labour was. This common fate pushed them together under the umbrella of the CCF. By contrast, in the United States, agricultural price-stabilization programs under Hoover and in Roosevelt's first term kept the conservative Farm Bureau at the head of organized agriculture, thereby greatly weakening agrarian commitment to a CCF-type party (Brody 1983; Robinson 1990: 326–46). As a result, when the Cold War descended on the labour movements of both countries, exponents of economistic unionism expelled the Communists in the United States, while in Canada, the CCF leaders played this role and inherited control of most of the major unions.

Public-Sector Union Expansion

After the doldrums of the 1950s, union membership in both countries began to grow again in the 1960s and 1970s. Most of this growth was due to dramatic increases in public-sector unionization. Public-sector union density in the United States went from 17.8 to 36.0 percent between 1968 and 1986; in Canada, density levels rose from 38.5 to 62.4 percent over the same period (Meltz 1989; Robinson 1990: 31). At the same time, public-sector employment in both countries was growing. By 1986, such employment accounted for 26.2 percent of all Canadian jobs and 17.2 percent of all American employment (Meltz 1989; Robinson 1990: 34). Taken together, these differences in density growth and sectoral employment account for almost 40 percent of union-density divergence-between 1968 and 1984 (Robinson 1991).

The unionization of federal government employees in the United States took place in the relatively benign context of reform from above by the Kennedy and Johnson administrations (Robinson 1990: 411–13; Troy 1983: Goldfield and Plotkin 1987). The experience of state and municipal government employees was much more varied. But here, too, employees and their leaders have generally sought their rights through legislative changes and, failing that, refrained from illegal mobilizations. As a result, most American public-sector workers—federal and state—still lack the right to strike (Meltz 1989).[11] Such a fundamental weakness gives unorganized workers less reason to become members, accounting in part for lower public-sector union-density levels in the United States.

American health-care workers and teachers are the exceptions that prove the rule. In the case of teachers, Goldfield and Plotkin (1987) found that by 1977, 29 states had collective bargaining laws granting teachers full collective-bargaining rights, while 21 states did not. Of the latter group, 10 had very weak teachers' unions, but the other 11 had reached the "take-off point" at which membership begins to increase exponentially *without* the aid of legislation, and 6 of these had achieved union-density levels of 65 percent or more. Moreover, in most of the 29 states that had strong bargaining laws, union membership growth had reached the take-off point *before* bargaining legislation was passed, suggesting that these laws sought to institutionalize and control a process that was already underway.

The history of American teachers' unionization suggests that enabling legislation was *not* necessary to successful organizing in most American states. This is not surprising, given the Canadian and British experiences in both the private and the public sectors. Further, when compared with the experience of American civil servants, it suggests that unions that rely on prior membership mobilization to acquire collective-bargaining and strike rights are the stronger for it, and get better legislation, than employee associations and unions that wait for legal changes before seeking to organize, bargain, and strike.

Canadian public-sector union density started from a much higher baseline in the 1960s because many workers, particularly at the municipal level, formed unions and demanded collective-bargaining rights during the World War II organizing wave. By 1944, civic employees in Montreal, including police and firefighters, had both organized and struck for better wages and working conditions (Morton and Copp 1984: 257). When the CCF became the government of Saskatchewan in the same year, the province broke new ground by granting its employees collective-bargaining and political rights.

Thereafter, union expansion took place either as a result of legal innovations associated with political breakthroughs by parties relying heavily on union backing—especially in Quebec in 1964 and again in 1976 and 1978 (Morton and Copp 1984: 306)—or following successful illegal strikes, as in the case of British Columbian civil servants (1960); federal postal, airline, railway, and seaway workers (1965–66); and Ontario hospital employees, nurses, and teachers (1974–75) (Robinson 1990: 413–17; Morton and Copp 1984: 244–64, 292–96; Calvert, 1988: 222–24).

In 1965, one third of all strikes in Canada were illegal wildcats, many involving public-sector workers. In 1966, 5,178,000 working days were lost to strikes, 0.34 percent of all working time. Over the next ten years, that level was surpassed six times, with the high point being 1.53 percent of working time lost in 1975. This compares with 0.60 and 0.54 percent of working time lost during the two previous record strike years of 1919 and 1946, respectively (Morton and Copp 1984: 294–95). By 1982, "nonessential" government employees had the right to strike in six of ten provincial jurisdictions—the exceptions being Alberta, Ontario, Prince Edward Island, and Nova Scotia—as well as the federal jurisdiction (Meltz 1989). All provinces accepted the principle that their employees had the right to form unions and engage in collective bargaining (Morton and Copp 1984: 261).

Thus, to a considerable degree, the process of public-sector organization in the two countries recapitulated the differences associated with the organization of the private sector. In the United States, reform from above brought about a more rapid initial membership expansion, but founded on a weaker moral economy. The exceptions were the teachers and health-care workers, who were forced to follow a more mobilizational model and acquired better labour laws thereby. In Canada, public-sector collective-bargaining and strike rights were generally the product of long political and economic struggles involving large-scale membership mobilizations. This process made them stronger unions, viewing legislation as a useful consolidation of their legal rights, rather than the source of their power.

Since Canadian public-sector union density increased by more percentage points, and the public sector represents a larger share of total employment in Canada, the incorporation of public-sector workers into the two labour movements had a bigger impact on the Canadian labour movement. By 1980, 45.8 percent of all Canadian union members came from the public sector; in the United States, the figure was only 34.9 percent (Meltz 1989; Robinson 1990: 31, 34). Thus, all of the generalizations that follow hold *a fortiori* for the Canadian labour movement.

Public-sector unionization in the 1960s and 1970s—along with organizing in the burgeoning private-service sector—increased the number of minorities, women, and office workers in both movements. The growth of female membership gives an idea of the pace and scale of these changes. In 1962, women still only made up 15.4 percent of all Canadian union members, whereas by 1956, they were 18.6 percent of all union members in the United States. By 1986, women constituted about 36.4 percent of Canadian membership and 34 percent of that in the United States (Coates, Arrowsmith, and Courchene 1989: 32; Milkman 1988: 172–73).[12] Increased membership diversity created new tensions (or intensified old ones) in the short run. Yet it also had a positive longer-run impact, changing the issues that unions brought to the bargaining table and their attitudes toward political coalitions with other social movements (Milkman 1988: 174–78; Briskin and Yanz 1985: 67–199, 259–376; Kumar and Ryan 1988).

The influx of public-sector workers also affected the political orientation of the labour movement, as was manifest in the positions of the two main labour federations. Public-sector employees are directly dependent upon government policy for their basic rights as well as their jobs, wages and benefits, and working conditions. They cannot achieve even the most limited "bread-and-butter" objectives without building and maintaining broad political support for the taxes that pay for the public provision of the services that are their jobs. Consequently, they are more politicized than their private-sector counterparts in some respects, and their politics are more likely to favour state intervention for a variety of social and economic purposes (Johnston 1990a, 1990b).

In Canada, the public-sector unions were large enough by the early 1970s to shift the balance of power from international to national unions, resulting in the passage of new rules by the CLC requiring international affiliates to modify their constitutions to ensure that Canadian members elected their union leaders. In 1981 these rules, together with growing public-sector union support for the New Democratic Party (NDP), precipitated the exit of the most conservative element of the Canadian labour movement—the twelve international building-trades unions—from the CLC. Nine of these went on to found a new, rival federation, the Canadian Federation of Labour (CFL), with about 210,000 members, in 1982 (Ryan 1986; Robinson 1990: 397–404, 441–45).

The exit of the building-trades unions meant that for the first time within the CLC, national affiliates had more members than international affiliates, and by 1988, the share of international unions had fallen to 36.8 percent of membership (Robinson 1990: 400). The exit of these unions, and along with them the most conservative elements of the CLC executive, shifted the political centre of gravity to the left. External events—above all, the suspension of collective bargaining and the imposition of wage controls from 1975 to 1978—were pushing in this direction in any case. The result was CLC adoption of what Smith (1990) calls its "maximal program." In essence, it held that the labour movement, through NDP governments, must gain greater control over private investment, so as to restore full employment and ensure adequate levels of investment in research and development and new technologies, world product mandating for Canadian branch plants, and restrictions on unproductive mergers and takeovers. To this end, the CLC and its affiliates became much more active in efforts to elect NDP members provincially and federally (Smith 1990: 263, 274–76, 291–302, 305–8: Robinson 1990: 445–52).

Thus, the organization of the public sector strongly reinforced the social unionism of the Canadian labour movement, gave it new momentum, a more diverse face, stronger links with some of the new social movements, and new issues to add to and sometimes modify its traditional list of social-change objectives. In the United States, the impact of public-sector unionization on the character of the movement was more muted, both because the scale of its growth was smaller and because its orientation was less social unionist. The particular political contexts in which the public-sector unions emerged have thus reinforced the previously established differences between the two labour movements.

Consequences of Labour-Movement Character Divergence

The two most important consequences of labour-movement character divergence have been (1) a more powerful Canadian labour movement (relative to its size) and (2) a higher level of union commitment to organizing the unorganized in Canada. The greater economic power of the Canadian labour movement was a product of social unionism's greater capacity to overcome free-rider problems and mobilize members in effective industrial actions. The greater political power of the Canadian movement was a function of its commitment to a third, pro-labour party, first the CCF, and then the NDP. Such a party was able to pull legislation to the left more effectively than American unions' efforts to "realign" the Democratic party from within (Bruce 1988).

The higher level of commitment to organizing was, in part, the legacy of the Canadian labour movement's tradition of primary reliance on economic power, rather than supportive state legislation. Greater reliance on economic power requires greater attention to taking wages out of competition by organizing the unorganized. This tradition was reinforced and legitimated by the fact that union members who see their unions as part of a larger social movement, with goals transcending their own particular economic interests, do not respond to union taxation to support organizing in the same way as economistic union members. They might agree that they would benefit more individually if their dues went more to servicing current members, but they also believe that they have a duty to help the unorganized and to build the movement by bringing in new members (Robinson 1990: chap. 4; Robinson 1991).

The labour-movement power gap, together with the higher level of commitment to organizing in Canada, accounts for the larger number of unorganized workers organized each year in Canada (relative to union membership).[13] This private and public-sector "organizing-performance" gap was, in turn, the most important cause of divergence in union densities in the two countries from the early 1960s to the late 1980s. Density divergence further strengthened the Canadian labour movement and further weakened the U.S. one. Thus, self-reinforcing spirals were set in motion in each country: increasing labour-movement power in Canada and decreasing power in the United States.[14]

Beyond its impact on organizing-performance and union-density divergence, the greater power of the Canadian labour movement has been responsible, to a considerable degree, for (1) the gradual emergence of more favourable labour laws in Canada,[15] (2) the development of a national public health system and other social policies favoured by the labour movement and rejected by its opponents,[16] (3) the much higher strike levels in Canada as the two economies began to go into crisis in the 1970s,[17] (4) the pursuit of economic policies that made the industrial restructuring of the late 1970s and the early 1980s less destructive in Canada,[18] and (5) the more successful fight against concession bargaining in the first half of the 1980s (Kumar 1991).

Future Prospects

The 1980s represented the greatest crisis faced by these labour movements since the employers' Open Shop drive of the 1920s and the Great Depression of the 1930s. The late 1970s were years of brutal economic restructuring and rising employer hostility to the very existence of unions, particularly in the United States. The resources—membership, material, and moral commitment—of the Canadian labour movement continued to increase, but growth now took place in an environment that was much more hostile to organized labour. As a result, the real power of the Canadian movement declined from the mid-1970s, as the inability to resist effectively the three-year suspension of collective bargaining from 1975 to 1978 and other erosions of union bargaining rights signalled (Panitch and Swartz 1988).[19]

In the United States, organized labour's resources and power have been in decline since the late 1960s, if not before,[20] so the labour movement was less well prepared for the severe tests of the 1970s and 1980s. The results of weakness in a time of crisis are visible in the union-density data. By the end of the 1980s, private-sector union membership stood at about the same level as its previous nadir of 1929 (under 12 percent). Only much higher public-sector organization keeps the aggregate at about 16 percent, which is near the 1920 level. Canadian union density, by contrast, has fallen from its 1980 high of 40 percent to about 36 percent.

If falling union density and reduced union influence in a weakened Democratic party have created a vicious circle of declining labour-movement power and rising employer resistance, is there any prospect for an end to the decline of the labour movement? What (if anything) can organized labour do to break out of the downward spiral that the union-density data continue to record? Neither the provision of higher levels of selective incentives nor changes in the labour laws address the basic problem: Economistic unionism cannot function effectively once employers begin to impose, with de facto if not de jure government permission, serious material sanctions against workers who seek to organize or exercise their collective-bargaining rights.

The only thing that can get organized labour in the United States out of the crisis of economistic unionism is the emergence of social unionism as the dominant form and corresponding changes in the economic and political priorities and strategies of the majority of unions. Are there reasons to think that such a change in the basic character of organized labour is happening or is likely to happen in the foreseeable future?

I believe that there are. Most important, perhaps, is a factor seen at work in the past: the impact of political exclusion on labour-movement character. The last twenty years of conservative government in the United States has already pushed American unions in that direction (Brecher and Costello 1988a, 1988b; Coleman 1988; Moody 1988). Change is evident in the rising priority assigned to organizing (Connecticut AFL-CIO 1989). This, in turn, is reflected in innovative organizing strategies,[21] substantial increases in the number of full-time organizers employed by several of the major unions, and improved organizing performance (Robinson, 1990). It is also reflected in two recent initiatives to create a third party in which organized labour will be a core constituent—as the NDP is in Canada. These are the first serious initiatives of this sort to come from the labour movement since the late 1940s.[22]

There are reasons to believe that this shift will continue. Unions that fail to move in this direction will steadily shrink in size and power relative to those that do; so there is a powerful survival-of-the-fittest logic behind the shift to social unionism. Also, with the Cold War at an end and the new challenge widely perceived to be economic competition from Japan and the European Community, public attention turns to a new set of issues, including the social failures, such as poor domestic health care and education, that undermine American capacity to compete effectively in the world. This shift opens up more political space for social unionism and a labour-backed party to recover the initiative in economic policy.

In addition to these externally generated trends and pressures, factors internal to the labour movement also point toward social unionism. One of the most important weaknesses of the labour movements in both countries has been the scarcity of strong, resource-rich unions in the largely unorganized private-service sector, where employment has been growing most rapidly. The richer, more powerful unions in the construction, transportation, manufacturing, and public sectors had no economic incentives to put resources into organizing such workers and were hampered as well by jurisdictional demarcations. Now, however, manufacturing-sector unions need to replace membership lost as a result of deindustrialization and are seeking to do so by moving outside their traditional jurisdictional boundaries.[23] At the same time, public-sector unions need to reduce the attractiveness of "contracting out" and "privatization," an attractiveness that stems from much lower wages and benefits, hence lower labour costs, in the largely unorganized private-service sector. The most effective way to do this if one cannot mount the political pressure to take such ideas off the agenda is to help those workers organize.

Another internal factor is the new generation of labour leaders who are inheriting the top political and staff positions in their unions. Many are veterans of other social movements in the 1960s and 1970s, and they will bring to the task of rebuilding the American labour movement the assumptions and skills acquired in that apprenticeship (Fellner 1990; Piore

1989). Finally, at the grass-roots level, the effects of the changing racial, gender, and ethnic composition of the labour movement will continue to intensify even within existing labour strongholds. For the unions that make significant progress in the private-service sector, these trends will be greatly reinforced.

Less clear than the factors pushing American unions toward social unionism is whether traditional social democratic discourse is capable of supporting the next generation of social unionism in Western Europe and North America. While its core values remain morally compelling, many of its economic prescriptions look increasingly obsolete as national economies open up and capital becomes ever more mobile. The policy instruments with which national governments once set their own economic priorities are now less effective, while the global institutions necessary to regulate the global economy along Keynesian lines do not exist and will be strongly resisted by many private multinational corporations. Meanwhile, there is intense pressure to move toward a Japanese-style, firm-level corporatism that threatens to destroy internal union solidarities.

Therefore, if there are powerful internal and external pressures toward social unionism in the United States, other pressures associated with the crisis of Fordism and global economic restructuring threaten the traditional economic and political strategies of social unionism in Canada and Western Europe. The next generation of social unionists will have to forge a new moral economy—this time together with the other social movements that are such an important part of modern politics—and a corresponding new set of political and economic strategies and policy instruments. There is no telling what the product of this creative process will be or what success the activists will have in mobilizing the moral commitment of union members, unorganized workers, and potential allies. There are no iron laws of necessity operating here, and it is always possible that labour-movement leaders will fail to meet these formidable challenges.

Two points, however, can be made with some confidence. First, the future of North America's unions lies primarily in the hands of the members and their leaders—their imagination, choices, sacrifices, and commitments will tell the tale, as they always have. Second, these choices will be shaped and constrained by the wider political and economic environment within which they must act. Given the similar nature of the economic environment in both countries and the high and growing levels of economic integration between them, it seems most unlikely that the divergence of the labour movements will continue much longer: Either the U.S. labour movement will successfully rebuild itself along social unionist lines, so that it will become more like the Canadian movement, or it will continue its decline, in which case the economic and political pressures on Canadian governments to "harmonize" their industrial relations and social-policy systems with those in the United States will intensify. In the medium run, such pressures will be very difficult to resist, given the scale of trade with the United States and the increasing mobility of goods, services, and capital between the two countries under the Free Trade Agreement. For better or worse, the Canadian and American labour movements are in this one together.

Notes

1. This paper is based on my dissertation, and the acknowledgments found there apply equally here. Funding was received from the Social Sciences and Humanities Research Council of Canada and Yale University. Thanks also to Rianne Mahon for her suggestions.

2. A "labour movement" includes unions, the political party or parties with which they are closely allied, other organized interests and social movements, and sympathetic intellectuals and members of the general public.

3. This is not to deny that some unions have used violence to gain employer recognition and member acquiescence. Only a small fraction of all unions, however, engage in such practices (Freeman and Medoff 1984: 207–17), and even that action is severely constrained by employer and government regulation, as the Teamsters have recently discovered (LaBotz 1990).

4. The old craft unions of the AFL, while often conservative and relatively unconcerned with the fate of workers in the mass-production industries, were not economistic unions in this sense. While they did seek to provide a range of selective incentives, such as pensions, and even fought generalized social programs that they thought might weaken their force (Rogin 1971; Brody 1967, 1968), they relied heavily on craft traditions and notions of fairness and solidarity (Montgomery 1980, 1987), along with the market power born of valuable skills, to survive in a very hostile climate where other forms of unionism were quickly crushed. For this reason, the use of the term "business unionism" to encompass both the early AFL craft unions and most of the post–World War II industrial and general unions is misleading.

5. The Knights of Labor and the Industrial Workers of the World repre-

sent earlier efforts to develop a mass-based social unionism. These efforts failed because the moral economy they sought to develop could not generate sufficiently strong commitments to withstand the levels of repression to which they were subjected. France's labour movement is probably the best-known case of sectarian unionism.

6. Valenzuela (1979), Lipset (1985), Collier and Collier (1986), and Marks (1989)—all argue that the political context within which labour movements emerge is critical to their character. Yet none of these analyses are grounded in the kind of moral-economy microfoundations developed here.

7. See Milton (1982: 25–68), Piven and Cloward (1979: 97–131), and Goldstein (1978) for levels of employer and government violence against unions before the Wagner Act. This level was by no means reduced to zero thereafter, as the massacre of unarmed picketers in the "Little Steel" strikes of 1937 demonstrated (Milton 1982: 107–111). Yet firing, discrimination, or beatings, rather than multiple murders, now became the norm.

8. There are important differences between the Québécois labour movement and that in the rest of Canada. For a good, comprehensive history of the Québécois movement in French, see Rouillard (1989). In English, see Lipsig-Mummé (1987, 1988).

9. Even then, the federal labour law was not as supportive of unionism as the American (Warrian 1987).

10. This argument holds *a fortiori* for Quebec and British Columbia, where Mackenzie King's 1944 program was rolled back by extremely conservative provincial governments following the termination of the federal government's war powers. There, the old ways continued until 1960 in Quebec and 1972 in B.C. (Calvert 1988; Phillips 1967; Rouillard 1989). This helps to explain why social unionism has generally been strongest in these provinces.

11. Meltz is writing of civil servants, rather than of public employees of a broader definition that encompasses all workers paid out of public funds.

12. Women in Canadian unions seem to have risen to executive positions more quickly than in the United States. In 1985 only about 7 percent of the officers and executive board members of the 11 U.S. unions with more than 200,000 female members were women (Milkman 1988: 175). Women, however, constituted 19.3 percent of all Canadian union executive board members in the same year, primarily because of the very high levels in national unions. Only 1.7 percent of the Canadian executive board members of international unions were women (Coates, Arrowsmith, and Courchene 1989: 35, 67–81).

13. Robinson (1992) uses multiple regression analysis to evaluate various explanations of divergent union-density trends in the OECD countries (those of the Organization for Economic Cooperation and Development) between 1970 and 1985. The finding is that labour-movement power differences are among the

most important factors accounting for density-trend variations: Stronger labour movements, other things being equal, experience growth, or at least lower rates of decline, in union density. Thus, the importance of labour-movement power in the North American case is not exceptional, but conforms to what seems to be a general rule for advanced capitalist economies.

14. The details of this analysis and the evidence supporting it can be found in Robinson (1990, 1991).

15. On the legal differences, see Weiler (1983, 1984). On the role of the CCF/NDP in generating these differences, see Bruce (1988).

16. For the Saskatchewan CCF's role in launching both public hospital insurance and full-fledged public health care in Canada, as well as a general survey of the evolution of Canadian social policy, see Guest (1980).

17. In Canada, the number of days per 1,000 employees lost to strikes involving more than 1,000 workers averaged 912 from 1971 to 1980, and 471 from 1981 to 1986; in the United States, the figures for the same years were 274 and 117, respectively (Kumar, Coates, and Arrowsmith 1988: 659).

While in Western Europe the strongest labour movements are associated with very low strike levels, nevertheless the relationship between labour-movement power and strike levels is not linear. Rather, it is more like an inverted U-curve. When unions are few and fragmented—too weak to hold successful strikes—then strike levels are very low. Conversely, when unions are so powerful that strikes will cost employers much more than they can hope to gain, employers will bargain much more assiduously, and again strike levels will be very low (Shalev 1980; Hibbs 1987). So it is in the medium ranges of labour-movement power where strike levels tend to be higher. And within this medium range, greater union power will be associated with more strikes (Snyder 1977).

18. For a good illustration of policy differences, compare the reaction of the federal governments of each country to the Chrysler bail-out (Gindin 1989). In the 1990–91 recession, however, the federal Conservatives greatly exacerbated restructuring difficulties by supporting an overly high Canadian dollar, in the context of the Free Trade Agreement.

19. I am distinguishing between power resources and power vis-à-vis particular actors such as governments or employers. Power resources are the moral and material resources that an actor can command, and they can be measured without reference to those of any other actors. Power, however, is a relational concept, having to do with A's capacity to get B to do what A wills (Lukes 1974). An organization's power resources might double, but if those of the organization whose behaviour it seeks to affect have tripled, then its real power vis-à-vis that actor has probably declined.

20. It is difficult to be precise, because there are different kinds of power resources: In most American unions, "stocks" of moral capital probably began

declining from the era of the No-Strike Pledge, and certainly from the Cold War purges of the late 1940s; on the other hand, union revenues—material re-sources—were still going up in most cases in the late 1970s. Also, different unions exhibit substantial variations in character and resource endowment within each country, so that what is true of national aggregates is false for some particular unions.

21. See, for examples, Craft and Extejt (1983), Kuttner (1987), and the case studies in volumes 8, 16, and 17 of the *Labor Research Review*.

22. The Labor Party Advocates is led by Tony Mazzocchi of the Oil, Chemical and Atomic Workers (OCAW) and aims to build a critical mass of or-ganizers who will promote the idea within the labour movement (Mazzocchi 1990). The other is advocated by Daniel Cantor and Joel Rogers (1990) in their paper entitled "Party Time."

23. The United Steel Workers in Quebec and in the United States have been doing just this with considerable success, especially in Quebec.

References

Abella, Irving. 1973. *Nationalism, Communism, and Canadian Labour*. Toronto: University of Toronto Press.

AFL-CIO Committee on the Evolution of Work. 1985. *The Changing Situation of Workers and Their Unions*. Washington, D.C.: AFL-CIO.

Behiels, Michael D., ed. 1987. *Quebec since 1945: Selected Readings*. Toronto: Copp Clark.

Berger, Suzanne, ed. 1981. *Organizing Interests in Western Europe*. Cambridge: Cambridge University Press.

Brecher, Jeremy, and Tim Costello. 1988a. "American Labor: The Promise of Decline," *Zeta* (May).

———. 1988b. "From Domination to Solidarity: Perspectives for a Labor/Com-munity Program," *Zeta* (July/August).

Briskin, Linda, and Lynda Yanz, eds. 1985. *Union Sisters: Women in the Labour Movement*. 2d ed. Toronto: Women's Educational Press.

Brody, David. 1967. "The Expansion of the American Labor Movement: Insti-tutional Sources of Stimulus and Restraint." In Stephen E. Ambrose, ed., *Institutions in Modern America*, 11–36. Baltimore: John Hopkins University Press.

———. 1968. "Career Leadership and American Trade Unionism." In F. C. Jaher, ed., *The Age of Industrialization in America*, 288–303. New York: Free Press.

———. 1980. *Workers in Industrial America*. New York: Oxford University Press.

———. 1983. "On the Failure of U.S. Radical Politics: A Farmer-Labor Analysis," *Industrial Relations* 22 (Spring): 141–63.

Bruce, Peter. 1988. *Political Parties and the Evolution of Labor Law in Canada and the United States*. Ph.D. dissertation, Department of Political Science, MIT.

Calvert, John. 1988. "The Divergent Paths of Canadian and American Labor." In Mike Davis and Michael Sprinker, eds., *Reshaping the U.S. Left*, 213–28. London: Verso.

Cameron, David. 1978. "The Expansion of the Public Economy: A Comparative Analysis," *American Political Science Review* 72 (December): 1243–61.

———. 1984. "Social Democracy, Corporatism, Labor Quiescence, and the Representation of Economic Interests in Advanced Capitalist Society." In John Goldthorpe, ed., *Order and Conflict in Contemporary Capitalism*, 143–78. Oxford: Oxford University Press.

Cantor, Daniel, and Joel Rogers. 1990. "Party Time." Unpublished ms.

Coates, Mary Lou, David Arrowsmith, and Melanie Courchene. 1989. *The Current Industrial Relations Scene in Canada, 1989*. Kingston, Ont.: Industrial Relations Centre, Queen's University.

Cochran, Bert. 1977. *Labor and Communism*. Princeton, N.J.: Princeton University Press.

Coleman, Vernon. 1988. "Labor Power and Social Equality: Union Politics in a Changing Economy," *Political Science Quarterly* 103: 687–705.

Collier, David, and Ruth Berins Collier. 1986. "The Initial Incorporation of the Labor Movement in Latin America: A Comparative Perspective." Paper prepared for the panel on Labor, Parties, and Political Change at the annual meeting of the Western Political Science Association.

Connecticut AFL-CIO. 1989. "Wynn Proposes New Organizing Ethic," *Connecticut Labor News* (Fall): 12 and 19.

Craft, James A., and Marian Extejt. 1983. "New Strategies in Union Organizing," *Journal of Labour Research* 4 (Winter): 19–32.

Crouch, Colin, and Alessandro Pizzorno, eds. 1978. *The Resurgence of Class Conflict in Western Europe since 1968*, London: Macmillan.

Dennis, Norman, and A. H. Halsey. 1988. *English Ethical Socialism: Thomas More to R. H. Tawney*. Oxford: Clarendon Press.

Dubofsky, Melvyn, and Warren Van Tine, eds. 1987. *Labor Leaders in America*. Urbana: University of Illinois Press.

Easterbrook, W. T., and Hugh Aitken. 1958. *Canadian Economic History*. Toronto: Macmillan.

Fellner, Kim. 1989. "In Search of the Movement: 1960s Activists in Labor." Photocopy.

———. 1990. "An Uneasy Marriage in the House of Labor," *The American Prospect* (Summer): 93–105.

Fishman, Robert. 1990. *Working-Class Organization and the Return to Democracy in Spain*. Ithaca, N.Y.: Cornell University Press.

Freeman, Bill. 1982. *1005: Political Life of a Union Local*. Toronto: Lorimer.

Freeman, Richard, and James Medoff. 1984. *What Do Unions Do?* New York: Basic Books.

Gindin, Sam. 1989. "Breaking Away: The Formation of the Canadian Auto Workers," *Studies in Political Economy* 29 (Summer): 63–89.

Golden, Miriam. 1988. *Labor Divided: Austerity and Working-Class Politics in Contemporary Italy*. Ithaca, N.Y.: Cornell University Press.

Goldfield, Michael. 1987. *The Decline of Organized Labor in the United States*. Chicago: University of Chicago Press.

Goldfield, Michael, and Jonathan Plotkin. 1987. "Public Sector Union Growth in the United States: Do the Laws Matter?" Photocopy.

Goldstein, Robert Justin. 1978. *Political Repression in Modern America*. Cambridge, Mass.: Schenkman.

Goldthorpe, John, ed. 1984. *Order and Conflict in Contemporary Capitalism*. Oxford: Oxford University Press.

Goodin, Robert E. 1982. *Political Theory and Public Policy*. Chicago: University of Chicago Press.

Griffith, Barbara. 1988. *The Crisis in American Labor: Operation Dixie and the Defeat of the CIO*. Philadelphia: Temple University Press.

Guest, Dennis. 1980. *The Emergence of Social Security in Canada*. Vancouver: University of British Columbia Press.

Hahn, Frank, and Martin Hollis, eds. 1979. *Philosophy and Economic Theory*. Oxford: Oxford University Press.

Hibbs, Douglas, Jr. 1987. *The Political Economy of Industrial Democracies*. Cambridge, Mass.: Harvard University Press.

Hirschman, A. O. 1986. *Rival Views of Market Society and Other Recent Essays*. New York: Viking/Elizabeth Sifton.

Horowitz, Gad. 1968. *Canadian Labour in Politics*. Toronto: University of Toronto.

Jamieson, Stuart. 1968. *Times of Trouble: Labour Unions and Industrial Conflict in Canada. 1900–1966*. Ottawa: Privy Council Office.

Jenkins, J. Craig. 1985. *The Politics of Insurgency: The Farm Worker Movement in the 1960s*. New York: Columbia University Press.

Johnston, Paul. 1990a. "Contrary Trajectories: Public and Private Sector Strikes and Union Growth in California, 1962–1985." Photocopy, Department of Sociology, Yale University.

———. 1990b. "State-Organized Social Reproduction and the Public Worker Movement." Paper presented to the section of the ISA Conference in Madrid on "Organizations, Institutions, and States."

Kumar, Pradeep. 1991. "Industrial Relations in Canada and the United States: From Uniformity to Divergence," Kingston, Ont.: Queen's University Papers in Industrial Relations, No. 2.

Kumar, Pradeep, Mary Lou Coates, and David Arrowsmith. 1988. *The Current Industrial Relations Scene in Canada, 1988*. Kingston, Ont.: Industrial Relations Centre, Queen's University.

Kumar, Pradeep, and Dennis Ryan, eds. 1988. *Canadian Union Movement in the 1980s: Perspectives from Union Leaders*. Kingston, Ont.: Industrial Relations Centre, Queen's University.

Kuttner, Robert. 1987. "Will Unions Organize Again?" *Dissent* (Winter 1989): 52–62.

Labor Research Review, vol. 8. 1986. *Labor's Crucible in the 1980s . . . ORGANIZE!* Chicago: Midwest Center for Labor Research.

———, vol. 16. 1990. *Organizing for Health and Safety*. Chicago: Midwest Center for Labor Research.

———, vol. 17. 1991. *An Organizing Model of Unionism*. Chicago: Midwest Center for Labor Research.

La Botz, Dan. 1990. *Rank-and-File Rebellion: Teamsters for a Democratic Union*. New York: Verso.

Lange, Peter, George Ross, and Maurizio Vannicelli. 1982. *Unions, Change, and Crisis: French and Italian Union Strategy and the Political Economy, 1945–1980*. London: George Allen and Unwin.

Lichtenstein, Nelson. 1982. *Labor's War at Home: The CIO in World War Two*. Cambridge: Cambridge University Press.

Lipset, Seymour Martin. 1985. "The Sources of Working-Class Politics." In *Consensus and Conflict*, 219–52. New Brunswick, N.J.: Transaction Books.

———. 1986a. "North American Labor Movements in Comparative Perspective." In Lipset, ed., 1986b: 421–54.

———, ed. 1986b. *Unions in Transition*. San Francisco: Institute for Contemporary Studies Press.

Lipsig-Mummé, Carla. 1987. "The Web of Dependence: Quebec Unions in Politics Before 1976." In Behiels, ed., 1987: 133–56.

———. 1988. "Quebec Labour, Politics, and the Economic Crisis of the 1980s: The Roots of Defensive Accommodation." Photocopy, Department of Industrial Relations, Laval University.

Lukes, Steven. 1974. *Power*. London: Macmillan.

MacDowell, Laura Sefton. 1983. *Remember Kirkland Lake: The Gold Miners' Strike of 1941–42*. Toronto: University of Toronto Press.

Mansbridge, Jane, ed. 1990. *Beyond Self-Interest*. Chicago: University of Chicago Press.

March, James, and Herbert A. Simon. 1958. *Organizations*. New York: Wiley and Sons.

Marks, Gary. 1989. *Unions in Politics: Comparative Union Politics in Great Britain, Germany, and the United States.* Princeton, N.J.: Princeton University Press.

Mazzocchi, Tony. 1990. "It's Time for a Labor Party." Circular. New York: Labor Institute.

Meltz, Noah. 1985. "Labor Movements in Canada and the United States." In Thomas Kochan, ed., *Challenges and Choices Facing American Labor*, 315–34. Cambridge, Mass.: MIT Press.

———. 1989. "Inter-state versus Inter-provincial Differences in Union Density," *Industrial Relations* (Spring).

Milkman, Ruth. 1988. "Women Workers, Feminism, and the Labor Movement." In Robert Cherry et al., eds., *The Imperiled Economy*, book 2, 171–86. New York: URPE (Union of Radical Political Economists).

———. 1990. "Gender and Trade Unionism in Historical Perspective." In Patricia Gurin and Louise Tilly, eds., *Women in Twentieth Century Politics*. New York: Russell Sage Foundation.

Mills, C. Wright. 1948. *The New Men of Power*. New York: Harcourt, Brace.

Milton, David. 1982. *The Politics of U.S. Organized Labor*. New York: Monthly Review Press.

Montgomery, David. 1980. *Workers Control in America*. Cambridge: Cambridge University Press.

———. 1987. *The Fall of the House of Labor*. Cambridge: Cambridge University Press.

Moody, Kim. 1988. *An Injury to All: The Decline of American Unionism*. London: Verso.

Morton, Desmond. 1986. *The New Democrats, 1961–86: The Politics of Change*. Toronto: Copp Clark Pitman.

Morton, Desmond, with Terry Copp. 1984. *Working People*. Rev. ed. Toronto: Deneau Publishers.

Olson, Mancur. 1965. *The Logic of Collective Action*. Cambridge, Mass.: Harvard University Press.

Panitch, Leo, and Don Swartz. 1988. *The Assault on Trade Union Freedoms: From Consent to Coercion Revisited*. Toronto: Garamond Press.

Phillips, Paul. 1967. *No Power Greater: A Century of Labour in BC*. Vancouver, B.C.: Boag Foundation.

Piore, Michael. 1989. "Administrative Failure: An Hypothesis about the Decline of the U.S. Union Movement in the 1980s." Photocopy, Department of Economics, MIT.

Piven, Frances Fox, and Richard Cloward. 1979. *Poor People's Movements: Why They Succeed, How They Fail*. New York: Vintage.

Pizzorno, Allesandro. 1978. "Political Exchange and Collective Identity in Industrial Conflict." In Crouch and Pizzorno, eds., 1978: 277–98.

Porter, John. 1965. *The Vertical Mosaic: An Analysis of Social Class and Power in Canada*. Toronto: University of Toronto Press.

Regini, Mario. 1984. "The Conditions of Political Exchange: How Concertation Emerged and Collapsed in Italy and Great Britain." In Goldthorpe, ed., 1984: 124–42.

Robinson, Ian. 1990. *Organizing Labour: Explaining Canada-U.S. Union Density Divergence in the Post-War Period*. Ph.D. dissertation, Department of Political Science, Yale University.

———. 1991. "Organizing Labour: A Labour Movement Power Explanation of Canadian-American Union Density Divergence, 1963–1986." Kingston, Ont.: Queens Papers in Industrial Relations, 1992, No. 2.

———. 1992a. "Labor Movement Power and Union Density: Explaining OECD Divergence, 1970–1985." Paper presented to the annual meeting of the A.P.S.A., Chicago, September 3–6.

Rogers, Joel. 1984. *Divide and Conquer: The Legal Foundations of Postwar U.S. Labor Policy*. Ph.D. dissertation, Princeton University.

———. 1992. "Don't Worry, Be Happy: The Postwar Decline of Private-Sector Unionism in the United States." In this volume.

Rogin, Michael. 1971. "Voluntarism: The Political Functions of an Anti-Political Doctrine." In Brody, ed., *The American Labor Movement*, 100–118. New York: University Press of America.

Rouillard, Jacques. 1989. *Histoire du syndicalisme québécois*. Montreal: Boreal Press.

Ryan, Dennis. 1986. "Division in the 'House of Labour': An Analysis of the CLC-Building-Trades Dispute." Kingston, Ont.: Industrial Relations Centre Research Essay Series No. 4, Queen's University.

Sabel, Charles. 1981. "The Internal Politics of Trade Unions." In Berger, 1981: 209–348.

Scott, James. 1976. *The Moral Economy of the Peasant*. New Haven, Conn.: Yale University Press.

Selznick, Philip. 1957. *Leadership in Administration: A Sociological Interpretation*. Evanston, Ill.: Row, Peterson.

Sen, Amartya. 1979/1990. "Rational Fools." In Hahn and Hollis, eds., 1979: 87–109, and in Mansbridge, ed., 1990: 25–43.

Shalev, Michael. 1980. "Trade Unionism and Economic Analysis: The Case of Industrial Conflict," *Journal of Labor Research* 1: 133–73.

Simeon, Richard, and Ian Robinson. 1990. *State, Society, and the Development of Canadian Federalism*. Toronto: University of Toronto Press.

Smith, Miriam. 1990. *Labour without Allies: The Canadian Labour Congress in Politics, 1956–1988*. Ph.D. dissertation, Department of Political Science, Yale University.

Snyder, David. 1977. "Early North American Strikes: A Reinterpretation," *Industrial and Labor Relations Review* 30: 325–41.

Thompson, Edward P. 1966. *The Making of the English Working Class*. New York: Vintage Books.

———. 1971. "The Moral Economy of the English Crowd in the Eighteenth Century," *Past and Present* 50 (Feb): 76–136.

Tomlins, Christopher. 1985. *The State and the Unions: Labor Relations, Law, and the Organized Labor Movement in America, 1880–1960*. Cambridge: Cambridge University Press.

Troy, Leo. 1983. "The Agenda of Public Sector Unions and Associations," *Government Union Review* 4 (Spring): 15–35.

Troy, Leo, and Neil Sheflin. 1985. *U.S. Union Sourcebook: Membership, Finances, Structure, Directory*. West Orange, N.J.: Industrial Relations Data and Information Services.

Valenzuela, Julio Samuel. 1979. *Labor Movement Formation and Politics: The Chilean and French Cases in Comparative Perspective, 1850–1950*. Ph.D. dissertation, Department of Political Science, Columbia University.

Wallace, Michael, Beth Rubin, and Brian Smith. 1988. "The Impact of American Labor Law on Working Class Militancy, 1901–1980," *Social Science History* 12: 1–29.

Warrian, Peter. 1987. *Labour Is Not a Commodity*. Ph.D. dissertation, Department of History, University of Waterloo.

Weiler, Paul. 1983. "Promises to Keep: Securing Workers' Rights to Self-organization under the NLRA," *Harvard Law Review* 96 (June): 1769–1827.

———. 1984. "Striking a New Balance: Freedom of Contract and the Prospects for Union Representation," *Harvard Law Review* 98 (December): 351–420.

Wilson, James Q. 1973. *Political Organization*. New York: Basic Books.

Yates, Michael. 1987. *Labor Law Handbook*. Boston: South End Press.

Young, Walter. 1969. *The Anatomy of a Party: The National CCF. 1932–61*. Toronto: University of Toronto Press.

Zieger, Robert H. 1987. "George Meany: Labor's Organization Man." In Dubofsky and Van Tine, eds., 1987: 324–49.

3   JOEL ROGERS

Don't Worry, Be Happy: The Postwar
Decline of Private-Sector Unionism
in the United States

He who would understand politics in the large may ponder well
the status of labor: a numerically great force in a society adher-
ing to the doctrine of the rule of numbers, yet without proportionate durable power as a class.
—V. O. Key 1953:53

Frankly I used to worry about the membership, about the size
of the membership. But quite a few years ago, I just stopped
worrying about it, because to me it doesn't make any difference.
—George Meany, USNWR 1972:28

It is a watchword of contemporary social science that "institutions matter." The slogan stands for the claim that how the affairs of social life are
organized is not only a consequence but also a cause of the interests,
resources, and patterns of interaction of social actors. Attention to the
effects of institutional structures can thus contribute to social explanation.

This chapter presents an account of some of the key institutional features of postwar U.S. industrial relations and uses that account to explain
the generation-long decline of private-sector U.S. unionism.[1] The discussion has three parts. In the first, I suggest a typology of industrial relations systems, based on differences in the density and centralization of
union memberships, and locate the "exceptional" U.S. case within that
typology. In the second, I characterize the narrow and fragile "accord"
that obtained between unions and employers in the U.S. private sector
during the first part of the postwar period—from 1945 until the early

48

1970s—and the factors that led to its collapse in the 1970s. In the third, I present a simple explanation of the decline of private-sector unionism and of the limited character of union response to its dwindling political power, consistent with the preceding analysis.

Constraints of space forbid any extensive discussion of the legal framework of private-sector unionism, an important institutional feature of the postwar system that figured prominently in union decline. For purposes of this discussion, then, I will simply premise the truth of the claim that that framework was, throughout the postwar period, extremely hostile to union growth. More particularly, I take the Labor Management Relations Act (LMRA),[2] the centerpiece of federal labor regulation over the past generation, to have hurt the labor movement in two important ways. First, the LMRA kept the costs of new union organization, particularly organization in the face of employer resistance, very high and offered little protection to organized workers in face of sham bargaining, relocation, and other changes in employer operation or other forms of management resistance or attack. This tended to confine unionization to those sectors of the economy claimed at the outset of the postwar period—the "traditional" union sectors, or union "core"—while leaving unions within this core highly vulnerable to changes in employer strategy. Second, the LMRA furthered the fragmentation of organized workers. It did so both by overtly limiting their coordination and by encouraging the pursuit of highly particularistic bargaining strategies in their dealings with employers. Of some consequence for understanding the national political strategy of labor during the postwar period, the latter included (often successful) strategies aimed at providing private equivalents of what in most advanced capitalist democracies was a social wage. A natural result of their pursuit was that unions were divided from one another and from unorganized workers, with the consequence that the labor movement as a whole was weakened as a national political force. But for individual unions such weakening only served to underscore the logic of particularism and the appeal of a "go it alone" strategy of self-help.[3]

If the LMRA had malign effects on private-sector union growth, however, it was hardly exogenous to other aspects of the postwar system. The LMRA's basic hostility to unions reflected the long-standing political weakness of American labor, which in both absolute and comparative terms became more pronounced over the postwar period. And the spe-

cific structure of industrial relations that it promoted, with all its atten-
dant difficulties for unions, reflected the interests generated on both sides
of the bargaining relation under conditions of low-density, decentralized,
and sectorally uneven worker organization. Indeed, while labor was far
from being an "equal partner" with business in elaborating the terms of
the LMRA, unions helped elaborate many of its key terms, including
some of those that eventually proved most debilitating to labor as a
whole. In short, the LMRA—in itself awful for the labor movement, if
not all unions within it—may be understood as product, as well as producer, of the nonlegal institutional setting sketched here.

U.S. Industrial Relations

As a general matter, the postwar private-sector industrial relations system
in the United States reflected the long-standing "exceptionalism" of
U.S. worker and employer organization and the characteristic strategies of unions and employers associated with low-density, decentralized
unionism.

Dynamics of Bargaining

Abstracting from the particulars of different industrial relations systems, the dynamics of bargaining between employers and unions can be
expected to vary discontinuously with the density and centralization of
union organization. At some risk of caricature, one may distinguish between a "low-density, decentralized case" (LDDC) and "high-density,
centralized case" (HDCC).[4] In the first, wages and benefits are not taken
out of competition, and unions are not coordinated. In the second,
wages and benefits are taken out of competition, and unions are coordinated. Across these cases, bargaining dynamics can be expected to vary
discontinuously for two reasons—the first arising from differences in the
competitive effects of unionization, the second from differences in the
strategies of gain undertaken by unions.

To clarify differences in competitive effects, some assumptions are immediately in order. Assume that the costs of unionization to employers
outweigh its benefits; call this difference the "union cost." Assume further, however, that the union cost can be borne by the market, that is,
that demand for the good produced is sufficiently inelastic that an increase in market price equal to the union cost does not significantly depress demand. Assume finally that employers exist in competition with

other employers and that all those with whom they are in competition use roughly identical techniques of production. On these assumptions, what matters to employers is not the union cost per se, but the degree to which those costs are generalized to rivals. Where only some firms in the particular sector are unionized (the LDDC), unionization appears as competitive disadvantage, and employers can be expected to resist it. Where all or most firms are unionized (the HDCC), unionization has little or no effect on competition, and employers thus lack an important incentive to resist.

On differences in union strategy, I assume that unions attempt to maximize the expected income of their members, but that in doing so they face important strategic trade-offs along two dimensions. The first dimension is time. Unions can concentrate on short-term gains, trying to enlarge their share of current product; or they can pursue long-term gains, attempting to enlarge future payoffs through the enlargement of future product. The second dimension is space (or "organizational space"). Unions can go it alone in wage demands, or coordinate their demands with other unions;[5] they can concentrate on extracting concessions from employers directly, or they can seek coalitions with other groups necessary to extract income through the state (i.e., through an increased social wage).[6]

The HDCC favors longer-term cooperative strategies with employers, and greater orientation to making gains through the state. The reasons are straightforward. In the HDCC, unions have more confidence that they will be able to extract future gains; because they comprise a larger and more coordinated share of the population, they can be expected to be less tolerant of "destructive" redistributive strategies that depress social product; and being both big and centralized, they have more developed capacities to make gains through the state. In the LDDC case, by contrast, unions have every incentive to free ride on their future interests, since they may not have a future; they have incentives to free ride on unorganized workers, since they bear a negligible portion of social costs of "destructive" redistribution; and they have little incentive to coordinate with other unions or seek general gains through the state, since their capacity for doing so is limited by their small numbers and lack of centralization.

What about employer attitudes toward the different cases? It seems safe to conclude that they, who in general may be assumed to favor no unionization over any unionization, also favor the HDCC over the

LDDC.[7] At a certain point of density and centralization, union effects on interfirm rivalry, the preferred strategies of unions, and employer attitudes toward unions all change direction. At this point, wages are taken out of competition, more secure unions exchange "militant economism" and "job control" for "political exchange" and cooperative strategies, and employers recognize that they both must and can live with unionization. Instead of devoting themselves to destroying unionization or resisting its spread, they cooperate in its maintenance and extension. Call this point, in Hegelian fashion, the line of "mutual recognition."[8]

Exceptional Disorganization

In the United States, which probably more closely approximates the ideal type of the LDDC than any other industrial relations system, this line has never been reached.[9] In comparative terms, American employers are "exceptionally" hostile to unions, in large measure because American workers are exceptionally disorganized. Here I note two familiar aspects of American worker disorganization—one bearing on the organization of formal politics, the other on union scope and structure—and indicate their relation and policy consequences.

Beginning with politics, the most salient phenomenon, virtually definitive of "American exceptionalism," is the absence of political organizations deriving their programmatic identity and organizational form from independent organizations of workers qua workers. There is no viable labor or social democratic party in the United States.[10] The electoral field is instead fully occupied by two business-dominated parties, featuring an almost premodern, "very archaic general structure" of weak vertical linkages between elites and masses, low capacities for mobilization, and a coalitional rather than programmatic thrust that is almost never articulated in explicit class terms.[11]

Lacking political vehicles of their own, American workers have long been disappearing as even a presence in the electoral system. As a general matter, and running counter to patterns in all other capitalist democracies, U.S. participation rates have trended downward since the late nineteenth century (since, in other words, the emergence of a substantial industrial working class). Recently they have hit record lows. Excluding the southern states, participation in the 1986 congressional elections dropped to its lowest level since 1798; and presidential election participation in 1988 dropped to 50 percent, lower than in any "modern" election but 1920 and 1924 (shortly after the denominator of the eligible electorate was abruptly swollen by the extension of the franchise to women).[12] Within this generally demobilized and increasingly "dealigned" universe, moreover, a large "hole" has opened up in that part of the electorate (the bottom third or so in income and education) that elsewhere provides the core support for social democratic and labor parties. Massive working-class abstention gives aggregate participation in the United States a decisive "class skew." Rates of U.S. working class participation are about 40 percent lower than both those of the U.S. propertied middle class *and* those of workers in other rich capitalist democracies.[13] In brief, U.S. workers do not appear much at all, and certainly do not appear as a class, in American electoral politics. They are thus singularly ill equipped to wage reform struggles through the state, to supplement their private incomes with a social wage.

Turning to economic organization, both the low-density and decentralization aspects of the LDDC find clear referents in the United States. Low density is obvious. Postwar U.S. union density reached a peak of 25.5 percent in 1953—the year V. O. Key observed that labor's numbers far exceeded its power. It has declined without interruption since then, dropping to 16 percent by 1990.[14] Considering only private-sector non-agricultural workers, the decline is even more striking. Unionization among that group fell from 38 percent in 1954 to 24 percent by 1978 and, on a different statistical series, to 12 percent by 1990.[15] This experience is also comparatively distinct. U.S. union density is lower than that in all other advanced industrial capitalist democracies, and no other system displays the postwar U.S. pattern of *uninterrupted* decline during the postwar period.

The decentralization of the U.S. case is also apparent. Whether one looks at the level at which bargaining proceeds, the control that central federations exert over member unions, the distribution of union resources across different levels of organization, or the sheer number of union organizations, there is scholarly consensus that the U.S. labor movement and industrial-relations system is among the most decentralized in the world, and certainly more decentralized than the continental Western European systems, such relatively decentralized cases as Italy and France included.[16]

The extreme decentralization of the U.S. union movement amounts to fragmentation, or a condition in which there is little effective coordination of component parts. To return once more to Key, this fragmentation is the most important reason that American labor's political strength is greatly outdistanced by its numbers. Numbers mean little without organization, and organization means little without coordination of those organized. It follows that increases in membership, without coordination, do not proportionately increase power, which is why, despite its absolute numbers, organized labor in the United States lacks "proportionate durable power as a class."[17] Instead of being more than the sum of its parts, with those parts coordinated in collaborative strategic action, the American labor movement is usually less.

More particularly, political and economic disorganization are related and have clear effects, both at the macro level of public policy and the micro level of collective bargaining. At the macro level, comparative studies indicate close correlation between union centralization and the strength of leftist parties,[18] and between the conjunction of centralized unions and leftist representation in government and a high social wage.[19] The extremely low and uneven quality of the U.S. social wage—the striking absence, in comparative terms, of such generic substantive entitlements as paid accident and sickness leave, vacation time, retraining, family leave, or national health insurance, and the heavy reliance instead on stingy, means-tested entitlement programs—is probably the most obvious policy outcome of U.S. worker disorganization. At the micro level of collective bargaining, the failure to achieve classwide gains through the state sharpens concentration on achieving more particular gains in narrow arenas, increases the appeal of "job control" versus "political" unionism, and the like.

Once embarked on this trajectory, moreover, it is difficult to get off. The particularity both of the gains sought within local arenas and of the organizations that seek them makes the articulation of general demands more difficult. And success in the achievement of particular demands tends to consolidate the pattern of organizational isolation while slowing the impetus to cross-sectoral coordination. The union strategies associated with the LDDC—a narrow political agenda, a focus on militant economism and job control—reinforce one another.

The Rise and Fall of the Postwar "Accord"

What I have just described as the LDDC has applicability to the whole of the U.S. economy and the U.S. labor movement within it during the postwar period. But in fact, of course, the labor movement is not organized on economy-wide lines, but on sectoral ones. During the first half of the postwar period, in a limited number of sectors, something approximating an "accord" (or "truce," or "ceasefire in place") was established.[20] This accord was *not* a perfect miniaturization of the HDCC. Gaining national political power sufficient to mount broad programs to increase the social wage required more than the coordination of union memberships in a limited number of sectors, and this was never something the postwar U.S. labor movement, confined to a few sectors, could achieve. Still, within those few sectors the U.S. approximated one aspect of the HDCC, namely, a modicum of cooperation between unions and employers.

The Limited Accord

The scope of the accord was severely limited. In addition to being concentrated in a few geographic regions (something of great consequence to the political power of labor at the national level), private-sector unionism was concentrated severely in a limited number of economic sectors. Entering the postwar period in 1947, the two broad sectors of construction and the major regulated industries (transportation, communication, and utilities) accounted for 34 percent of total private-sector union membership, while manufacturing provided another 48 percent.[21] These shares remained substantially unchanged until the late 1970s. Disaggregated data on membership within manufacturing, available since 1958, suggest further concentration. Four manufacturing sectors alone, combined with construction and the regulated industries, account for 72 percent of all private-sector union members in 1958, 71 percent in 1968, and 66 percent as late as 1978,[22] or consistently about twice their share of total private-sector employment.[23] In short, throughout the postwar period the vast bulk of private-sector unionism was confined to a clearly defined, distinctly limited, and shrinking portion of the total economy— really a handful of economic sectors. With little risk of exaggeration, one can thus speak of the postwar "accord" with labor not as an economy-wide phenomenon but as a sector-specific one.

This leads to the accord's content—the terms and conditions of cooperation between labor and management. While on an economy-wide basis unions never climbed past the line of "mutual recognition" with employers, in particular sectors they did. They achieved densities sufficient to take wages out of competition, thus removing the chief employer reason for resisting unionization. And in most of these core sectors, employer hostility was further reduced, or rendered ineffective, by other factors. In manufacturing, many of the lead firms had exceptionally strong market positions. They were willing to pay "monopoly rents" to unions because they had monopoly power themselves. Faced with strong domestic demand and operating in a relatively closed market, they could simply pass the union premium along to consumers—other firms or individuals—in the form of higher prices. In the heavily regulated transportation, communications, and utility sectors, this same effect was achieved through direct government regulation, which limited entry by rivals and set standardized prices for consumers that covered the additional costs of unionization. Finally, in some important cases, most notably mining and construction, firms were tied to particular locales and simply had to deal with an external labor market successfully organized by unions. In the core, in short, unions benefited heavily from monopoly pricing, and in some cases from the "locational immobilities" of firms.[24]

Within this limited core, unions and employers forged stable relationships, marked by significant cooperation.[25] The wage terms of collective-bargaining agreements were typically tied, as in the historic "Treaty of Detroit" negotiated by the United Auto Workers and General Motors, to productivity increases.[26] Collective-bargaining agreements were widely extended to three-year terms, with the inclusion of cost-of-living adjustment clauses (COLAs) for union members, no-strike clauses for management, and the agreement of both parties to submit disputes over contract terms to arbitration.[27] Despite their enormous complexity, the subject matter of collective-bargaining agreements was narrowed to "bread-and-butter" issues, leaving management's prerogative to make "strategic" decisions intact. And within firms, unions devoted themselves to elaborating the rules of "job control"—increasing the "cost of movement" of workers in the internal labor market, and thus compensating for the general lack of regulation of the external one.[28] From these efforts, employers gained stability without serious loss of autonomy, and union members gained benefits unavailable to the rest of the labor force.

The End of "Labor Peace"

This "accord" between unions and select employers in the private sector held in place in the United States until the early 1970s. Despite some shifting around, union density in the core sectors remained quite stable. The basic institutional arrangements of the accord—wage increases tied to productivity increases, generalization of wage and benefit costs throughout unionized sectors, binding arbitration to settle disputes over collective-bargaining agreements, union assistance in governing the internal labor market—remained in place.

Beginning in the early 1970s, however, particularly after the recession year of 1973, signs of stress began to appear. As in most advanced capitalist nations, U.S. economic performance deteriorated. Rates of profit and GNP and productivity growth dropped sharply, and median family income and weekly earnings stagnated or declined. Of even greater consequence, the U.S. economy was suddenly internationalized. The additive share of imports and exports in the GNP, which had been relatively slight (about 10 percent) and stable for the previous 50 years, doubled during the 1970s. Most U.S. firms (about 70 percent) were just as suddenly exposed to international competitive pressures. Throughout the decade of the 1970s, many lost market share to foreign competitors.[29] Even where they retained share, however, U.S. firms found themselves operating in a qualitatively more competitive environment.[30]

One effect of these changes on the calculus of American business was predictable. They became much more sensitive to costs, since those costs could no longer be passed along to captive domestic consumers, and more intent on cutting costs, beginning with the price of labor. This was true both in unionized sectors of manufacturing, which suddenly faced substantially increased competition from abroad, and nonunionized sectors of the economy, which became even more bent than they were before on resisting unionization. As a general matter, the ensuing attack on workers in both union and nonunion sectors was reflected in the decline in worker incomes reported above.[31] But while union workers, because they were organized, were better able to resist such downward pressures—a fact reflected in a better than 50 percent rise in the union "premium," or difference between union and nonunion wages, during the 1970s[32]—that ability made them even more squarely an object of attack.

In addition to rolling back wages, or unionization, or both, for their own workforces, firms sought to roll back various regulatory protections that imposed costs on them. Of particular consequence here were the efforts to "deregulate" the highly regulated, and heavily union, service sectors of transportation and communication, where government sponsored barriers to entry and artificially inflated prices.

These developments, all untoward for the union sector, coincided with

an equally unfavorable diffusion of new technologies of profit extraction—computerized switching devices in communications, prefabrication
in construction, strip-mining in mineral extraction, use of containers in
shipping, vacuum-packed meat boxes in meat cutting, numerically controlled machine tools in machining. Their diffusion permitted firms to
shift production away from externally organized markets—thus overcoming the "locational immobilities" that had benefited labor—or to
break union monopolies on the generation of needed skills by organizing
alternative sources of skill or deskilling the relevant production process.[33]

Last, increased competition and uncertain demand (the apparent satu-
ration or fracturing of traditional mass markets) persuaded many firms of
the need for increased "flexibility" in production. The term is protean in
meaning—referring at one extreme to felicitous paths of "flexible specialization" in high value-added market niches, at the other to simple sweat-
ing of workers and implementation of the business maxim "internalize
scarcity, externalize risk."[34] Whatever the meaning of "flexibility," however, it was clear that its implementation required something almost diametrically opposed to the "high-cost-of-movement" governance mechanism typical of the unionized internal labor market. And this provided
further animus against unions.

On all these dimensions, then, the calculus of American employers
changed in the 1970s. They broke the truce that had existed since the
close of World War II and began attacking unions within the traditional
core. The response of a weakened and highly fragmented labor movement was always slow, generally ineffective, and never aimed at a much
broader mobilization of the sort needed to withstand this attack. Indeed,
labor's failed response only served to underscore the appeal, to those
unions that remained, of the particularism that had long characterized
labor's political efforts—a particularism, again, that followed "naturally"
from its LDDC status.[35]

Given the weakness of labor's response and the absence of any independent check by the law, employer attacks soon registered in an acceler-
ation of union-density decline. In the 1970s, major losses were sustained
in the core sectors of manufacturing and construction. In the 1980s, the
decline became a rout, as losses in these sectors were joined by massive
attrition in the newly deregulated services of transportation and communications, and the employer attack snowballed. As unions weakened, they
were less able to take wages out of competition among employers, leading
to further employer attacks, leading to further weakening, and so on.[36]

In brief, the elaborate system of rules and understandings, compromise and consent, that had marked U.S. industrial relations for a generation was suddenly transformed.

Patterns of Decline

However incomplete the characterization provided here, something like this account of the structure and collapse of the postwar accord with unions has a certain obvious appeal. It fits well with what is known about other changes in American political economy in the 1970s and makes sense of the common perception that there was a distinct and relatively stable set of dealings between unions and employers that held for a long period and then rather suddenly collapsed into "one-sided class war."

Such an account, however, does not immediately fit the facts of continuous and, until the late 1970s, virtually linear decline in private-sector union density over the postwar period, the comparable steady decline in union success rates in NLRB (National Labor Relations Board) representation elections (widely taken as a proxy for the "balance of class forces"), and the comparable decline in union organizing efforts, as measured by the percentage of the unorganized workforce participating in NLRB representation elections. Notice of such continual declines has led some theorists to conclude that the *real* sources of private-sector union decline in the postwar period predated that period; they are owing to bad strategic choices unions made in the 1930s and 1940s (perhaps coupled with a postwar-1950s purging of radicals from their ranks).[37]

This view has much to recommend it. Clearly, the political choices that unions made in the 1930s, 1940s, and early 1950s affected their options, and their willingness to act on them, in subsequent decades. Clearly too, the continuous decline in postwar union density establishes the tautological truth of the claim that union organization was insufficient to maintain density shares. As a guide to understanding what happened in the postwar period, however, I find the view less than satisfying. Commonly the view is accompanied by invidious characterizations of the "false consciousness" or blank "irrationality" of the American labor movement, and here it just as commonly suffers from a compositional fallacy, falsely assuming that what is rational for workers as a class must be rational for individual members of that class and their unions. More immediately, the view is offered in opposition to the claim that union-employer dealings were stable for a long period; it does not capture or explain the perception that in fact they were.

The problems with this alternative view, as well as the problem from which it arises (the apparent lack of fit between the account of stable dealings through the early 1970s and the fact of continuous density decline), can be addressed through a brief analysis of union-density decline. Killing many birds with a single statistical stone, this analysis rests on a sector-specific explanation of the composition of that decline, and on the division of the postwar period into distinct subperiods.[38]

To see the force of this analysis, consider what the accord account offered above would imply for union-density decline. This requires pressing two assumptions in that account into sharper relief.

The first, implicit in my earlier account of bargaining dynamics and American exceptionalism, is that unions customarily organize workers (rather than workers organizing unions), and that in doing so unions behave in strategic ways. They choose an optimal level of organization and choose optimal sites for organization, taking into account the payoffs accruing from the addition of new members and the likely response of employers to organizing efforts.

The second assumption, noted at the outset, is that postwar labor regulation, centered in the LMRA, set the costs of organizing extremely high and provided no serious deterrent to employer attacks on unions. As a practical consequence of this, where unions are not able to compel employer recognition and bargaining through economic force, they have little or no redress against resistant employers.

Together these assumptions lead to a natural hypothesis, namely, that in the postwar period, unions were quite reluctant to organize in sectors where they did not already command significant power. Always admitting exceptions, as a general matter it would only be in such sectors that they could expect some mitigation of employer resistance—since only there would they have already made progress in taking wages out of competition. And only there, where there was resistance, could they expect to be able to overcome it through economic force.

In the framework of the accord analysis offered above, we can join these assumptions with what we know about the structure and scope of unionism to "predict" a certain pattern in union decline in the postwar period. Briefly, we know that coming into the postwar period, unions were organized in a limited and distinct number of sectors, with union power within those sectors concentrated in blue-collar (as against white- or pink-collar) jobs within them. If, as argued above, these union strongholds remained relatively stable through the early 1970s, then we would expect that most of the decline in overall union density would be accounted for simply by a decline in the share of total employment taken by these strongholds, not by a decline within them.[39] Returning to the argument above, I claimed that these stable sectoral dealings were disrupted in the early 1970s and I attached particular importance to international price pressures. This would lead us to expect a decline in the importance of the "structural" variables of sector employment and occupation, and to expect that some defensible proxy for international price pressures would become a significant predictor of intrasector union decline, once occupation is taken into account, via controls. Finally, I argued that the postwar system began disintegrating rapidly in the 1980s. During this period, we would thus expect yet further decline in the power of the structural variables (and perhaps even a drop in the significance of the internationalization variable). The picture should become highly scrambled, as befits a period of wreckage and transition. The "system" would no longer display systemic properties.

Statistical analysis shows exactly these results, and thus offers confirmation of the account offered above.

Disaggregating the private economy into five sectors, a basic "shift-share" analysis of sectoral employment—predicting union density on the basis of shifts in the share of total employment claimed by different sectors (with different degrees of unionization)—shows great power in predicting density until the early 1970s, but much less power since then, and even less since the early 1980s.[40] Using Bureau of Labor Statistics (BLS) data, sectoral employment shifts account for 54–60 percent of the decline over the 1956–72 period; for the years 1972–78 sectoral shifts account for only 29–35 percent.[41] Using different data from the Current Population Survey (CPS), but the same industry breakdown, only 22–27 percent of the decline between 1974 and 1980 and only 13–17 percent of the decline between 1980 and 1984 can be accounted for by such sectoral employment shifts.

Supplementing the sectoral variables with occupational data (the shift across white-, blue-, and pink-collar employment) strengthens the analysis, without disturbing the pattern of decline across periods in the power of structural variables. Using CPS data, industry and occupation shifts together account for 51–56 percent of the decline between 1974 and

1980 (roughly a 30 percent increase over industry alone), but only 17–21 percent of the decline between 1980 and 1984.

While the BLS data do not permit the same kind of comparison for the earlier period, the later period results allow a confident assertion that the two variables together would increase the amount of accounted-for decline substantially above the industry-alone figure for 1956–72, bringing it from 54–60 percent to as high as 75 percent of the total decline.

Moving to intrasector decline (controlling for occupation) of the sort that became evident in the 1970s, one finds that over the period 1974–80, when about 50 percent of the decline in density remained unaccounted for by structural variables, 60 percent of unaccounted-for decline is attributable to decreases in unionization among blue-collar workers in manufacturing, with about 20 percent attributable to decreases among blue-collar workers in construction. Thus, about 80 percent of that which is not accounted for by the structural analysis can be explained by changes in union density in just two occupational/industrial groups— blue-collar workers in manufacturing and blue-collar workers in construction. A third of the decline among the former, in turn, is accounted for by a simple "internationalization" variable, used as a proxy for international price pressures in those sectors.[42]

For the period 1980–84, when the "unaccounted-for" portion of the decline increased to about 83 percent, substantial declines in unionization spread to all industries. In addition to continued declines among blue-collar workers in manufacturing and construction, all of the occupational groups in the regulated industries and blue-collar workers in the service sector (both less subject to direct international competitive pressures) experienced declines in unionization. The internationalization variable thus fails a significance test. The picture is decidedly scrambled—albeit subject to reconstruction through more qualitative sector-specific histories, notice of the effects of deregulation, and the like.[43]

To summarize, simple structural variables (employment by sector and occupational group) can account for about 75 percent of the decline in unionization through 1972. These variables, joined by a measure of internationalization, can account for about 60 percent of the decline during the 1974–80 period. During the 1980s, they account for only about 20 percent of the density decline. It seems clear that the common perception, shared by the accord account, that there was a period of relative stability that was then interrupted, is correct. And if my assumption about the hostile legislative environment for organizing is correct, then union behavior during the period has at least the appearance of ratio-nality. Faced with a hostile external climate, unions hunkered down in their heavily organized sectors and essentially stayed put. They organized relatively little in general and confined much of their organizational ef-forts to maintaining density within their sectors.[44] This they succeeded in doing in virtually all sectors until the early 1970s, and even in many sec-tors until the very late 1970s.

In retrospect, the fragility of postwar private-sector U.S. unionism is obvious. Given the extremely unfavorable framework of self-help pro-moted by the LMRA, a shift in employer toleration of unions was regis-tered almost immediately in a sharp rollback of private-sector union power. As late as 1972, however, when George Meany was observing that he was not worried about the size of membership, the vulnerability of private-sector unionism was, perhaps, less apparent. Guided by the par-ticularistic logic of the LDDC, the U.S. labor movement looked at itself in the early 1970s and basically liked what it saw. The reasons for its contentment were as straightforward as the reasons why it would soon be shattered. Even as the overall level of private-sector unionism was declining, and even as the economy (and with it, much of American society) was moving away from the labor movement, union density within the shrinking "core" sectors was still high, union dealings with employers were still relatively stable, and union gains were still consider-able. The limits of the LMRA, and of the fragile accord it regulated, had not yet been tested. The limits of the LDDC itself, and the style of trade unionism to which it gave rise, had barely been contemplated. As they looked to the future, then, it is understandable why American trade-union leaders found the most reassuring maxim—"Don't worry, be happy"—also to be the wisest. Much less clear, as I contemplate the future now facing the U.S. labor movement, is whether intervening events have generated support among them for a more radical, encom-passing, political, and, of necessity, more productivist strategy of renewal, or whether most unions will, within the logic of the LDDC, simply play out with American business an endgame of steadily declining power.

Notes

1. This is a much-shortened version of a paper delivered at the conference, "North American Labour Movements into the 1990s: Similarities or Differ-ences?" Cambridge, 3–5 February, 1989. It draws on Rogers (1990). In revised

form, it appears as "In the Shadow of the Law: Institutional Aspects of Postwar U.S. Union Decline," in Christoper Tomlins, ed., *New Directions in Legal History*, Johns Hopkins University Press, 1992.

2. 29 U.S.C. Sec. 141–97.

3. These assertions about the LMRA are defended at length in Rogers (1990). See as well U.S. Congress (1984) and Morris (1987).

4. This two-fold, rather than four-fold, typology of systems is permitted by the very high correlation of centralization and density. For eighteen OECD (Organization for Economic Cooperation and Development) countries, for example, the Pearson correlation coefficient between average union density over 1965–80 and Cameron's (1984: 165) measure of "confederation power in collective bargaining," for example, is .7708. More interesting complications arise with consideration of variations in political structure, however, which add an important dimension to the interactions described here. See note 6, below.

5. The opportunities for free riding here are of course legion and form the basis of the "destructive" redistributive coalitions of which Olson (1965; 1982) warns.

6. Clearly, the preexisting political structure affects this choice as well. The structure of the state and electoral competition in the United States (separated powers at the national level, extreme federation of government functions, single-member districts for most elected offices, etc.) make a legislation-centered union strategy more difficult, as do related differences in the typical structure of benefit delivery for those benefits that have been gained. Differences in these areas are critical to distinguishing the United States from other "liberal" cases, the case of Canada included.

7. The analysis here is intended to "dance in the middle of the floor." Hypothetical extreme cases of 0 and 100 percent unionization may both be assumed to pose efficiency problems and additional flips in the attitudes of employers. At the low end of unionization, what is generally true of employers in real-world circumstances is probably not true of all employers; at least in some industries, some minimal degree of (weak) unionization is probably desired. And certainly at the high end, as union density and centralization approach unity, employers again begin to worry, for workers with that much power might opt to run the economy for themselves. As Przeworski (1987: 37) wryly observes, "Capitalists would prefer no unions than unions; if they cannot have the former they should prefer stronger over weaker unions; yet they fear the political consequences of strong unions. This is not an easy preference profile to act upon: hence the ambivalent posture of capitalists toward workers."

8. Two clarifications may be needed here. First, crossing this point, of course, may and commonly does require intense conflict between unions and employers, or changes in the legal framework facilitating increased unionization.

Second, passage itself is as much process as event. Before the full logic of the HDCC is reached, and it becomes self-stabilizing with employer cooperation, one can expect a period of continued gaming and testing.

9. One contender for pride of place might be the enterprise union system of Japan. Other features of that system, however, permit the coordination of interests (including incomes policies) lacking in the LDDC. This "corporatism without unions" is sufficiently different to defy easy comparison. A more formidable class of contenders is populated by the other "liberal" industrial-relations systems (e.g., the United Kingdom, Canada, and New Zealand). Differences in state structure and the rules on party competition (see note 6, above), however, make it easier for labor in those states to mount a more encompassing strategy through the state than in the United States.

10. Contrary to the suggestion in Greenstone (1969), I take the relation between labor and the Democratic party to be fundamentally different than relations between union movements and social democratic parties in Western Europe. The best single measure of labor's postwar power within the Democratic party was its ability to compel party support of legislation favorable to its own organization. On this measure, labor's relations with the Democrats have been incomparably worse than relations, however strained, between social democratic parties in Europe and their respective labor movements. Labor lost repeatedly in the postwar period, on Taft-Hartley, Landrum Griffin, the promised repeal of the right-to-work provision in Taft-Hartley, common situs picketing, and labor law reform, suffering throughout from massive Democratic defections. More subtle measures of comparison (e.g., the representation of labor officials in party organizations, staffing ties, regularity of consultation with labor officials, etc.) only underscore the difference. Unions have of course been active in national politics and have often extracted benefits from the party system. But the characteristic organizational form that takes—the capacity for sanctions of party leaders, the intimacy of relations, and the range of objects sought—all differ in quite fundamental ways from the "typical" social democratic case. On labor's relations with the Democrats, see Ferguson and Rogers (1981; 1986) and Davis (1986). For rich evidence of continuing close ties between trade unions and parties in Europe, see the range of studies in Gourevitch et al. (1984); Lange, Ross, and Vanicelli (1982); and Flanagan, Soskice, and Ulman (1983). For an account of "electoral socialism" that examines the constraints unions put on the choices of party leaders—constraints largely absent in the U.S. case—see Przeworski and Sprague (1986).

11. Duverger (1959). That both major parties are business-dominated makes it rather difficult, of course, to use the category of class in organizing electoral appeals. (But not impossible, as canned populist appeals indicate each electoral season.)

12. "Modern" here means since the emergence of a national party system in 1828.

13. This discussion draws from Burnham (1982). See as well Przeworski and Sprague (1986) for historical data on levels of working-class voting for several West European nations.

14. The 1953 peak figure is from BLS (1979: Table 165); Troy and Sheflin (1985) estimate the peak at the same year, with a marginally higher 25.9 figure. The 1990 figure comes from BLS (1991: 228). Note that this uses a slightly different estimating technique.

15. The 1954 and 1978 figures are based on BLS (1980: Tables 72, 162, and 165). I have replicated the calculations from these data reported in Freeman and Medoff (1984: 222). For the 1990 figure, from the Current Population Survey, see BLS (1991: 229).

16. Wallerstein (1985: 42) has merged these various studies, converting their results to a single 0–7 scale on centralization (7 being most centralized). The United States and Canada both rank at 0. For select West European states, the rankings are: Austria 7, Netherlands 5.7, Norway 5.5, Sweden 5.5, Belgium 5.4, Finland 5.1, Denmark 3.0, Switzerland 2.2, West Germany 1.2, France 0.7, Italy 0.7. This scaling does not reflect differences in the structure of political systems, the degree of leftist representation in government, or the structure of social programs—all of which can mitigate the effects of decentralized union organizations on the ground. Again, taking such differences into account (see note 6, above), I would argue that Canada (and other "liberal" systems) are less fragmented than the United States.

17. Key (1953: 53).

18. Surveying eighteen OECD countries over the period 1965–82, for example, Cameron (1984: 167) reports a .79 correlation between these two variables.

19. This literature is now enormous. For a recent review, and significant contribution in its own right, see Wilensky and Turner (1987).

20. See Edwards and Podgursky (1986), an excellent treatment of the postwar accord with labor, that influences my own throughout.

21. Troy (1969).

22. BLS (1980). The four main manufacturing sectors contributing to unionization were: (1) food, beverages, and tobacco; (2) clothing, textiles, and leather; (3) metals, machinery, and equipment; and (4) transportation equipment.

23. BLS (1980: Table 162).

24. Edwards and Podgursky (1986). See as well Mishel (1986) for a review of the "permissive" economic environment in which unions prospered.

25. For a recent, clear, and very compressed description of the elements of cooperation and their functionality, see Kochan (1988).

26. Piore and Sabel (1984) provide a good discussion of this basic wage pattern, as do Kochan, McKersie, and Katz (1987).

27. On the growth of COLAs, see Hendricks and Kahn (1985).

28. Piore's (1986) discussion of this, with useful contrasts to European restrictions, is particularly good.

29. For reviews of the decline in U.S. competitiveness, see Dertouzos et al. (1989); Scott and Lodge (1985); Eichengreen (1988). Note that while the U.S. share of world trade continued to decline during this period, U.S. multinationals generally retained market share (Lipsey and Kravis 1986).

30. This phenomenon, and its effects on the calculations of American business elites, is discussed at length in Ferguson and Rogers (1986).

31. Real average weekly earnings in private nonagricultural industry declined continuously during this period, from $198 in 1973 to $166 in 1989. See CEA (1990: Table C-44).

32. Freeman and Medoff (1984: 53).

33. The point is emphasized in Edwards and Podgursky (1986).

34. Piore and Sabel, generally identified with the promise of the first extreme, acknowledge the distinct possibility of the second (1984: 278–79).

35. For labor's failed response, see Ferguson and Rogers (1986); Davis (1986); Moody (1988).

36. The widespread phenomenon of "concession bargaining" underscored the decline in labor's bargaining power. At least as striking, however, was the ensuing drop in pattern bargaining. On this, perhaps the best evidence comes from two Conference Board surveys of employer wage-determination practices, conducted in 1978 and 1983 (Freedman 1985). In the first, firm managers identified "industry patterns" as most critical to their own wage determination. In the second, industry patterns receded markedly in significance, dropping to fourth overall among managerial considerations. Coming to the fore were narrower concerns: (in descending order of importance) productivity or labor-cost trends in their particular firm, expected profits, or local labor-market conditions and wage rates. Over 1978–83 the number of firms citing one of these as their primary consideration increased a remarkable 64 percent.

37. See, for example, Goldfield (1987), a leading proponent of the thesis of an essentially continuous decline. Bad choices in the 1930s and 1940s, Goldfield argues, cemented a conservative labor movement incapable of resisting a steadily increasing attack by employers and unwilling to make sufficient investments in organizing.

38. The analysis that follows is drawn from joint work with Sigurt Vitols. See Rogers and Vitols (1989).

39. Note here that this is a "structural" analysis, but not one that assumes some inherent properties in occupational or sectoral groupings that make them more or less immune to unionization. What is really doing the work in explana-

tion here is not the structural variables per se but the political context in which they operate. It is that context—extremely inhospitable to the spread of unionization beyond the sectors organized at the outset of the postwar period—that gives them their predictive power.

40. The five sectors are: mining, construction, manufacturing, transportation/communications/utilities, and services. This provides a more disaggregated analysis than that commonly offered (e.g., by Farber [1985]), while also avoiding a common mistake in such accounts (again, see Farber [1985]), viz., the inclusion of the public sector. The structural-decomposition technique I share with Farber does not work well when some sectors go up in density and others go down. When this is the case (as with the public sector during the postwar period), there is some canceling out, and the percent of decline "explained" or "accounted for" by the shift-share analysis is consequently overstated.

41. I report these data in ranges because the results are dependent upon whether one uses as the "weight" the size of sectors in the first year or the last year in a subperiod; since sectors change sizes, they have different weights in the two periods. A more complete explanation is provided in Rogers and Vitols (1989).

42. We used the ratio of the sum of imports and exports to domestic shipments.

43. On deregulation's effects, see Hendricks (1986).

44. This picture of organizing is confirmed by Voos (1982).

References

BLS (Bureau of Labor Statistics). 1979. *Handbook of Labor Statistics*. Washington, D.C.: Government Printing Office.

————. 1980. *Handbook of Labor Statistics*. Washington, D.C.: Government Printing Office.

————. 1991. *Employment and Earnings* 38 (January).

Burnham, Walter Dean. 1982. *The Current Crisis in American Politics*. New York: Oxford.

Cameron, David R. 1984. "Social Democracy, Corporatism, Labour Quiescence and the Representation of Economic Interest in Advanced Capitalist Society." Pp. 143–78 in J. Goldthorpe, ed., *Order and Conflict in Contemporary Capitalism: Studies in the Political Economy of Western European Nations*. New York: Oxford University Press.

CEA (Council of Economic Advisers). 1990. *Economic Report of the President*. Washington, D.C.: Government Printing Office.

Davis, Mike. 1986. *Prisoners of the American Dream: Politics and Economics in the History of the U.S. Working Class*. London: Verso.

Dertouzos, Michael L., Robert K. Lester, Robert M. Solow, and the MIT

Commission on Industrial Productivity. 1989. *Made in America: Regaining the Productive Edge*. Cambridge, Mass.: MIT Press.

Duverger, Maurice. 1959. *Political Parties*. 2d ed. New York: Wiley.

Edwards, Richard, and Michael Podgursky. 1986. "The Unraveling Accord: American Unions in Crisis." Pp. 14–60 in Richard Edwards, Paolo Garonna, and Franz Tödtling, eds., *Unions in Crisis and Beyond: Perspectives from Six Countries*. Dover, Mass.: Auburn House.

Eichengreen, Barry. 1988. "International Competition in the Products of U.S. Basic Industries." Pp. 279–353 in M. Feldstein, ed., *The United States in the World Economy*. Chicago: University of Chicago Press.

Farber, H. S. 1985. "The Extent of Unionization in the United States." Pp. 15–43 in T. A. Kochan, ed., *Challenges and Choices Facing American Labor*. Cambridge, Mass.: MIT Press.

Ferguson, Thomas, and Joel Rogers. 1981. "The Reagan Victory: Corporate Coalitions in the 1980 Campaign." Pp. 3–64 in Thomas Ferguson and Joel Rogers, eds., *The Hidden Election: Politics and Economics in the 1980 Presidential Campaign*. New York: Pantheon.

———. 1986. *Right Turn: The Decline of the Democrats and the Future of American Politics*. New York: Hill and Wang.

Flanagan, Robert J., David W. Soskice, and Lloyd Ulman. 1983. *Unionism, Economic Stabilization, and Incomes Policies: European Experience*. Washington, D.C.: Brookings Institution.

Freedman, Audrey. 1985. *The New Look in Wage Policy and Employee Relations*. New York: Conference Board.

Freeman, R. B., and J. L. Medoff. 1984. *What Do Unions Do?* New York: Basic Books.

Goldfield, Michael. 1987. *The Decline of Organized Labor in the United States*. Chicago: University of Chicago Press.

Gourevitch, Peter, Andrew Martin, George Ross, Christopher Allen, Stephen Bornstein, and Andrei Markovits. 1984. *Unions and Economic Crisis: Britain, West Germany, and Sweden*. Boston: George Allen and Unwin.

Greenstone, D. J. 1969. *Labor in American Politics*. New York: Alfred A. Knopf.

Hendricks, W. E. 1986. "Collective Bargaining in Regulated Industries." *Advances in Industrial and Labor Relations* 3:21–42.

Hendricks, W. E., and L. M. Kahn. 1985. *Wage Indexation in the United States: Cola or Uncola?* Cambridge, Mass.: Ballinger.

Key, V. O. 1953. *Politics, Parties, and Pressure Groups*. 3d ed. New York: Crowell.

Kochan, T. A. 1988. "Adaptability of the U.S. Industrial Relations System." *Science* 240:287–92.

Kochan, T. A., R. B. McKersie, and H. C. Katz. 1987. *The Transformation of American Industrial Relations*. New York: Basic Books.

Lange, Peter, George Ross, and Maurizio Vanicelli. 1982. *Unions, Change, and*

    Crisis: French and Italian Union Strategy and the Political Economy, 1945–1980. Boston: George Allen and Unwin.

Lipsey, R. E., and Irving Kravis. 1986. "The Competitiveness and Comparative Advantage of U.S. Multinationals, 1957–83." National Bureau of Economic Research (NBER) Working Paper No. 2051. Cambridge: NBER.

Mishel, Lawrence. 1986. "The Structural Determinants of Union Bargaining Power." *Industrial and Labor Relations Review* 40: 90–104.

Mishel, Lawrence, and David Frankel. 1991. *The State of Working America*. Armonk, N.Y.: M.E. Sharpe.

Moody, Kim. 1988. *An Injury to All: The Decline of American Unionism*. London: Verso.

Morris, Clarke, ed. 1987. *American Labor Policy: A Critical Appraisal of the National Labor Relations Act*. Washington, D.C.: Bureau of National Affairs.

Olson, Mancur. 1965. *The Logic of Collective Action*. Cambridge, Mass.: Harvard University Press.

———. 1982. *The Rise and Decline of Nations*. New Haven: Yale University Press.

Piore, M. J. 1986. "Perspectives on Labor Market Flexibility." *Industrial Relations* 25: 146–66.

Piore, M. J., and C. F. Sabel. 1984. *The Second Industrial Divide: Possibilities for Prosperity*. New York: Basic Books.

Przeworski, Adam. 1987. "Capitalism, Democracy, Pacts." Unpublished revision of a paper prepared for the Conference on Pacts in the Process of Transition to Democracy. Sao Paulo, June.

Przeworski, Adam, and John Sprague. 1986. *Paper Stones: A History of Electoral Socialism*. Chicago: University of Chicago Press.

Rogers, Joel 1990. "Divide and Conquer: Further 'Reflections on the Distinctive Character of American Labor Laws.'" *University of Wisconsin Law Review* 1990: 1–147.

Rogers, Joel, and Sigurt Vitols. 1989. "Explaining the Postwar Decline in Private Sector U.S. Union Density: Structural Variables in a Political Context." Unpublished.

Scott, B. R., and G. C. Lodge, eds. 1985. *U.S. Competitiveness in the World Economy*. Boston: Harvard Business School Press.

Troy, Leo 1969. "Trade Union Growth in a Changing Economy." *Monthly Labor Review* 92 (September): 3–7.

Troy, Leo, and Neil Sheflin. 1985. *U.S. Union Sourcebook: Membership, Finances, Structure, Directory*. West Orange, N.J.: Industrial Relations Data and Information Services.

U.S. Congress. 1984. *Has Labor Law Failed?* Hearings before the Subcommittee on Labor-Management Relations of the House Committee on Education and Labor, and the Manpower and Housing Subcommittee of the House Committee on Government Relations. 98th Congress, 2d Session.

USNWR (U.S. News and World Report). 1972. "U.S. Needs '30,000 New Jobs a Week Just to Break Even': Interview with George Meany, President, AFL-CIO." 21 February: 27–28.

Voos, P. B. 1982. "Labor Union Organizing Programs, 1954–1977." Cambridge, Mass.: Ph.D. dissertation, Harvard University.

Wallerstein, Michael. 1985. "Working Class Solidarity and Rational Behavior." Chicago: Ph.D. dissertation, University of Chicago.

Wilensky, Harold, and Lowell Turner. 1987. *Democratic Corporatism and Policy Linkages: The Interdependence of Industrial, Labor-Market, Incomes, and Social Policies in Eight Countries*. University of California, Berkeley: Institute of International Studies. Research Series No. 69.

4   JANE JENSON AND RIANNE MAHON

Legacies for Canadian Labour
of Two Decades of Crisis

The Canadian labour movement gained new strength after 1945, and it is the rights and authority gained then that unions have fought to protect in the troubled last two decades. Yet as the country entered the 1990s it became increasingly clear that the postwar efficacy of the movement arose from a particular conjunction of circumstances and state policies on which unions can no longer count. Canadian unionists, as those in all other advanced industrial societies, face a world that is in many ways unfamiliar and in which long-standing strategic predilections work less effectively.

The search for new responses has brought mixed results in Canada. While labour became weaker in some ways, facing stagnating and even declining densities in some sectors, it has not been subjected to organizational decay as the American movement has. Canadian unions, moreover, have begun to show signs that they are carving out a new and innovative political position for themselves. They have begun to develop new workplace and collective strategies and to intervene in broad questions of national development and strategy, either alone or in alliance with other popular forces. This too is a shift from the postwar pattern in which unions tended to concentrate their political efforts on lobbying the state on issues of particular import to them, leaving broader political matters to Canada's social democrats, the New Democratic Party (NDP).

This chapter examines the characteristics of the Canadian labour movement in the postwar period in order to ascertain why it has taken this path into the 1990s, one which diverges in so many ways from that followed by the American movement with which it shares much history and organizational experience.

The Foundations of Permeable Fordism

As was the case for so many other countries, Canada emerged from the Great Depression and World War II with a restructured economy and altered social relations. The new economic relations can be characterized as "Fordism," a form of social regulation based on the extension of mass-production industries, which in turn were dependent upon the extension of markets—primarily domestic markets—for their goods.[1] In this way mass consumption of many kinds of goods, and particularly automobiles and consumer durables, was an integral part of postwar regulation. A crucial part of the regulatory power of Fordism was its social compromise around a wage relation that granted unions certain collective rights in exchange for leaving production decisions to capital. In this way, a new status for representatives of labour was at the heart of the mode of regulation.

This social compromise did not fall from the sky, nor was it determined simply by technology or economic systems. Politics, in the broadest sense of the term, had a crucial role to play. It was through concrete political struggle that a social compromise was worked out, and therefore its content and the balance of class forces it institutionalized differed in each country, according to the specific character of that country's politics.[2]

Canada's Fordism reflected the particularities of the country's model of development and particularly its relationship to the United States. The postwar Fordism developed in Canada was a specific kind, being very permeable to international effects. It was designed domestically but always with an eye to the international economy, in a way that made it more permeable to international trade than was the case with most other countries.³ This institutionalized arrangement could be called permeable Fordism.

Thus, although mass consumption played a part in Canada's postwar economic expansion, the accelerator was less investment in domestic consumer durable industries producing for an expanding home market than the inflow of foreign capital related to the extraction and export of Canadian resources, whose product was primarily destined for the U.S. market. Canada's mass-production industries, moreover, were largely assembly operations, established by foreign (mainly U.S.) capital and dependent on the import of technology and key capital goods from parent companies. These miniature-replica branch plants were rarely able to achieve economies of scale. The exceptions to the rule were those industries, such as auto, defence production, and agricultural machinery, which were able to rationalize their operations as a result of special bilateral agreements that gave them access to both markets.

This accumulation strategy, fostered by the state, made Canada's goods-producing sector particularly vulnerable to developments in the United States. Both the resource and the manufacturing sectors were dependent on the flow of foreign capital and technology from U.S. sources. The resource sector depended on secure access to the U.S. market, and manufacturing depended on the continued existence of the tariff to entice branch plants to locate north of the forty-ninth parallel.

The industrial relations system was also permeable to continental effects. By 1949, 70.9 percent of unionized workers belonged to unions headquartered in the United States and that number remained steady until 1965. Canada's postwar industrial relations legislation was also modelled on the Wagner Act. It is, therefore, not surprising that collective-bargaining practices in many respects resembled the American pattern—highly decentralized and focussed on securing wage increases in accordance with productivity rises, while posing a limited, and highly bureaucratic challenge to capital's prerogatives in the workplace via a complex grievance procedure. Both differed from the pattern set in certain Western European countries where national wage setting through bi- or tri-partite mechanisms became the norm. In addition, both labour movements had to rely largely on collective bargaining to secure "fringe benefits," since their welfare states remained undeveloped relative to their Western European counterparts. In this sense, Fordist regulation in both countries can be described as centred in the private sector, with the state

acting more as an overseer than as an active partner. Even in the formative years, however, there were significant differences between the two.

Canadian industrial relations legislation may have incorporated important elements of the Wagner Act, but it also built on previous legislation
that more profoundly circumscribed the rights of unions (Panitch and
Swartz 1988; McBride 1987). It imposed elaborate certification procedures
and required unions to win the support of the majority of those eligible
to vote. Contracts were legally enforceable, and strikes were prohibited
during the life of the agreement. Union leaders and membership were
subject to fines and other penalties if these rules were not followed. Once
a contract had expired, moreover, unions had to go through a lengthy
process of conciliation before they could go on strike. Finally, the state
retained the right to intervene in the settlement of grievances, should the
parties themselves prove unable to settle a dispute.

Canada's "Wagner Act" also came later, and then only after a series of
bitter strikes that escalated dramatically during the war. In retrospect, the
lateness and difficulty with which Canadian workers secured the right to
bargain collectively did have certain positive effects (Robinson 1990;
Swartz in this volume). The state's resistance to labour's demand for new
collective-bargaining rights actually acted as a spur to organization.
Thus, while the American unions' organizing drive began to falter in
1943—four years prior to the passage of the Taft-Hartley Act—the organizing drive in Canada was sustained into the fifties, until the internal
struggle to purge the Communists halted it, just as it did in the United
States. From the prewar density of 14.5 percent of all nonagricultural paid
workers in 1935, it had expanded to 24.2 at war's end, reaching a high of
33.7 percent in 1955.

The Liberal government's tough stance toward the labour movement
during the war also opened a space for unions' alignment with the social
democratic Cooperative Commonwealth Federation (CCF). It would be
wrong, however, to overemphasize the strength of the link between the
unions and the CCF, especially in the formative years of Canadian Fordism. Certainly the CCF's strong showing in 1943–44 might have led the
old parties to compete for working-class votes in a way the Democrats
were never forced to do (Robinson 1990). Yet the mode of regulation in
Canada's permeable Fordism clearly depended less on partisan mobilization of the labour movement, with the state facilitating a compromise
between capital and labour, than on a combination of private-sector bar-

gaining and federal-provincial negotiations. In Canada, with all parties claiming—and gaining—votes from workers, the CCF had no privileged support from working-class voters or even from the unions.[4]

The threat of labour's support for the CCF proved enough to wring certain promises out of the Liberal government. Yet while a universal family-allowance scheme was introduced and the unions won new collective-bargaining rights, the battle for a universal pension program continued into the fifties and even then offered substantially lower benefits than Roosevelt's Social Security Act. Nor was the government fully committed to Keynesian economic policies. While postwar economic growth was strong, it remained cyclical, and several recessions occurred in the 1950s.[5] Only in the mid-1960s would state full-employment policies work to keep unemployment at low levels. The mid-sixties would also see the expansion of social-policy expenditure and, with it, the growth of public-sector employment.

In the immediate postwar years, full-blown Fordism was inhibited by the results of federal-provincial negotiations. Thus, after the war, health insurance was allowed to founder on the shoals of federal-provincial politics, where the lone CCF government in Saskatchewan was unable to make its voice heard in a sea of conservative governments. More importantly, although the industrial-relations legislation introduced during the war (PC 1003) applied to the whole country, it was superseded by the Industrial Relations and Disputes Investigation Act (IRDIA) in 1948, which made the provinces the primary site of regulation.

While the return to divided jurisdiction did not sanction the passage of "right-to-work" legislation, as the Taft-Hartley Act did, it did permit substantial interprovincial variation in labour rights throughout the first postwar decade. Thus, Alberta, British Columbia, and Newfoundland imposed restrictions on picketing, secondary boycotts, and sympathy strikes; Alberta prohibited strikes in "essential" services; British Columbia and Manitoba imposed government supervision of strike votes; and Ontario, Newfoundland, and British Columbia permitted state interference in the internal affairs of unions. It was in Quebec, however, that unions really suffered a rollback of wartime gains in the 1950s.

In the face of such provincial hostility and employer intransigence, it took a series of major strikes in both the familiar sectors of a Fordist regime of accumulation (automobiles, steel) and the resource sectors (wood, asbestos) just to achieve a firm-by-firm adjustment to the new conditions of collective bargaining. Divided jurisdiction also enhanced the importance of the provincial federations of labour at the expense of national trade-union centrals. Thus even with the formation of the Canadian Labour Contress (CLC) in 1956, through the merger of the craft-based Trades and Labour Congress and the industrial unions of the Canadian Congress of Labour (CCL), the Canadian union movement remained weak at the national level. Nor were the provincial federations substantially stronger, deprived as they were of a role in collective bargaining.

Nevertheless, the CLC did face one crucial task immediately, and that was to regularize the union movement's relationship with social democracy. The CCF, founded in the 1930s as the party of farmers, labour, and socialists, faced serious organizational decline in most provinces and at the federal level after 1945. The CLC, with the support of an important faction within the CCF, set out in the late 1950s to re-create the party, bringing about a metamorphosis of the CCF into a partisan force modelled on the British Labour Party.[6]

A major innovation for the NDP, and a highly controversial one, was that union locals could affiliate with the new party. This change was intended to solidify a base of support for the NDP, give it a solid source of funds, and symbolize its new status as the party of labour. Unfortunately for the NDP, the plan went somewhat awry. While some union locals did affiliate and the CLC did become a major source of campaign dollars, the electoral support of working people never materialized.[7] The NDP systematically attracted only about one-fifth of the electorate in federal elections, and its success among unionized workers and their families was much less than that of the Liberals (Clarke, Jenson, LeDuc, and Pammett 1979: 109).

Therefore, as unions entered the 1960s, they did so linked to a weak third party that had not succeeded in forging a loyal following among the majority of union members.[8] Nevertheless, the political scene was rapidly changing, as pressures increased in several parts of the country for completion of the social-policy package long promised but as yet not implemented.

1960 to 1974: From Strength to Uncertainty

The 1960s were to prove the high point of Fordism in all advanced capitalist economies, and Canada was no exception. Strong growth brought about a situation of low unemployment and created the material conditions for the expansion of the welfare state, and political conditions created the "political will" to make use of this opportunity. Although the NDP failed to make the hoped-for breakthrough nationally, it gained a stronger voice in federal-provincial negotiations via victories in Manitoba (1969), Saskatchewan (1971), and British Columbia (1972). It was also able to strengthen the position of the Left within the governing Liberal party, especially under the minority governments of 1963–68 and again in 1972–74. As in other advanced capitalist countries, however, in Canada the sixties also provided the early warning signs of the crisis of Fordism.

In Europe, a wave of rank-and-file rebellion against Fordist production relations broke out, as did youth rebellion against the narrow values of a society based on mass consumption. In Canada the workers' rebellion began early (1966) and continued into the mid-seventies.[9] This wave of strikes produced certain legislative changes, notably the replacement of the IRDIA by the more liberal Canada Labour Code and the even more favourable labour reforms introduced by the NDP governments in the three western provinces.[10] Mounting inflation, in a period of marked labour unrest, also induced the federal government to try to implement an incomes policy of the sort familiar in Western Europe but which had not been part of Canada's mode of regulation. In 1969 the Liberal government introduced the Prices and Incomes Commission, an experiment in voluntary wage and price controls that quickly collapsed.

While wages bargaining in the private sector was becoming politicized, workers in the growing public sector were also waging a struggle for collective recognition. Federal public-sector workers finally won the right to bargain and to strike in 1967, five years after Kennedy had granted their U.S. counterparts the right to bargain but not to strike. The difference in outcomes can be attributed, in part, to the impact of the Quebec Liberals on their federal counterparts,[11] but it was the struggles of the postal workers that really forced the issue.

The sixties' rank-and-file rebellions in Europe and in North America—and in the public, as well as the private, sector—can be seen as an expression of the political crisis of Fordist production relations. The economic limits were also to become increasingly visible by the early seventies. Productivity rises depended on increasingly expensive capital outlays (Leborgne and Lipietz 1988). Inflation, with its deleterious effects on interest rates, only exacerbated the productivity crisis by raising the price of borrowed capital. In Canada, these problems threatened to become all the more unmanageable because its permeable brand of Fordism rendered it so vulnerable to developments in the United States. Repatriation of profits by foreign corporations meant that Canada was dependent on continuing imports of capital; if anything threatened that supply, the economic health of the country was in jeopardy. Thus, Nixon's reaction to America's mounting economic problems sent its own shock-wave through the Canadian economy before the first oil crisis produced a commodities boom that fuelled inflationary growth in resource-exporting countries like Canada.

A political consequence of this situation was the nationalist flavour that the anglophone Canadian New Left was to assume. The left nationalists initially found their home in the NDP, where the "Waffle" excited the imagination of many young radicals. But the Waffle's critique aimed at both dimensions of permeable Fordism: It was not content to criticize Canada's trade and investment ties with the United States but also took aim at foreign domination in the labour movement. The Waffle's political attack resonated within the union movement. Several unions broke away from international unions, and the Canadian Council of Unions, a small but dynamic left-nationalist trade-union central formed in response to the fifties' purges, scored some important victories (Palmer 1983).

Initially, the CLC unions responded in an ambivalent fashion to the nationalist challenge. On the one hand, they joined forces with the old guard in the NDP to expel the Waffle. On the other hand, the CLC did introduce new guidelines or "minimum Canadian standards" to give Canadian sections of the internationals greater autonomy. This occurred, moreover, at the point when certain public-sector unions, like the Canadian Union of Public Employees (CUPE), had grown to become some of the largest affiliates. Taken together, the two developments strengthened horizontal connections among Canadian unions and paved the way for a lively internal debate that would lend to CLC pronouncements a decidedly left-nationalist cast (Smith 1990).

Nationalism also constituted an important element in Quebec's New Left, but while the latter shared its anglophone counterpart's critique of U.S. imperialism, it drew more deeply on the spirit of Quebec *indépendantisme* unleashed by the Quiet Revolution after 1960. Inspired by different national projects, the francophone and anglophone wings of the labour movement thereby became increasingly distinct organizations following divergent strategies.

The differences between the two labour movements have deeper roots. It was in Quebec that the unions faced the toughest assault against their wartime gains, and the bitter battles fought—from the Asbestos strike in 1949 to Murdochville in 1958—served to forge alliances between the unions and progressive intellectuals that bore fruit in the Quiet Revolution and its political progeny, the Parti Québécois.[12] Yet the unions were never docile partners. From the late sixties through the seventies, all three union centrals in Quebec embraced more of the New Left's radical analyses than the labour movement did in the rest of Canada.

One consequence of the increasing divergence between the Quebec labour movement and the CLC and the tensions between nationalists and the internationals in the rest of Canada was that it remained difficult for the unions, the NDP, and other parts of the Left to mount a unified response to the restructuring of the Canadian economy that was in full swing by the mid-1970s.

Facing the Challenge of Restructuring

The burgeoning crisis of the institutional basis of permeable Fordism has also entailed a strategic crisis and a search for new alternatives on the part of the main collective actors. Some of the solutions explored during the first years of the crisis (notably liberal nationalism) have been abandoned, but other elements have been retained and woven into the broader strategy favoured by both business and the state, the outlines of which began to become visible in the eighties.

The state's initial response to the crisis of permeable Fordism bore the marks of the previous decade of unrest even while it signalled elements of the tougher phase to come. Thus, the Liberal governments of the late seventies and early eighties embraced a form of monetarism and had increasing resort to "permanent exceptionalism" as a way of regulating collective bargaining.[13] At the same time, they played to the growing economic nationalism that was finding a home in the unions as well as among the general population. A renewed effort to repatriate the constitution and the proclamation of the Charter of Rights and Freedoms sought to overcome growing regional opposition and to forge a new national unity at the political level (Jenson 1989).

More specifically, the state sought to strengthen "responsible unionism" through corporatist experiments at the macro, sectoral, and micro levels (Albo 1990: 490; McBride 1987). These initiatives fed into the growing debate within the labour movement, wherein those favouring "social corporatism" faced mounting criticism from activists who preferred to mobilize the rank and file to defend living standards, advance workplace rights, and strike alliances with other social movements for social reforms (Heron 1989; Smith 1990).

In the eighties, however, both the state and business began to explore the parameters of an alternative model of development that builds on the continentalism of permeable Fordism but abandons the latter's more progressive features. The moves toward privatization, deregulation, "targeted" (as opposed to universal) social programs, and contracting out—hallmarks of neoconservatism throughout the West—thus form part of a broader package including the consolidation of a continental mode of regulation that would incorporate the Canadian economy into the regime of polarized growth that has already taken root in the United States (Davis 1984; Mahon 1991). The Canadian-U.S. Free Trade Agreement and its extension to include Mexico have to be seen in this context.

The model of development favoured by business and the state poses a serious challenge to the labour movement. It aims to achieve cost competitiveness by increasing the intensity of work (eliminating "waste time" by reorganizing the work process) and lowering real wages. While all workers are the target of such initiatives, the new strategy seeks to establish a new dualism or "two-tier" economy consisting of a smaller core of multiskilled workers and a large pool of "irregular" workers, many of whom are women and members of ethnic and racial minority groups. The latter provide the "numerical flexibility" underlying the new competitiveness while the former are offered flexible wages, tied to plant and corporate profit performance, teamwork, and enterprise unionism.

Corporations and governments have pursued these objectives with some success. Thus, real wages have fallen throughout the eighties (Albo 1990), but the fall in real income has not been evenly distributed. In addition to marked interregional differences (Kumar 1991), income polarization has grown, with younger workers the main losers (Myles, Picot, and Wannel 1988). Unemployment has remained above the U.S. rate—and well above that experienced in countries like Sweden and Japan. More importantly, the pattern of job growth has reflected the deeper roots of the increasingly polarized structure of income distribution (ECC 1991). The level of union density has also fallen from the 1983 peak of 40 percent, albeit not as dramatically as it has in the United States. The decline reflects the shrinkage of jobs in the goods-producing sectors; the rising incidence of contracting out, especially in the public sector; the unions' failure to make substantial inroads into the burgeoning private-service sector; and the impact of antiunion industrial-relations reforms.[14]

Nevertheless, the struggle to shape the terms of a post-Fordist compromise is far from over, and the attacks on unions and other popular groups have prodded the latter to begin to explore new strategic alternatives of their own.

More specifically, the unions have shown a significant capacity to resist. Thus, although union density has fallen, it remains just a little below the 1983 peak (36.2 percent in 1990). The rate of organization in the public sector has held up particularly well: It is almost complete in government services and remains markedly higher than in the United States in important areas like education, 70 percent versus 35 percent, and health, 55 percent versus less than 20 percent (Kumar 1991). The relative size of Canada's public sector and the public-sector unions' greater success have given the labour movement a greater capacity to resist the tendency toward income polarization than their U.S. counterparts (Jackson 1988). Canadian unions, moreover, have kept up their drive to organize the private-service sector, which has produced a disproportionate number of the "bad" jobs caught in the Economic Council's study (Robinson 1990; Meltz in this volume).[15] Finally, a number of unions have merged across old jurisdictional boundaries, thereby increasing resources available for collective bargaining and new organizing (Kumar 1991).

Canadian unions have also resisted concession bargaining and have taken a critical stance toward the new "teamwork." Individual unions have been encouraged to "fight back" by the stance taken by the provincial and national federations.[16] As a result, they have been more successful in defending Fordist rights than most U.S. unions. Most, however, are coming to realize that defence of the status quo is not enough. What is needed is a new agenda that speaks to the needs of workers as workers, with interests both broader and more diverse than recognized in the Fordist era, and as citizens, with concerns that extend beyond the workplace.

It would be an exaggeration to suggest that the labour movement as a whole has not only managed to formulate a new strategy but has also been able to make that strategy the operative guide to practice, from the shop floor to solidaristic action across national frontiers. Nevertheless, there are some promising signs that, if developed and sustained, hold out the prospect of a different future.

First, the unions have begun to go beyond resistance to employer initiatives to formulate their own version of a post-Fordist workplace and labour market. In this, they have actually been aided by the remnants of the state's earlier efforts to encourage "responsible unionism," notably funds set up by federal and provincial governments to enable the unions to undertake (or commission) research on technological change and adjustment[17] and more recent initiatives designed to elicit the labour movement's cooperation in building a competitive economy.[18] While earlier such initiatives unleashed an internal fight between those in favour and those opposed to corporatism, this time the labour movement has been more inclined to treat such "opportunities" as a chance to develop and push its own agenda in collective bargaining and via "social bargaining."[19]

Labour's common agenda on these issues has proved more difficult to pursue at the national level, but significant progress is being made in certain provinces. For instance, the 1989 Ontario Federation of Labour (OFL) convention led to the passage of a statement on training that staked out a distinctive union position, and this agenda is being taken beyond convention rhetoric. The OFL's training committee has continued to meet and to deepen the areas of agreement, and this has strengthened their hand in negotiating the parameters of the proposed new training and adjustment board. In addition, the OFL and its affiliates are running the research projects, funded under the Ontario government's "TARP" (Technology and Adjustment Research Project) program, in a manner designed to develop and disseminate a labour agenda not only on training but also job redesign, "homework," and adjustment. The participating unions meet on a regular basis to help each other to develop their respective projects. The ensuing discussions also raise the level of understanding and consensus regarding a new conception of workplace and labour-market politics.

Trade-union renewal involves more than the elaboration of labour's version of post-Fordist production relations. It also involves winning the hearts and minds of existing and prospective members, and this has its own challenges, given the changed nature of the labour force. While in the past unions could afford to take the white male worker as the norm, this is no longer the case. Women, who accounted for less than 20 percent of the membership in the mid-sixties, now constitute over one-third.

The Canadian workforce has also become more ethnically and racially heterogeneous.

Some unions were quick to adjust their strategies to meet the needs of these new members,[20] but it took the birth of "working-class feminism" (Maroney 1987) to push others to take up new issues—from pay and employment equity to parental leave, day care, and sexual harassment (Briskin and Yanz 1983; Saint-Pierre in this volume; Kumar 1991). The unions have also begun to take up issues of direct relevance to ethnic and racial minorities by engaging in struggles against racism and for language and other forms of assistance.[21]

These changes in the substantive issues taken up by unions have been accompanied by changes in their internal structure and external alliances. Many vestiges of the bureaucratic unionism sanctioned by Fordist collective-bargaining practices of course remain. Yet unions have begun to democratize under pressure from the push for Canadian control of the labour movement (Robinson 1990); the women's movement's call for empowering processes and forms of interaction (Briskin 1990); and the challenge of union hegemony vis-à-vis the members on the shop floor, posed by the employers' attempt to establish de facto enterprise unionism.[22]

It is the labour movement's external political strategy, however, that has drawn the most attention. In the past, the unions relied on a combination of lobbying and a loose connection with the NDP to push their wider political interests. The Liberal government's initial search for a route out of the crisis had pushed the CLC to a new effort to win rank-and-file support for the NDP in the late seventies (Brodie and Jenson 1988: 305). The CLC sustained this partisan activity in subsequent federal campaigns, but the effects on electoral outcomes were limited.

The labour movement did not confine itself to electoral politics, however. By the mid-1980s it had become a central actor in the "popular sector." The unions have been developing their links with progressive social movements through the issues they have brought to the bargaining table and their support for particular demands in the political arena. We have already noted some of the issues pertinent to the women's movement and antiracist groups. Unions like the Steelworkers, the Paperworkers, and the CUPE have also begun to link their demands at the bargaining table to broader environmental issues, and the OFL's proposed social investment fund—which the Ontario NDP government has signalled its intent to support—will channel money into cooperative housing and help to bankroll environmental initiatives.[23] The CAW has also put contributions to a "social justice" fund into its most recent agreements with the Big Three and eventually hopes to be able to allocate some $2.2 million to Third World support and domestic solidarity projects.

The unions' most prominent move, however, was to play an active part in the coalition of social movements—including the organized women's movement, the churches, native peoples, nationalists, and environmentalists—that opposed the Canadian-U.S. Free Trade Agreement (FTA). Building on the notion of a continued commitment to social programs and economic redistribution, the Pro-Canada Network—now Action Canada Network—sought to mobilize opposition to the strategy for restoring Canada's competitiveness pushed by the Progressive Conservative government. The network was an important rallying point for mobilizing extraparliamentary opposition to the FTA. It also was heavily involved as a force parallel to the opposition parties in the 1988 election, which centred on the agreement. Unfortunately, the network remained a rather loose coalition, united around a defence of what had been, rather than an alternative vision of the future (Breton and Jenson 1991). Thus, the FTA was depicted as a threat to the Canadian welfare state, to jobs (especially for women), to Canadian culture, and to the environment.[24]

While the network may have lacked a real alternative vision to counterpose to the polarized model of post-Fordist growth that the FTA favoured, it did provide a vehicle for political intervention more responsive than support for the NDP, and this became particulary apparent in the 1988 election (Bernard in this volume). The NDP's electoral weakness manifested the party's incapacity to consolidate a strategic position that would allow it to make use of the opening provided by the mounting political crisis. Its difficulties arose from the ways in which the two crucial dimensions of the crisis—constitutional and economic—cut into its internal alliance structure. Evolving disputes around these two dimensions severely divided the fragile coalition that the federal NDP had always been (Bradford and Jenson 1992).

Internal pluralism has made any consistent response to economic restructuring very difficult for the party to organize. Cleaved internally by tensions between proponents of a "parliamentary road to socialism" and those advocating more radical stances, as well as by those who see the

NDP as a party of the official labour movement and those who want it to combine all progressive forces, the NDP has also had to contend with strong regional caucuses. Its historic commitment to centralized solutions, moreover, rendered it incapable of establishing itself as a force in Quebec. It was the Parti Québécois that stepped into the vacuum and came the closest to being labour's political ally.

One result of these unresolved internal tensions has been a sort of "avoidance strategy," papering over real conflicts with a discourse of contentless populism (Bradford and Jenson, 1992). The 1988 election starkly revealed the vacuity of the NDP's position; its union supporters in the Pro-Canada Network worked side by side with other popular forces to defeat the FTA while the NDP blithely ignored its "natural constituents" and followed the advice of those committed to a narrow electoralist strategy. The unions, led by Bob White, president of the CAW and vice-president of the CLC, were quick to chastise the party for its stance, calling for a new relationship between the party and the social movements it claimed to represent and a greater recognition of the importance of extra-parliamentary struggles. Politics, in other words, is something more than electoral mobilization; it also involves coordinated struggles in the trenchworks of civil society.

That it was the CAW which led the charge is significant. In 1984, the Canadian region of the United Auto Workers decided to break away from the international union to form an independent Canadian body, and the CAW has since become an important symbol of the growing independence of the Canadian labour movement. Since the mid-1960s, nationally based public-sector unions have been the largest and increasingly provide the leadership cadres of the CLC and provincial federations. With the establishment of the CAW representing workers in the Fordist sector par excellence, the Canadian labour movement appeared to be announcing that it had moved from one form of labour movement to another. That this announcement occurred as a result of a conflict over restructuring and concession bargaining just clarified that times had changed, that unions faced a new set of circumstances, and that the CAW, at least, was determined to find its own route out of the new situation. It is of some importance for the future, then, that White since June 1992 will lead the CLC as a whole. His election to the presidency was controversial both because of strategic differences with other candidates and because that congress brought the breakaway of the FTQ.

The CAW's important decision, with all that it symbolized for the labour movement as a whole, represents one of the ways that the Canadian labour movement has come to differ from its counterpart in the United States. But brave words and great deeds have never been sufficient to solve the problems associated with a crisis. Fully aware of that, Canada's labour movement has embarked upon a multifront war of manoeuvre to try and find its own way out of the economic and political crisis.

Notes

1. This notion of Fordism, and the description of its mode of regulation, is drawn from the work of the French regulationists, especially Lipietz (1987a; 1987b). For a description of the Fordist characteristics of Canadian economic policy, see Boismenu (1990).

2. For an elaboration of this point and a detailed discussion of the politics of Fordism in Canada, see Jenson (1989).

3. One of the characteristics of Fordism elsewhere was its relatively low level of international trade and the centrality of domestic markets for the model of development (Lipietz 1987a: ch. 2).

4. On the rocky relationship of the CCF with the voters and unions after the war, see Brodie and Jenson (1988: ch. 8).

5. The United States too suffered recessions in the 1950s. Given the level of continental integration that al eady existed, the coincidence of economic downturns is hardly surprising. In Europe and Japan, in contrast, the effect of business cycles was mitgated (Gonick 1987: 325).

6. For this story, see Horowitz (1968) and Brodie and Jenson (1988: 230–45).

7. As late as 1966, the overall rate of affiliation remained as low as 11.8 percent, although in certain former CIO unions, like steel and auto, the rate exceeded 50 percent. CLC leaders—including those heading former TLC unions—were more supportive, but they were not able to bring the rank and file with them (Robinson 1990: 371–72).

8. It is worth noting that almost half of NDP voters were unionized workers, which was a rate of appeal somewhat higher than that achieved by either of the other two parties. Nevertheless, the overall failure to attract more than 20 percent of all voters meant that most workers voted for another party (Brodie and Jenson 1988: 253).

9. In 1966, there were 316 work stoppages, one-third of which were wildcat strikes, directed as much against the union leadership as against the Fordist

practices they effectively sanctioned. The strike wave continued, reaching a peak between 1971 and 1975, when one-quarter of all the industrial disputes recorded since 1900 occured (Heron 1989: 105).

10. Of particular note here is the progressive occupational health and safety legislation introduced by Saskatchewan in 1972. Provinces like Quebec and Ontario were to follow Saskatchewan's lead several years later. See Tucker (1992) for a discussion of some of the limits of even these reforms.

11. Saskatchewan's CCF government had recognized the collective rights of government workers at the same time that workers in the private sector won their rights (1944), but political conditions for an extension of these rights to public-sector workers in other parts of the country were not yet ripe. By the 1960s, public-sector workers in other provinces were pressing for recognition, and the fact that, as part of the "Quiet Revolution," the Quebec Liberals were prepared to grant their employees full bargaining rights could not but affect the federal party, whose electoral fortunes very much hinged on its support in Quebec.

12. See Tanguay in this volume on the union-party relationship.

13. For Panitch and Swartz, the turn to incomes policies, combined with the dramatic rise in the incidence of back-to-work legislation, signals a turn from the generalized rule of law to "a form of selective, ad hoc, discretionary state coercion (whereby the state removes for a specific purpose and period the rights contained in labour legislation)" (1988: 31).

14. For instance, the level of organization in the Alberta construction industry fell from 80 percent in 1982 to 10 percent in 1987 as a result of new legislation passed in 1983 that allowed construction companies to set up nonunion subsidiaries and as a result of the lockout inspired by that legislation in 1984 (Heron 1989).

15. We can also expect to see some important changes to the legislation governing the largest provincial labour market, where the Ontario Federation of Labour has been able to impress upon the NDP government the importance of this issue. See the *Ottawa Citizen* (5 July 1991) for a list of the proposals submitted to the minister of labour by the labour representatives on his advisory panel.

16. Thus, debate at the 1984 CLC convention led to the imposition of a five-cents-per-member charge to create a fund supporting campaigns of resistance.

17. The federal government began funding union education in the late 1970s. While it failed to move on its own commission's recommendations regarding paid educational leave, it did establish the Technology Impact Research Fund in 1984 (renamed Technology Impact Programme in 1986), which has supported a large number of research projects. Unions like the Canadian Auto

Workers (CAW) have used these funds to get a better understanding of the threats and possibilities opened up by restructuring and to develop appropriate strategies in the auto, aerospace, telecommunications equipment, and airline sectors.

The Ontario Liberal government also established a Technology and Adjustment Research Fund of $5 million over a five-year period, to be administered by the OFL. The majority of the members of the management committee are also trade unionists.

18. The most dramatic initiative was the creation of the Canadial Labour Force Development Board in the spring of 1991. (See Mahon [1990] on the background to this.) Parallel discussions are also taking place in Ontario, where the victory of the NDP has given the unions more substantial opportunities to influence the structure and mandate of the proposed Ontario Training and Adjustment Board (OTAB). There are also a host of sectoral initiatives, some of which—notably the oft-cited Electrical and Electronic Manufacturers Adjustment Council—have proved divisive for the labour movement. Others, however, have pushed the unions to expand their horizons and to develop their own strategic and organizational capacity.

19. "Social bargaining" rejects the view that bi- and tripartite mechanisms are based on a common interest and the need to develop a consensus concerning how to pursue this. Instead, it extends the "adversarial" relation found in collective-bargaining situations to the sectoral and even societal level. Thus, some agreements may be reached through negotiation, but this by no means belies the enduring differences between the parties.

20. The Canadian Union of Postal Workers (CUPW) has been in the forefront here, pushing for "solidaristic wages," organizing part-time workers, and leading the way in the struggle for paid maternity leave. See White in this volume for a discussion of the reasons behind this.

21. In addition to antiracist stances taken by individual unions, broader groupings like the Metro Toronto Labour Council have been very active in trying to develop support for immigrant workers. The International Ladies Garment Workers locals in Montreal and Toronto have not only thrown off their quiescent stance vis-à-vis the employer but, at the same time, have been restructured to become multiethnic, multiracial organizations (Heron 1989).

22. See Kumar (1991) for a discussion of some of these changes. Stinson's (1991) analysis of the Ontario hospital workers gives insight into the way restructuring and feminism have pushed the CUPE to change its practices. Many of the OFL's TARP projects are premised on the need for a new dialogue with rank and file and some actually build local involvement into the research design itself.

23. In their 1990 contract with Inco, Canada's major nickel producer, the

Steel Workers managed to establish a senior-level labour-management committee to identity environmental problems in the workplace and the surrounding
environment and recommend solutions. For the union, such moves link the
union's growing interest in occupational health and safety to the broader concern about the environment in which people—including workers—live. CUPE,
the union organizing most municipal workers, has taken up the issue of waste
management, linking its demands to its critique of privatization and contracting
out. The Paperworkers' TARP project is explicit in its concern to find technological options that both provide better jobs and are ecologically sound.

24. Action Canada can also be criticized for failing to recognize the
longer-term necessity of working solidaristically with progressive forces in the
United States. This seems to be changing. The announcement of a new round
of talks to extend the FTA to Mexico prompted the formation of a related
group, Common Frontiers, which aims to develop ties with opposition forces
in Mexico. There is also increasing talk of the need for a "social charter" to accompany any future deals.

References

Albo, Greg. 1990. "The 'New Realism' and Canadian Workers." In Jim Bicker-
    ton and Alain Gagnon, eds., *Canadian Politics: An Introduction to the Disci-
    pline*, Peterborough, Ont.: Broadview Press.
Boismenu, Gérard. 1990. "Une economie politique pour la compréhension de la
    crise et ses enjeux." In Gérard Boismenu and Daniel Drache, eds., *Politique
    et régulation: Modèle de développement et trajectoire canadienne*, Montreal:
    Méridien.
Bradford, Neil, and Jane Jenson. 1992. "The Roots of Social Democratic Popu-
    lism in Canada." In Frances Fox Piven, ed., *Labor Parties in Postindustrial
    Societies*, New York: Oxford University Press.
Breton, Gilles, and Jane Jenson. 1991. "After Free Trade and Meech Lake: *Quoi
    de neuf?" Studies in Political Economy* 34.
Briskin, Linda. 1990. "Women, Unions, and Leadership," *Canadian Dimension*,
    January–February.
Briskin, Linda, and Lynda Yanz. 1983. *Union Sisters*, Toronto: Women's Press.
Brodie, Janine, and Jane Jenson. 1988. *Crisis, Challenge, and Change: Party and
    Class in Canada Revisited*, Ottawa: Carleton University Press.

Clarke, Harold, Jane Jenson, Lawrence LeDuc, and Jon Pammett. 1979. *Political Choice in Canada*, Toronto: McGraw-Hill Ryerson.

Clement, Wallace. 1984. "Canada's Social Structure: Capital, Labour, and the State, 1930–1980." In Michael S. Cross and Gregory S. Kealey, eds., *Modern Canada: 1930–1980s*, Toronto: McClelland and Stewart.

Davis, Mike. 1984. "The Political Economy of Late Imperial America," *New Left Review* 123.

Economic Council of Canada (ECC). 1990. *Good Jobs, Bad Jobs*, Ottawa: Government of Canada.

Gonick, Cy. 1987. *The Great Economic Debate: Failed Economics and a Future for Canada*, Toronto: Lorimer.

Heron, Craig. 1989. *The Canadian Labour Movement: A Short History*, Toronto: James Lorimer.

Horowitz, Gad. 1968. *Canadian Labour in Politics*, Toronto: University of Toronto Press.

Jackson, Andrew. 1988. "The Rise of the Service Sector and the Quality of Jobs: A Labour Perspective," *Labour Issues*, Paper No. 3, Canadian Labour Market and Productivity Centre.

Jenson, Jane. 1989 " 'Different' but Not 'Exceptional': Canada's Permeable Fordism," *Canadian Review of Sociology and Anthropology* 26:1.

Kumar, Pradeep. 1991. "Industrial Relations in Canada and the United States: From Uniformity to Diversity," Queen's University Papers in Industrial Relations, No. 2.

Leborgne, Danielle, and Alain Lipietz. 1988. "New Technologies, New Modes of Regulation: Some Spatial Implications," *Space and Society* 6(3).

Lipietz, Alain. 1987a. *Mirages and Miracles*, London: Verso.

———. 1987b. "Rebel Sons: The French Regulation Approach," *French Politics and Society* 5(4).

Lipsig-Mummé, Carla. 1991. "Future Conditional: Fragmentation and Realism in the Quebec Labour Movement," *Studies in Political Economy* 36.

Mahon, Rianne. 1984. *The Politics of Industrial Restructuring: Canadian Textiles*, Toronto: University of Toronto Press.

———. 1990. "Adjusting to Win? The New Tory Training Initiative." In Katherine Graham, ed., *How Ottawa Spends, 1990–1991*, Ottawa: Carleton University Press.

———. 1991. "Post-Fordism: Some Issues for Labour." In Daniel Drache and Maric Gertler, eds., *The New Era of Global Competition: State Policy and Market Power*, Montreal and Kingston: McGill-Queens University Press.

McBride, Steven. 1987. "Hard Times and the Rules of the Game: The Legislative Environment of Labour-Capital Conflict." In Robert Argue, Charlene

Gannagé, and D. W. Livingstone, eds., *Working People in Hard Times*, Toronto: Garamond.

Maroney, Heather Jon. 1987. "Feminism at Work." In H. J. Maroney and Meg Luxton, eds., *Feminism and Political Economy: Women's Work, Women's Struggles*. Toronto: Methuen.

Myles, John, Garnett Picot, and Ted Wannell. 1988. "Wages and Jobs in the 1980s: Changing Youth Wages and the Declining Middle," *Statistics Canada Research Paper* 17.

Palmer, Bryan. 1983. *Working Class Experience: The Rise and Reconstitution of Canadian Labour*, Toronto: Butterworth.

Panitch, Leo, and Donald Swartz. 1988. *The Assault on Trade Union Freedoms: From Consent to Coercion Revisited*, Toronto: Garamond.

Robinson, Ian. 1990. Organizing Labour: Explaining Canada-U.S. Union Density Divergence in the Postwar Period, Ph.D. dissertation, Yale University.

Smith, Miriam. 1990. Labour without Allies: The Canadian Labour Congress in Politics, 1956–1988, Ph.D. dissertation, Yale University.

Stinson, Jane. 1991. "Swimming against the Tide: The Ontario Council of Hospital Unions' Effort to Negotiate Pay Equity," Honours Essay, Interdisciplinary Studies, Carleton University.

Tucker, Eric. 1992. "Worker Participation in Health and Safety Regulation: Some Lessons from Sweden," *Studies in Political Economy* 37.

Wolfe, David. 1984. "The Rise and Demise of the Keynesian Era in Canada: Economic Policy 1930–1982." In Michael Cross and Greg Kealey, eds., *Modern Canada: 1930–1980s*, Toronto: McClelland and Stewart.

Unionism in a Different Context:
The Case of Quebec

Unions in Quebec share many characteristics with those in the rest of Canada. Nevertheless, the existence of some major differences in the legislative and political context warrant special attention. This chapter documents the specificities of the Quebec situation. These follow both from the cultural distinctiveness of an overwhelmingly francophone population and from past actions of provincial governments as well as the labour movement itself. Apart from Montreal, where the proportion is somewhat lower, francophones make up over 90 percent of the Quebec population. This homogeneity of language and its cultural effects are reflected in all aspects of society, including the union movement and labour relations in general.

Nevertheless, Quebec is also part of North America. The same economic forces affecting the whole continent have contributed to the restructuring of Quebec's economy, albeit in its own ways. Agriculture employs only 5 percent of the population, while the service sector has expanded to become almost 70 percent of total employment. Of these jobs, 700,000 to 800,000 are in the public sector (including provincial and municipal administration, education and health services). The unemployment rate is also high, almost double that of Ontario, Canada's other major industrial province. The structure of business has dramatically changed in recent decades, at times in contradictory ways. Most new firms are generally in the small and medium category, but there have also been mergers, creating large, transnational corporations. The Quebec economy remains grounded on primary resource production—pulp and paper and hydro-electricity—as well as light manufacturing (especially textiles and clothing), transportation, and engineering services. With such an economic structure, Quebec is inevitably greatly affected by world competition.

The political context of Quebec has also undergone important alterations recently. The 1976 election of the Parti Québécois (PQ) had a major impact on all aspects of the province's life, and especially the labour movement (Tanguay, this volume). Then the 1980 referendum asked Quebec residents to choose between remaining in the Canadian confederation or negotiating an arrangement of sovereignty-association. While the federalist option won a small majority, almost 60 percent of those voting said no to sovereignty-association. Moreover, many observers contend that among francophone Québécois the result was the other way around.

The referendum did not settle the constitutional controversies, of course. The Constitution of 1982 had the support of the federal government and all of the provinces *except Quebec*. In essence this outcome meant that Quebec was left out of Canada. The 1987 election replaced the PQ with the Liberals, who then tried to negotiate a new constitutional accord. Nevertheless, these efforts collapsed with the defeat of the Meech Lake Accord in 1990, and subsequent events indicated that the political pendulum had swung sharply toward support for the independence or sovereignty option in Quebec.

It is this general context of economic restructuring and political controversy that the labour movement in Quebec now faces. Thus, it is a context that is simultaneously part of the North American experience and somewhat distinct, in large part because of the different history of the movement in the postwar period.

The Diversity of the Quebec Labour Movement

A first important point to note is that both unionization rates and collective-bargaining coverage are higher in Quebec than in the rest of Canada. If these percentages hover around 35 percent and 40 percent for Canada as a whole, in Quebec they are closer to 40 percent and 45 percent (Meltz, this volume, especially Table 10-1). Only British Columbia has slightly higher rates (Kumar 1988: 19–22). Moreover, unlike the other Canadian provinces, where there is usually a single central body that groups most of the union locals (for example, the Ontario Federation of Labour), in Quebec there are four centrals to which local unions are affiliated. Each federation has its own philosophy and is often concentrated in a specific sector. The presence of international unions is also weaker in Quebec than in any other Canadian province. About one-third of all Canadian unionists belong to U.S.-based unions. In Quebec the comparable statistic is 25 percent, despite the presence of the United Food and Commercial Workers and the United Steelworkers of America, two major international unions that play a prominent role in the provincial labour movement.

Most locals of international and Canadian unions are affiliated with the Fédération des travailleurs et des travailleuses du Québec (FTQ), which represents 35 percent of all union members in Quebec. Until 1992 these unions normally affiliated with the Canadian Labour Congress (CLC). Close to 25 percent of all union members are affiliated with the Confédération des syndicats nationaux (CSN). The other two federations are the Teachers' Federation, the Centrale de l'enseignement du Québec (CEQ), and the Centrale des syndicats démocratiques (CSD), which represent, respectively, 10 percent and 5 percent of all unionists (Fleury 1988a: 15; Racine 1990: 23). The remaining 25 percent of union members belong to unaffiliated unions, either independent locals or small groupings, often confined to a single industry.[1]

Public-sector unions are extremely important in Quebec. They represent 45 percent of all union members, and most of the unions are quite militant.[2] The unionization rate is very close to 100 percent of the sector, which includes the provincial administration, health and education institutions, most public utilities, public agencies—such as the Quebec Liquor Board—and a high proportion of municipal administrations.

Finally, one industry in the private sector warrants special mention. In order to work in the industry, all construction workers, without exception, must be members of a recognized trade union. Without such membership they cannot obtain the permit necessary to work on any construction site. This unionization rate of 100 percent is again very different from that of the other Canadian provinces and even more so from that of the United States.

With four central bodies, of unequal size and authority, and a large group of independent unions, one can hardly speak of *the* labour movement in Quebec without severely oversimplifying. It is important, therefore, to recognize the differences among the four and the issues to which they give rise. One such issue is that of solidarity. The CSD broke away from the CSN in 1972. More recently the CSN came close to another split. Its private-sector members could not help but realize that the more public-sector members obtained in their bargaining with the government, the more income tax private-sector workers had to pay.

One basic distinction among the four centrals derives from variations in their membership base. Most important is whether they organize primarily public- or private-sector workers. Unions in these two sectors do not have the same power, their members do not share the same benefits, and they display little solidarity with each other; this affects the federations' stances. A majority of the membership of unions affiliated with the FTQ are in the private sector. Only 50,000 of the FTQ's 300,000 affiliated members are public-sector employees. By counting the 60,000 members of CUPE (Canadian Union of Public Employees) working in public utilities and the municipal sector, however, the proportion of FTQ membership in the private sector falls to a little under two-thirds. The situation is reversed in the CSN, which has two-thirds of its 200,000 members in the public sector. This sectoral variation in itself might partly explain the different ideological tendencies of the two centrals, because public-sector unions tend to be more radical.

Although small in size with only 75,000 members, the Quebec Teachers' Federation (CEQ) has had more influence than its numbers alone would explain. Ideologically, the CEQ has always been closer to the CSN than to the FTQ. Like the CSN, the CEQ took a radical position in the early 1970s. Both also moved toward a middle-of-the-road stance in the 1980s, although for different reasons. Many teachers supported the Parti Québécois, and when this political party came to power in 1976, it was difficult for the CEQ to continue its militant propaganda criticizing all governments. Many of the members of the Legislative Assembly and even cabinet ministers were former teachers, and all were close friends of CEQ members. The militancy of the CEQ staff was dampened for a while. Nevertheless, it returned to the forefront after budgetary constraints moved the Parti Québécois government to make tough wage decisions in 1981–1982.

The four federations also differ in terms of their organization, even within the same central. Some FTQ unions are more democratic than others, some more radical, some more active, and others more businesslike, depending on the business agent acting on their behalf. Differences within the CSN, the CEQ, and the CSD may be less apparent, but they too exist. Such a variety of attitudes and practices on organizational matters, coupled with the cross-sectoral and cross-federation differences, therefore do not generate a very unified labour movement.

Political Action of the Quebec Labour Movement

This labour movement has been in a sense both more and less politically involved than the Canadian labour movement as a whole. It has been *less* involved because most federations have no direct affiliation with a political party, whereas the Canadian Labour Congress does support the New Democratic Party. On the other hand, the Quebec labour movement has been *more* active in fiercely opposing legislation put forward by provincial governments.

From 1945 until almost 1960—the Duplessis era—common-front reaction to government initiatives was the norm. Premier Maurice Duplessis tried to implement vehemently antiunion legislation. The almost solid front against this action eventually led to its repeal. Nevertheless, there was not total union opposition to Duplessis; a certain number of international unions managed to maintain the favour of the premier. Lack of union opposition came in very handy for certain government contracts, for example, on the Quebec North Shore.

Since 1960 the situation has been very different. The CSN has always maintained an officially neutral position with regard to political parties. This official nonpartisanship gave the federation a definite advantage when public-sector unionization took off in the 1960s. The law explicitly stated that government employees could not affiliate with a union central maintaining official ties to a political party. In practice, this excluded the FTQ-affiliated unions because of that federation's ties to the New Democratic Party at the federal level.

Despite the lack of formal ties to a party, however, the CSN has been much more ideologically engaged than the FTQ. Indeed this political engagement has contributed to the decision of several groups, including some civil servants, to abandon the CSN and establish unaffiliated or independent unions.

Despite the differences over whether to provide official support for political parties, however, Quebec unions took quite similar positions in the 1970s on the national question, openly backing the Parti Québécois position. Then, during the Meech Lake controversy and after, they supported advocates of independence or sovereignty for Quebec (Lipsig-Mummé, this volume).

It should be noted, however, that the rank and file has not always shared the politics of the union leadership. In the early 1960s, all Quebec unions—and especially the CSN—took an open and clear stand against the Parti créditiste. Following an all-out union campaign against the Créditistes in the 1962 federal election, the party won an unexpectedly large number of seats and provided almost half of Quebec's representation in the House of Commons. The Créditiste candidates were elected mainly outside of the big-city ridings, in highly industrialized and unionized small urban centers. This pattern was testimony to rank-and-file unionists' support for that party (Tanguay, this volume). Again, while the federations strongly advocated sovereignty in the late 1970s and called for a yes vote in the 1980 referendum, the no prevailed by a good 10 percent margin.

Central labour bodies have always been keen on organizing political action committees, but these were never influential in the partisan arena itself. Political action by labour unions has been most successful in obtaining or defeating legislative proposals. The experience, then, is one of a mixed bag of political failures and successes for this labour movement.

A Disunited Labour Movement

One indication of the divisions within the labour movement is the upsurge of independent or, more precisely, unaffiliated unions in Quebec. Between 1971 and 1985, the proportion of unaffiliated union members went from 10 percent to more than 25 percent of total union membership in the province. It has remained at that level for the past few years (Fleury 1988b: 64–71).

The construction or building-trades unions' situation testifies to internal division. When the present centralized structure with mandatory union membership was created in December 1968, two groups of construction unions existed. The internationals of the construction and building-trades unions were tightly organized by trade into over twenty different unions and grouped primarily in local and provincial building-trades councils. These local unions were affiliated with the FTQ. The other group consisted of the construction locals affiliated with the CSN. Thus, there were two central bodies in the construction industry. This was reflected in the law itself, which recognized these two groups and their representatives as a joint bargaining agent for all construction workers in the province.

In time, other divisions appeared. When the CSD split from the CSN in 1972, a certain number of construction workers moved over to the new federation. Then in the late 1970s the internationals suffered a major split. After union membership became mandatory, some of the traditional building-trades unions refused to recognize the new members as full members. These so-called B members seceded from the internationals and formed their own unions, which affiliated directly with the FTQ. Meanwhile, another small organization was set up on the Quebec North Shore. These events eventually brought to five the union federations in the construction industry. Currently, membership in the FTQ construction unions represents 40 percent of the total construction labour force, while the Building Trades Council in good standing with the internationals accounts for 30 percent, the CSN construction unions organize 15 percent, the CSD 10 percent, and the North Shore group 1 percent or 2 percent (Fleury 1988a: 21).

Another case of major division appeared in the public sector in early 1988. The Liberal government offered all unions with collective agreements in the public sector an extension of the existing terms for one year, postponing their expiry date from 31 December 1988 to 31 December 1989. This offer was in exchange for a general 4 percent increase to everyone. Unions affiliated with the FTQ accepted the deal, but the CSN and CEQ affiliates refused. The result was a one-year gap between the expiry dates of the collective agreements. Moreover, the CSN and CEQ engaged in bargaining for large raises, gearing up for a major confrontation with the government.

Whether or not this situation will damage the heretofore prevailing solidarity in the public sector is uncertain. It does not seem unlikely, however, that one group, most likely the CSN, will try to prove to all public-sector employees that it can obtain more for its members than can the FTQ. Such an outcome would again raise the argument, which was heard twenty years ago, that the CSN should organize the whole of the public sector, leaving the private sector to the FTQ. Such an explosive situation would likely obliterate all hopes for future labour solidarity.

Quebec Labour Legislation as an
Explanation for Difference

There is no doubt that legislation has made a large contribution to the higher union density in Quebec as compared to the rest of Canada and the United States. The legislative protection of union security in Canada and in Quebec has followed a somewhat different path than that of the United States. In particular, Canadian labour relations legislation resembles some provisions of the Wagner Act before it was restricted by Taft-Hartley. Laws in most Canadian provinces explicitly allow for the inclusion of union-security clauses in the collective agreement and for union dues checkoff by the employer. The Quebec Labour Code (section 47) goes further by making checkoff mandatory as soon as union certification takes place.

In the public sector (including educational and health services but excluding municipal employees), unionization and collective bargaining became, in practice, mandatory by law. Technically, it was a little more complex. The changes to the Labour Relations Act in 1964 meant government employees were covered by the more general law, the Labour Code. To implement this change a new Civil Service Act (Loi de la fonction publique) was adopted in 1965 (Statutes of Quebec 1964: s. 47). The union representing civil servants was certified by the act itself, which recognized by name the Syndicat des fonctionnaires provinciaux du Québec (SFPQ) as the sole bargaining agent for all blue- and white-collar government employees. Any other smaller group had to apply for certification to the provincial cabinet. A joint committee was established to investigate such applications, with final certification being a cabinet decision. These procedures made it clear that the provincial government wanted to bargain collectively with all its employees, since all groups could apply for such ministerial certification.

Other public-sector employees faced a slightly different set of procedures. Unions representing employees in education and health services had a longer process to follow; they had to go through the regular channels. Nevertheless, within two decades all groups were certified and bargaining with the provincial government. Moreover, collective agreements included a union-security clause, making it compulsory for any current employee to remain and any new employee to become a union member. Full union representation is thus guaranteed. The result is that in the public and parapublic sectors, unionization and collective bargaining reached almost 100 percent coverage by the mid-1980s. The number of jobs in these sectors (reaching approximately 500,000) is a major part of the explanation for Quebec's high union density.

Similarly important is legislation in one industry of the private sector. The construction industry in Quebec voluntarily placed itself under a special form of industrial relations first developed in 1934. It was a system permitting juridical extension of collective agreements (Statutes of Quebec 1934: ch. 56). The original design was intended to avoid internal competition over wages. Under the Construction Industry Labour Relations Act, adopted in December 1968, one collective agreement (including a union-security clause) became mandatory for all employers and employees of the industry (Statutes of Quebec 1968: ch. 45, s. 28). In practice, the law made union membership compulsory for all construction workers in Quebec.

The act included a qualified closed-shop provision for the construction industry. Individual employees still have the freedom to select the union—more correctly—the central of their choice. At the end of every agreement, moreover, employees have the right to change their union affiliation. Nevertheless, before beginning to work, each new employee must choose one of the five central bodies recognized by the act. Once a choice of central is made, the member is assigned to the appropriate union. Since no one can work in the construction industry without already being a member of one of the recognized trade unions, this legislation also guarantees 100 percent coverage in this sector of the economy, which employs about 100,000 Quebec workers.

In addition to these particular pieces of labour legislation affecting fully 600,000 workers, it should also be noted that union certification is even easier in Quebec than in other Canadian provinces. The vast majority of certifications are made by certification agents. Following a request by a union, these agents visit the workplace to verify the representativity, making sure that it has an absolute majority of members in the bargaining unit. As far as the bargaining unit is concerned, if the employer and the union agree on its definition, even if they disagree on whether a few employees are included or not, the certification agent immediately provides the certification requested by the union.

If there are difficulties, especially disagreement about the definition of the bargaining unit, the matter goes before a labour commissioner. These commissioners act like a labour relations board but with one major difference: The decision can be appealed. The labour court has not received many appeals of decisions made by labour commissioners, however.[3] Thus, as far as certification is concerned, even formally the process in Quebec is much simpler and more rapid than in other Canadian provinces. In many cases it does not even go before the equivalent of a labour relations board.

One final specific legislative provision must be noted for its singular nature. The law (the anti-scab legislation) forbids any employer whose employees are on a legal strike to replace the strikers with anyone but local management (Quebec Labour Code 1964, as amended 1977: s. 109.1 [a–g]). The employer may neither contract out work usually done by the striking employees nor use nonstriking employees (office or otherwise; unionized or not) to do the work of strikers. The employer cannot bring in employees from other plants of the same company or hire new employees. No other Canadian jurisdiction has an anti-scab law of this sort.[4] The Quebec law was enacted to prevent violence on the picket lines and has, in fact, almost eliminated violence on the grounds of or in the areas surrounding workplaces on strike.

In light of this background information about the character of the labour movement and the legislative environment, union responses to economic and other changes can now be examined. These responses have centred around three major types of activities: organizing, collective bargaining, and involvement in social issues.

Union Response: Organizing

In order to contain the decline of its membership in the private sector, the labour movement in Quebec, as in the rest of Canada, has been using card-signing campaigns, collective-bargaining efforts, and judicial decisions.

Card-Signing Campaigns. The card-signing campaigns of yesteryear seem to be fading away. Nevertheless some still survive, as certification statistics testify. These statistics reveal that card-signing is practised more by "new" unions than by more-established ones.[5]

Overall the number of certifications has been slightly on the decrease recently. Nonetheless, the rate is still fairly impressive. Over the past decade most certifications have been of small units, averaging around thirty employees each, with the most recent trend being toward still smaller units. Lately there have been more certifications in the private sector than in the public sector, probably because few opportunities for unionization remained. The sectors in which certifications are occuring are, in order, trade, manufacturing, and services; in other sectors they are minimal (Quebec 1988a).

Such numbers do not necessarily represent a net increase, however. Each year there are a substantial number of decertifications, representing more than one-third of the total (Ministère du Travail du Québec 1988a: 28). Moreover, some certification cases result simply from transfers to another union, probably more as a result of the employee's choice than because of direct raiding.

It appears that despite the rhetoric about them, organizational campaigns as a mainstay of union strategy do not really exist anymore. There are a few exceptions, of course. For example, when a large plant opens, an organizational campaign will usually take place at that time. Nevertheless, in the small-unit category it looks more likely that organization is more "on demand" from the employees rather than as the result of union initiative.

Collective-Bargaining Efforts. Some organizational activity occurs via collective bargaining with the employer. A number of unions have tried to expand their coverage simply by convincing the employer that the bargaining unit should be expanded to include a group of unorganized employees. Both parties then send a letter to the certification officer and the deal is legally completed. Probably the most important example of this practice relates to the growing tendency among unions to cover part-time and casual employees. Despite public criticisms of such types of employment, union leaders at the local level recognize that the phenomenon is here to stay and that these employees can represent an important source of new members. Another example comes from the public sector. As municipalities hire more and more persons to conduct recreation activities, there are efforts to incorporate these employees into the category of blue-collar workers of the city, even if a good number of them are only casual employees.

Judicial or Quasi-Judicial Channels.   Another important organizing activity of trade unions in Quebec is conducted before labour commissioners or even before a regular court. The law provides that if a plant or part of a plant—and this may include subcontracting—is sold or transferred to another employer, any existing certification or collective agreement continues in full force and is binding on the new employer as forcefully as it was on the previous one (Quebec Labour Code 1964 and amendments: s. 45). The law also provides that labour commissioners have the authority to decide if the transfer of rights and obligations applies in any case submitted to them. Every year, labour commissioners in Quebec decide a few hundred such cases, ensuring that the rights of the former union and of employees continue in full force despite the new employer (Quebec Labour Code 1964 and amendments: s. 46).

Not all such disputes are settled at the level of the commissioner; some have gone all the way to the Supreme Court of Canada, which recently made a landmark decision on the subject. The 1988 case involved a school board and two maintenance companies. The school board had contracted out the maintenance of its schools and other buildings to a private entrepreneur. During the academic year the employees of the maintenance company went on strike for several months. When the time came for renewal of the maintenance contract the school board called for bids, as it did every year. The company that had had the contract for several years—and that was then on strike—lost out to another bidder. The employees of the successful company were in a different union, however. Therefore, the union organizing the employees of the first company asked the labour commissioner to decide who held the certificate and had the right to bargain for the employees involved. The labour commissioner found that section 45 of the Labour Code applied and that the original union was the representative of the new employees. The labour tribunal confirmed the opinion of the labour commissioner. Nevertheless, the Supreme Court of Canada overturned both decisions, finding that because there was no direct relationship between the two service employers, successor rights did not apply. The court decided that because the school board was the only link between the two employers, its simply awarding a maintenance contract did not create a juridical relationship between the two maintenance companies.

All these kinds of organizing activities appear more defensive than offensive and it is difficult to assess their final results in numerical terms. While the next group of responses seems more aggressive, it is nevertheless also hard to translate their effect statistically.

Union Response via Collective Bargaining

Restructuring of the Quebec economy has also influenced collective bargaining, including its methods, targets, and results. Indeed, unions now bargain not only for improved working conditions for their members but also for their own survival as the representatives of workers.

Bargaining for Union Security. Possibly because of the declining density in the private sector, unions have been inclined to press for tighter union-security provisions. There may also be another reason, however. Because the required majority is more easily undermined in smaller units, unions trying to organize such sectors often insist on a union shop. Therefore, as smaller units become more prevalent, they may account partly for the relative rise in claims for union-shop provisions.

Traditional *trade* unions, organizing skilled and craft workers, have become tougher at the bargaining table to protect their usual rights: the hiring-hall system, hot cargo provisions, employers' contribution to union training programs, control of admission to the trade, union-administered fringe benefits. At the same time, concern about the needs of apprentices, helpers and casual employees is very low if not nonexistent. The *trade* unions have remained true to themselves; they care for their own membership and for little else.

Another protective device many unions have employed is to bargain for tight subcontracting provisions. Unions have not been equally successful in this realm. Public-sector unions (especially the municipal employees unions) have achieved the best protections. The problem of subcontracting is more acute, or at least more evident for them. Garbage collection and snow removal are only two prominent examples where subcontracting has been widely used. The Canadian Union of Public Employees is a leader in using such a strategy of limiting subcontracting. An issue that arises, of course, with this strategy of restricting subcontracting is, What happens to the subcontractors' employees? They are not likely to be at the top of the list if the municipality does decide to hire new employees. Whereas the bargaining power of the employer may be less in the public sector and municipal administrators can sometimes shift the burden of higher costs to the taxpayers, the game is different in the private sector. Subcontracting clauses are not as stringent there.

Another strategy, again in the public sector, involves a recognition that there be a minimum number of employees in the unit. Some unions have obtained in some collective agreements the acceptance of a kind of "employment floor," below which the number of employees and union members will never go. The Canadian Broadcasting Corporation has guaranteed NABET (National Association of Broadcasting Employees and Technicians) a minimum number of 2,103 employees in the bargaining unit. This number was reached about ten years ago. Radio-Québec has gained a similar guarantee that there will be not fewer than 215 employees in the union representing its general employees, from office workers to stage employees. The agreement goes further, indicating there are to be 81 employees in the office group, 56 in the stage-related jobs, and so forth. The municipality of Laval—the second largest city in the province—has granted a similar guarantee to a local of CUPE that represents its blue-collar and other workers.

Bargaining on Working Conditions and Wages. Here there has not been any major breakthrough. Nevertheless, efforts continue to obtain improvements or at least maintain the status quo in traditional bargaining areas. For example, employment guarantees exist in collective agreements with larger corporations for protection against the effects of sweeping technological changes. Moreover, there has been very little concession bargaining in Quebec, in comparison to the other provinces or the United States. It would be incorrect to say there was none, but it was infrequent and the concessions were generally minor, affecting work rules, wage indexation arrangements, paid vacations, and the like. There were a few cases of a freeze, but very rarely setbacks in wage rates. Two-tier wage scales are also less prevalent. Whereas the presence of such concessions in American collective agreements is said to hover around 10 percent, the Quebec statistic is less than half that figure, just below 4 percent (Pes and Blanchet 1988: 79–89).

Union Response via Involvement in Social Issues

Employment guarantees for those who are already employed and wage systems favouring such workers confirm that the labour movement is preoccupied with its own members. It is natural that it be so. The objective of trade unions in their day-to-day and year-to-year operations is to better the working conditions and wages of their own members. A problem arises, however, if the same movement attempts to speak for the unemployed and for all those in the lower income brackets, by claiming to defend all workers.

The mismatch between these two activities of the trade-union movement is, of course, visible. Therefore, the strategic decision, however necessary, of representing union members more effectively than the unemployed, coupled with the problems that public-sector strikes inflict on the population in general, has tarnished the labour movement's reputation. Public-opinion polls confirm this observation.

Image Making. The union response to this declining status has been ambiguous. In their daily activities, especially in collective bargaining and conflict situations, unions tend to ignore the public and fight as fiercely as they can for their own objectives. If and when they feel public opinion may help their cause, however, they launch advertising campaigns to present and defend their positions. But the other side does the same. In major strikes and conflicts, the public has become accustomed to reading in the papers advertisements representing both antagonists in a kind of press war.

In the late 1980s, the promotional documents informed the viewer how public servants filled extremely useful jobs, how teachers really cared for the students, how public utilities workers did help in cases of power failures and could help in other disaster situations. These video sequences were aired between beer, shampoo, or chocolate bar commercials. They were clearly identified as a kind of promotional commercial sponsored by an equally clearly identified union. These television advertisements showed, first, that such unions have the financial resources to produce them and, second, that they do care about their reputation. A third message is that they are preparing public opinion for the next round of bargaining.

Pension Funds. Besides this public-image innovation, however, it is in economic and financial matters that the labour movement in Quebec has been most imaginative over the last decades. For example, there have been some cases in which a plant with serious economic difficulties has been taken over by its employees in a cooperative form or otherwise. Many of these employees have often managed to save the plant and to keep their jobs at the same time.

Even more innovative—one of the gems of the Quebec labour movement over the past few years—has been the establishment of the so-called Solidarity Fund of the FTQ. Under the leadership of this central body, several national and international union locals have contributed to build a $200 million fund over the last seven years.

The fund has a double mission. Some years ago, many Quebec industries were in severe difficulty because of the economic recession. FTQ leaders analysed the situation to be one in which there was very little risk capital available to rescue ailing industries and thus keep hundreds of jobs for their own members as well as for all other workers. They envisaged a risk-capital fund that would operate on sound economic principles but not only for the benefit of its investors, because an additional goal would be keeping jobs for local workers. Since then the Solidarity Fund has helped many firms through difficult economic times, including their own restructuring. It is estimated that over its first four years of activity it has saved or created 11,000 jobs (*La Presse*, 21 February 1988; 9 March 1988). Nevertheless, it is less clear whether it is financially profitable.

The other objective of the fund is to provide a pension income to the many wage earners not enrolled in a company pension plan. Any money invested in the fund by workers must remain in the fund until their retirement. Employers on the whole have also supported this fund. Many employers have agreed to add a 1 percent increase, or a $.15-per-hour increase, to be directed, on behalf of each employee, to the Solidarity Fund. In the month of February 1988 alone, for example, the fund collected $45 million this way.

The second central body in Quebec, the CSN, has created a different scheme. Its objective is primarily to generate pensions for its members. The CSN has set up a collective Registered Retirement Savings Plan. The project operates much in the same way as the Solidarity Fund. Employers designate a certain portion of the wage increase to the CSN fund, earmarking it for the individual employee. This is again a way of ensuring some income at the time of retirement, and it usually benefits employees who do not have a company pension plan.

Administering Services. A certain number of CSN local unions have innovated in another way by participating in the administration of some services. Two cases come to mind in the quasi-public sector. One of them involves day-care centres, while the other is in the ambulance service of Greater Montreal.

About forty day-care centres are involved in this program. They are private organizations in that each has its own board of directors, but they are public corporations heavily subsidized and therefore heavily dependent on the province for grants. In principle, each local union bargains over the working conditions of its members at each day-care centre. But the power relations in this bargaining situation are subtly different. First, CSN officials have prepared a model, or pattern agreement that is supposed to guide every local union in setting out its own demands (CSN 1988). The employer side is represented by delegates from the board of directors of each centre. The board members represent mostly parents, but by government decision, the board must also seat two representatives of the local union. Moreover, since many of the jobs involved are similar to those performed in hospitals or homes for the elderly, the working conditions of which are determined by provincial collective agreements, the specific content of most of the clauses is simply lifted from the provincial agreements to those of the day-care centres. Finally, for other clauses, it is pretty much the will of the union that prevails, because the board's power is close to nil. Therefore, although a traditional bargaining situation theoretically still exists, the practical situation is much closer to a formula for self-management than anything else.

A comparable experiment was set up in 1988 for ambulance services in the Montreal area. The twenty owners of companies operating ambulance services were replaced by a public corporation (Corporation d'urgences-santé de la région de Montréal métropolitain) (Quebec 1988b: ch. 47). All the employees of the former ambulance owners or companies are now employees of the corporation. Three of nine members on the board of the corporation are named by the employees, that is, by the attendants and the drivers of the ambulances. The other members are persons whose functions are related to local ambulance services (e.g., a representative of the general hospitals of the area). On the face of it this last factor would not encourage the system to become one of self-management by the union. On the other hand, since owning ambulance services has become less attractive, several owners have tried to sell their companies. Some employees have formed cooperatives to buy the vehicles and their equipment. These employees then have a dual status. They are involved in negotiating the employment contract with the corporation, as members of the local union, and the services contract with the minister of health services, as cooperative owners of the vehicles and equipment. The scheme is too recent to permit an evaluation and too limited to discuss the possibility of a future trend.

This general overview of some union responses to economic restructuring and other changes in Quebec suggests a few brief concluding remarks. No labour movement moves in a single direction, even if the common denominator is the betterment of working conditions of the workers it represents. Where the labour movement will go depends on decisions taken not only by union leaders but also, and mainly, by union members. It also depends on some decisions of governments and tribunals. In the current situation some hard decisions are coming up. One is whether trade unions are special organizations with a social mission important enough to provide a rationale for the benefits that labour legislation has granted them.

If the general population, and government as its representative, decides that trade unions have become little more than an insurance business for generating better working conditions for less than half of the workforce, it might decide that trade unions should be treated as any other private insurance organization. For example, in the many cases where the law recognizes a presumption in favour of the union against the employer and where the burden of proof before a court is accordingly oriented, the government may decide that this privilege is no longer justified. In the same way, other rights, like the compulsory dues checkoff and the closed shop, may be challenged. Moreover, the courts may decide that such privileges are in conflict with the Canadian Charter of Rights and Freedoms. Existing decisions are not yet clear, but the threat is there.

Nevertheless, the outcome of state decisions, at least, will depend on the power of unions, just as the decisions of governments and the courts will provide a new framework within which leaders and union members will have to act in the restructured future of Canada and Quebec.

Notes

1. For additional details on the configuration of the union movement in Quebec, see Lipsig-Mummé in this volume.

2. The effects of this militancy in the rest of Canada are discussed in Swartz in this volume.

3. The same labour commissioners also deal with the unfair labour practices, and again it is possible to appeal their decisions before the labour court.

4. The only other legislation dealing with strikebreaking is in British Columbia, which forbids the use of professional strikebreakers but contains no other restriction (British Columbia *Industrial Relations Act* 1979: ch. 212, ss. 1, 3 (3)d). For a discussion of the political implications of this law see Lipsig-Mummé in this volume. In 1992 the Ontario government introduced legislation similar to Quebec's.

5. For a comparison to the U.S. practices see Freeman in this volume.

References

CSN. (Confédération des syndicats nationaux). 1988: Syndicat des travailleuses et travailleurs en garderie de Montréal: Projet-type de convention collective.

Fleury, Gilles. 1988a; Le Monde syndical au Québec en 1987. *Les Relations du travail en 1987*. Supplement to *Marché du travail* 9 (January).

———. 1988b: Un Portrait du syndicalisme indépendant. *Marché du travail* 11 (September).

Kumar, Pradreep. 1988: *Estimates of Unionism and Collective Bargaining Coverage in Canada*, Queen's Papers in Industrial Relations, Kingston, Ont.: Queen's University.

Ministère du Travail du Québec. 1988: *Rapport annuel 1987–1988*. Quebec: Les Publications du Québec.

Pes, Johanne, and Anne-Marie Blanchet. 1988: La Rémunération à double ou à multiples paliers dans les conventions collectives en vigueur au Québec. *Marché du travail* 9 (March).

Quebec. 1964 and amendments: Labour Code. Statutes of Quebec.

———. 1988a: *Synthèse des activitiés du bureau du commissaire général du travail, 1er avril 1972 au 31 mars 1988*. Conseil Consultatif du Travail et de la Main d'oeuvre.

———. 1988b: *Lois du Québec*.

Racine, Francine. 1990: Le Syndicalisation au Québec en 1990. *Les Relations du travail en 1990*. Supplement to *Marché du travail* 11–12 (December).

The Political and Legal Context
of Trade Union Action

Cooperation for What?
The Democratic-Labor Alliance in the
Reagan-Bush Era

To say that the Democratic-labor alliance that has operated in American politics since the New Deal is now "in crisis" is easy.[1] But why? In what respects is this alliance in crisis?

The crisis has to do with both political vulnerability and incapacity for organizational renewal. In the 1980s the alliance became much more vulnerable to public arguments that it was a somewhat illegitimate force in American politics. Implicit in postwar Keynesianism was a public role for unionism as a force pushing for increased purchasing power and, more broadly, for a social program of taking wages out of market competition. The Democratic-labor alliance stood for such broad, social goals, and its goals—for instance, support of social security or minimum wage legislation—were widely perceived as collectively useful. Despite continuing public support for key features of the American welfare state in the 1970s, and even more in the 1980s, the political and economic environment of the alliance changed. The political unification of business and the discovery of the "competitiveness" problem, among other factors, helped to make the alliance vulnerable to charges that growth and international competitiveness were now antithetical to the alliance's historic concern for protecting wage earners from the economic insecurities that a market economy continually generates. The alliance now seems (I stress *seems*) more like a rent-seeking coalition.

This new political vulnerability has itself contributed to an incapacity for organizational renewal. Yet this incapacity for organizational renewal is also linked to the particular responses of the two partners in the alliance to the sweeping, largely political reconstruction of the labor market that, in the 1980s, placed more wages into competition. Weaknesses in Republican macroeconomic management during the 1980s provided opportunities for the alliance to respond to this political project, using policy proposals that addressed both Democrats' electoral needs and labor's organizational imperatives, as perceived by labor leaders. Yet, despite an elaborately planned effort intended to culminate in the 1984 presidential election, the Democratic-labor alliance was unable to fashion successful responses either to the general phenomenon of Reaganomics or to its disruption of the social democratic system for regulating the labor market that had been in place for decades. This failure added to the forces undermining the renewal of the Democratic-labor alliance.

However, there is more to the incapacity for organizational renewal, namely, a long-standing "crisis of mobilization" that faces both of the alliance's partners and that was already apparent by the late 1960s. Labor leaders have been unable to halt the decline in union density—a decline sharply hastened, of course, by the disruption of the historic U.S. system for regulating the labor market. Yet that incapacity was clear well before the 1980s. A parallel incapacity can be found among Democrats. Since the 1960s, they have been unable and unwilling to increase levels of voter turnout among those that would seem to be likely Democratic constituencies. Furthermore, these incapacities reinforce each other: As unions weaken, there are fewer resources for mobilizing existing and potential Democratic voters, and as there are fewer strong Democrats in the electorate, the prospects for a political environment more favorable to unions become bleaker (Myerson 1989: 305–10; Greenstone 1977).

A full account of the sources of these twin incapacities is beyond the scope of this chapter. But I will briefly suggest how and why both "divided government"—that is, the institutional fact in the Reagan-Bush era of Republican control of the presidency and Democratic control of the House of Representatives and, beginning in 1987, of the Senate—and increased corporate involvement in congressional electoral politics in the

1980s somewhat paradoxically encouraged strategies among Democrats and labor leaders that actually deepened the "crisis of mobilization."

The basic political resource of all labor parties or party-labor alliances is "social democratic mass," comprising the power that comes from sheer numbers and the partisan, or populist, political consciousness of those who can be counted among a social democratic mass. Of course, even when these variables are at maximum values—enough to maintain a high degree of continuous, labor-party control over electoral and policy-making processes—the struggle to achieve new, social democratic goals remains an uncertain process. Nevertheless, numbers and consciousness are necessary resources for a labor party or party-labor alliance. The diminution of these resources and the incapacity of Democratic politicians and trade-union leaders to renew them reinforce the new, Republican-corporate control of politics and the economy.

Below I treat the circumstances that made the Democratic-labor alliance more vulnerable in the 1980s to arguments against its legitimacy and briefly illustrate some of the logic of this vulnerability. This outline is crucial to understanding a key aspect of the 1984 presidential campaign— the explosiveness of the "special interest" issue that emerged in the wake of the AFL-CIO's heightened involvement in presidential nominating politics. I then consider the political reconstruction of the American labor market; the weaknesses in Republican, macroeconomic management that made possible a countervailing strategy in 1984: and the Democratic-labor alliance's actual, countervailing strategy in 1984's presidential electoral politics and the political and organizational logic of this strategy.

In short, I offer a case study of a particular version of an organizational alliance, central in the development of modern capitalist democracies. Viewed from the vantage point of the interdependence of the advanced industrial democracies, the importance of this case is obvious. The economic interdependence of advanced industrial democracies can perhaps promote, through international economic bargaining, policy agreements that will strengthen the Democratic-labor alliance. It is more likely, however, that international diplomacy will instead reinforce the alliance's weakness. Conservative policymakers in the United States—unhindered by any substantial pressure from the Democratic-labor alliance—will continue (as the U.S.-Canadian and the proposed North American free trade agreements suggest) to structure economic interdependence in ways that block an international emphasis on labor rights, coordinated expansion, managed trade, and regulation of financial markets. The political weakness of party-labor alliances and trade unions in such newly industrializing economies as Japan, South Korea, and Taiwan further helps to skew attention in the arena of international economic diplomacy away from social democratic concerns. Thus, the current and future weakness of the Democratic-labor alliance is crucial for understanding the international context of labor parties and party-labor alliances in the advanced industrial democracies.

More generally, the case is interesting for what it suggests about organizational decline. The Democratic-labor alliance is perhaps exceptional in the extent to which its leaders appeared, even before the Reagan-Bush era, either unable or unwilling to solve the long-run imperative of assuring the alliance's organizational strength. The Democratic party will, of course, continue to exist as a major party, and organized labor will continue to work within the Democratic party. But the "swan song" of the historic alliance, the one created during the New Deal, seems to have been 1984.

A New Political and Economic Context

Public Disapproval of Labor Unions.   A basic attitudinal change in the United States since the 1950s has been an increase in public disaffection with unions. From 1937 to 1957 public approval of unions was high, peaking at 76 percent in 1957. It has since dropped to roughly 55 percent. While the public very strongly supports the right to organize, it holds labor leaders in especially low esteem. Since 1971 about half the public has considered trade unions too powerful. Union members themselves have come to resemble the public in their views of unions. In 1984 three-fifths of both union members and the public agreed that "union leaders express their own views, not those of their members, when taking stands on public issues," and in 1985, 54 percent of union members did not express any "trust and confidence" in unions (Goldfield 1987: 34–37; Lipset 1986: 287–322; esp. 304–5).

Change in Voter Behavior.   Party and electoral politics seems periodically to go through upheavals in voter behavior. In the 1980s the Republican party beat the Democratic party at registering voters, and the number of voters professing identification with the party increased.

Young people, if they were electorally active at all, seemed more pro-Republican than before. In addition to these national trends, the dynamics of Southern public opinion strongly favor the Republican party in presidential elections. Opposition to the Republican party must not only overcome those features of national electoral politics that favor the Republicans, it must have a successful regional thrust as well. The Republican party's growing strength in the South since the 1950s gives the Republican party a decided advantage in presidential elections unlikely to crumble soon (Cavanaugh and Sundquist 1985: 33–68; Beck 1988: 145–71; Black and Black 1987: chs. 1–3, 8, 10–14).

Change in Consensus on Macroeconomic Target Variables. For two or three decades after the Great Depression most economic policymakers and economists worried about the level of unemployment. This was the "consensus target variable" of macroeconomic policy, to be adjusted by countercyclical policy measures. But in the inflationary 1970s attention shifted to inflation as it became a more serious problem. Generational change, the agenda-setting efforts of monetarist economists discontented with Keynesianism, and programs such as unemployment insurance helped to undermine the degree to which the public worried about unemployment. Unemployment has been redefined as a cyclical, sectoral, and racial problem.[2] Inflation, in contrast, is perceived as an economy-wide phenomenon that affects every individual and that arouses public anxiety more than unemployment. "Fighting inflation" has become a major, new responsibility for macroeconomic managers. The rate of annual increase in inflation is now a "consensus target variable" to be adjusted by central bank regulation of monetary transactions (Peretz 1983: 85–89; Kiewiet 1 `3: 58–60; Greider 1987).

Change in International-National Linkages. In the past two decades the U.S. economy and the international economy have become ever more tightly integrated. After the breakdown of the Bretton Woods system in the mid-1970s, the dollar continued to be used for international transactions. An international market in the dollar and other currencies developed, posing new constraints for economic policymakers. Second, the U.S. share of world markets in an array of industrial goods, ranging from cars to computer chips and supercomputers, has dropped. Certain markets no longer have U.S. manufacturers competing in them at all. The percentage of industry insulated from foreign price competition, and from low-wage producers, has sharply dropped. In the process, millions of manufacturing jobs have shifted from the historic areas of union strength in the United States to regions where unions have historically been much weaker. Finally, U.S. business itself has become highly transnational; it thus has less of a sense of sharing the fate of its domestic workforce (Ferguson and Rogers 1986: 79–83; Norton 1986: 1–40).

Delegitimation of the Democratic-Labor Alliance

These changes make possible new and delegitimating arguments against the Democratic-labor alliance. The increasing public dissatisfaction with trade unions and the decline in union density mean that there are increasingly fewer people in the electorate who self-consciously conceive of the Democratic-labor alliance either as an institution that serves their individual interests or as an institution that can play a legitimate role in addressing national-policy problems. To the contrary, this alliance can more easily be described in public—as it was during the 1984 presidential campaign—as a "special interest" and likely to worsen national problems. These trends may also suggest why increasingly fewer politicians are willing or able to develop the kind of political style that could reconstitute the legitimacy of trade unions (Raskin 1986: 3–38).

The pro-Republican trend in the behavior of the active, voting electorate has only reinforced the consequences for the Democratic-labor alliance of increasing public disaffection with trade unions and of declining union density. The national electorate, while still populist in many ways, has become skeptical of government intervention in society and the economy and expresses strong support for the system of free enterprise. The Southern electorate, as evidenced in presidential politics, was and is more hostile to government intervention in the economy and more warmly espouses individualistic values in the marketplace than does the national electorate (Black and Black 1987).[3]

The emergence of the rate of inflation as a "consensus target variable" implicitly casts that Democratic-labor alliance in a new light. Collective bargaining's upward pressure on the wage bill is only one of the sources of inflation, but it is easily presented as a problem for the economy. Though the wage concessions and give-backs have characterized collective bargaining in this decade, the Democratic-labor alliance has become more implicitly threatening to the apparent majoritarian interest in low inflation (Lipset, 1986: esp. 316–18).

With the rise of new Asian industrial economies and the jump in the U.S. trade deficit in the 1980s, the standard microeconomic argument that trade unions interfere with allocative efficiency, comparative advantage, and flexible adjustment has tended to find a more receptive audience. Business leaders have become more used to dealing with foreign workforces that have apparently lower expectations, which may contribute to the view that U.S. workers ought to be more "flexible." In addition, the real, Taylorist rigidities of high-volume mass production that were built up from the 1930s into the 1950s now seem increasingly obsolete as manufacturers have learned to compete in markets that require continual adaptation in response to the emergence of new market niches for customized versions of basic products (Piore 1989; Norton 1986).

In capitalist democracies the public has a tendency to regard business leaders as embodying "general interests." After all, the material welfare of all depends on their decisions, even if they are not coordinated decisions (Cohen and Rogers 1983: ch. 3; Gourevitch 1986: ch. 6). As business views have changed, the Democratic-labor alliance has gradually metamorphosed into a putative "special interest," hostile to the "national interest."

Finally, the mobility of international capital and the development of an international currency market have made it possible for deficit spending to be plausibly presented as irresponsible. Capital, the argument goes, will flee economies that are potentially inflationary, drying up investment capital. A corollary of such a view is that the historic stake of the Democratic-labor alliance in the incremental growth of governmental activism is irresponsible. Of course, deficit spending increased in the 1980s, with little diminution in the confidence of international currency markets in the dollar. Yet the threat of loss of confidence has structurally limited the agenda-setting capacity of actors in the Democratic-labor alliance (Weisskopf 1989: 12–14; Block 1987: 13–31, esp. 23–27).

The Political Reconstruction of the Labor Market

With the election of Ronald Reagan in 1980 came a sweeping, political reconstruction of the U.S. labor market. Several aspects of this reconstruction first emerged in the 1970s. The Carter administration took certain steps on which the Reagan administration built. For the most part, the Carter administration was inactive amid the wrenching, regional transfer of manufacturing jobs from states and communities where unions were historically strongest to those where they were historically weakest. The pace of change, however, picked up very quickly in the 1980s.

To put the essence of this second phase of the reconstruction of the American labor market very briefly, the wages of more and more wage earners were placed "in competition" through a combination of (1) social policy changes; (2) changes in industrial relations policy; (3) changes in antitrust policy and regulation of transportation; and (4) private, corporate attacks on unionism (symbolically encouraged by President Reagan himself in the 1981 PATCO [Professional Air Traffic Controllers Organization] strike, in which the federal government permanently replaced striking air traffic controllers). Structures were politically created in ways that in turn forced more and more wage earners to encounter the insecurities and risks endemic to an idealized "free market" in labor.[4] The net effect of this change was a lowering of worker expectation about the risks and rewards of entering the labor market, manifested in concession bargaining and in a drop in work stoppages. It placed great pressure on unions to expend scarce resources on protecting existing organizations, which militated against a strategy of organizing the unorganized. The political reconstruction of the labor market will be described in greater detail below.[5]

Social Policy.   The value of the minimum wage, a policy dating to the Fair Labor Standards Act of 1938, dropped in the 1980s, relative to the average wage. Unemployment insurance (UI), dating to the Social Security Act of 1935, has been drastically changed. It was intended to enable workers to retain their occupational status and purchasing power during business cycle downturns. The Reagan administration expanded Carter administration assaults on the UI system, increasing taxes on UI benefits and sharply decreasing the scope of the system's coverage. Thus, during the recession of 1974–75, about 78 percent of the unemployed received UI, while during the Reagan recession, which saw significantly higher unemployment, about 45 percent of the unemployed received UI. This percentage dropped further in the 1989–91 recession. In 1981 Congress prohibited striking workers from receiving food-stamp benefits. Public-sector employment funded under the Comprehensive Employment and Training Act of 1973 was sharply cut. Means tests for welfare were tightened.

Industrial Relations Policy.   President Reagan acted forcefully to reorganize the National Labor Relations Board. Prior to this reorganization, key features in the legal structure of industrial relations policy facilitated increased employer resistance to unionism. Simply maintaining the legal and administrative status quo was a policy that menaced unionism. Under Reagan, the NLRB acted to hinder unionism. Its decisions made it more difficult to generate new membership, thereby discouraging attempts to organize.

Antitrust and Transportation Regulation. The relaxation of antitrust enforcement during the Reagan administration made it easier for firms to merge, to engage in hostile takeovers, and to engage in leveraged buyouts. These reorganizations, in turn, contributed to plant closings that shed labor and to increased corporate debt loads that invited corporate attacks on unions. Although the deregulation of transportation began under Democratic aegis during the late 1970s, the Reagan administration continued strongly to press for it. Deregulation brought the wages of nonunion firms—in the airline industry, for example—into competition with unionized companies, leading to concession bargaining and attacks on unions.

Corporate Resistance to Unionism. Managerial attitudes clearly changed in the 1970s. "Union avoidance" became an increasingly conscious strategy, founded on using temporary workers, subcontracting, and part-time workers. The failure in 1977–78 of the AFL-CIO's campaign for a modest labor reform signaled the rupture of postwar labor-management compromises. In the early 1980s firms demanded concession bargaining in large part, of course, because of the recession. Yet a significant number of firms did not face financial distress and still demanded concession bargaining. In the 1980s and 1990s many corporate leaders are convinced that changes in workplace organization in a more competitive, international environment could and should be done without bothering to consult a weakened labor movement.

The Mixed Results of Reaganomics

The political reconstruction of the labor market that began in the 1970s and that quickened during the 1980s menaced not only organized labor but also the Democratic-labor alliance. After a slight increase in absolute terms of labor membership through the 1970s, union membership declined very sharply in absolute terms from 1980 to 1984. This decline struck directly at the overall organizational strength of the alliance (Ginsberg and Shefter 1990: 117). Nevertheless, the limits of Republican macroeconomic management provided opportunities for a countervailing strategy. Actors committed to causing a resurgence of the Democratic-labor alliance could attempt politically to define the costs of Reaganomics in ways that were favorable to them and the alliance. It was instrumentally rational for them to act on the assumption that they faced opportunities as well as constraints.

As is well known, the longest expansion in the postwar American political economy occurred from 1982 to mid-1990. There were, however, limits to Reaganomics. During the Reagan era a deep recession occurred, the worst since the 1930s. Unemployment moved up to 11 percent and did not return to prerecession levels, already high by historic standards, until 1984. Rates higher than 11 percent were recorded in certain states, and there were still higher rates in certain urban areas (Greider 1987: Appendix B).[6] Moreover, the recession had serious short-run effects on the export competitiveness of the U.S. economy because the value of the dollar relative to the currencies of other major trading partners increased during the recession, a phenomenon that compounded itself as foreign investors in securities chased a tight dollar. As the dollar climbed, the American trade deficit worsened. Increasingly "uncompetitive" factories closed. Export distribution networks closed down (Bergsten 1988: Figures 2.1 on 38 and 4.1 on 86; Obey and Sarbanes 1986: Appendix Figures A.9, A.11, A.16). After the Reagan recession, the problem of the "twin deficits" emerged: a combination of high government deficits and high trade deficits (Bergsten 1988: ch. 3; Lipset 1986: 421–54, esp. Table 1).

Reaganomics, in other words, had a series of economic stresses and problems associated with it, and one cyclical crisis of some magnitude. These stresses and crises created uncertainty about the future both among elites and among voters. As a result, there was a window of opportunity for the leaders of the Democratic-labor alliance to seize power back from the Reaganites and in so doing to halt the political reconstruction of the labor market.

Mondale and the Rise of Industrial Policy, 1981–84

In an authoritative study of the rise of the "industrial-policy idea," Jim Shoch has shown that between 1981 and 1984 industrial policy was taken very seriously by Democratic party, business, and trade-union leaders as a way of building a winning coalition for 1984. Shoch shows that the industrial-policy idea was at the center of a series of meetings, special conferences, and planning sessions within and without Congress devoted to developing a basis for cooperation behind a new, macroeconomic program that could be presented to the electorate as a positive alternative to Reaganomics (Shoch 1988).[7]

A brief definition of the industrial-policy idea is in order. Some proponents of industrial policy were "preservationists"—they wanted to save industries from international competition. Equally important, however, were "modernizers" who argued their case in microeconomic and structural terms. They proposed that a new world structure in which industrializing nations could exploit the diffusion of technologies and their lower labor costs meant that older, industrialized economies could retain their comparative advantage only if they developed ways to renovate—with government assistance to workers, firms, and sectors—their potential advantages in technology and high worker productivity.[8]

Shoch's evidence about the scope and seriousness of planning for industrial policy is consistent with evidence Hilary Silver has presented regarding the politics of the Greenhouse Compact in Rhode Island, a comprehensive industrial policy that, after extensive debate between fall 1983 and June 1984, was voted on by the Rhode Island electorate. Due to accumulating economic stresses, a key political entrepreneur, Ira Magaziner, who was influential in developing the concept of industrial policy, was able to persuade business and union leaders in Rhode Island that the state should have its own industrial policy. Although it failed to win public approval, the Greenhouse Compact may have been intended by Magaziner and perhaps by his Democratic and trade-union allies to demonstrate the idea's general political utility beyond Rhode Island. If the Greenhouse Compact had succeeded in June 1984, this might have had national ramifications (Silver 1987: 333–68).

The depth of the Reagan recession, in combination with the rise of the dollar, seems largely to explain the degree to which industrial policy became accepted in the early 1980s among Democrats, labor, and certain business leaders as not just a theory but a program with political utility. Coming on the heels of the turbulent 1970s, the worst recession since the 1930s left political actors open to thinking about their economic interests in new ways. As the basis for a presidential campaign and a new, macroeconomic program, industrial policy promised certain payoffs to these three actors.

Payoff to Business.   Industrial policy meant public assistance to industries damaged by the strength of the dollar and foreign competition. In return for tax concessions, short-term trade protection, loans, and the certainty of labor peace, business leaders would modernize and invest in new products and processes that would recapture foreign and domestic market shares.

Payoff to Labor.   By becoming a partner in government-guaranteed and -guided modernization, the labor leadership could present itself to its constituency as having traded concessions on wage demands and shop floor rules for increasing market shares over the long run and guarantees of job security. These guarantees were especially important in the context of the Reagan recession. Labor leaders could also acquire a public status as de facto macroeconomic planners. Most important, perhaps, the industrial-relations system would be regularized. Industrial policy would end the turmoil of the emerging, new labor market and industrial-relations system being constructed in the early 1980s, and generate a more secure labor market and a more predictable system of industrial relations.

Payoff to Democrats.   Industrial policy gave Democrats a way to change their public image as incompetent macroeconomic managers. As a framework for regaining foreign market shares, industrial policy implicitly contained a nationalism that could help Democrats to portray themselves as agents of the "national interest."

With the exception of Senator Glenn (Democrat, Ohio), all of the Democratic presidential candidates of 1984 were interested, to one degree or another, in industrial policy as a campaign theme. The politician who went furthest in brokering an industrial-policy coalition was former Senator and Vice-President Walter Mondale. Mondale already had experience in assembling an industrial-policy coalition. Through working with business and labor, Mondale had played a role in the federal bailout of Chrysler Corporation and its United Auto Worker unions during the Carter administration. Unlike many Democrats, Mondale was comfortable working closely with labor leaders who rose to prominence in the 1970s. Mondale's political base had for many years been in a strong state-level version of the Democratic-labor alliance, the Minnesota Democratic Farmer-Labor party. For reasons peculiar to the development of parties in that state, the Minnesota DFL was and is among the most social democratic of the state-level party-labor alliances. Finally, following the 1980 election, an ostentatious program of "self-education" helped Mondale to appear open to business demands (Reich and Donahue 1985: 99, 124–25, 129, and ch. 7; Blumenthal 1984: 16–20; Valelly 1989; Ferguson and Rogers 1986: 154–57, 162–65).

The Debacle of the 1984 Election

Whether the industrial-policy idea was good strategy for the Democratic-labor alliance is still the subject of considerable controversy, not least because it plainly had a conservative, defensive character that aimed to hang on to the historic strengths of organized labor in industry through a renewed social compact with business. Yet a key political implication of the proposal warrants consideration: If the Democrats were to win the White House on an industrial-policy platform, organized labor stood to gain the prospect of order and security in the industrial-relations system and, more generally, the labor market. In other words, the forces eating away at the sources of the alliance's "social democratic mass" could be momentarily slowed or stopped, which itself is a necessary condition for any more progressive strategy of turning back or dissolving these forces.

It is impossible to know whether the industrial-policy idea could, in fact, have been the basis of a policy mandate from the electorate to the Democratic-labor alliance. Public-opinion polls showed public hostility to the AFL-CIO's endorsement of Mondale. The American public and many unionists themselves actively dislike labor leaders and "big labor"; the AFL-CIO endorsement unintentionally tapped these long-standing antipathies. Mondale's opponents in the Democratic party had strong incentives to charge that he was a hostage of "special interests" (a charge later picked up by the Republican campaign). Yet there is some ground for believing that a very well conceived campaign of education might have convinced the public of the merits of industrial policy. In 1984 unemployment was, by historic standards, still high, and there was a detectable level of public anxiety about America's economic future (Lipset 1986; Shogan and Schneider 1983: 41–44).

Still, this is little more than counterfactual speculation. Mondale, the very figure who seemed able and willing to put together a renewed Democratic-labor-business coalition, abandoned industrial policy. His decision may have had to do with pressure from his business supporters, who became less interested in industrial policy as the economy began to recover. In addition, the opposition to industrial policy by the great majority of reputable economists may have affected his thinking. Third, the political failure of the Rhode Island Greenhouse Compact (June 1984) may have played a role. The corporatist mechanisms of consultation among business, government, and labor that were envisioned by industrial-policy analysts never really existed in America, except for two years during the New Deal in the guise of the National Recovery Administration. In the 1970s there were corporatist experiments in New York City and one or two other local settings, but these experiments could not resolve the conflicts that emerged in 1983 and 1984 over the merits of industrial policy's institutional design (Gourevitch 1986: 232; Blumenthal 1983).

Perhaps the most important factor was public opinion. The poll evidence regarding public hostility to the AFL-CIO endorsement surely played a role; an emphasis on industrial policy in the general campaign would obviously highlight ties between the Democratic party and organized labor, putting Mondale on the defensive amid charges of subordination to "special interests." The issue would not only threaten efforts to win over independents, it would also threaten to expose tensions between blue- and white-collar unionists; unionists and nonunion, middle-class Democrats; and unionized and nonunion workers (Lipset 1986; Shogan and Schneider 1983).

Ironically, the factors that have delegitimated the Democratic-labor alliance made labor seem really like a "special interest." Labor's first preconvention endorsement in sixty years was driven by the AFL-CIO leadership's accurate assessment of the inhospitality of labor's political environment, even during the Carter years, and its interest in industrial policy (Myerson 1984: 285–94). As a rational campaigner, Mondale had little choice but to drop industrial policy as a campaign theme, even though the platform contained an endorsement of it.

In trying to find some general policy stance that seemed more promising than industrial policy, Mondale opted for an ill-starred emphasis on raising taxes in order to cure the Reagan deficit and some emphasis on the unfairness of Reagan budget cuts in Great Society programs. Mondale effectively presented himself to the electorate in much the way a fiscally orthodox Republican of the 1950s did. In doing this he seemed to recycle Carter's emphasis in 1979 and 1980 on budget balancing and taxation. Given the way of defining the costs of Reaganomics that he chose, and given the rise in personal income that occurred in 1984, it hardly seems surprising that Reagan's lead over Mondale in public-opinion polls was huge and stayed huge (Edsall 1987: 103–5; Kiewiet and Rivers 1985: 69–90).

Here another irony deserves emphasis. Previous decades of Democratic-led, Keynesian macroeconomic management hurt Mondale and helped Reagan. This history constrained Mondale's postconvention effort at politically defining Reaganomics' costs. By 1984, the expansion seemed to be delivering on precisely those "target variables" that Keynesian economists considered central: growth in GNP, declining unemployment, and increase in real family income. The previous success of the Democratic party, and of the Democratic-labor alliance, in constructing the interests and attitudes of the electorate thus became a constraint. Decades of Keynesianism have led, unsurprisingly, to a lot of incumbent-favored voting. Thus, despite the electorate's worries in 1984 about the country's economic future, once Mondale abandoned the issue of industrial policy, incumbent-favored voting assured Reagan of a victory.

Industrial policy was an issue that might (but one has to emphasize *might*) have changed the terms of economic-policy debate in 1984 from a debate whether the expansion had a fiscal flaw to a debate about America's long-run competitiveness. In contrast to this contingency, industrial policy seemed certain to sink Mondale's candidacy into continual, defensive posturing in the face of the "special interest" issue.

The Impact of Divided Government and Business Mobilization

While Michael Dukakis did not lose as badly in 1988 to George Bush as Mondale did in 1984 to Ronald Reagan, the fact that the Democratic party ran two apparently weak candidates in two successive presidential elections, in combination with another fact—Bush's unexpected strength as a president—underscores the seeming durability of "divided government" in the United States. Divided government has exacerbated the dual "crisis of mobilization" described at the outset of this chapter.

Although there is considerable academic and political debate about its likely efficacy, one possible strategy for regaining control of the presidency that the Democrats have rejected is mobilizing nonvoters. To be sure, the Democrats have paid some lip service to voter mobilization, sponsoring "get out the vote" initiatives in 1984, and in 1989 and 1990 pushing a national voter-registration policy through the House of Representatives. The relatively greater success in 1984 of Republican initiatives for mobilizing voters, however, suggests that the Democrats are not serious about voter mobilization. Instead, they have focused—although usually with little success—on defining issues that can help them win among the 50 percent or so of the electorate that is still actually voting in presidential elections. And they have focused on strategies for weakening the executive branch in the legislative-executive rivalry that is invited by divided government (Ferguson and Rogers 1986: 189–92; Ginsberg and Shefter 1990).

Furthermore, holding on to Congress requires a defensiveness that militates against the development of a mobilization strategy and of policy stances that might appeal to nonvoters: "To be a legislative party requires congressional Democrats to get reelected, and to do that they need "permanent," well-funded campaigns and predictable electoral bases. . . . Building a war chest primarily from well-heeled donors to scare away potential challengers is not an activity that encourages deep reflection on social change" (Valelly 1990: 147). In addition, divided government creates pressure for responsibility that makes it much harder for congressional Democrats continuously to present a clear-cut, social democratic policy stance to the electorate. Instead, they must often compromise with the Republican party, being in effect a partner in a coalition government. Divided government can thus undermine voter awareness of efforts by congressional Democrats and key state-level leaders to define the party's political identity (Kuttner 1991: 25–36).

As for organized labor's leaders, here too there are new incentives for defensive, short-run strategies. These have somewhat undercut the local, revitalizing effects of shop steward involvement in 1984 presidential politics, a strategy developed partly in reaction to the initially top-down character of Mondale's AFL-CIO alliance. Business mobilization into politics in the 1970s in response to a burst of new regulatory initiatives that rivaled the scope of the Progressive Era's regulatory thrusts has led to a new role for business in congressional electoral politics and in the policy-making process. The networks of business lobbyists in Washington have become much denser, and business lobbyists themselves have become more aggressive and sophisticated in their activities. In response to increased business involvement in congressional electoral politics and more aggressive lobbying, organized labor has become much more heavily invested in elections and lobbying itself, in large part through raising the real, inflation-adjusted price of union membership in order to expand funds for political action (Bennett 1991: 1–12; Masters and Delaney 1987: 336–53; Ornstein, Mann, and Malbin 1990: 99–109).

The political strategy that greater funds for political action have made possible is largely defensive: investing in the congressional Democratic party and presidential campaigns in order to prevent the larger political environment from becoming even more inhospitable. The strategy has provoked strong counterattack under the guise of campaign finance reform. On the plus side have been legislative efforts to remedy some of the consequences of the labor market's reconstruction in the 1970s and 1980s, such as the plant-closing notification legislation of 1988 and Congress's attention to making the permanent replacement of strikers illegal.

On the whole, however, organized labor's investment in the congressional Democratic party and in presidential elections has been defensive. It also comes at the cost of decreased investment, in real terms, in organizing new members (Freeman 1985; Fellner 1990: 103–5).

A Doomed Alliance?

What explains the evidence of failure, incapacity, and defensiveness that seems to abound both in the record over the past decade of the Democratic-labor alliance's politics and—as some analysts have shown—in preceding decades (Goldfield 1987; Piven 1991)? There is no guarantee that actors within organizations will successfully address crises that face their organizations. But the apparent irresolvability of the Democratic-labor alliance's crisis is striking. Does the explanation for it lie in lack of creativity, strategic vision, or political will? Or is the alliance's fate largely outside its leaders' control?

I cannot pretend to have the right answer to these questions. But Rogowski's (1989) work on how trade affects domestic politics suggests that the extraordinary expansion of global trade in the post-1945 decades has imposed serious, structural limits on this alliance. Relative to the economies of Europe and Japan in the postwar decades, labor in the United States has been a scarce factor, while capital and land have been abundant factors. Over the long run, this ratio of labor scarcity to capital and land abundance implies political weakness for labor because in a period of rapidly expanding trade, expansion favors the abundant factors in a political economy. Conversely, contraction of world trade economically and politically favors labor. It would seem more than a coincidence that since 1955 union density in the United States has steadily dropped, amid the unprecedented, rapid expansion of world trade, whereas in the 1930s and 1940s, until the international trade system was put back together, union density spurted upward. It was in these decades that the Democratic-labor alliance was politically strongest.

If there is some merit to Rogowski's theory and to its implications for the Democratic-labor alliance, then it may be the case that without a contraction of world trade the Democratic-labor alliance is fated to decline. Union density may well be a single digit by the end of this century. No matter what actors in the alliance do, perhaps they can do little more than slow its decline. Even relatively sophisticated strategies, such as the industrial-policy strategy put together by labor leaders and Walter Mondale in anticipation of the 1984 presidential election, seem impossible. Rogowski wonders, indeed, whether the Democratic-labor alliance has not become a "regional party of industrial decay." To most economists, and to much of the public, if one is to take the survey data seriously, this is just what the Democratic-labor alliance looked like in 1984 as it focused for a time on industrial policy.

While I do not completely accept the bleak implications of such a highly deterministic theory of how expansion or contraction of trade affect domestic politics in any given political economy, it does explain broad trends in the twentieth-century history of the Democratic-labor alliance. It also suggests a very harsh hypothesis: that in the case of this alliance, politics cannot matter and has perhaps not mattered for several decades. At the very least, the recent record of the alliance's politics suggests that if politics *can* matter in the coming years, it will require extraordinary creativity, cooperation with other labor movements, such as Mexico's and Canada's, and a mix of strategies and successes that incrementally renew the alliance.

Notes

1. For genuinely thoughtful, helpful comments on the second of two earlier drafts of this chapter, I thank Jane Jenson, Frances Fox Piven, Martin Shefter, and Jim Shoch. I am also grateful to Andrew Martin, Richard Samuels, Charles Stewart III, and Donald Swartz for probing criticism on the first of the previous drafts. I thank Carla Kruger and Gail Mantelman for invaluable re-

search assistance. None of them is responsible for any errors of fact or interpretation.

2. On the racial aspects of unemployment see Wilson (1987: ch. 2).

3. For the statistical details, see *Public Opinion*, December-January 1980, 20–21; April-May 1980, 21–27; June-July 1980, 32–33, 35; August-September 1980, 36.

4. For a poignant account focusing on an individual worker, see David Wessel, "As Recession Bores In, Many Factory Workers Still Feel the Last One," *Wall Street Journal*, 4 April 1991, A-1.

5. The arguments and data for the discussion that follows come from Cohen and Rogers (1983: 35, 54), du Rivage (1992), Farber (1987: 915–20), Freeman (1985: 45–64), Ferguson and Rogers (1986: 83–86, 127–37), Ginsberg and Shefter (1990: ch. 4), Moe (1987: 236–302), Norton (1986), Piore (1989), Rosenberg (1989: 63–85), and Weiler (1990).

6. On state-level and urban unemployment, see Osborne (1988: 45–46, 149) and Wilson (1987: ch. 2).

7. A similar, albeit briefer, account is Blumenthal (1983).

8. For a good introduction, see Reich (1983).

References

Beck, P. A. 1988. "Incomplete Realignment: The Reagan Legacy for Parties and Elections." In C. O. Jones, ed., *The Reagan Legacy*, Chatham, N.J.: Chatham House Publishers.

Bennett, James. 1991. "Private Sector Unions: The Myth of Decline," *Journal of Labor Research* 12, Winter.

Bergsten, C. F. 1988. *America in the World Economy: A Strategy for the 1990s*, Washington D.C.: Institute for International Economics, November.

Black, Earl, and Merle Black. 1987. *Politics and Society in the South*, Cambridge, Mass.: Harvard University Press.

Block, Fred. 1987. "Social Policy and Accumulation: A Critique of the New Consensus." In Martin Rein, Gösta Esping-Andersen, and Lee Rainwater, eds., *Stagnation and Renewal in Social Policy-The Rise and Fall of Policy Regimes*, Armonk, N.Y.: M. E. Sharpe.

Blumenthal, Sidney. 1983. "Drafting a Democratic Industrial Plan," *New York Times Magazine*, 28 August.

———. 1984. "Made in Minnesota: The Origins of Mondale's Candidacy," *The New Republic* 6, August.

Cavanagh, T. E., and J. L. Sundquist. 1985. "The New Two-Party System." In J. E. Chubb and P. E. Peterson, eds., *The New Direction in American Politics*, Washington, D.C.: Brookings.

Cohen, Joshua, and Joel Rogers. 1983. *On Democracy: Toward a Transformation of American Society*, New York: Penguin.

du Rivage, Virginia. 1992. "Flexibility Trap: The Proliferation of Marginal Jobs," *American Prospect*, Spring.

Edsall, T. B. 1987. "Right Turn?" *Tikkun*, May–June.

Farber, Henry. 1987. "The Recent Decline of Unionization in the United States," *Science* 13, November.

Fellner, Kim. 1990. "An Uneasy Marriage in the House of Labor," *American Prospect*, Summer.

Ferguson, Tom, and Joel Rogers. 1986. *Right Turn: The Decline of the Democrats and the Future of American Politics*, New York: Hill and Wang.

Freeman, Richard. 1985. "Why Are Unions Faring Poorly in NLRB Representation Elections?" In T. A. Kochan, ed., *Challenges and Choices Facing American Labor*, Cambridge, Mass.: MIT Press.

Ginsberg, Benjamin, and Martin Shefter. 1990. *Politics by Other Means: The Declining Importance of Elections in America*, New York: Basic.

Goldfield, Michael. 1987. *The Decline of Organized Labor in the United States*, Chicago: University of Chicago Press.

Gourevitch, Peter. 1986. *Politics in Hard Times: Comparative Responses to International Economic Crises*, Ithaca, N.Y.: Cornell University Press.

Greenstone, J. D. 1977. *Labor in American Politics*, Chicago: University of Chicago Press.

Greider, William. 1987. *Secrets of the Temple: How the Federal Reserve Runs the Country*, New York: Simon and Schuster.

Kiewiet, D. R. 1983. *Macroeconomics and Micropolitics: The Electoral Effects of Economic Issues*, Chicago: University of Chicago Press.

Kiewiet, D. R., and Douglas Rivers. 1985. "The Economic Basis of Reagan's Appeal." In J. E. Chubb and P. E. Peterson, eds., *The New Direction in American Politics*, Washington, D.C.: Brookings.

Kuttner, Robert. 1991. "Congress without Cohabitation," *American Prospect*, Winter.

Lipset, S. M. 1986. "Labor Unions in the Public Mind" and "North American Labor Movements: A Comparative Perspective." In S. M. Lipset, ed., *Unions in Transition: Entering the Second Century*, San Francisco: ICS Press.

Masters, M. F., and J. T. Delaney. 1987, "Union Political Activities: A Review of the Empirical Literature," *Industrial and Labor Relations Review*, 40, April.

Moe, Terry. 1987. "Interests, Institutions, and Positive Theory: The Politics of the NLRB," *Studies in American Political Development* 2.

Myerson, Harold. 1984. "Labor's Risky Plunge into Politics: From Top-Down to Bottom-Up," *Dissent*, Summer.

————. 1989. "Why the Democrats Keep Losing: The Abandonment of Economic Populism," *Dissent*, Summer.

Norton, R. D. 1986. "Industrial Policy and American Renewal," *Journal of Economic Literature* 24, March.

Obey, David, and Paul Sarbanes, eds. 1986. *The Changing American Economy: Papers from the Fortieth Anniversary Symposium of the Joint Economic Committee of the United States Congress*, New York: Basil Blackwell.

Ornstein, N. J., Thomas E. Mann, and Michael J. Malbin. 1990. *Vital Statistics in Congress, 1989–1990*, Washington, D.C.: Congressional Quarterly for the American Enterprise Institute.

Osborne, David. 1988. *Laboratories of Democracy: A New Breed of Governor Creates Models for National Growth*, Boston: Harvard Business School.

Peretz, Paul. 1983. *The Political Economy of Inflation in the United States*, Chicago: University of Chicago Press.

Piore, Michael J. 1989. "Fissure and Discontinuity in U.S. Labor Management Relations." In Samuel Rosenberg, ed., *The State and the Labor Market*, New York: Plenum Press.

Piven, F. F. 1991. "The American Democratic Party." In F. F. Piven, ed., *Labor Parties in Post-Industrial Societies*, Cambridge: Polity.

Raskin, A. H. 1986. "Labor: A Movement in Search of a Mission." In S. M. Lipset, ed., *Unions in Transition: Entering the Second Century*, San Francisco: ICS Press.

Reich, Robert. 1983. *The Next American Frontier*, New York: Times Books.

Reich, Robert, and J. D. Donahue. 1985. *New Deals: The Chrysler Revival and the American System*, New York: Times Books.

Rogowski, Ronald. 1989. *Commerce and Coalitions: How Trade Affects Domestic Political Alignments*, Princeton, N.J.: Princeton University Press.

Rosenberg, Samuel. 1989. "The Restructuring of the Labor Market, the Labor Force, and the Nature of Employment Relations in the United States in the 1980s." In Samuel Rosenberg, ed., *The State and Labor Market*, New York: Plenum Press.

Shoch, Jim. 1988. The Politics of the U.S. Industrial Policy Debate, 1980–84: A Theoretical and Historical Perspective. Unpublished paper, MIT Political Science.

Shogan, Robert, and William Schneider. 1983. "Labor's Gamble: The Presidential Endorsement and the Polls," *Public Opinion*, June–July.

Silver, Hilary. 1987. "Is Industrial Policy Possible in the United States? The Defeat of Rhode Island's Greenhouse Compact," *Politics and Society* 15(3).

Valelly, R. M. 1989. *Radicalism in the States: The Minnesota Farmer-Labor Party and the American Political Economy*, Chicago: University of Chicago Press.

————. 1990. "Vanishing Voters," *American Prospect*, Spring.

Weiler, Paul. 1990. *Governing the Workplace: The Future of Labor and Employment Law*, Cambridge, Mass. Harvard University Press.

Weisskopf, Tom. 1989. "Taking on the Deficit: Progressives Must Make Deficit Reduction a Priority," *Dollars and Sense*, June.

Wilson, W. J. 1987. *The Truly Disadvantaged: The Inner City, the Underclass, and Public Policy*, Chicago: University of Chicago Press.

7 ELAINE BERNARD

Labour, the New Democratic Party, and the 1988 Federal Election

The 1988 federal election was supposed to be the big breakthrough for Canada's social democratic party, the New Democratic Party (NDP). In the period leading up to the election, the polls indicated that the NDP was a serious contender for official opposition at the federal level for the first time in its almost thirty-year history. Long relegated to third-party status while the Liberals and Progressive Conservatives contested power, the NDP at last seemed to be on the verge of overcoming its marginal status in the federal arena. Senior party strategists even spoke guardedly about the possibility of the NDP forming a minority federal government.

The 1988 election, however, proved to be a major disappointment for both the party and Canada's labour movement. The NDP did make some important breakthroughs: It elected the most members of Parliament (43) in its history and won its largest-ever share of the popular vote (20 percent) in a federal election. While failing to win a seat in Quebec, it managed to poll a remarkable 14 percent in a province where the party had not even previously bothered to contest every seat. Yet the NDP did not become the official opposition, nor was it ever really a contender for power during the election. Without a single seat east of Oshawa, On-

137

tario, it was still a "Western" party.[1] Worse yet, in an election that had come to focus on the Canadian-U.S. Free Trade Agreement (FTA) and the future of Canada, the largest and most expensive NDP election campaign in history was judged a failure by most party and labour activists.

The activists were angry, not because their hopes had been raised so high in the preelection period, but because of the NDP's failure to lead a clear and consistent assault against the agreement with the United States. The free trade pact was not seen as simply another political or economic issue but an all-inclusive expression of the neo-liberal program for Canada, designed to entrench the market as the guiding force, thereby subordinating Canada's social and economic policy even more to the needs of corporations. Labour and progressive groups vigorously opposed the FTA, predicting that tens of thousands of Canadians would lose their jobs as enterprises moved south of the border. Worse, they feared that the new trade regime would undermine Canadian sovereignty and prevent future governments from using state regulation, universal government-funded social programs, and social planning to achieve a greater degree of equality and social justice among regions and individuals (Breton and Jenson 1991).

In the wake of the failed NDP federal election campaign, recriminations abounded. Few criticisms were aimed at the popular party leader, Ed Broadbent, but labour leaders, the newly elected caucus, the party's federal executive, and several provincial sections of the party expressed their frustration. Among the most stinging criticisms were lengthy critiques circulated to the federal executive of the party by two prominent labour leaders, Robert White, president of the Canadian Auto Workers, and Gérard Docquier, Canadian director of the United Steelworkers of America. White and Docquier were leaders of the two largest labour affiliates of the party. Both condemned the small group of party staff who ran the election campaign for what White termed the "disastrous" election. Docquier noted that the "link between the trade union movement and the party at the strategic level failed completely," while White complained that labour's "financial and people support is accepted gratefully, but its ideas and leadership are completely ignored." Both leaders viewed the failure of the NDP to campaign strenuously against the free trade issue to have been a critical misjudgment. For White, the party "never really came to grips with the importance of free trade, were scared of it as an election platform, and while it was mentioned in the campaign, it certainly did not get the priority or attention, or emotion it deserved."[2]

Widespread criticism of the 1988 campaign led the Canadian Labour Congress to set up a special task force on labour-party relations and to review the election.[3] After its first formal meeting, the task force decided "to focus its work on the broad picture of party-labour relations rather than limit it to the last election" (CLC 1989: 2). In the end, the task force reaffirmed labour's essential commitment "to the concept that labour and the NDP are partners in the pursuit of social justice" (CLC 1989: 48). It found that "both the leadership and membership of unions have come to see political action as a natural extension of collective bargaining" (CLC 1989: 2). Recognizing that neither the party nor the labour movement was a monolith and that there would continue to be disagreements within and between the two, the report called for the strengthening of links between the party and labour, with special attention to be paid to labour liaisons within the elected caucus and improved labour participation on the election strategy committee.

The 1988 federal election was indeed a watershed for labour and the NDP, but certainly not the one either group had hoped for. In spite of the unions' anger and disappointment over the performance of the NDP in the election, their decision in the postelection period was to remain with the party and continue to support political action through this affiliation. In face of the new political environment dominated by a neo-liberal agenda—free trade, privatization, and deregulation—labour decided to concentrate on improving relations with, and strengthening its influence within, the party.

Labour and the NDP

These decisions once again reaffirmed a three-decade-long strategy of the labour movement in Canada. Founded in 1961, the New Democratic Party united the small, predominantly western Canadian farm-labour-socialist party, the Cooperative Commonwealth Federation (CCF), with the recently united labour central to form a social democratic labour party.[4] Its founders hoped that the NDP would quickly grow beyond its predecessor's prairie roots and minor-party status.[5]

While impressive gains were made after 1961 in provincial elections in western Canada—including the formation of governments in Saskatchewan, Manitoba, British Columbia, and the Yukon—in federal politics the NDP peaked at 17 percent of the popular vote. The NDP remained a minor party at the federal level, generally represented by a caucus of a few dozen members of Parliament, mostly from western Canada and Ontario.

In the western provinces, the success in provincial elections did much to end the criticism of labour's affiliation with and official endorsement of a political party.[6] With approximately 90 percent of Canada's workers covered by provincial labour laws and regulations, election of provincial NDP governments resulted in significant workplace and labour-law reform. While organized labour occasionally criticized and conflicted with NDP provincial governments, especially when they failed to implement party policy and to move quickly on matters of particular interest to labour, for the most part labour has been a stalwart party supporter in the West.

Nevertheless, the NDP's minor-party position at the federal level, its weakness in Ontario and the Maritimes, and its failure to garner support in Quebec led some within the labour movement periodically to question the wisdom of official labour affiliation to a political party that was essentially not a contender in national politics. In provinces where the NDP was weak, such critics charged that workers who voted for it were throwing their votes away. There was also the feeling that affiliation to one political party compromised labour when it lobbied the government in power. Finally, there continued to be some opposition by union members who felt that affiliation to a political party constituted an attempt by labour leaders to tell members how to vote.

In spite of these drawbacks and criticisms, the NDP has not had to face a serious challenge from the labour movement in recent years, the angry reaction after the 1988 election notwithstanding. Most labour leaders argue that the advantages of having a party sympathetic to labour far outweigh the disadvantages.[7] At both the federal and provincial levels, the NDP has played an important role in legitimating an alternative view of Canadian society. Where the NDP has held power provincially, labour has been able to win important reforms.[8] Even when the party is in opposition, it has assisted in legitimating labour's concerns and has helped delay or force a government to withdraw legislation that labour opposes.

Nevertheless, the NDP is more than a political party for labour. It is a political coalition that provides a permanent structure for labour and other progressive groups, such as the women's movement, environmentalists, students, and the peace movement, to work together. There is a constant tension within the party, rooted in the very different organizational practices and beliefs of groups and individuals affiliated with the NDP. Yet, by and large, the party serves as a vehicle by which all of these groups can work together politically to influence each other and enhance mutual dialogue, while at the same time providing the necessary pressure and cohesion to keep these disparate groups together.

At times, the mutual influence between the popular movements and labour is readily apparent. The CLC, for example, admits that the women's movement within the party successfully pressured the party to adopt "the principle of gender parity on the party executive and committees," while influencing the CLC in its somewhat more modest "parallel course in promoting women within the trade union movement" (CLC, 1989: 24). Labour in Canada is less isolated from popular movements than its counterpart in the United States, and at least some of this is attributable to the fact that the NDP provides a common arena in which activists can work together.

The NDP has given labour a powerful voice in politics. All political parties help define what is considered a legitimate political issue, how politics are conducted, and what relations and conflicts may be resolved through the political process (Brodie and Jenson 1988: 11). The NDP assists labour in shaping its concerns and making them part of the national or provincial political agenda. In contrast to its "special interest" status in the United States, the labour movement in Canada is able to widen the sphere of issues and concerns that should be addressed in electoral politics.

In shaping Canada's political discourse, the fact that the NDP is only a minor party with little prospect of coming to power has not necessarily been detrimental. It has even been argued that since the party is not likely to govern at the federal level at any time soon, it can afford to challenge the political consensus by taking unpopular positions based on political principles. Few would argue, however, that the NDP has not tried to make itself as politically attractive as possible within the constraints of the shared views of its membership. Indeed, internally the party is often criticized for its failure to stand on principle and for abandoning its policy when in power, as well as for its aversion to extraparliamentary activity and mobilization of its constituency for anything other than narrow electoral goals (Bradford and Jenson 1992). A former British Columbian CCF member of Parliament once explained that the experience of Canadian social democratic politics suggests that Lord Acton's famous dictum—"All power corrupts"—must be revised to reflect the fact that for the NDP, it is the "lively anticipation of power which corrupts" (Cameron 1949: 3).

The Anticipation of Power

In the lead-up to the 1988 election, there was a fair amount of "lively anticipation of power" by party strategists who were confident that the arithmetic of a three-party race was at last going to break in favour of the NDP. Since most governments in Canadian jurisdictions can win legislative majorities with less than 50 percent of the popular vote, the NDP's rise in popular opinion seemed to augur well.

This situation contrasted sharply with that of 1984. During that previous federal election, the newly selected Liberal party leader, John Turner, called an election, only to be soundly defeated. Progressive Conservative (PC) leader Brian Mulroney swept into office with the second largest majority of any federal party in Canadian history. There had been no talk of an NDP breakthrough in that election; the party was pleased simply to have withstood the Tory sweep. The collapse of the Liberal vote (down to 28 percent for a total of forty seats), however, placed the NDP on a new footing in federal politics, with 19 percent of the vote and thirty seats.

In by-elections following that election, the NDP further closed the gap between itself and the Liberals, so that by 1987 the NDP caucus had only eight fewer members than the Liberals. While the Liberals retained the important designation of Official Opposition, the NDP was able to capture considerable media attention as the more effective critic of the Tory government. After many years in government, the Liberals were internally divided and inexperienced in their role as opposition. In contrast, the NDP caucus was united and experienced in playing the parliamentary role of "loyal opposition." As a reflection of the new relationship of force between the opposition parties, the NDP was able to achieve some improvements on its status in Parliament, such as a higher profile for its parliamentary committee assignments and a larger time allotment in the all-important Question Period. Its more effective performance in the role of opposition helped to increase the media coverage dedicated to NDP leader Ed Broadbent and the members of his caucus. While the Liberals seemed plagued by a continual stream of highly publicized internal divisions and criticisms of their leader, the NDP leader basked in widespread popularity both inside and outside of the party. Broadbent's approval ratings continually led the party's, and for two years he topped the polls as the public's choice for prime minister. By September 1987, Broadbent's support had reached an all-time high, surpassing the combined total of Turner and Mulroney (Whitehorn 1989: 43).

In the run-up to the 1988 election, party strategists developed a campaign strategy they hoped would bring about the historic breakthrough. The key elements of this campaign strategy were leadership—capitalizing on Ed Broadbent's personal popularity—and the representational issue of "who speaks for whom," using such populist formulations as "fairness for ordinary Canadians." It avoided controversial issues, especially party positions on defence and economic policy. Finally, there was a special Quebec strategy that included the recruitment of francophone candidates, a fully bilingual campaign, and significant presence by the leader in Quebec throughout the campaign.

With Ed Broadbent consistently leading both the NDP and the other party leaders in the polls, it was hoped that his personal appeal would create a coattails effect for New Democrats across the country. Both the former Liberal government and the Mulroney Conservative government were tarnished with scandals and charges of conflict of interest and patronage; honesty, integrity, and fairness became the watchwords in the NDP's leadership-based strategy.

In line with the hopes for a historic breakthrough, the party adopted an election budget of $7 million, just $1 million short of the maximum expenditure authorized by Elections Canada, the federal regulatory agency. The most expensive media buy in the history of the party, over $3 million was slated for a television advertising campaign, with Broadbent as the main focus. In recognition of the need to win seats in Quebec, an unprecedented $1 million worth of advertisements were delivered in French.

The Quebec part of the strategy was judged to be crucial. The NDP had never won a seat in Quebec and was generally discounted as a serious contender for federal government because of its continuing failure to win support in the province. In the intensely nationalistic political

environment of the province of Quebec, the NDP had always been regarded as a western Canadian, anglophone-based, federalist party. Reflecting the nationalist concerns of their members, organized labour in
Quebec was not affiliated with the NDP, thus denying it the "labour
party" character it enjoyed in anglophone Canada. But by the late 1980s,
with the electoral defeat and right-wing swing of the nationalist Parti
Québécois and the disenchantment with the pro-federalist Liberals, many
Québécois trade unionists seemed ready to give the NDP serious consideration (Lipsig-Mummé in this volume). By 1987, party polling showed
an unprecedented 30 percent approval rating in Quebec.

Organizationally, the NDP designated 144 seats out of a total of 295 as
priority ridings, enough to deliver a minority government.[9] These potentially winnable ridings included 59 seats in western Canada (the traditional base of the party), 39 seats in Quebec, 35 seats in Ontario (mostly
large cities and communities with large concentrations of organized labour) and 11 seats in Atlantic Canada.

While the NDP had always prided itself on its organizational talent,
this campaign threatened to stretch its cadre of organizers and campaign
managers to the limit. In provincial elections, the party had developed a
system of pooling organizers from unions, party staff, and volunteers
from across the country to fight relatively short provincial campaigns.
Yet the large number of priority seats designated in this federal election
exceeded the party's ability to provide trained and experienced organizers.

The focus of the campaign was the leader's tour. Ed Broadbent jetted
across Canada weekly, returning to Toronto on Sundays for strategy
meetings. A majority of his time was devoted to Ontario, the location of
one-third of the seats in Parliament (99), followed by western Canada,
with the remainder spent in Quebec and the Atlantic provinces. Candidates were schooled in the correct campaign language for discussing policy issues. The political message was to be packaged in "representational"
terms. "Ed Broadbent and the New Democrats speak for ordinary Canadians" was one of the central campaign themes. "A fair deal for Canada"
and "New Democrats speak up for average Canadians" were the two
phrases on the cover of the party's main brochure for the election.[10] Campaign material avoided using terms that might frighten voters, such as
"socialism" or "democratic socialism," and in their place opted for populist appeals to "fairness for average Canadians and their families" (NDP
1988).

In light of the new national standing of the NDP, party strategists suspected that party policy would receive unprecedented scrutiny by opponents and by the media (Whitehorn 1989: 46). Candidates were therefore cautioned to avoid controversial issues and to follow the lead of the national campaign in using the neutral language of "fairness."[11]

This concentration on such themes marked a significant shift in strategy, which held major implications for the 1988 campaign. For a number of years the NDP had been engaged in extensive polling and opinion research at both the federal and provincial levels. These data consistently indicated that when issues were viewed in representational terms, the NDP did well. "Who do you believe will best look out for the interests of you and your family?" was a familiar question asked in various forms in polls. A majority of people polled identified themselves as "average," "ordinary," or even "working" Canadians, and responded positively about the NDP when questions were posed as "Who do you believe will best look out for the interests of ordinary Canadians?" Conversely, when issues were posed in terms of "managing the economy," the NDP did poorly. Party strategies determined that the leader and candidates should avoid discussing economic issues as such and instead should attempt to deal with them in "representational" terms.

Free Trade and Meech Lake

It is ironic that this carefully drawn strategy was developed for the 1988 election, which turned out to be one of the most issue-oriented, controversial, and even class-divided in Canadian history. The 1988 federal election has come to be characterized as the free trade election. During the almost two years that Canada had been involved in negotiating the Free Trade Agreement (FTA), every turn in the negotiations was prominently covered in the Canadian media. Although the Tory government gave no indication it would call an election over the issue, the FTA did have to pass Parliament. The Liberals' threat to block it in the Senate, where they remained dominant, forced the September 1988 election and made the FTA the central issue of the election (Clarke et al. 1991: chs. 1, 4, 7).

A second major issue that was emerging in the period leading up to the election was the Meech Lake Accord. This package of changes in Canada's constitution had been negotiated by the eleven first ministers in June of 1987. As a constitutional amendment, the accord had to pass all ten provincial legislatures and the federal parliament within a three-year deadline. As Mulroney and the first ministers attempted to force the package through their respective legislatures, however, opposition began to grow across the country.

The accord was ostensibly designed to meet Quebec's objections to the Constitution Act of 1982. Historically, Canada's constitution was an act of the British Parliament, the British North America Act of 1867. In 1982 Prime Minister Pierre Trudeau "brought the constitution home" over the objections of the Province of Quebec, which refused to sign the repatriation document. While Quebec was legally bound by the new constitution, its refusal to sign the 1982 Constitutional Act created powerful political pressure to "bring Quebec into the political fold." The Meech Lake Accord essentially granted to Quebec the designation of "a distinct society" and granted to Quebec—and all other provinces—a series of reforms of the federal-provincial division of powers.

Opposition to the Meech Lake Accord began shortly after its signing, with different regions and groups attacking the reforms, in many cases for conflicting reasons. In a rare display of unanimity, the leaders of the three major political parties all endorsed the accord. Yet opposition developed even within their own parties. In Quebec, many unions and the Quebec NDP opposed the reforms because they did not go far enough in recognizing Quebec's status as a distinct society and, indeed, its national character and right to self-determination. At the same time, the British Columbia NDP, while not opposed to the recognition of Quebec as a distinct society, rejected the accord for a variety of reasons: the undemocratic and closed process through which the agreement was concluded; the silence on the rights of indigenous peoples; and the fear that the amendments would undermine universal social programs and rights.

Taken together, the Free Trade Agreement and the Meech Lake Accord were changes that promised to restructure significantly the economic and political character of the country. The two agreements provided reference points for a lengthy public debate on the nature of the Canadian nation and society. Nevertheless, while Meech Lake was being debated in the period leading up to the election, NDP strategists felt that the party could safely ignore it in the campaign because the constitutional reform had been endorsed by all three party leaders. Free trade, however, was rapidly becoming a central election theme, and this created difficulties for the NDP's narrowly conceived representational strategy.

While the labour movement mobilized its membership in opposition to the Free Trade Agreement, the party strategists considered the FTA a concern that fell into the category of "managing the economy" and, as such, not an issue the NDP would do well on. Therefore, NDP strategists warned candidates off the terrain of free trade. In the most expensive and ambitious election campaign in the history of the NDP, discipline was to be maintained and candidates were to follow the lead of the federal campaign committee. If free trade was to be mentioned at all, it was to be in a context of its threat to Canada's social programs.

NDP strategists feared that any electoral support generated by opposition to the agreement would necessarily be divided with the Liberals, who also rejected the specifics of the deal. Thus, even if 60 percent of the electorate opposed the FTA, such vote splitting would mean the Tories' reelection. This analysis led party strategists to develop an approach that sought to contest the election on what they perceived to be the more favourable issues: leadership, fairness, and representation.

Going into the 1988 election, representatives of organized labor on party leadership bodies—including the Federal Executive and Federal Council—supported the overall election strategy as outlined by the Strategy and Election Planning Committee (SEPC).[12] There was some concern from unionists that the party was not taking an aggressive enough stand against free trade but in general they, like other party members, were optimistic about the NDP's chances of making a historic breakthrough in federal politics. A strong showing by the NDP, with the real possibility of forming a minority government, would aid labour in defending itself against the Tories' neo-liberal agenda and might indeed result in parliamentary rejection of the FTA.

During the first few weeks of the fifty-one-day campaign, the NDP strategy appeared to work. By the third week, the party was in second place, with just under 30 percent of the popular vote. Yet with the televised leaders debates (one in French and one in English) the NDP campaign began to falter. The Liberal leader's impassioned opposition to the government's FTA managed to make free trade the central issue of the campaign.[13] The NDP, having not even mentioned the FTA in Broadbent's opening campaign speech and now locked into an election strategy committed to downplaying the free trade issue, was quickly overshadowed by the Liberals. Promising to make opposition to the trade deal "the political cause of his life," the Liberal leader, John Turner, proved to be a far more effective campaigner than the NDP had predicted.

In Quebec, the NDP campaign quickly unravelled because of the national question. In the first week, the campaign started with good momentum with the endorsement of the NDP by Louis Laberge, president of one of the province's three powerful labour centrals, the Fédération des travailleurs et des travailleuses du Québec (FTQ). Behind the facade of public unity, however, the Quebec NDP leadership was internally divided and subordinated to the Ottawa-run central campaign. Although the Quebec leadership was opposed to the Meech Lake Accord, the federal party was in favour of the accord. Québécois were understandably confused much of the time as to who really spoke for the NDP in their province. When several leaders of the Quebec party held a press conference and confirmed their support of controversial provincial legislation, stressing the use of French in the province, Broadbent was called upon to repudiate their statements. Broadbent, however, refused to comment on the statements, saying that as a non-Québécois it would be inappropriate to do so, which only heightened the confusion about the NDP's policy in Quebec. While voters in the rest of Canada began to see the free trade deal as a challenge to their sovereignty, in Quebec—whose sovereignty had been denied for so long—the FTA was widely seen as opening United States markets to emerging Quebec industry and business (Breton and Jenson 1991). Thus, in spite of an extensive and sophisticated French advertising campaign, the NDP once again became marginalized in Quebec.

In the party's traditional stronghold in western Canada, the strength of the well-organized and experienced provincial sections, along with the emergence of a right-wing protest group, the Reform Party, helped keep the race a two-way split between the Tories and the NDP. Here the NDP adjusted to the free trade focus of the election and took the offensive against the Tories over their proposed value-added tax, the Goods and Services Tax (GST).

Overall, the NDP's variations on the representational issue, its attempt to raise the alarm over the undermining of Canada's social programs, and its emphasis on fairness failed to fire the public's imagination, appearing disconnected from and of secondary importance to the central question in the election—the "Mulroney-Reagan free trade deal." In the last few weeks before the election, the NDP attempted to develop a campaign that would link the Conservatives and Liberals to big business and reassert the NDP's populist (though not necessarily labour) values. Voters were asked to "reject the values of Mulroney's Wall St. and Turner's Bay

St. and instead support the NDP's values of Main St." Whether a case of too little, too late, the new theme failed to revive the party's faltering fate. At the same time, in face of growing opposition to the trade deal, large corporations and the business community poured millions of dollars into an unprecedented political advertising favouring the Tories' Free Trade Agreement in the final weeks of the campaign (Whitehorn, 1989: 49).

Although a majority of Canadians voted against free trade and the Tories, the arithmetic of a three-party system worked for Brian Mulroney and the Conservatives. They received a majority of seats with only 43% of the popular vote.[14] In Quebec the Tories obtained majority support with 53% of the popular vote.

The election did not, of course, conclude the debate on free trade or the Meech Lake Accord. While it assured the implementation of the free trade deal, the labour movement and opponents of the deal have continued their campaign against the FTA and the market-driven restructuring that underlies the arrangement. The Canadian Labour Congress has estimated the job loss resulting from the deal is over 150,000 and rising. The issue of Canadian sovereignty, so central to the free trade debate, has continued to surface in discussions and debates on Canada's economic policy and options.

In the postelection period, party leader Ed Broadbent resigned and was replaced by Yukon M.P. Audrey McLaughlin. Having served just two terms in Parliament, McLaughlin was relatively unknown in national politics. Many prominent NDPers, including Ontario provincial party leader Bob Rae and former provincial leader Stephen Lewis, declined to enter the federal leadership race, underlining the general feeling that the focus of party activity had again moved to the provincial arena.

The CLC Executive Council did not support a candidate in the leadership race, although some powerful individual labour leaders such as Bob White threw their weight behind McLaughlin. McLaughlin's election as party leader marked the first time that a major party in North America had elected a woman as national leader, but also led to speculation that her role was to be that of an interim leader until the next federal election.

McLaughlin herself does not see hers as simply an interim role. She has worked diligently to rebuild the federal party's presence in Quebec and Ontario. Her name recognition has increased, and she has led the party in public-opinion polls.

The NDP's Future

Since the 1988 federal election, Canada has been an increasingly divided and uncertain society. The far-reaching public-policy debates taking place in the country have forced Canadians into a wide-ranging discussion about the nature of their society, social programs, constitution, economic treaties, and, indeed, the social contract that underlies Canadian society. From the ongoing discussions of free trade and its implications for the Canadian economy, through the Meech La⁻ᵉ Accord, to the three-month native barricade at Oka, Quebec, in the summer of 1990 and the demand for settlement of land claims, many of the fundamental assumptions of Canadian society are being challenged. Free trade, in particular, has moved Canadians toward a new receptivity to social democratic ideas and policies. In face of the threat of free trade to unleash the full force of the market, Canadians have sought protection through renewed determination to maintain their social safety net and universal social programs. As well, the challenge to Canadian sovereignty generated by the pact with the United States has contributed to a new national consciousness in anglophone Canada that seeks to emphasize the difference between the two countries. Most importantly, there is a new openness to the idea that the role of the state is to assure the welfare of its citizens, not simply to create an environment within which business can prosper. This is the essence of the NDP's social democratic approach, and it appears to have found new fertile ground in post–free trade Canada.

While the party's cautious election strategy in 1988 prevented the NDP from taking advantage of the increased public interest in social justice, its surprising, historic 1990 breakthrough in Ontario—where the NDP won 74 of a total of 130 seats and 38 percent of the popular vote—suggests that this new discourse can assist the NDP. The most powerful and influential region in the country, Ontario accounts for almost one-third of Canada's population and produces just under one-half of the country's GNP. The NDP's victory there provides a dramatic indication of the strength of the new political consciousness.

The Ontario victory also represents an important breakthrough for labour and its strategy of increased participation in the NDP at all levels. Still stinging from the NDP's defeat in the 1988 federal election, the Ontario labour movement made sure that organized labour was involved in all aspects of the provincial election campaign.

The Ontario victory significantly redraws the political landscape in Canada. As the government of Ontario, the NDP and its labour allies played a major role in the ongoing constitutional discussions. With one-third of the caucus unionists, including senior staff from many of the largest unions in the province, organized labour will have a powerful voice, not simply in the party's elected offices but also within the caucus. Moreover, the election of NDP governments in Saskatchewan and British Columbia, although they may not always agree with the position of the Ontario government, will provide greater weight for perspectives different from those promoted by the neo-liberal Tories.

Yet the challenge for the federal NDP over the next few years remains. It is, quite simply, to address the crisis in Canada brought on by the Free Trade Agreement, the continuing constitutional impasse, and the onset of a new global recession. The NDP must assume a leadership role in forging a new social contract among regions, communities, and nations within Canada, and in discussion of a North American Free Trade Agreement (NAFTA) at the international level.

Yet, as the lesson of the 1988 election also demonstrates, failure to rise to the challenge of providing leadership on strategic issues of economic policy can result in the party's marginalization and risks alienating its labour supporters. Increasingly the latter have the option of bypassing party politics to engage in more autonomous action under the umbrella of coalition politics in Action Canada (formerly the Pro-Canada Network) (Jenson and Mahon, Chapter 4 in this volume).

Therefore, while the NDP may not need to address each item on the Tory economic agenda, it must discover ways of moving beyond opposition to the current market-driven restructuring. A strategy that begins to reassert the social values that should influence economic decision making is needed. Without such a shift, the thirty-year alliance between labour and social democracy in Canada may be at risk.

Notes

1. In the 1988 election the NDP won 19 seats in British Columbia, 1 in Alberta, 10 in Saskatchewan, 2 in Manitoba, 10 in Ontario, and 1 in the Yukon, for a total of 33 seats from the West and the North.

2. Letter from Robert White to NDP Officers and Executive Members, 28 November 1988 (seven pages), and Letter from Gérard Docquier to NDP Executive Members, 5 December 1988 (twelve pages).

3. Set up in December 1988 by CLC President Shirley Carr, the task force consisted of Reg Baskin of the Energy and Chemical Workers Union as chair, John Fryer of the National Union of Provincial Government Employees, Leo Gérard of the United Steel Workers of America, Jack Munro of the IWA-Canada, Nancy Riche, vice-president of the CLC, Jeff Rose of the Canadian Union of Public Employees, Bob White of the Canadian Auto Workers, and Pat Kerwin of the CLC, secretary to the committee.

4. While the Canadian Congress of Labour (CCL) had endorsed the CCF as labour's political arm, the Trades and Labour Congress (TLC) was always reluctant to do so. Whether to engage in independent labour political action was one of the significant long-standing policy issues between the two labour centrals.

5. The CCF averaged 11.1 percent of the vote in federal elections from 1933 through 1958.

6. The CCF/NDP has formed provincial governments in the following provinces: British Columbia, 1972–1975 (reelected, fall 1991); Saskatchewan, 1944–1964, 1971–1982 (reelected, fall 1991); and Manitoba, 1969–1977, 1981–1987. The NDP won an Ontario election for the first time in September 1990 and formed the territorial government in the Yukon until 1992.

7. One important exception to the support of labour affiliation with the NDP is the building-trades central, the Canadian Federation of Labour. Splitting from the CLC in the early 1980s over the issue of representation and organizational norms, the CFL has not affiliated with the NDP.

8. The task force report (1989) lists a variety of legislative firsts achieved by the CCF/NDP under the following titles: health care, pensions, labour legislation, labour standards, anti-scab strikebreaking, pay equity, housing, public enterprises, and family support.

9. By comparison, in the 1984 election only 50 seats were given a priority designation.

10. The other side of the representational question—the fact that John Turner and Brian Mulroney spoke for the interests of big business and major corporations—was not addressed until late in the campaign.

11. In a few instances, changes were even made to long-standing party policy. With an eye on the earlier British elections, where Margaret Thatcher and the British Conservatives had ridiculed the Labour party's defence policy, NDP strategists modified the party's traditional demand for Canada's withdrawal from the North Atlantic Treaty Organization (NATO). In a lengthy document issued by the International Affairs Committee called "Canada's Stake in Common Security," Canadians were assured that withdrawal from NATO would be postponed until the NDP's second term of office.

12. The SEPC is a committee of the federal executive charged with design-

ing the party's election campaign. For the 1988 election it consisted of a chair, the party leader, the federal president, the federal treasurer, the federal secretary, the principal advisor to the leader, and a representative from each of the following: federal caucus, the participation of women committee, the Canadian Labour Congress, and each provincial section.

13. It should be noted that once the Conservatives were forced to call an election, they too tried to minimize the issue of free trade, preferring to run on their economic record in general (Clarke et al. 1991: ch. 1).

14. The popular vote was distributed PC 43 percent, Liberals 32 percent, NDP 20 percent with the remaining 5 percent divided among a number of small parties.

References

Bradford, Neil, and Jane Jenson. 1992. The Roots of Social Democratic Populism in Canada. In Frances Fox Piven, ed., *Labor Parties in Postindustrial Societies*, New York: Oxford University Press.

Breton, Gilles, and Jane Jenson. 1991. "After Free Trade and Meech Lake: *Quoi du neuf?*" *Studies in Political Economy* 34.

Brodie, Janine, and Jane Jenson. 1988. *Crisis, Challenge, and Change: Party and Class in Canada Revisited*, Ottawa: Carleton University Press.

Cameron, Colin. 1949. "An Analysis of the Election Results," *CCF News*.

Canadian Labour Congress (CLC). 1989. *Report of the Task Force on the Labour/ Party Relationship*, Ottawa: CLC.

Clarke, Harold, Jane Jenson, Lawrence LeDuc, and Jon Pammett. 1991. *Absent Mandate: Interpreting Change in Canadian Politics*, Toronto: Gage.

New Democratic Party (NDP). 1988. *A Fair Deal for Canada*, Ottawa: NDP.

Whitehorn, Alan. 1989. "The NDP Election Campaign: Dashed Hopes." In Allan Frizzell, Jon Pammett, and Anthony Westell, eds., *The Canadian General Election of 1988*, Ottawa: Carleton University Press.

An Uneasy Alliance: The Parti
Québécois and the Unions

During the 1980s, with the American labour movement trapped in a spiral of organizational decay and political impotence, Canada's trade unions appeared to many academics and trade unionists south of the border to be the picture of good health. One popular explanation for the divergence focuses on the relative strength of social democratic values—and their carriers, political parties—in the two countries. According to S. M. Lipset (1986: 451), for example, "the divergence in the trajectories of union density across the border reflect [*sic*] the undermining of the social democratic forces unleashed by the Great Depression in the south, and their maintenance in the north."[1] In Quebec, however, "social democratic forces lacked significant strength . . . until the emergence of the Parti Québécois [*sic*] in the 1970s, a development which paralleled a sharp increase in trade union density in the province" (Lipset 1986: 444).

This chapter argues that the relationship between social democracy and trade-union strength—whether one measures the latter restrictively, as rates of union density, or more generally, as legislation favourable to organized labour—is a great deal more complex than Lipset and others suggest. I leave aside the larger question whether Lipset's argument has any validity for Canada as a whole,[2] in order to focus exclusively on Quebec, a province that was governed by the social democratic Parti Québécois (PQ) between 1976 and 1985. My analysis will concentrate on the PQ's labour policies during its first term in office (1976–81), a period when the influence of the party's social democratic wing was at its peak.

After the defeat of the referendum on sovereignty-association in 1980 and the PQ's unexpected reelection in 1981, the Lévesque administration "went bad"—from the trade unions' perspective—and dealt with public-sector workers as brutally as Bourassa's Liberals had done in the early 1970s. The bitter conflict between the PQ government and the teachers' unions in the winter of 1982–83, sparked by the Lévesque administration's ultimately suicidal decision to fight the recession on the backs of its own employees, clearly demonstrates that self-styled social democratic parties do not always act as the friends of labour.[3] A careful examination of the PQ's labour policies during its *first* term in office, however, also shows that social democratic parties[4] do not *necessarily* work to promote the organizational interests of the labour movement. Whether they do or not depends to a large extent on their overarching political objectives, the ideological and organizational cohesiveness of the party, and the nature of the party's ties to the trade unions.

The most important reason for the PQ's ambivalent relations with organized labour was the nature of its nationalist project. To be successful, sovereignty-association required the support of a broad coalition of classes in Quebec, the working class included. Thus the PQ government during its first term in office made a number of policy concessions to the trade unions (especially those representing private-sector workers, for reasons that will be made clear below), in hopes of attracting their support for its vision of independence. Whenever a conflict arose between the interests of one class (labour) and the needs of the nation as the government perceived them, however, the PQ invariably gave precedence to the larger collectivity.

This decision to favour the nation over the representatives of workers was apparent during the first round of public-sector bargaining conducted by the PQ in 1979. When the trade unions balked at signing a collective agreement, thereby jeopardizing the PQ's timetable for the referendum, the government implemented legislation that enabled it to do an end run around the union leadership and appeal directly to the nationalist sympathies of rank-and-file workers. This distinction between workers qua workers and workers as Québécois, who were presumed to have an objective interest in Quebec's independence, constituted one of the most important—and until 1982–83 one of the most effective—weapons in the PQ's arsenal of tactics for dealing with the trade unions. I will argue below that this facet of the *péquiste* ideology was tinged with authoritarian overtones.

In summary, the PQ's labour policy between 1976 and 1981 consisted of a mixture of progressive reforms and coercive measures. While the PQ's legislative record during this period cautions against the Panglossian view of Lipset and others that social democratic parties always promote the organizational interests of the working class, it is by no means a confirmation of the diametrically opposed—and equally specious—argument that these parties inevitably end up crushing labour or finding novel ways to exploit the workers. The relation between social democracy and trade-union well-being is a complex one, mediated by a host of variables.

This chapter is divided into three sections. The first provides a rapid overview of the origins and ideological development of the Parti Québécois up to its election win in 1976. I focus on the tensions within the party between the radicals and the moderates, and the impact that these divisions had on the PQ's relations with organized labour. The second section examines Bill 45, the so-called anti-scab law, which is undoubtedly the PQ's most progressive legacy to the labour movement; the third section looks at the government's handling of public-sector bargaining in 1979. As I will show, the government's efforts to "civilize" labour relations in the public sector were not really that much more successful than those of previous governments, notwithstanding the party's talk of its "special relationship" with the trade unions.

The National Question, Social Democracy, and the Parti Québécois

At its birth the Parti Québécois was a fragile coalition of socialists, social democrats, reform-minded liberals, and reactionary populists. These fractious elements were held together in uneasy coexistence by a common commitment to some form of sovereignty for Quebec and by the force of René Lévesque's charismatic personality (Murray 1976; Fraser 1984). In view of the widely divergent ideological leanings of the PQ's founding members, it is hardly surprising that, from its inception, the party has been racked by recurrent doctrinal disputes. Vera Murray has argued that these periodic conflicts were symptoms of the dominant cleavage within the party, one between *technocrats* and *participationists*. The technocratic faction, centred around Lévesque, was the most influential group in the party hierarchy, at least during the early years of its existence. It consisted mainly of the ex-Liberals who had created the Mouvement souveraineté-association (MSA), the forerunner of the PQ, as well as former high-ranking civil servants like Claude Morin and Jacques Parizeau. Members of the participationist faction tended to be new to politics, had often been active in either the labour movement or the numerous citizens' movements that had sprung up during the 1960s, and were committed to quite radical reform of Quebec's economy and society (Murray 1976: Milner 1978: ch. 7). Roughly speaking, the moderate, technocratic faction dominated party policy making from 1968 to 1970. After the election of Robert Bourassa and the Liberals, and in the wake of the October Crisis of 1970, the PQ program underwent a marked radicalization as the participationist faction exerted a growing influence on party ideology. This radicalization came to an abrupt halt with the election victory of the PQ in 1976, a phenomenon that is by no means unfamiliar in countries where social democratic parties have taken power.

The nature of the PQ's early electoral successes reinforced the popular notion that it was a party of the working class. In the first provincial election it contested in 1970, for example, six of the seven victorious PQ candidates were from working-class constituencies in east-end Montreal (Hamilton and Pinard 1976: 4). As well, a number of provisions in the party program were clearly inspired by social democratic thought: the desire to ease union certification procedures, to establish industrywide collective bargaining, and to make the unions, along with business, one of the state's major *interlocutors*, thereby giving them a voice in economic planning. On more than one occasion, Lévesque and other party notables invoked the vision of creating a North American version of Swedish-style social democracy once independence had been achieved (Lévesque 1978: 48). In addition to this social democratic strand in the PQ's ideology, individual labour leaders like Robert Dean (United Auto Workers), Jean Gérin-Lajoie (*Métallos*), Michel Bourdon (CSN-Construction), and Guy Chevrette and Guy Bisaillon (both of the CEQ [Centrale de l'enseignement du Québec]) have played prominent roles in the party organization, as have labour lawyers such as Robert Burns, Pierre Marois, and Clément Richard.

Despite these ideological and personal links between the Parti Qué-bécois and the labour movement, the technocrats within the party have always made a virtue out of the PQ's structural independence from the trade unions. They have also exhibited a certain ambivalence toward organized labour. PQ leaders feared that excessively intimate ties with the unions could tarnish the party's image of moderation and responsibility, since some voters would inevitably associate it with the incidents of violence that periodically flared up on the picket line, or with the inflammatory rhetoric of certain labour leaders. Moreover, Lévesque and other party notables were convinced that independence would come about only if the PQ succeeded in forging a coalition of *all* classes; thus they felt that the party should avoid becoming too closely identified with the interests and demands of a single social class.[5]

One could describe the PQ's brand of social democracy, or at least the one associated with the dominant faction in the party, as a mixture of statism, technocracy, and liberal corporatism. The party spoke of the need to encourage greater citizen participation in planning the economy, but was careful to add that it was talking about

> "organized" citizens, who assert their opinions within groups where they feel at home and adequately represented. . . . Thus it is collectively, through the massive participation of the most representative categories of the population, that the Plan will open the way to the democratization of the economy, to the increasingly informed participation of citizens in guiding the regime, and in the complex decision making that this entails. (Parti Québécois 1972: 123; translation by Brian Tanguay)

Trade unions would obviously be one of the most important participants in this planning exercise and would have to act *responsibly* if the PQ's economic schemes were to succeed. Party leaders, and especially Lévesque, were always suspicious, however, that the unions were more interested in demanding their rights than in performing their duties toward the collectivity. To Lévesque and the party hierarchy, the union leaders were too self-interested, too susceptible to "class egoisms,"[6] to be completely trustworthy allies in the struggle for Quebec's independence. As a result, although many in the government styled themselves the friends of labour, they simultaneously harboured a deep suspicion of the trade-union leaders, who were considered to be out of touch with the supposedly more moderate rank and file. This ambivalent attitude helps to explain the sharp twists and turns in the PQ government's relations with organized labour between 1976 and 1985.

The PQ's ambivalence toward the unions was mirrored by the attitudes of the labour federations themselves. During the Bourassa era the ideological ties between the PQ and organized labour became increasingly intimate, especially in the wake of the October Crisis of 1970. So strong was the labour movement's loathing for the Bourassa regime that before the 1976 election the three major union federations either openly (in the case of the FTQ [Fédération des travailleurs et des travailleuses du Québec]) or tacitly supported the Parti Québécois.

When the PQ registered its unexpected triumph, there was unrestrained joy in the labour movement, with the president of the Confédération des syndicats nationaux (CSN), Norbert Rodrigue, calling it a "victory for ordinary people over the dark forces of Anglo-Saxon capitalism" (quoted in Francoeur 1976; cf. Bauer 1977: 307). Despite this heady rhetoric, however, many labour leaders, especially those in the public sector, were suspicious of the PQ and dismissed it as a "bourgeois party" whose independence project would inevitably subordinate social questions to the overriding issue of national sovereignty. By contrast, many rank-and-file workers in the three union federations were much more openly sympathetic toward the PQ and its program. This ideological rift between the union leadership and the base was exploited on a number of occasions by the Lévesque government, which attempted to appeal directly to individual workers as Québécois, without the intermediation of their elected representatives (Tanguay 1990: chs. 7–9).

The PQ was elected in 1976 on a wave of discontent directed at the scandal-ridden and highly unpopular Bourassa administration. The PQ's decision in 1975 to divorce a vote for the party from support for independence, by pledging to hold a referendum on sovereignty some time during its first mandate, had proven pivotal in attracting voters who were unhappy with the Bourassa administration yet not entirely enamoured of the prospect of independence (Hamilton and Pinard 1978: 772–73).

After its election the PQ moved cautiously to demonstrate its administrative competence (providing "good government"), to assuage the fears of wary investors in the United States who were more than a little worried by the prospect of a separatist, social democratic government in Canada's second most populous province, to give substance to its self-proclaimed "favourable prejudice toward workers," and to prepare the terrain for the successful passage of the promised referendum on sover-eignty-association. To achieve these often conflicting goals required con-siderable policy dexterity—critics called it incoherence—on the part of the government. Given the numerous constraints on the Lévesque gov-ernment's freedom of action, labour policy became extremely important in the effort to win over unionized and unorganized workers alike to the PQ's independence project. As Yves Bélanger (1982: 53) has argued, once the PQ took power, labour relations "undoubtedly became the sphere in which the 'favourable prejudice toward workers' and the party's social democratic inclinations were most apparent. Founded on a *bonne entente*, collaboration, and tripartism (State-Capital-Labour), the PQ's labour policies essentially aimed at strengthening its ties with workers while neutralizing the labour movement and its method of operation" (transla-tion by Brian Tanguay). Labour relations reforms would simultaneously serve other objectives as well, party leaders reasoned: They would keep the party's restive left wing happy and help to improve Quebec's sorry record of industrial militancy.[7]

Because of these conflicting objectives, the PQ government proceeded with a major overhaul of the Labour Code, the first substantive amend-ments (aside from those dealing with the construction industry or the public sector) to this legislation since 1969. These far-reaching reforms— they were by no means mere sops to labour, as I will show—are exam-ined in the following section.

The Anti-Scab Laws: The Parti Québécois Courts Organized Labour

The appointment of Jacques Couture as minister of labour in the first Lévesque cabinet caused considerable anxiety among Quebec's business community. This fear was no doubt fuelled by Couture's pronouncement that the government would move forward on its pledge to introduce anti-scab legislation, in order to ensure that the strike was a truly effec-tive weapon in the hands of organized labour. Too often, Couture re-marked, the right to strike was rendered valueless by employers' use of strikebreakers—professional scabs or other workers hired after collective bargaining with the union had already begun. Any government that purported to be social democratic, Couture claimed, would have to alter the balance of power between workers and management to the benefit of labour by guaranteeing that a strike would entail a complete stoppage of production (O'Neill 1977a, 1977b).

The PQ government's firm intention to introduce anti-scab legislation as quickly as possible, despite the vociferous opposition of the business community, was in part the legacy of the protracted (twenty-month) strike at the United Aircraft plant in Longueuil, a suburb of Montreal, in 1974 and 1975. Rouillard (1989: 454) labels this dispute "one of the longest and most violent in the history of Quebec trade unionism." In economic terms, the lengthy strike was at best a qualified success, since the UAW failed to achieve many of its principal demands. Most importantly, the settlement did not contain a provision for the Rand Formula (deduction of union dues from the paychecks of all members of a bargaining unit, whether they belong to the union or not), which had been one of the union's main priorities. At the political level, however, the UAW was much more successful, since the strike led to a marked radicalization in the PQ's position on labour relations. René Lévesque overcame his antipathy to such events and actually took part in a solidarity rally for the United Aircraft workers, and the PQ began to agitate for effective anti-scab measures that would prohibit the kind of manoeuvring undertaken by United Aircraft management to avoid true collective bargaining. It was hoped that this type of legislation would prevent acts of violence similar to those that had occurred on the picket lines in Longueuil.

The UAW achieved a complete victory—albeit a belated one—only when the PQ government introduced Bill 45 in July 1977. This piece of legislation, according to Rouillard (1989: 457), was the "direct consequence" of the United Aircraft dispute. Robert Dean (1989), formerly Quebec director of the UAW, claims that the main provisions of Bill 45 were "tailor-made to fit the demands of the United Aircraft workers." The bill contained six major reforms of the Labour Code, three of them quite contentious. The least controversial reform involved an easing of certification procedures by providing for secret ballot votes once the union seeking certification could demonstrate that it had signed up at least 35 percent of the workers in the bargaining unit in question. Secondly, the new bill stipulated that after a strike or lockout, every worker would have the right to return to his or her previous job unless the employer had sufficient cause not to rehire the employee. In the latter case, the burden of proof would fall on the employer. A third reform provided for the compulsory arbitration of first contracts in the event of a dispute. Quebec thus became the third province, after British Columbia (1973) and Manitoba (1976), to allow for such a procedure; Ontario (1986) and the federal government (1978) enacted similar legislation not long after (Girard and St. Onge 1982: 28–31).

The fourth reform enacted by Bill 45 provided for the checkoff of union dues and agency fees from all workers in a bargaining unit, whether or not they were members of the union (the Rand Formula). Quebec was the second province, after Manitoba (1972), to enshrine in law this important inducement to union security; Ontario followed suit in 1980 (Lascelles 1980: 2–6). Unlike the other jurisdictions that have implemented similar union-security clauses, however, Quebec made no attempt to attach conditions to the Rand Formula in order to protect *individual rights*, such as placing restrictions on the union's use of these funds (for political purposes, for example), allowing exemptions from the dues checkoff for individual employees on religious or political grounds, or guaranteeing the right of individual workers to contest "unreasonable" dues (Lascelles 1980: 15–22).

One of the most innovative and controversial reforms implemented by Bill 45 was its anti-scab provision. The bill prohibited the hiring of workers to replace those on legal strike, something that very few jurisdictions have done. Although British Columbia and a number of American states have outlawed the use of *professional* strikebreakers, no jurisdiction has gone as far as Quebec in placing limits on management's ability to continue production during a work stoppage (Dion 1977b).[8]

Bill 45, with its prohibition on the use of scabs (broadly defined), went some way toward ensuring that a legal strike really would bring about a stoppage in production and altered fairly dramatically (in theory at least) the traditional balance of power between unions and management. The legislation therefore had important *symbolic* value, even if only a tiny minority of industrial disputes involved the use of strikebreakers or degenerated into violence. This point was made by Liberal MNA (member of the National Assembly) Claude Forget, who claimed that Bill 45's anti-scab provisions were not designed to deal with a pressing problem in Quebec's labour relations but rather were intended to shore up the PQ's self-styled image as the friend of labour (Descôteaux 1977). According to

Gérard Dion (1977a, 1977b), Ministry of Labour statistics indicated that 95 percent of collective agreements in the province were signed without violence or the use of scabs. Although both Forget and Dion make valid points, the anti-scab provisions in Bill 45 were much more than cosmetic modifications of the law designed to deal with a nonexistent problem.

The sixth and final reform contained in Bill 45 consisted of a number of guarantees of union democracy. The proposed legislation compelled unions to include in their statutes a provision for the holding of secret ballot votes among the membership (of the union, not the entire bargaining unit) before a strike could be legally initiated or a collective agreement ratified or rejected. The bill made no provision for external (government) supervision of these votes.

Reaction to the first draft of Bill 45 was immediate, vociferous, and polarized. The three major union centrals all gave qualified approval to the proposed law. Although they were by and large satisfied with those sections of the bill outlawing the use of strikebreakers, providing for the arbitration of first contracts, and imposing the Rand Formula, they were adamantly opposed to any state interference in their internal affairs (the guarantees of "union democracy" contained in Bill 45).

As for the business community, its reaction to the draft law verged on the apoplectic. All of the major business associations condemned the proposed changes to the Labour Code,[9] particularly the anti-scab measures and the imposition of the Rand Formula, calling them the confirmation in policy of an unholy alliance "between the PQ government and the union establishment at the expense of the small wage earners of Quebec."[10] According to the Conseil du Patronat du Québec (CPQ), the first version of Bill 45 represented the government's craven capitulation to the demands of the trade unions. The CPQ's main complaint was that the proposed law would increase the powers of union *organizations* (through the guaranteed financial security of the Rand Formula and the anti-scab measures) without placing any offsetting obligations on them, either to their members or to the nation as a whole. In their opinion, the bill would strengthen collective rights (those of the unions) at the expense of individual liberties, effectively making union members "prisoners" of their own organizations (Conseil du patronat du Québec 1977: 22–26). Gérard Dion went so far as to claim that Bill 45 would strengthen unions and union leaders so much that it would create a system of *"syndicarchie"* (government by unions) in Quebec (1977a, 1977b).

After the outcry raised by the first draft of Bill 45 had died down somewhat, a second version was introduced into the National Assembly in late November 1977. It contained two important amendments: The first diluted the anti-scab provisions by stipulating that employers would be permitted to "take the necessary means," including the hiring of relief personnel, to prevent the destruction or serious deterioration of their property. The second series of amendments tightened the rather sketchy guarantees of union democracy contained in the original bill.

Clearly, for organized labour in Quebec the second draft of Bill 45 represented a considerable retreat from the first version. This apparent dilution by the PQ of its "favourable prejudice toward labour" in the face of business pressure had serious repercussions on governmental unity. Some of the more progressive members of the PQ caucus publicly announced their opposition to the amendments, particularly the changes to the anti-scab provisions, which they viewed as a potential escape hatch for employers seeking to break a strike. Despite the uproar, however, the revised version of Bill 45 was eventually passed in December 1977.

What impact did Bill 45 have on the balance of power between unions and management in Quebec? Many of the reforms enacted by the bill can be characterized as important, if far from revolutionary, concessions to organized labour. Changes in the certification procedures, though on the whole favourable to the unions, made almost no dent in the overriding problem that troubled most labour leaders in the province—the disconcertingly low levels of unionization in Quebec's private sector. In fact, as Table 8-1 shows, union density in Quebec declined to its lowest level in fifteen years during the PQ's second term in office, hardly a confirmation of Lipset's contention that social democratic parties invariably promote trade-union growth.

Imposition of the Rand Formula, without any of the qualifications that are attached to it in other jurisdictions, represented an important symbolic victory for trade unions in Quebec. Nonetheless, the number of workers actually affected by this clause was quite small, since the vast majority of collective agreements already contained such a provision. Similarly, the right of striking workers to return to their jobs and the allowance for the compulsory arbitration of first contracts were significant concessions to organized labour that in all likelihood would reduce the length and severity of a key category of work stoppages in the province. Disputes over first contracts were often the most protracted and

TABLE 8-1. Rate of Unionization in Quebec, 1964–84

	Total Union Membership	Annual Increase in Membership (%)	Rate of Unionization[a] (%)
1964	454,338		29.0
1965	512,981	+ 12.9	31.2
1966	568,520	+ 10.8	32.4
1967	580,201	+ 2.0	32.1
1968	702,161	+ 21.0	39.1
1969	694,972	− 1.0	40.0
1970	704,413	+ 1.4	41.1
1971	742,263	+ 5.4	42.1
1972	748,082	+0.8	41.9
1973	765,619	+ 2.3	39.5
1974	830,350	+ 8.4	41.3
1975	846,139	+ 1.9	38.0
1976	846,619	+0.1	37.0
1977	850,750	+0.5	37.0
1978	815,882	− 4.1	36.9
1979	849,318	+4.1	36.4
1980	868,666	+ 2.3	36.0
1981	880,199	+ 1.3	38.3
1982	838,003	− 4.8	37.3
1983	852,517	+ 1.7	36.3
1984	848,096	− 0.5	34.0

Source: Fleury (1985: 4).
[a]Union membership as a percentage of paid, nonagricultural workforce.

bitter of labour relations conflicts, while the issues of "return-to-work protocols" and the firing of workers for their activities during a strike, as the United Aircraft dispute attested, were also extremely contentious ones.

It was the anti-scab provisions, however, that had the greatest impact on the system of labour relations in Quebec. After three years of experience with the new bargaining regime, organized labour made the following assessment of the anti-scab measures: "The anti-scab provisions have actually contributed to lessening somewhat the legislative imbalance in favour of employers. But they are far from the changes . . . needed to fully respect the right to strike and to protect workers adequately" (Centrale de l'enseignement du Québec 1981: 10; translation by Brian Tanguay).

A study of the anti-scab measures carried out by the Quebec Department of Labour in 1982 confirmed this analysis (Garant 1982). This document indicated that the use of scabs was even more widespread after the passage of Bill 45 than it had been before: Between 1972 and July 1977, scabs were employed in 27 out of 755 labour disputes (3.6 percent); in the three years (1978–80) after the enactment of Bill 45, scabs were utilized in 56 out of 1,101 disputes (5.1 percent). The increase after 1978 in the average size of labour disputes involving scabs indicates that it was the larger corporations that were most easily able to circumvent the law (see Table 8-2). By far the most common tactic for avoiding the anti-scab provisions was to hire a subcontractor. The law specified that no "person" was to be hired to replace a worker on legal strike, but it was unclear whether corporate entities (*personnes morales*) were included under this designation. A number of contradictory judicial decisions on the legality of hiring individual entrepreneurs or corporations to do the work of strikers had been handed down between 1978 and 1980, and the author of the study implied that this legal loophole required the attention of the government (Garant 1982: 50–51, 78).

TABLE 8-2. Impact of Anti-Scab Measures on Industrial Disputes

	1972–1977		1978–1980	
	All Disputes	Disputes Involving Scabs	All Disputes	Disputes Involving Scabs
Number of disputes	755	27	1,101	56
Average length (days)	36.4	171	33.2	111
Average size	521	166	454	479
Total number person-days lost (millions)	9.07	1.12	9.84	1.10
Average number person-days lost (thousands)	12.0	41.5	8.94	19.6

Source: Garant (1982: 61).

Despite the many violations of the spirit (and sometimes the letter) of the law, Garant concluded that the anti-scab provisions had had tangible benefits. The average length of *all* disputes in the province had declined from 36.4 to 33.2 days (see Table 8-2), and Garant cautiously noted that the anti-scab provisions had played at least some role in this trend (1982: 76). Moreover, the average length of strikes involving scabs had decreased markedly from 171 days to 111 days, suggesting that though employers used strikebreakers as often as they had in the past, the government had been reasonably successful in prosecuting these illegal activities and putting a stop to them.

In June 1983, the Parti Québécois government moved to close off the loopholes in Bill 45 and tighten up its anti-scab provisions. Bill 17, ratified on June 23, prohibited the contracting out of work normally performed by workers who are on a legal strike and banned the use of management personnel to replace striking workers. All three union federations applauded the bill; not surprisingly, the various business organizations in the province were outraged by the government's move. According to the CPQ, the Quebec Labour Code was already one of the most restrictive in North America. Any further legal burdens placed on the province's corporations, it noted, could only assist the competition in other jurisdictions, where labour relations policy was less biased in favour of trade unions (Conseil du patronat du Québec 1983: 1–3). In a highly publicized case occurring not long after Bill 17 was enacted, Menasco, a manufacturer of airplane parts (and a subsidiary of New York–based Colt Industries) announced its intention to shut down its Quebec operations and relocate across the Ottawa River in Hawkesbury, Ontario, citing the oppressive nature of Bill 17 as the primary reason for its departure. Spokesmen for the firm claimed that the new law effectively removed a company's right to attempt to survive a legal strike (which was then in effect at the plant); only the complete withdrawal of Bill 17 would make it reconsider its decision to leave (Gibbens 1983).

Bill 17 was passed at the height of the worst recession in Quebec since the 1930s and not long after the bitter conflict between the government and the Common Front unions during the 1982 round of public-sector bargaining. The timing of this law is important because the reforms were so clearly at odds with the coercive labour relations strategy pursued by the PQ in the public sector, and with the repressive measures then being implemented in the private sector by right-wing governments in British

Columbia and Alberta (see Panitch and Swartz 1988: 41–42; Magnusson et al. 1984: 281–85).

Bill 17 can be seen, in large part, as an attempt by the government to cement the mutually beneficial relationship that had developed between it and the FTQ—the labour federation that would derive the greatest benefits from the tightening of the anti-scab provisions in the Labour Code.[11] Throughout the PQ's tenure in office, the FTQ remained the government's staunchest ally, enthusiastically taking part in the numerous socioeconomic summits that were a feature of the Lévesque administration's search for a new social contract, while the other two federations agonized over the dangers of corporatist co-optation and attacked the PQ for engaging in class collaborationism (Tanguay 1984; Fournier 1986). Even after the Lévesque government's brutal attack on the public-sector unions in 1982–83, Louis Laberge, the FTQ president, urged his union to endorse the PQ in the 1985 provincial election, only to be rebuffed by the federation executive.

Bill 45 and Bill 17 constituted significant improvements for organized labour in Quebec and altered in important ways the balance of power between unions and management in the province. Admittedly, these changes were far from revolutionary and were accompanied by an increase in state intervention into the internal affairs of trade unions. This does not, however, make the legislation any the less significant: Quebec was the *only* jurisdiction in the country to have made these concessions to organized labour. The ugly scenes of picket-line violence at the Gainers plant in 1986 and at the Canada Post terminals in 1987, as well as the precipitous drops in private-sector union membership in those jurisdictions that have pursued union-avoidance strategies (British Columbia and Alberta, in particular), should serve as cautionary reminders to anyone who casually pooh-poohs Quebec's labour reforms.

The Parti Québécois and Public-Sector Labour Relations: The Limits of Social Democracy

While relations between the Lévesque government and the private-sector FTQ remained cordial and mutually beneficial throughout the PQ's entire nine-year stay in power, public-sector labour policy during this period was an unmitigated disaster. Between 1968 and 1985, public-sector bargaining in Quebec was both extremely centralized and highly politicized, largely as a result of conscious government policy. Each round of negotiations, involving a union Common Front representing anywhere from 200,000 to 300,000 workers in the public and parapublic sectors and the relevant cabinet ministers, was in many ways a political struggle for the hearts and minds of the electorate, with the stakes being the place and role of the provincial state in Quebec society. Crippling strikes and public disenchantment with the administration's handling of negotiations were more or less the norm during each round, and no government had been able to survive more than two rounds of bargaining before the PQ was elected.

Trading on its privileged relationship with labour, its progressive ideology, and a nationalist vision that was shared by many in the trade unions, the Parti Québécois promised to restore labour peace when it was elected in 1976. And the first round of public-sector bargaining conducted by the government, in 1979, was remarkably expeditious and serene when compared to the debacles of the Bourassa era. This was a crucial time for the Lévesque administration, coming just months before the referendum on sovereignty-association was to be held. For political purposes, then, it was necessary for the government to conclude the negotiations with its employees as quickly as possible, so that the referendum would not be put in jeopardy by a highly publicized labour dispute.

This political context explains Finance Minister Jacques Parizeau's remarkable generosity toward the Common Front. Early in the negotiations, before any real bargaining had taken place, Parizeau acceded to a number of the unions' main demands, notably on maternity leave, isolation pay, and job security (which was already very close to ironclad). Clearly intended to purchase labour peace, these concessions also had the effect of undercutting the Common Front's militant rhetoric about the PQ being a bourgeois government every bit as rotten and authoritarian as the Bourassa regime before it.[12]

Not all of the unions were bought off by Parizeau's danegeld, however, and the PQ was forced to introduce emergency legislation to avert a public-sector strike. Bill 62, passed on 12 November 1979 (only two days before some crucial by-elections were to be held), imposed a two-week moratorium on public-sector strikes. During this cooling-off period, the government tabled its final offers to the unions in the National Assembly. These proposals were then submitted to government employees for a secret-ballot vote. Labour Minister Pierre-Marc Johnson claimed that Bill

62 was not a run-of-the-mill back-to-work law, of the sort that had been used so frequently by the Liberals when they were in power. After all, he argued, the legislation did not, strictly speaking, abolish the right to strike, nor did it impose draconian penalties on unions or workers. It simply suspended the right to strike for a brief period, because union leaders were spoiling for a strike—for political reasons, he implied, namely to create chaos during the by-elections scheduled for November 14. A general strike at this stage of bargaining, Johnson claimed, would be premature and unwarranted, since considerable progress was being made at the negotiating tables, progress that the union leaders were ignoring because of their own political ambitions (Québec 1979: 3484–85).

Johnson's justification of Bill 62 provides an important insight into the PQ's vision of the provincial state as protector of the unorganized, defender of the collectivity, and most legitimate representative of the trade-union rank and file (even more legitimate than their elected officials):

> To what extent can we allow old bargaining habits, which have led to repeated failures since 1966, to lead us inadvertently into an unlimited general strike? This is too important and too serious for the government, in the name of all the citizens, not to feel in certain respects that it is the *trade union of the population*, and that in this capacity, it has responsibilities toward its base, the population. . . . What we are saying is that . . . the use of the right to strike at this stage is premature or ill-timed, and, in view of the consequences that a strike would have on the population . . . it seems appropriate not to outlaw the right to strike but merely to postpone its use, to allow the completion of the work of the representatives of all employees and of the representatives of a government which, to this point, has demonstrated that *its favourable prejudice toward workers is not necessarily a favourable prejudice toward union organizations*, but rather a prejudice that favours the entirety of the population, especially those who are the most poorly paid (Québec 1979: 3484–85; translation by Brian Tanguay, emphasis added).

If public-sector employees were given the opportunity to vote on the government's offers, Johnson was implying, instead of being held hostage to the radical posturing of the union leadership, then the entire dispute could be settled. Bill 62 was the government's way of short-circuiting the normal course of collective bargaining, of circumventing the union hierarchy in order to speak directly to the rank and file.

More than anything else, Bill 62 constituted an extraordinary governmental intrusion into the internal affairs of the public-sector unions in Quebec. The legislation implicitly questioned the representativeness of the trade-union leadership. As one editorialist for *Le Devoir* noted, in enacting Bill 62, the PQ was presuming that the Common Front employees were "misinformed, despite the deluge of publicity that had been unleashed, or that they were being led into a strike by leaders who refused to consult them" (Leclerc 1979; translation by Brian Tanguay). Claude Ryan, then leader of the Liberal opposition in the National Assembly, pointed out that the PQ government was arrogating to itself a privilege that any employer in the province would wish to have: "When I was an employer myself, I would have loved to be able to say to my unions, 'You are going to submit my offers to a secret-ballot vote of your members.' That would be fantastic for an employer. It is an awesome weapon to give to any employer" (Québec 1979: 3488; translation by Brian Tanguay). That a self-styled social democratic government would enact legislation like Bill 62 serves to underscore the latent authoritarianism in the PQ's approach to labour relations. If necessary, the government was implying, the state itself would assume the responsibility of representing workers or other groups in society, especially when the elected leaders of these groups espoused a philosophy or adopted tactics that jeopardized the PQ's political objectives. As Pierre-Marc Johnson so eloquently put it in the quote cited above, the PQ government may have had a favourable prejudice toward *workers*, but it did not have a favourable prejudice toward *union organizations*.

This authoritarian streak in the PQ ideology was also apparent in another piece of emergency legislation that was passed during this pre-referendum round of bargaining. Although Bill 62 did have the intended effect on labour unity—the Common Front slowly crumbled, and the government signed a series of deals with separate unions—some groups of employees remained recalcitrant. Of these, the 11,000 highly paid Hydro-Québec workers posed one of the biggest threats to the government's objectives by threatening to let the province freeze in the middle of winter. After a three-week strike, the PQ again intervened, this time with Bill 88.

Statements made by a number of cabinet ministers during the debate on the proposed bill are extremely important for what they reveal about the PQ's thinking on trade unions, the state's role in labour relations, and the *duties* incumbent on organized labour in the struggle for independence. Lévesque, for instance, was clearly embarrassed by his government's failure to conclude the 1979 round of public-sector bargaining without emergency legislation; but taking up a theme that had first been laid down during the debate over Bill 62, he claimed that government intervention was necessary because union leaders were ignoring the wishes of the rank and file (Québec 1979: 4675). Lévesque and his principal allies in cabinet claimed that the union leadership's refusal to submit salary proposals contained in a mediator's report to their membership constituted an abuse of their power. This abuse, Finance Minister Jacques Parizeau argued, was made all the more repugnant by the fact that a small number of relatively well-off workers—Hydro-Québec technicians were earning upwards of $40,000 a year—were depriving the vast majority of the population of one of the most essential services (Québec 1979: 4658). It was necessary once again, the PQ leaders argued, for the government to act as the "trade union of the population" by compelling the union executives to consult their membership.

It was Yves Bérubé, the minister of natural resources, who most eloquently underscored the PQ's plight in attempting to legislate against public-sector workers, the party's "natural allies" in the struggle for independence. Responding to Claude Ryan's taunting remark that the PQ was finally discovering how difficult it was for *any* party in power, notwithstanding its putative favourable prejudices toward the workers, to solve the problem of public-sector labour relations, Bérubé unwittingly laid bare the class nature of the PQ's entire nationalist project:

> I became involved in politics because I was confident that people can, at a given moment, demonstrate sufficient pride, confidence in themselves, unselfishness, and a sense of responsibility toward the rest of their compatriots in order to say: I am standing up and assuming my responsibilities. . . . Obviously, it is hard when . . . it is our *natural allies* who do not understand. I say natural allies because it is in fact in the labour movement that I found most of the militants who became involved in the Parti Québécois. It is hard because *there are some militants who believe in Quebec but who still suffer from class egoisms*. They do not realize that . . . when you spend your time gazing at your navel and reducing all social problems to your own material existence, it is society itself that you destroy. . . . Class egoisms exist. It is necessary for our society to mature. It will mature only if we

show it the path of transcendence. (Québec 1979: 4671; translation by Brian Tanguay, emphasis added)

Bérubé was claiming that responsible *indépendantistes* ought to subordinate their "class egoisms" to the interests of the collectivity. If they did not, then the state would be compelled to show them the path of enlightenment.

This chilling invocation of Big Brother would take on even greater significance in the 1982 round of bargaining, when Bérubé was minister of the treasury board and in charge of negotiations.

In summary, during the 1979 round of public-sector bargaining, just as had been the case with private-sector labour policy (the anti-scab law), the PQ very carefully tailored its actions to further the overriding objective of sovereignty-association. With the referendum looming on the political horizon, the PQ government pursued a mixed strategy in collective bargaining with the Common Front. On the one hand, government negotiators exhibited a fair degree of generosity toward the public-sector unions: Witness Parizeau's substantial concessions on maternity leave, isolation pay, and job security. On the other hand, the PQ did not hesitate to resort to emergency legislation (Bill 62 and Bill 88) when negotiations appeared in danger of stalling and possibly jeopardizing the carefully orchestrated buildup to the referendum. As the CEQ observed,

The PQ government undertook major initiatives in accordance with a well-defined political strategy; it prepared the terrain for the referendum by holding highly publicized economic summits and by the continuous production of programs of publicity and propaganda. Each political intervention was directly or indirectly a call to consensus, harmony, social peace, cohesion, pride, etc. (Centrale de l'enseignement du Québec 1981: 114; translation by Brian Tanguay)

Once the referendum had been held, and defeated, the delicate balancing act performed by the PQ government between 1976 and 1980 was no longer necessary. According to the CEQ, however, the fear that the PQ might radically alter its style of governing was unrealistic and unfounded. If the PQ somehow managed to survive the upcoming provincial election it would likely continue in its reformist ways, acting as a "good government," content to manage the status quo.

In the case of public-sector labour relations, the CEQ's prognostication proved sadly inaccurate. With the collapse of its independence project, the Parti Québécois was left adrift, without philosophical or ideological bearings; it was a party without a *vision*. For not only did the 20 May referendum vote signal the demise of the party's constitutional option, it also prefigured the collapse of most of the social and economic policies pursued by the PQ during the first few years of its mandate. No longer was it necessary to perform the high-wire act required before 1980 to reconcile the mutually antagonistic interests of different classes in Quebec, which the PQ had done in hopes of building a fragile independence coalition. With its twin national and social projects virtually dead, the PQ underwent a rapid metamorphosis after May 1980, from a programmatic and social democratic party to a party *comme les autres*. Its primary objectives after the defeat of the referendum were to cling to power, to defend Quebec's interests as jealously as possible within the Canadian federal system, and to foster the development of francophone-owned businesses.

These sweeping changes in the philosophy and style of intervention of the second Lévesque government reflected what might be called the "Union-Nationalization" of the PQ.[13] After its miraculous reelection in 1981, the few remaining social democrats in the PQ caucus were shunted aside, opening up a window of opportunity for the hard-liners in the party, whose commitment to social democracy had always been tenuous at best. As long as the fate of the referendum on sovereignty-association had remained undecided, the authoritarian inclinations of the party elite had been kept more or less in check by the need to retain the support of the labour movement (although there were certainly glimpses of this tendency even in such ostensibly pro-labour legislation as Bill 45). With the defeat of the referendum, and with the consequent transformation of the Parti Québécois into a political party *comme les autres*, there was no longer any need to mollify union leaders, and an attack on public-sector wages became the most attractive option for coping with the recession.

As this chapter has shown, social democratic parties do not always promote the organizational interests of trade unions. In the case of the Parti Québécois governments between 1976 and 1981, private-sector unions received tangible policy benefits from the regime—the anti-scab provisions in Bill 45, most importantly—but did not experience any sustained growth. In fact, union density in the province declined to its lowest levels in fifteen years during the PQ's second term in office, largely as a result of the government's failure to promote the organization of the burgeoning categories of employees in the service industries. Nonetheless, the PQ's policies were far more favourable toward private-sector unions than were those in a number of other jurisdictions during this period—notably Alberta and British Columbia. The reason for this favouritism is found in the privileged relationship that had grown up between the PQ government and the FTQ.

In the public sector, the PQ government's attitude toward the unions was characterized by a subterranean authoritarianism. This remained beneath the surface during the 1979 round of bargaining, largely because the strategic requirements of the impending referendum required concessions to the unions, not coercion. After the defeat of the referendum in 1980, however, and the marked shift in the balance of power in the party that attended its surprising 1981 election victory, the path was open to a highly coercive strategy designed to crush the union leadership, which was seen as putting its own sectional interests before the needs of L'Etat du Québec. In the conflict between nation and class, while the PQ was in power, the latter was no match for the former. The unions in Quebec would do well to remember the behaviour of the PQ while it was in power, now that another party, the Bloc Québécois, with few real roots in social democratic ideology, is attempting to mobilize workers as Québécois.

Notes

1. This argument is echoed by, among others, Meltz (1985: 325–27), Williams (1985), and Huxley, Kettler, and Struthers (1986: 123–25, 131).

2. It might be noted in passing, however, that the behaviour of the federal Progressive Conservative government since its election victory in 1984, and in particular its ill-fated attempt to break the inside postal workers' union during a bitter 1987 labour dispute, has hardly exemplified the "Tory" concern for the disadvantaged that Lipset claims is a feature of Canada's "collectivist" political culture.

3. For a more detailed examination of this conflict and its roots in the PQ's ideology and organization, see Tanguay (1990: ch. 9). For further descriptions of this conflict, see Lipsig-Mummé (this volume) and Hébert (this volume).

4. Before 1981 there is little question that the PQ merited this label as much as the New Democratic Party (NDP), even if the latter opposed the PQ's application to join the Socialist International.

5. The fact that there were several tendencies within the PQ, some of them less sympathetic to organized labour than others, did not make the party any less social democratic than, for instance, the Parti socialiste (PS) in France, the Labour party in Britain, or the NDP in Canada. Each of these parties has grouped under one label a variety of ideological currents, and each has been racked by recurrent and bitter disputes over the kind of relationship that ought to exist between the party and the trade unions. On the various tendencies within the French PS, see Jenson and Ross (1983: 73–78); for conflicts within other European social democratic parties, see individual chapters in Paterson and Thomas (1977).

6. This phrase was used by Yves Bérubé in 1979 during debate in the National Assembly on a piece of back-to-work legislation and will be examined more fully below.

7. In 1976, over 6.5 million person-days were lost in strikes and lockouts, a figure that made Quebec a rival of Italy for the title of world leader in industrial militancy. See Niosi (1979: 56).

8. For the details of this legislation, see Hébert in this volume.

9. The biggest and most important business association is the Conseil du patronat du Québec (CPQ), representing primarily large firms. The Chambre du commerce de la province du Québec, the Association des manufacturiers canadiens, and the Centre des dirigeants d'entreprise (CDE) are the other major business organizations in the province.

10. Gérard Dion, quoted in Conseil du patronat du Québec (1977: 8); translation by Brian Tanguay.

11. Data provided by Garant (1982: 67) indicate that although in principle the anti-scab regulations apply to all provincial employers, private and public alike, they have their greatest impact on the private sector: Over 90 percent of the disputes involving scabs (between 1978 and 1980) occurred in the private sector.

12. For excellent discussions of the PQ's strategy during this round of bargaining, see Lemelin (1984: ch. 9) and Demers (1982: ch. 3).

13. This term refers to the parallels between the PQ government from 1981 to 1985 and the Union Nationale administrations of Maurice Duplessis (1936–39, 1944–60).

References

Bauer, Julien. 1977: L'Attitude des syndicats. *Etudes internationales* 8:2 (June), 307–19.

Bélanger, Yves. 1982: Alliance de classes et nature de classe du PQ: Etude de quelques législations du PQ. In Centre de formation populaire, *Au-delà du parti québécois*, Montreal: Nouvelle Optique, 43–68.

Centrale de l'enseignement du Québec. 1981: *Un gouvernement de plus en plus conservateur: Réflexion critique sur l'exercice du pouvoir du gouvernement du parti québécois de 1976 à 1981.* Quebec, 26 March.

Conseil du patronat du Québec. 1977: *Mémoire au ministre du travail et aux membres de l'assemblée nationale sur le projet de loi no 45 amendant le code du travail.* Montreal, October.

————. 1983: *Mémoire à la commission parlementaire du travail sur les amendements proposés au code du travail.* Montreal, June.

Dean, Robert. 1989: *Interview.* Montreal, 27 January.

Demers, François. 1982: *Chroniques impertinentes du 3ème Front commun syndical.* Montreal: Nouvelle optique.

Descôteaux, Bernard. 1977: Le caucus du PQ est divisé sur la loi anti-scab. *Le Devoir,* 24 November, 1.

Dion, Gérard. 1977a: Comment assurer le caractère démocratique et l'efficacité des scrutins secrets dans les syndicats? *Le Devoir,* 5 November, 5.

————. 1977b: Les mesures anti-briseurs de grève et le précompte syndical. *Le Devoir,* 7 November, 5.

Fleury, Gilles. 1985: *Evolution de la syndicalisation. 1964–1984.* Quebec: Ministère du Travail, de la Main-d'oeuvre et de la Sécurité du revenu.

Fournier, Pierre. 1986: *La concertation au Québec: Étude de cas et perspectives.* Quebec: Commission consultative sur le travail et la révision du code du travail.

Francoeur, Louis-Gilles. 1976: Les syndicats accueillent avec joie la victoire du PQ. *Le Devoir,* 16 November.

Fraser, Graham. 1984: *PQ: René Lévesque and the Parti Québécois in Power,* Toronto: Macmillan.

Garant, Louis. 1982: *Les briseurs de grève et le Code du travail.* Quebec: Ministère du Travail, de la Main-d'oeuvre et de la Sécurité du revenu, March.

Gibbens, Robert. 1983: Pressure Building on Quebec to Revoke Nonunion Labor Bill. *Globe and Mail,* 12 September, B5.

Girard, Michelle, and Yvan St. Onge. 1982: *Etude sur l'arbitrage des premières conventions collectives.* Quebec: Ministère du Travail, de la Main-d'oeuvre et de la Sécurité du revenu, 12 July.

Hamilton, Richard, and Maurice Pinard. 1976: The Bases of Parti Québécois Support in Recent Quebec Elections. *Canadian Journal of Political Science* 9:1 (March), 3–26.

————. 1978: The Parti Québécois Comes to Power: An Analysis of the 1976 Quebec Election. *Canadian Journal of Political Science* 11:4 (December), 739–75.

Huxley, Christopher, David Kettler, and James Struthers. 1986: Is Canada's Experience "Especially Instructive"? In Seymour Martin Lipset, ed., *Unions in Transition,* San Francisco: Institute for Contemporary Studies, 113–32.

Jenson, Jane, and George Ross. 1983: Crisis and France's Third Way." *Studies in Political Economy* 11 (Summer), 71–103.

Lascelles, Michael. 1980: *Legislative Provision for the Compulsory Check-Off of Union Dues and Agency Fees: A Review of the Issue*. Ottawa: Labour Canada.

Leclerc, Jean-Claude. 1979: Un constat d'échec. *Le Devoir*, 13 November.

Lemelin, Maurice. 1984: *Les négociations collectives dans les secteurs public et parapublic*. Montreal: Editions Agence d'ARC Inc.

Lévesque, René. 1978: *La passion du Québec*, Montreal: Editions Québec/Amérique.

Lipset, Seymour Martin. 1986: North American Labor Movements: A Comparative Perspective. In Seymour Martin Lipset, ed., *Unions in Transition*, San Francisco: Institute for Contemporary Studies, 421–52.

Magnusson, Warren, W. K. Carroll, Charles Doyle, Monika Langer, and R.B.J. Walker, eds. 1984: *The New Reality*. Vancouver: New Star Books.

Meltz, Noah. 1985: Labor Movements in Canada and the United States. In Thomas Kochan, ed., *Challenges and Choices Facing American Labor*, Cambridge, Mass.: MIT Press, 315–34.

Milner, Henry. 1978: *Politics in the New Quebec*, Toronto: McClelland and Stewart.

Murray, Don, and Vera Murray. 1978: *De Bourassa à Lévesque*, Montreal: Editions du Quinze.

Murray, Vera. 1976: *Le Parti québécois: De la fondation à la prise du pouvoir*, Montreal: Hurtubise HMH.

Niosi, Jorge. 1979: Le Gouvernement du PQ deux ans après. *Les Cahiers du socialisme* 2 (Fall), 32–71.

O'Neill, Pierre. 1977a: Anti-scab, Couture recherche l'équilibre. *Le Devoir*, 10 February, 3.

———. 1977b: Le Ministre du travail se défend d'être anti-patronal. *Le Devoir*, 15 February, 7.

Panitch, Leo, and Donald Swartz. 1988: *The Assault on Trade Union Freedoms: From Consent to Coercion Revisited*, Toronto: Garamond Press.

Parti Québécois. 1972: *Prochaine étape . . . quand nous serons vraiment chez nous*, Montreal.

Paterson, William, and Alastair Thomas. 1977: *Social Democratic Parties in Western Europe*, London: Croom Helm.

Québec. Assemblée nationale. 1979: *Journal des Débats*, 4^c session, 31^c Législature, November-December.

Rouillard, Jacques. 1989: *Histoire du syndicalisme québécois* Montreal: Boréal.

Tanguay, A. Brian. 1984: Concerted Action in Quebec, 1976–1983: Dialogue of the Deaf. In Alain Gagnon, ed., *Quebec: State and Society*, Toronto: Methuen, 365–85.

————. 1990: Rediscovering Politics: Organized Labour, Business, and the Provincial State in Quebec, 1960–1985. Ph.D. dissertation, Ottawa: Carleton University.

Williams, Lynn. 1985: Discussion. In Thomas Kochan, ed., *Challenges and Choices Facing American Labor*, Cambridge, Mass.: MIT Press, 335–37.

9 PETER G. BRUCE

State Structures and the Processing of Unfair Labor Practice Cases in the United States and Canada

The Canadian workforce is more than twice as unionized as its U.S. counterpart largely because Canadian public policies have restricted legally defined unfair labor practices (ULPs) by employers to about one-tenth the U.S. rate (Weiler 1983; Robinson 1990).[1] The frequency of ULPs in the United States, of which discriminatory discharges are the most frequent and potent, has led to widespread fear of supporting a union (Weiler 1989). Most studies show that such ULPs are highly effective at defeating union drives when they are not quickly remedied by government action (Freeman and Medoff 1984). Yet the U.S. National Labor Relations Board (NLRB) is slow and sparing in providing such remedies. This has led to such a rapid proliferation of ULPs in recent years that approximately one worker for every thirty-five involved in a union representation campaign has been found by the NLRB to have been the victim of a discriminatory discharge and has been offered reinstatement (LaLonde and Meltzer 1991). U.S. employers also violate the law almost as frequently by refusing to bargain with a certified union. Freeman and Medoff (1984) conclude from this that between one-quarter and one-half of the decline in private-sector unionization in the United

States in the postwar era has been due to ULPs and ULP-related forms of employer resistance to unions.

Although many differences in union-recognition law in Canada and the United States have been adequately analyzed, some have been over-looked—particularly differences in the frequency with which labor boards on both sides of the border dismiss ULP cases and the speed and fairness with which they expedite their ULP litigation. This chapter analyzes these differences in detail. It shows why they are important, how they stem from differences in governmental structure, how they interact with other aspects of union-recognition policy, and how they affect outcomes in certification cases and ultimately union growth. Before proceeding with that analysis, however, I will elaborate briefly why union density (i.e., the proportion of the workforce unionized) is important, since the significance of this measure has been called into question.

Does Density Matter

Panitch and Swartz (1988) assert that the Canadian state has curbed the right to strike so frequently and severely in recent decades that union density misleads as an indicator of labor movement power. This curbing of union freedoms supposedly derives from the Canadian state deploying its political powers in reshaping the labor market to make industry more competitive and to relieve governments of their fiscal crises. Supposedly these processes are taming Canadian union leaders and rendering them unable to undertake the mobilizing tasks of trade unionism, including uniting the working class for socialist struggle. As such processes advance, Canada as well as the United States becomes threatened with effective, if not formal, deunionization. Thus, in their view, union density is merely a nominal indicator of union power and any comparison between U.S. and Canadian union density is about as useful as one between pygmies and dwarves.

These charges have some merit. Canadian governments have curbed the rights of workers to strike with increasing frequency through back-to-work legislation and by designating increasing proportions of public-sector workers as "essential" and thus barred from striking. Canadian courts have also failed to interpret the Charter of Rights and Freedoms as guaranteeing the right to strike.

While these limits on union freedoms have been serious and frequent, however, the critics' analysis exaggerates their extent. Such violations have generally been confined to the public sector, which in the United States, for the most part, has not had the right to strike. This confinement undermines the broader claim that such seemingly repressive measures are constraining unionism throughout the economy. Relatedly, rather than simply reflecting a generalized campaign by government and capital against unions, these curbs are sometimes responses to public sentiment. Nearly two-thirds (62%) of Canadians opposed the right of public-sector workers to strike by the early 1980s (CIPO 1965, 1982).

While strikes decreased in many countries in the 1980s, moreover, Canadian labor's overall ability to strike appears to have increased relative to that of other labor movements. In 1985 and 1986 Canada's strike volume led all other OECD nations, and ranged from 35 percent to 65 percent higher than Italy's, the second most strike-prone democracy. Canada's strike volume has also been approximately three to four times that of the United States in the last fifteen years (Arrowsmith and Courchene 1989: 125).

This relatively high strike volume suggests that the curbs on public-sector union freedoms are an exception to a more general pattern in which Canadian governments act with a more neutral and mixed approach toward the regulation of labor and strike activity than the U.S. government. So too does the fact that many Canadian governments have recently introduced laws that encourage union organization and facilitate striking (Sack and Lee 1990; Weiler 1990).

The use of union density as an indicator of union power thus seems warranted. Union density should be viewed as a real rather than nominal indicator of labor strength, both political and economic. As numerous scholars have pointed out, there is usually a direct relationship between union density and the development of social democratic parties and the welfare state. Generally one can infer that the stronger a labor movement's union density, the stronger its political and economic power (Kettler, Struthers, and Huxley 1990; Cameron 1984; Stephens 1980).

Although Canada's higher union density is sometimes explained solely in terms of differences in public-sector union growth (Troy 1988, for example), the slower decline of Canadian private-sector unionism—a decline that has proceeded at approximately half the U.S. rate (Meltz 1989, in this volume)—has been just as important. Private-sector unionists constitute approximately half of all union members in Canada (Troy

1988; Dion and Hébert 1989). It is plausible to hypothesize that if Canadian unions had to contend with the higher rates of employer antiunion discrimination and weak legal remedies found in the United States, private-sector union density would probably have fallen more quickly.

Understanding the promptness and fairness with which ULP cases are processed is crucial for comparing the effectiveness of these countries' collective-bargaining policies and for understanding differences in their political development. Most previous studies have stressed automatic (card check) certification procedures as a key preventive means of minimizing antiunion discrimination by Canadian employers. But these practices do not function in isolation. They are complemented by others that allow workers easy access to ULP hearings and limit employer appeals and judicial review. These give Canadian workers a chance to make an adequate case and allow for prompt enforcement of the laws after ULPs occur.

One might argue, then, that if ULP litigation could be protracted for as long or that if complaints of ULPs could be dismissed as arbitrarily in Canada as in the United States, Canadian employers would have more incentive to commit ULPs, even despite certification by card checks, or "instant elections." Likewise, even if these latter practices were introduced in the United States, employers might still be able to defeat unionization by engaging in ULPs and utilizing opportunities for arbitrary dismissal and strategic delay if this aspect of the NLRB's procedures went unreformed, especially if antiunion employers bolstered their resources for surveillance and undertook coercive actions sooner. Thus, the enforcement aspect of union-recognition policy requires analysis for an adequate understanding of how Canadian law protects workers' organizational rights more effectively.

The more effective enforcement of these rights is founded on legislation giving Canadian labor relations boards more power relative to the courts. This law has not only eliminated appeals and strictly limited judicial review in almost all provinces; it has also prevented the courts from competing with labor boards to regulate collective bargaining. Such practices differ markedly from those in the United States. Thus, analyzing how ULPs are processed also requires an analysis of differences in governmental structures and functions.

Most regulation of collective bargaining falls within provincial jurisdiction in Canada. This chapter therefore compares ULP case processing at

the Ontario Labour Relations Board (OLRB) with that at the NLRB.
Not only is Ontario the largest and most industrialized province, but
most of its procedures are shared by other provincial labor relations
boards.[2]

This analysis compares key administrative differences: (1) the place of
formally heard cases in the disposition of all ULP cases in both jurisdictions; (2) the disposition of ULP case loads, and especially differences in
the limits they put on workers seeking access to hearings; (3) the speed
with which ULP cases are processed; and (4) the division of powers
among judiciaries, legislatures, and administrative boards and the impact
these have on fairness and efficiency in the processing of ULP cases.

Similarities in Rights Enforced and Procedures

In the United States and Canada, proscriptions against ULPs constitute
the protected rights of private-sector workers (Halliday 1982; Weiler
1983). These rights are virtually identical in both countries because Canadian collective-bargaining legislation adopted the spirit, and sometimes
the letter, of sections 7 and 8 of the Wagner Act and has changed little
since. Both countries ban, inter alia, discriminatory discharges and demo-
tions, refusals by management to bargain with unions, and antiunion
threats.

Despite these similarities, key differences follow from the administration of the law. Canadian labor relations boards regulate ULPs more
effectively through the use of certification by cards rather than elections,
through first-contract arbitration, "anti-scab" laws, insistence on the inclusion of agency-shop or stronger union-security clauses in all employment contracts, and the enforcement of stronger bans on employers contracting out or terminating a business to avoid unionization (Weiler 1983,
1984; Carter 1982, 1983; Dion and Hébert 1989). These regulations contrast with U.S. administrative practices and laws such as relatively tooth-
less remedies for employers refusing to bargain; NLRB jurisprudence
accepting employers' rights permanently to replace strikers, shut down,
or subcontract work to avoid a union; and "right-to-work" laws. ULPs
are also processed more quickly in Canada (Halliday 1982). This particular administrative difference, however, and the differences in governmental structure and public policy underlying it, have received little analysis.

It is useful to begin a comparative analysis by detailing the steps followed for processing ULP cases, especially those alleging the most typical offenses of discriminatory discharges and closely related violations. In both the United States and Ontario the worker files a ULP complaint (or charge), and then officials seek to effect a settlement between the parties in conflict. And in both places cases go to formal litigation in a trial-like "hearing" if settlement fails. However, qualification for a hearing at the OLRB is almost automatic, whereas at the NLRB parties must satisfy stringent criteria to qualify. A second major difference is that in Ontario a case is heard directly before a labor relations board, and that is usually its final stage. In the United States, cases are first heard by administrative law judges whose "recommended orders" can almost automatically be appealed to NLRB headquarters in Washington. From there, cases can then be easily appealed to the courts (Weiler 1983). The result is that there are potentially three stages in the United States versus one in Ontario.

The Importance of Hearings to the Disposition of All ULP Cases

Adequate deterrence and prompt enforcement of the law regarding ULP violations is essential for fair and efficient labor-board administration. The two main functions of labor relations boards are (1) to act as "fair ballot associations" and test the sentiment of workers for unionization through formal votes or by card or membership counts, and (2) to act as "public law enforcers" in remedying and deterring ULPs, in order to guarantee workers uncoerced choices regarding unionization, and in exerting other collective-bargaining rights (Miller 1980). That the NLRB fails to protect workers' rights effectively is suggested by the fact that ULP charges against management have grown geometrically in the United States in recent decades, and are much higher than in Canada. To use a rough indicator that adjusts for these nations' population differences, in 1980 six times as many U.S. workers charged they were discriminatorily fired per certification case than workers in Ontario, and twenty-five times more than workers in British Columbia (Weiler 1983).

Of ULP cases alleging antiunion discrimination by management, discriminatory discharges are the most typical. They have constituted approximately 90 percent of all section 8(a)3 violations of the Labor Management Relations Act in the United States (Cooke 1985). Section 8(a)3 charges, in turn, have constituted a majority of all ULP charges alleging antiunion discrimination in most years since 1950 (NLRB, *Annual Reports* 1948–86). The cases falling under Ontario's equivalent section 66, which also prohibits discriminatory discharges, constituted about one half of the OLRB's ULP caseload in the first half of the 1980s (Haywood 1987).

Promptness is crucial in the processing of discriminatory discharge cases, due to the sorts of remedies they require, including reinstatement of workers or the declaration of a "bargaining order."[3] Prompt reinstatement (within several months) after a firing tends to encourage workers to return to the job or to encourage union victory in a certification contest. But more time elapsed reduces the likelihood of both of these outcomes (Aspin 1966; Gagnon 1984; Freeman and Medoff 1984). Meanwhile, other remedies—for example, compensating workers with back pay—are generally ineffective and thus favor employers (Weiler 1990).

The time that it takes ULP cases to go through a formal hearing and obtain a remedy is thus crucial to the outcomes of all ULP cases, despite the fact that only a small fraction are formally litigated, since cases that are heard (or tried, in the more formal U.S. setting) set the bargaining contexts for those resolved informally through settlements or withdrawals. The pace of litigation determines costs to workers and employers of fighting ULP cases. Short hearings benefit workers, and long hearings favor employers. Few workers have the money or time to fight ULP cases over a period of years, and they will be more likely to withdraw their cases if hearings and decisions drag on; conversely, employers will be less likely to settle on terms favorable to workers, because slow hearings and decisions offer chances for strategic delays. Even if eventually found guilty, delay often helps employers undercut union support so effectively that they can defeat a union drive while losing the legal case. These tendencies are reinforced in the U.S. system, which (unlike the OLRB) expects workers fighting ULP cases to seek employment actively as their cases progress (MacDowell 1988).

Beyond these antiunion biases, delays in individual ULP cases can cumulate into general administrative bottlenecks. Thus, justice delayed is justice denied for other workers, too. Of course, simple eligibility for a hearing, as well as prospects for its quick resolution, affect the bargaining strategies of both unions and management, since workers and unions have little to bargain with if their cases are dismissed at the outset. Conversely, companies have more incentives to fire workers who face impediments in gaining a hearing.

Differences in Access to Hearings

Variable access to a hearing and the speed of decisions lead to differences in the ways these labor boards dispose of cases. Despite similarities in rights to organize, the processing of ULP cases in the United States involves more dismissals and withdrawals and a smaller proportion of settlements and cases heard than in Ontario.

Although it is difficult to find comparable data, the *Annual Reports* of the OLRB in fiscal years 1980–81 and 1982–83 provide statistics that can be straightforwardly compared with the NLRB's. Those years the OLRB reported the number of ULP cases withdrawn and settled (a statistical practice it has since discontinued). These can be compared to NLRB reports of the disposition of all cases for those years.

As Table 9–1 and data in subsequent *Annual Reports* show, the OLRB provides a more hearing-centered process. Compared to the NLRB, it has had approximately five to seven times more of its total ULP caseload go through a formal hearing. It has also dismissed cases in the prehearing stage at about one-tenth the U.S. rate. The NLRB's high dismissal rates not only deny many workers opportunities to win ULP cases but also give workers an incentive to withdraw their cases or to make settlements on comparatively disadvantageous terms (McClintock 1980). Conversely, in the OLRB process, the prospect of a guaranteed hearing within four weeks of filing a complaint provides a stronger bargaining position for workers and unions.

The boards try to limit the number of cases going to litigation to a manageable number, and voluntary settlements are regarded as essential to this goal at both the NLRB (Miller 1980) and the OLRB (Adams 1985). While both boards praise settlements as a means of limiting bottlenecks due to too much litigation, the NLRB settles less (30 percent of cases versus 70 percent in Ontario) and uses more prehearing dismissals (approximately 30 percent versus 3 percent) to accomplish this.[4] A dismissed case reduces litigation as much as a settled case. So does a withdrawn case. Often a case is withdrawn in the United States after the charging party is notified that the case is likely to be dismissed. Thus cases either withdrawn or dismissed in the United States are indicators that, after investigation, they were found to be "without merit" (Miller 1980). Table 9–1 shows that the combined withdrawals and dismissals at the NLRB equaled approximately two-thirds of all ULP cases in the 1981–83 period. This proportion has remained virtually constant in subse-

TABLE 9-1. ULP Cases Disposed of by Different Methods at the OLRB and NLRB, by Percentage

OLRB

Year	Formal Action	Dismissed[a]	Withdrawn	Settled	Total
1980–81	21.0	3.0	9.0	67.0	100
1981–82	18.0	3.0	10.0	69.0	100
1982–83	15.0	3.0		82.0[b]	100

[a]Estimates.
[b]Withdrawn and settled.

NLRB

Year	Formal Action	Dismissed	Withdrawn	Settled	Total
1981	3.6	33.8	34.4	28.3	100
1982	3.3	31.6	35.4	29.6	100
1983	3.0	31.1	34.5	31.1	100

Sources: The OLRB statistics are from its *Annual Reports.* See 1980–81, p. 40; 1981–82, p. 59; 1982–83, p. 68. The NLRB statistics are from Table 7 of its *Annual Reports,* listed under CA cases, i.e., cases complaining of ULPs by management for 1981–83.
Note: The cases involving "formal action" have had hearings.

quent years (see NLRB *Annual Reports,* Table 7, for the 1980s). By contrast, the OLRB equivalent of cases "without merit" equaled less than one-seventh of its ULP cases.

Legal and Procedural Reasons for More Dismissals at the NLRB

Board criteria for determining which cases "merit" a hearing are clearly different. The NLRB requires (1) a factual investigation and (2) analysis of whether such facts as appear to be provable are legally sufficient for the prosecutor to continue an effort to remedy the violation (Miller

1980). The investigation is mandatory and the NLRB is required to seek "all" the facts—the "entire picture" of the case—in order to decide whether there is violation (Kammholz and Strauss 1980; NLRB 1983). The exact criteria for finding "all" the facts and judging them are unclear, however. They are not defined by any statutory standards, but obviously a considerable production of evidence is required (McClintock 1980).[5]

On the other hand, Ontario cases are *automatically* scheduled for a hearing. A screening panel's informal review makes efforts to weed out frivolous or misconceived cases, but this is not an investigation like the NLRB's. No effort is made to ascertain whether the main facts are provable. Instead, the OLRB screenings are concerned only with the logic of the complaint. The assumption is that the complainant can prove factual allegations. The review simply asks if the law provides a legal remedy for the alleged practice (Dissanayake 1986).

The NLRB's requirement that the investigation produce all of the evidence, or enough to create the "entire picture" of the case, places a greater burden on the charging party and shows that the NLRB's investigation is really a prehearing hearing. In *NLRB v. Wright-Line* (1980) the court recognized "the practical reality that the employer is the party with the best access to proof of its motivation" in section 8(a)3 cases (NLRB, *Decisions* 1980), while in *National Automatic Vending* (1962) Canadian jurisprudence found that the key "facts lie peculiarly within the knowledge of one of the parties," that is, business (*Canadian Labour Law Cases* 1962).

In the NLRB investigatory process, the utilization of compulsory tools normally used to produce evidence in a hearing is very limited. The investigator's assessment is usually based only on the charging party's evidence, despite the likelihood that many of the most important facts are in the employer's possession (Kammholz and Strauss 1980). The employer is under no compulsion to produce all of the relevant facts. Thus, NLRB investigation procedures often depend on the willingness of employers *voluntarily* to produce the evidence that could undermine their own arguments (see Kowal 1985).

The Ontario Labour Relations Act in contrast states that the OLRB "shall give full opportunity to the parties to any proceedings to present their evidence and make their submissions" (*Revised Statutes of Ontario* 1980, c. 228, s. 102{13}; Finkelman 1985). Generally, these norms have been construed to give a complainant a right to a hearing in the OLRB process, since it is often only through a hearing and associated means, such as cross-examination and subpoena powers, that a full production of evidence can be achieved.

The Inadequacy of Equalizing Weapons

In NLRB investigations, the complainant is supposed to have legal weapons with which to offset the biases inherent in the access to information noted above—that is, the investigatory subpoena and right to appeal dismissal decisions. The former's purpose is to allow the charging party to subpoena records that the employer does not wish to divulge. In fact, however, the use of this tool depends on the discretion of the same general counsel whose subordinates are responsible for dismissing cases, and its use has been granted only on "rare occasions" (Kammholz and Strauss 1980). The NLRB's investigation process also lacks judicial review. Neither the board in Washington nor the courts may hear appeals from cases dismissed in investigations. Such appeals are heard only by the general counsel's own staff. Thus, the general counsel's office has total control over appeals of dismissal of NLRB cases, 94 percent of which are rejected (McClintock 1980).

Workers and unions have at times asked for judicial review of the general counsel's decisions to dismiss section 8(a)3 cases, especially in light of the abundant opportunities for appeal offered to management after these cases are heard. Although the Supreme Court has never directly addressed the matter, circuit courts have asserted that such power was necessary for administrative efficiency. Not turning investigations into full-blown hearings was also necessary, according to the courts, to maintain the "amiable and peaceful settlement of labor disputes." The courts have also justified these powers on the grounds that they were consistent with the legislative intent of the Taft-Hartley Act. These reasons largely lack validity, however, given the ease of appeal in almost every other area of U.S. law and the fact that the Taft-Hartley Act took no position on these issues (McClintock 1980).

Structural Reasons for More
Dismissals at the NLRB

The OLRB is able to hear a larger proportion of its ULP cases than the NLRB because: (1) it covers a smaller population; (2) it has a smaller caseload of ULPs due to better regulation; and (3) the charging parties pay their own expenses. In the United States, the NLRB handles an extremely large volume of cases covering virtually the entire private-sector workforce. In 1983, for instance, it handled 27,454 ULP cases versus 674 at the OLRB. Since in Canada the protection of workers' rights falls under the jurisdiction of ten provincial labor relations boards and a federal labor relations board, the total case intake is shared eleven ways, in a country with one-tenth the population of the United States.

Despite the different territorial and demographic structures of these boards, however, the OLRB and NLRB spend almost identical amounts per workers covered under their respective jurisdictions—approximately $.75 per voting-age citizen (Bruce 1988). These similar per capita expenditures show that the OLRB does not hear a larger proportion of its ULP cases because it spends more money than the NLRB. Instead, these overall spending similarities show that the OLRB can hear a larger proportion of cases because it cuts other costs. Most significantly, it cuts costs because its overall caseload is smaller, and especially because the overall frequency of ULPs per certification case is many times lower than in the United States. This phenomenon is largely a function of the more effective regulation of ULPs by the OLRB, through automatic certifications and through faster ULP case processing itself. The latter enables the OLRB to play an educational role in setting clear expectations among the regulated parties and the public that violations of the law will be discovered and remedied in a timely way (Adams 1985). This provides more incentives than the U.S. process for employers to obey the law.

The third factor that limits the number of complaints and allows the OLRB to hear more of its ULP cases is that the parties, rather than the government, bear the costs of prosecuting their own cases. In the United States the government prosecutes and provides counsel. Doubtless, the Canadian system limits a number of frivolous cases before they begin. It also constrains pressures from taxpayers to limit rights to a hearing. Indeed, when surveyed in the 1960s, most Canadian industrial-relations experts opposed suggestions that the government prosecute ULP cases, on the grounds that this would impose too great a burden on taxpayers (Christie and Gorski 1968). In the United States, cost is a major incentive for the NLRB to dismiss large numbers of cases (Miller 1980).

Of course, this is not an aspect of the Ontario procedure that could be tried in the United States unless other changes were forthcoming. If financial responsibility for prosecution were transferred to complainants in the United States, this could eliminate deserving cases in which workers could not afford the costs of counsel, as well as frivolous ones, unless the unions were willing to provide support to workers fighting ULP cases. The Ontario system works, in large part, because the unions have committed their lawyers to this aspect of the organizing process. In the United States, however, while union organizers often accompany workers and play a semiactive role in section 8(a)3 hearings, the unions generally do not commit their lawyers to prosecuting. Instead, they view this as the NLRB's responsibility (Kowal 1987). Unions in the United States would have to make a quantum leap in their organization and financial commitments to make this sort of system work.

Delay in ULP Cases

It is difficult to compare differences in the promptness with which the NLRB and OLRB process cases involving discriminatory discharges and closely related offenses. Neither board publishes these figures. Data may, nevertheless, be obtained and compared by other means.[6] The median time elapsed for section 8(a)3 cases was virtually identical (with less than 3 percent difference) to the median time elapsed for all ULPs heard in the same years (Bruce 1988). Assuming that time elapsed for section 8(a)3 cases is equal to or greater than those for all ULP cases (recorded in the NLRB's *Annual Reports*),[7] the median time elapsed for section 8(a)3 cases would have ranged from 658 days in 1983 to 769 days in 1986.

Although per-case time spent by both boards has lengthened in recent years, comparison of Tables 9-2 and 9-3 shows that the NLRB in the mid-1980s took four to five times longer than the OLRB to deal with

TABLE 9-2. Median Time Lapse at NLRB for All ULP Cases Heard, and Estimated Median Time Lapses for 8(a)3 Cases Heard

Year	Days
1983	658
1984	660
1985	720
1986	769
1987	709

Source: Table 23 of *Annual Reports* of the National Labor Relations Board.

TABLE 9-3. Median Time Lapse at OLRB Section 66 Cases Formally
Heard

Year	Days
1983–84	137
1984–85	146
1985–86	183
1986–87	187

Source: OLRB Records. From computer printouts and notes dated 27 January
1987. From Len Haywood, research director, Ontario Ministry of Labor.

such a case. As Table 9-3 shows, the discriminatory discharge and related
cases at the OLRB took 137 to 187 days over approximately the same
years. In earlier decades, the NLRB took between 325 and 483 days (Miller 1980), which was also several times longer than recent OLRB decisions.[8]

Although the OLRB does not publish statistics recording the time
elapsed between the stages of its "heard" cases, it does publish goals for
these stages. These allow impressionistic estimates for comparison with
the NLRB's more exact figures. Because the target times are viewed critically by Ontario's trade unions and parties in the legislature, and because
the board's case-monitoring system requires fairly realistic targets, these
give at least a rough approximation of the time cases take.[9]

Table 9-4 compares the length of each stage, for fiscal years 1983–84 of
the OLRB and 1983 of the NLRB. This time period was chosen because
it was one of those for which the OLRB provided overall data about
time for section 66 cases and for which the board's registrar had volunteered estimates of the time taken for these cases to go through various
stages. Table 9-4 shows that the biggest differences were in stage 3, the
decision-writing period, and stage 4, the period of appeal between the
issuance of the administrative law judge's (ALJ) decision and the decision of the NLRB itself in Washington, a process that has no counterpart
in Ontario.

The overall lengths of time these boards took are so grossly different
that the differences by stage, even allowing for considerable imprecision
in the OLRB figures, are obvious. Since the median time elapsed for ALJ

TABLE 9-4. NLRB and OLRB Time Lapses by Stage in All ULP Cases Heard (Fiscal Year 1983–84, OLRB; Fiscal Year 1983, NLRB)

Major Stages Completed	NLRB Days	OLRB Days
1. Filing of charge to issuance of complaint	45	28[a]
2. Complaint to close of hearings[b]	156	88
3. Close of hearing to issuance of ALJ's decision[c]	118	21[a]
4. ALJ's decision to issuance of board decision	324	
5. Filing of charge to board decision	658	137

Sources: U.S. National Labor Relations Board, *Annual Report*, 1983, Table 23. OLRB data from notes and computer printouts dated 27 January 1987, provided by Len Haywood, research director, Ontario Ministry of Labour. Interview with OLRB Registrar Donald Aynsley, April 1984.
[a]Estimate.
[b]Beginning to close of hearing at the OLRB.
[c]Close of hearing to board decision at the OLRB.

decision writing at the NLRB (stage 3) almost equals that for the overall time elapsed in OLRB cases, it is probable that NLRB decision-writing time would be much longer than the OLRB's, even if the OLRB's time targets severely underestimated actual decision-writing time. Also, the appeal from the ALJ to the NLRB, which has no equivalent in Ontario, accounts for four to eleven months of extra delay (Miller 1980; NLRB, *Annual Reports* 1980–86). Once the NLRB's process of internal appeals has been exhausted, it is comparatively easy for antiunion employers to use appeals to the courts for strategic delays and to make the thousand-day ULP case commonplace (Weiler 1983).

Reasons for Differences in Delay

These time records reflect the more pervasive influence of courts and judicial review in the NLRB's process. U.S. courts have disagreed with the NLRB over principles for deciding section 8(a)3 cases (*NLRB v. Wright-Line* 1980). Court decisions and influences have also led to more ambiguous criteria for determining a violation, more constraints on drawing inferences from records, and more emphasis on determining the employer's state of mind in NLRB decisions than those of the OLRB

(Bruce 1988). These differences all lead to more delay in decision writing in the United States. Furthermore, the greater power of the courts in the U.S. constitutional system was responsible for the establishment of the NLRB's internal appeals stage (Bowman 1942) as well as for the ease of appeal to the courts per se. Thus, while the large territory and population of the United States made it imperative for the board to delegate responsibility to ALJs who could serve local populations, judicial review—and NLRB timidity in the face of it—militated against these officials gaining powers to make final decisions.[10] So did the power of the coalition of Republicans and Southern Democrats, which defeated legislation in 1961 that proposed such reforms (Bruce 1988).

The more judicialized character of the U.S. process also contributes to more delay in the decision-writing and hearing stages at the NLRB due to the power and independence of the ALJs. While the OLRB has been able to administer its officials' work according to a systematic "management-by-objectives" program (OLRB 1981–82), the "make-believe-judges" (Miller 1980) at the NLRB have successfully resisted being "administered" in this or even less formal ways by the NLRB's general counsel. Delay, therefore, in NLRB processing of ULP cases is largely structural, derivative of the relatively greater power of the court vis-à-vis administrative agencies (tribunals) in the U.S. political system.

Judicial Review and Appeals

Canadian legal scholars point out that appeals of these decisions are barred in most provinces.[11] Only review is possible (Wanzycki 1969). Canadian courts are effectively prevented from "deciding the issues" in ULP cases, and this has prevented them from developing a jurisprudence of their own to rival that of labor relations boards. The latter have thereby become the sole authority in ULP cases. This is quite different from the division of authority between the NLRB and courts in the United States.

Moreover, even the restricted judicial review that does occur in Canada is less frequent than in the United States. For instance, the OLRB, between 1982–83 and 1984–85, had four or fewer of its ULP cases reviewed per year, out of a total of approximately 70 section 66 cases.[12] In the United States, by contrast, approximately one-third of all ULP cases against management that were decided by the NLRB were appealed to the courts in the early 1980s, as Table 9-5 shows.

TABLE 9-5. Judicial Review of OLRB ULP Cases

	Total ULP Cases with Judicial Review	Number of Section 66 Cases Heard	% Reviewed
1982–83	0	67 (est.)[a]	0
1983–84	4	70	6
1984–85	2	65	3

Sources: "Court Activity" sections of relevant OLRB *Annual Reports*, and OLRB records of section 66 cases heard, provided by Mr. Haywood, 29 January 1987.
[a]From average of subsequent two years.

Judicial Review of NLRB ULP Cases

	Compliance[b]	Circuit Court Decrees[c]	% Appeals to Courts
1980	3.7%	1.4%	38%
1981	3.6	.9	25%
1982	3.3	1.0	30%
1983	3.0	.9	30%

Source: From NLRB *Annual Reports*, Table 7.
[b]Total percentage of CA cases (ULPs against management) heard and remedied.
[c]These are a subset of CA compliance cases, i.e., CA cases that get appealed to the courts after the NLRB's decision.

To determine why judicial review and appeals of labor relations boards decisions are more limited in Canada, one needs to answer two main questions: (1) How do Canadians and U.S. citizens differ regarding the roles they think courts, administrative boards, and legislatures should play in the implementation of labor relations act? and (2) What specific legal rules bar appeals from Canadian labor boards and limit the proportion of cases reviewed more stringently than in the United States?

Canadian legal and industrial-relations circles generally assume that labor relations board officials have more expertise than judges in industrial-relations matters, and hence that their decisions should be final and without appeal to the courts (Adams 1985). Otherwise, losing parties would have the chance to win decisions on second attempts in inferior tribunals and to delay cases in which prompt remedies are essential. The view is that to the extent that judicial review is necessary, it should be limited as strictly as possible.

The Canadian assumption is that judges' expertise in such matters is reduced by their upper middle-class backgrounds, long years of formal education, lack of practical experience in industrial conflicts, and remoteness from the parties in conflict (Weiler 1976). Therefore, in Canada, all hearings are held by labor boards rather than by ALJs or similar delegated authorities, as is the case in the United States.[13] It is also widely assumed in Canada that appeals and easier review of ULP decisions would undermine the promptness required for justice to be effective in the implementation of collective bargaining (Adams 1985). Given these assumptions, most Canadian labor relations acts have banned appeals and restricted reviews of ULP decisions.

The types of cases that can be reviewed by the courts are very limited. Labor relations board decisions need not be made with "substantial evidence" (Adams 1985). In the United States this ambiguous requirement allows courts to intervene frequently to reweigh evidence and rewrite decisions. Although a Canadian labor relations boards's decision may raise questions of law or evidence, unless these are linked to questions of jurisdiction (such as, Is the board the appropriate tribunal to hear the case?) or of "natural justice" (such as, Did the procedures of a hearing give the parties a fair right to be heard?) it will not be subject to review. Thus, only poorly made decisions will be reviewed.

These restrictions on appeals and judicial review stem from statutory "privative clauses," so called because they deprive the courts of jurisdiction. Currently, all statutes regulating collective bargaining outside Quebec are covered by such clauses (Adams 1985). While "finality clauses" in American statutes assert that the decision of labor relations boards should be "final" and that the courts should defer to these agencies' special competence, especially if their fact-finding efforts are supported by "substantial evidence," these clauses in fact lay NLRB decisions wide open to appeals and review.

A major reason why privative clauses have succeeded at preventing Canadian courts from remaking labor board decisions is that they fit well with the British parliamentary form of government and its traditions, which generally have limited the power of the courts more than the U.S. constitutional system.[14] Although parliamentary tradition facilitated the weakening of court powers over labor boards in Canada, the strictness of these constraints was not an inevitable product of these constitutional factors.

198 PETER G. BRUCE

Such restrictions on the courts emerged from political conflicts and from the learning experiences of policy elites.[15] Instead of evolving directly from Canada's governmental structure and Tory traditions, the first labor-law privative clauses were advocated by the Cooperative Commonwealth Federation (CCF). The Liberals, Conservatives, and even the Communists advocated a Canadian version of the Wagner Act, which would have allowed the courts to hear ULP cases (Bruce 1988). The CCF, on the other hand, sought to give labor boards the power to make final decisions free from judicial intervention and appeals, since its policy experts perceived that easy appeals inhibited the effectiveness of the Wagner Act in the United States. The CCF fully achieved this goal in Saskatchewan in the 1940s. The model for labor board power that it established eventually spread to other jurisdictions.

Ontario workers charging antiunion discrimination have a much better chance of gaining a hearing and of having their cases expedited promptly than do their U.S. counterparts. These differences give employers fewer incentives to engage in ULPs in Ontario. This in turn contributes to union growth. Such practices also probably contribute to the effectiveness of other aspects of Ontario's union-recognition policies, particularly certification without elections.

Differences in the structure of the Canadian and U.S. governments, particularly the relative power of administrative agencies (tribunals) vis-à-vis the courts, and the extent to which the courts intervene in the labor relations board's decision making are among the most important factors determining the promptness with which ULP cases are processed. These administrative variations, in turn, derive both from differences in constitutional origins and in the nature of partisan conflict in these nations. Pressures for more dismissals in the United States derive from a variety of factors not obtaining in Ontario: (1) the much larger number of ULPs that the NLRB must process, even allowing for differences in population; (2) the jurisdiction of a single labor relations board over virtually all private-sector ULP cases; and (3) the fact that the government, rather than the parties involved, prosecutes these cases at the taxpayers' expense.

Notes

1. I would like to thank former NLRB Regional Attorney Harold M. Kowal for several years of dialogue about ULP cases. That dialogue stimulated and assisted much of the analysis in this paper, especially regarding the NLRB's in-

vestigation process. I would also like to thank Richard O. MacDowell of the Ontario Labour Relations Board for helpful comments on an earlier draft.

2. For example, restrictions on appeals of board decisions in ULP cases, the prosecution of ULP cases by the parties rather than the government, and less formal and courtlike procedures are found at most other Canadian labor boards (Adams 1985). Quebec's procedures differ from those of Ontario in several significant ways, however (Hébert, in this volume).

3. Such orders certify a union automatically, without a vote, and sometimes without majority support, when gross abuses are found.

4. The OLRB data lack a category for prehearing "dismissals" that corresponds to the NLRB's category. Although the OLRB has a "dismissals" category, this refers only to cases dismissed *after a hearing*, not cases deemed unqualified for a hearing (as in the NLRB statistics). This is a minor gap, however, since the cases dismissed as unqualified by the OLRB's screening panel have constituted less than 5 percent of all ULP cases in each year in the 1980s, and usually no more than 3 percent (Dissanayake 1986). Subtracting from the total the number of cases "dismissed" (in the NLRB's sense), withdrawn, and settled yields the total number of ULP cases that were heard, since all cases are disposed of in one of these ways. Since 1982–83 the OLRB has included withdrawn cases in its "settlement" category. Although this prevents as detailed a comparison with the NLRB as for the earlier years, the *Annual Reports* show that approximately 20 percent of all ULP cases in Ontario are still heard.

5. Instead, the NLRB's requirements for evidence suggest that the normal tools for evidence production in a hearing—i.e., subpoenas, cross-examinations, and rights to judicial review—are the standard.

6. Section 8(a)3 cases can be tabulated from the texts of these decisions, which are all published in *Decisions and Orders of the NLRB*. These usually record the date on which charges were filed or, at least, the first date of hearing, along with the date on which the decision was reached. Although calculating time lapses from first day of hearing, rather than from when a charge was first filed, underestimates the time lapse, it nevertheless allows minimum estimates. Analysis is based on a representative sample of decisions for several years in the 1980s.

7. The NLRB does not break down stages of section 8(a)3 cases by time, although it does so on a aggregate basis for all ULP cases. Since median overall time lapses for all ULP cases have been similar to those for section 8(a)3 cases, and since structural differences (especially the availability of appeals) largely account (see Table 9-4) for differences in delay in the stages where differences are most pronounced, it is reasonable to infer that the differences by stage for section 8(a)3 cases are broadly similar to the differences by stage for all ULP cases. Such inference thus allows a rough comparison of the efficiency of these boards in processing their sections 8(a)3 and 66 cases by stage.

8. The OLRB apparently has no easily accessible record of similar data for earlier periods.

9. Between 1983 and 1985 the OLRB generally scheduled hearings for 28 days after the filing of a complaint (Aynsley 1984). The OLRB registrar also maintained that 95 percent of ULP decisions were written within three weeks of the hearings' completion. Although no OLRB time targets were available for the stage from the beginning to the close of a hearing, this can be calculated by subtracting the sum of the target times for the two stages noted above (i.e., from the filing of a complaint to the start of a hearing, and from the end of a hearing to the completion of the board's decision) from the median total time lapse.

10. These officials were known as trial examiners until 1971.

11. Quebec, with its civil-law tradition, is the exception to these generalizations about courts and appeals.

12. Since the number of all ULPs heard was not available, using the total number of section 66 cases as a substitute overestimates the proportion of all ULPs reviewed. All of the OLRB cases reviewed are summarized in its *Annual Reports* in the "Court Activity" section.

13. Quebec is an exception here.

14. Canadian privative clauses have antecedents in similar clauses in British statutes, the earliest of which date back to the beginnings of parliamentary sovereignty. These prevented courts from interfering in the implementation of policies by Parliament and administrative tribunals (Royal Commission 1968). Indeed, with the development of the welfare state and other forms of regulation, judicial review of administrative agencies has become so restricted (through privative clauses and the norms associated with them) in Britain that it has become almost extinct (Shapiro 1981).

15. It is also worth noting that judicial review has been more prevalent in Canada than Britain (Mullan 1974). Labor laws has provided a pioneering example of limited judicial intervention in Canada. Labor lawyers such as Laskin (1952) and Finkelman (1965) have provided key rationales justifying these changes.

References

Adams, George W. 1985: *Canadian Labour Law: A Comprehensive Text*. Aurora, Ont.: Canada Law Books.

Arrowsmith, David, and Melanie Courchene, eds. 1989: *Collective Bargaining Reference Tables: The Current Industrial Relations Scene in Canada*. Kingston, Ont.: Industrial Relations Centre, Queens University.

Aspin, Leslie. 1966: *A Study of Reinstatement under the National Labor Relations Act*. Ph.D. dissertation, MIT.

Aynsley, D. K., registrar, Ontario Labour Relations Board. Interview, April 1984.

Bowman, D. O. 1942: *Public Control of Labor Relations: A Study of the National Labor Relations Board*. New York: Macmillan.

Bruce, Peter G. 1988: *Political Parties and the Evolution of Labor Law in Canada and the United States*. Ph.D. dissertation, MIT.

———. 1989: "Political Parties and Labor Legislation in Canada and the United States." *Industrial Relations* 28, 2: 115–41.

Cameron, David R. 1984: "Social Democracy, Corporatism, Labour Quiescence, and the Representation of Economic Interest in Advanced Capitalist Society." In John Goldthorpe, ed., *Order and Conflict in Contemporary Capitalism*, 143–78. New York: Oxford University Press.

Canadian Institute of Public Opinion (CIPO). "Gallup Report." 4 December 1965 and 22 September 1982.

Canadian Labour Law Cases, 1960–64, para. 16,278, p. 1162ff.

Carter, Donald D. 1982: "Legal Restraints upon Employer Conduct during the Collective Bargaining Process: A Study of the Law Relating to Employer Unfair Labour Practices in Canada." Kingston, Ont.: Industrial Relations Centre, Queen's University. Research and Current Issues Series, no. 42.

———. 1983: "The Labour Code of Quebec: Some Reflections and Comparisons." Paper delivered at the Fourteenth Colloquium on Industrial Relations at the University of Montreal.

———. 1986: "The Impact of the Canadian Charter of Rights and Freedoms on Industrial Relations." *Annual Conference Proceedings* 34. Montreal: Industrial Relations Centre, McGill University.

Christie, I., and M. Gorski 1968: *Unfair Labour Practices: An Explanatory Study of the Efficacy of the Law of Unfair Labour Practices in Canada*. Study no. 10, Task Force on Labour Relations. Ottawa: Queen's Printer.

Cooke, William N. 1985: "The Rising Toll of Discrimination against Union Activists." *Industrial Relations* 24, 3: 421–42.

Dickens, William F. 1980, *Union Representation Elections: Campaign and Vote*. Ph.D. dissertation, MIT.

Dion, Gérard, and Gérard Hébert. 1989: "L'avenir du syndicalisme au Canada." *Relations Industrielles/Industrial Relations* 44, 1: 5–23.

Dissanayake, Nimal, solicitor, OLRB. Interview, October 1986.

Finkelman, Jacob. 1965: *The Ontario Labour Relations Board and Natural Justice*. Kingston, Ont.: Industrial Relations Centre, Queens University.

Finkelman, Jacob, and Shirley Goldenberg. 1983: *Collective Bargaining in the Public Sector: The Federal Experience in Canada*. Vols. 1 and 2. Montreal: Institute for Research on Public Policy.

Freeman, Richard, and James Medoff. 1984: *What Do Unions Do?* New York: Basic Books.

Gagnon, Denis. 1984: "L'efficacité des ordonnances de réintegration." *Marché du travail* 5, 10.

Halliday, Alasdair. 1982: *The Effects of Legislation on Trade-Unionism in Canada and the United States*. B.A. thesis, Harvard University.

Haywood, Len, research director, Ontario Ministry of Labour. Computer print-outs and notes dated 27 January 1987.

Huxley, Christopher, David Kettler, and James Struthers. 1986: "Is Canada's Experience Especially Instructive?" In Seymour Martin Lipset, ed., *Unions in Transition: Entering the Second Century*, 113–22. San Francisco: Institute for Contemporary Studies.

Kammholz, Theophil C., and Stanley R. Strauss. 1980: *Practice and Procedure before the National Labor Relations Board*. Philadelphia: American Law Institute–American Bar Association.

Kettler, David, James Struthers, and Christopher Huxley. 1990: "Unionization and Labour Regimes in Canada and the United States: Considerations for Comparative Research." *Labour/Le Travail* 25: 161–87.

Kowal, Harold M. 1985: *A Tract for Workers Who Fear Discrimination because of Union Organizing or Other Collective Activity*. Unpublished book. Copyright 1985.

———, regional attorney, NLRB, 1948–78. Interviews, November 1986, June 1987.

Lalonde, Robert J., and Bernard D. Meltzer. 1991: "Hard Times for Unions: Another Look at the Significance of Employer Illegalities." *University of Chicago Law Journal* 58: 953–1014.

Laskin, Bora. 1952: "Certiorari to Labour Boards: The Apparent Futility of Privative Clauses." *The Canadian Bar Review* 30, 4: 986–1003.

Lemelin, Maurice. 1984: *Les négotiations collectives dans la secteur publique*. Montreal: L'Arc Presse.

Lipset, Seymour Martin. 1986a: "Labor Unions in the Public Mind." In Lipset, ed., *Unions in Transition: Entering the Second Century*, 287–322. San Francisco: Institute for Contemporary Studies.

———. 1986b: "North American Labor Movements: A Comparative Perspective." In Lipset, ed., *Unions in Transition: Entering the Second Century*, 421–51. San Francisco: Institute for Contemporary Studies.

MacDowell, Richard, vice-chair, OLRB. Interview, August 1988.

McClintock, Michael. 1980: *NLRB General Counsel: Unreviewable Power to Refuse to Issue an Unfair Labor Practice Complaint*. Arlington, Va.: Carrollton Press.

Meltz, Noah. 1985. "Labor Movements in Canada and the United States." In Thomas A. Kochan, ed., *Challenges and Choices Facing American Labor*, 315–34. Cambridge, Mass.: MIT Press.

―――. 1989: "Unionism in the Private Sector: A Canada–United States Comparison." Paper delivered at the Center for International Affairs' Conference on North American Labor Movements into the 1990s, Harvard University, February 1989.

Miller, Edward. 1980: *An Administrative Appraisal of the NLRB*. Rev. ed. Philadelphia: University of Pennsylvania Press.

Mullan, D. J. 1974: "Reform of Judicial Review of Administrative Action—The Ontario Way." *Osgoode Hall Law Journal* 12, 1: 122–79.

National Automatic Vending. No. 63 *Canadian Labour Law Cases*, 1960–64, para. 16,278, p. 1162ff.

NLRB v. Wright-Line. No. 251 NLRB *Decisions and Orders*, 1980, p. 1083 ff.

Ontario Labour Relations Board (OLRB). *Annual Reports*, 1980–87.

Panitch, Leo, and Donald Swartz. 1984: "Towards Permanent Exceptionalism: Coercion and Consent in Canadian Labour Relations." *Labour/Le Travail* 13: 133–57.

―――. 1988: *The Assault on Trade Union Freedoms: From Consent to Coercion Revisited*. Toronto: Garamond Press.

Revised Statutes of Ontario. 1980, c. 228, s. 102 {13}. Queen's Printer, Toronto.

Robinson, Edward Ian. 1990: *Organizing Labour: Explaining Canada-U.S. Union Density Divergence in the Post-War Period*. Ph.D. dissertation, Yale University.

Rose, J. B., and G. N. Chaison. 1987: "The State of the Unions Revisited: The U.S. and Canada." In Harish Jain, ed., *Emerging Trends in Canadian Industrial Relations*, proceedings of the twenty-fourth annual meeting of the Canadian Industrial Relations Association. Quebec City: Laval University, Canadian Industrial Relations Association.

Royal Commission. 1968: *Inquiry into Civil Rights Report No. 1* (McRuer Report). Vol. 1. Toronto: Queen's Printer.

Sack, Jeffrey, and Tanya Lee. 1990: "The Role of the State in Canadian Industrial Relations." *Relations Industrielles/Industrial Relations* 44, 1: 195–221.

Sack, Jeffrey, and C. Michael Mitchell. 1985: *Ontario Labour Relations Board Law and Practice*. Toronto: Butterworth's.

Shapiro, Martin. 1981: *Courts: A Comparative Legal and Political Analysis*. Chicago: University of Chicago Press.

Snyder, David. 1977: "Early North American Strikes: A Reinterpretation." *Industrial and Labor Relations Review* 30, 3: 325–41.

Stephens, John D. 1980: *The Transition from Capitalism to Socialism*. Atlantic Highlands, N.J.: Humanities Press.

Troy, Leo. 1988: "Is the U.S. Unique in the Decline of Private Sector Unionism?" Paper delivered at Laval University's Conference on Comparative Labor Movements. Quebec City, August.

Troy, Leo, and Neil Sheflin. 1985: *Union Sourcebook*. West Orange, N.J.: IRDIS.
U.S. National Labor Relations Board. *Annual Reports*. Fourth (1938) to Fifty-
    first (1986). Washington, D.C.: GPO.
———. 1983: *Case-Handling Manual*. Vol. 1, *Unfair Labor Practices*. Washing-
    ton, D.C.: GPO.
———. *Decisions and Orders of the NLRB*. Various years. Washington, D.C.:
    GPO.
Wanzycki, Jan K. 1969: *Judicial Review of Labour Relations Boards in Canada*.
    Ottawa: Canada Department of Labour, Queen's Printer.
Weiler, Paul. 1976. "The Administrative Tribunal: A View from the Inside."
    University of Toronto Law Journal 26: 193, 198ff.
———. 1983. "Promises to Keep: Securing Workers' Rights to Self-organization
    under the NLRA." *Harvard Law Review* 96, 3: 1769–1827.
———. 1984. "Striking a New Balance: Freedom of Contract and Prospects for
    Union Representation." *Harvard Law Review* 98, 1: 351–420.
———. 1985. "The Contemporary Crisis in American Labor Law." Unpublished
    paper, Harvard University. Delivered at MIT's Sloan School Seminar on
    Industrial Relations, spring 1985.
———. 1989. "The Representation Gap in the North American Workplace."
    Larry Sefton Memorial Lecture, Woodsworth College, University of
    Toronto.
———. 1990. *Governing the Workplace: The Future of Labor and Employment
    Law*. Cambridge, Mass.: Harvard University Press.
Willis, John. 1968: "The McRuer Report: Lawyer's Values and Civil Servants'
    Values." *University of Toronto Law Journal* 18: 351–60.
Wood. W. D., and Pradeep Kumar. 1987: *The Current Industrial Relations Scene
    in Canada*. Kingston, Ont.: Industrial Relations Centre, Queens Univer-
    sity.

The Challenge of a Changing Labor Force

10 NOAH MELTZ

Unionism in the Private-Service Sector:
A Canada—United States Comparison

Aside from a few countries, such as those of Scandinavia, there has recently been a general decline in union density, that is, the percentage that union members represent of paid workers (Freeman 1989; Troy 1990).[1] Until 1984, Canada was also an exception to the trend, but recent figures indicate that union density has begun to fall in Canada as well.[2] An important factor in the decline has been the continuing shift of workers to the private-service sector where union density has traditionally been very low.

Nevertheless, while union density has been low in these industries, it has consistently been higher in Canada than in the United States. The purpose of this chapter is to examine the factors underlying the low union densities in the private-service sector and to consider possible reasons why the union density in this sector in Canada has been higher than that in the United States.

Several general conclusions can be drawn. In both countries, for at least the past two decades, union density in the private-service sector has been consistently one-fifth that of the other sectors. The low level is due to a combination of factors: the small size of establishments in this sector, the concentrated time periods in which demand for services requires a relatively high proportion of part-time workers, a high turnover of labour, and a workforce characterized by an above-average employment of younger persons.

The most important conclusion is that the differences between Canada and the United States in union density in the private-service sector are virtually identical to the differences in union density for all other sectors. As a result, there do not appear to be any particular explanatory factors that apply only to the private services. Instead, general factors, such as differences in labour legislation and its enforcement, are the major contributors to the differences in union density.

This chapter is organized into five sections. The first compares union density in the private-service sectors in the two countries for 1986. The second examines the trends in union density in these sectors over time. The third considers possible factors behind the low union-density rates. The fourth examines recent developments in the private-service sector in Canada and the United States. The last section explores some issues for the future of trade unions in the private-service sector.

Unionization in the Private-Service Sector

For purposes of this chapter, the term private-service sector will include: trade; finance, insurance, and real estate; and commercial (nonpublic) services.[3] Excluded from this sector are industries that tend to have a high degree of direct or indirect government support: transportation, communication, and utilities; education, health, and public administration (government).[4]

Whereas there was a rapid growth in employment in education in the 1960s and early 1970s and a rapid growth in employment in health care in the 1970s and early 1980s, the fastest growing industries are now the private services, particularly commercial services (business, financial, consumer, and personal). In 1986 this sector represented half of the paid employment in the United States and almost 40 percent in Canada (see Table 10-1). In the past two decades the share of total employment in the private-service sector has grown by 8 percent in the United States and by almost 7 percent in Canada.

Not only does the private-service sector bulk large in the workforces in both countries, but it is also characterized by the lowest union density

TABLE 10-1. Union Membership as a Percentage of Paid Employment by Industry (Union Density) and Percentage Distribution of Nonagricultural Wage and Salary Workers, Canada and the United States, 1986

	Union Density		Distribution Of Employment	
	Canada	U.S.	Canada	U.S.
Private services				
Trade	12.9	7.2	17.9	20.8
Finance, insurance, and real estate	9.2	2.6	6.0	6.7
Commercial services[a]	8.9	6.3	15.5	22.0
All private services	10.7	6.2	39.4	49.5
Other sectors				
Mining (Nonag. primary)	32.4	17.5	2.4	0.9
Manufacturing	41.6	24.0	19.3	21.3
Construction	34.8	22.0	4.4	5.2
Transportation and public utilities	58.4	35.4	8.2	6.0
Government (including education and health)	62.4	36.0	26.2	17.2
Education[a]	66.7		8.2	
Health[a]	55.2		9.7	
All other sectors	52.0	29.1	60.6	50.5
Total	35.7	17.7	100.0	100.0

Sources: Canada: Statistics Canada, Labour Market Activity Survey, 1986, special tabulations. United States: *Employment and Earnings*, January 1987, vol. 34, no. 1.

[a]In the United States, privately funded education and health establishments are included in commercial services, while those publicly funded, as well as other public establishments, are included in government. To attain approximate comparisons with the United States, all health and education employment in Canada was considered to be publicly funded and was included with government.

(excluding paid workers in agriculture). In both countries the private-service sector has a union density one-fifth that of the other sectors. In Canada in 1986, private services had a union density rate of 10.7 percent compared with 52.0 percent for the other sectors (see Table 10-2). In the United States the figures are 6.2 percent and 29.1 percent, respectively.

TABLE 10-2. Union Membership as a Percentage of Paid Employment (Union Density) Canada and the United States, 1968–1986 (Selected Years)

	Canada				United States			
	1968	1976	1984	1986	1968	1976	1984	1986
Private services								
Trade	11.0	8.5	12.5	12.9	9.2	6.8	7.9	7.2
Finance, insurance, and real estate	2.6	2.7	9.2	9.2	1.3	1.0	2.7	2.6
Commercial services[a]	8.3[b]	9.5[b]	9.0	8.9	9.8[b]	10.9[b]	7.3	6.3
All private services	8.8	7.9	10.6	10.7	8.5	7.8	6.9	6.2
Other sectors								
Other primary	54.7	41.5	34.2	32.4	42.5	42.4	17.7	17.5
Manufacturing	43.7	43.5	45.0	41.6	43.3	41.6	26.0	24.0
Construction	55.0	52.1	38.0	34.8	70.1	68.0	23.5	22.0
Transportation and public utilities	57.0	50.0	60.0	68.4	71.3	65.7	38.7	35.4
Government (including education and health)[a]	38.5	45.9	63.6	62.4	17.8	20.3	35.8	36.0
Education & health[a]	26.2	47.6	62.2	60.5				
All other sectors	45.6	46.1	54.0	52.0	41.2	39.1	30.4	29.1
Total	33.6	32.7	37.5	35.7	27.8[c]	24.6	19.1	17.7

Sources: *Handbook of Labor Statistics*, December 1980, U.S. Dept. of Labor Bureau of Labor Statistics; *Corporations and Labour Union Returns Act*, reports for 1968 and 1976; and Statistics Canada, Labour Market Activity Survey (LMAS), 1984 and 1986, special tabulations.

[a]See note, Table 10-1.

[b]The estimate of members of international and national unions in the private-service sector was prepared from the CALURA reports for 1968 and 1976 by adding the number of members in unions associated with this sector. An estimate of 10 percent of Services Employees International Union (SEIU) members was attributed to this sector on the advice of the SEIU research department. An additional 10 percent was added to the figures for Canada based on the approximate differences between U.S. internationals and the U.S. total in service in 1968.

[c]Includes union members not classified by industry.

From the equality of the ratios within each country, it follows that the ratio of private-service sector densities in Canada to those of the private-service sector in the United States is similar to the ratio between the countries for the other sectors, that is, approximately one and three-quarters to one.[5]

Trends in Union Density

Table 10-2 shows that in both countries, for the past three decades, union density in the private-service sector has been very low relative to the other sectors. In addition, in the United States the general trend over the period has been a decline in the rate for the sector as a whole and for two of the three components, trade and services.[6] In Canada, the long-term trend has not been the same as that in the United States. Trade, finance, and services all increased their union densities in the 1980s compared with the 1960s, whereas only finance in the United States was higher in 1986 than in 1968.

TABLE 10-3. Private-Services Union Density vs. Union Density in Other Sectors, Canada and the United States, Selected Years

	Canada				United States			
	1968	1976	1984	1986	1968	1976	1984	1986
Union Density								
Private services	8.8	7.9	10.6	10.7	8.5	7.8	6.9	6.2
All other sectors	45.6	46.1	54.0	52.0	41.2	39.1	30.4	29.1
Private Services Density as a percentage of all other services	19.3	24.2	19.6	20.7	20.6	19.9	22.7	21.3
Average private-services density as a percentage of all other services		20.9				21.1		

Sources: See Table 10-2.

The most remarkable observation concerning the long-term trends is the virtually identical relationship between the rates of private-service-sector union density to that in all other sectors in both Canada and the United States. This long-term stability is shown in Table 10-3. Although there is some small variation among the observations and between Canada and the United States, the fluctuations appear to be around a mean of 21 percent of all other sectors in both countries. This stability and identical relationship implies that there are factors inherent in the private-service sector in both countries that produce the low levels of union density relative to other industry sectors.

The stability of the relationship and its similarity in both countries also suggest that the factors governing the overall relationship of union density between Canada and the United States apply equally to the private-service sector and to all other sectors. Just as union density as a whole diverged between Canada and the United States from the 1960s to the 1980s (Meltz 1985), so union density diverged in the private-service sector. Apparently nothing unique in the private-service sector in Canada can explain the increase in union density in Canada and the decrease in the United States. However, before I examine this divergence, I turn to the impact of changes in the structure of employment.

The impact on overall union density of the shift in employment toward the private-service sector is shown in Table 10-4. The change in union density in the two countries from 1968 to 1986 and from 1984 to 1986 is divided into three sources: the shift in employment to the private-service sector; the change in union density within the private-service sector; and the change in union density in the other sectors. The impact of the shift in employment to the private-service sector was calculated by estimating the net change due to the loss in union membership from the reduction in other sector membership (assuming the union density in other sectors remained unchanged) and the gain from the increase in private-sector membership (again assuming the union density in the private-service sector remained unchanged).[7] The change in union density in the private-service sector was calculated by combining the change with the final-year (1986) proportion of employment in private services. The change in the union density in the other sectors was estimated by combining the change with the final-year (1986) proportion of employment in the other sectors.[8]

Between 1968 and 1986 the shift to the private-service sector in the

TABLE 10-4. Sources of Change in Union Density in Canada and the United States, 1968–1986

	1968–1986				1984–1986			
	Amount (%)		Distribution (%)		Amount (%)		Distribution (%)	
	Canada	U.S.	Canada	U.S.	Canada	U.S.	Canada	U.S.
1. Shift in employment to private service sector	− 2.5	− 2.7	− 119	27	−.7	−.3	37	23
2. Change in union density in private service sector	0.7	− 1.1	33	11	0	−.3	0	23
3. Change in union density in other sectors	3.9	− 6.1	186	62	− 1.2	−.7	63	54
Total change:[a]	2.1	− 10.1	100	100	− 1.8	− 1.4	100	100

Sources: See Table 10-2.
[a]Numbers may not add to totals due to rounding. Method of calculation: see text.

United States accounted for a little over a quarter of the decline in union density. In the case of Canada, union density would have been 2.5 percent higher had there not been a shift toward the services. From 1984 to 1986 the shift to private services again contributed approximately a quarter of the 1.4 percent decline in the United States. For Canada, the shift to private services, which was slightly larger than in the United States (1.5% vs. 1.2%), contributed almost four-tenths of the 1.8 percent decline in union density (see Table 10-1).

In the case of both countries, the largest part of the change in union density came from the change in union densities within sectors. Nevertheless, the shift to the private services still contributed between a quarter and over a third of the overall changes in union density.

The Low Private-Service-Sector Union Densities

There are a number of factors common to the two countries that contribute to explaining the continuing low levels of union density in the private-service sector. The workforces of both trade and commercial-service industries are composed of high proportions of groups that have below-average union density: younger workers, part-time workers, and women. The demand for workers in these industries tends to be concentrated in certain time periods requiring a relatively high proportion of part-time workers. When the baby boomers reached their teens they provided a pool of young workers available for part-time work. Since the labour force has aged, some of the retail outlets, for example McDonald's, are now employing some older workers on a part-time basis, as well as younger workers. Younger workers aged 20 to 24 have a union density rate of 21.0 percent compared with 36.1 percent for those aged 25 to 34 and 43.2 percent for those 35 to 44.[9] Part-time workers have half the density rate of full-time workers, 20.6 versus 38.5 percent, while female full-time workers have a density rate somewhat below that of males, 34.2 versus 41.5 percent. Other aspects are also associated with low union density. Turnover tends to be higher in these sectors (at least as measured by low job tenure, Statistics Canada 1988), and the average size of establishments is small (except for department stores).

Finance, insurance, and real estate also have characteristics that tend to be associated with lower union density. The establishment size in banking and real estate tends to be small. While insurance companies have large establishments, both they and banks tend to have workers who either identify with management (Lowe 1981) or dissociate themselves from unions (Schaefer 1988). There has been a strong paternal tradition within both banks and insurance companies and long-standing practices of promoting from within the organization. While wage rates used to be below average in banks and insurance companies, over the past decade there have been substantial increases (see Statistics Canada: Survey of Employment, Payrolls, and Hours; and Labour Market Activity Survey).

Management in both countries seems to have actively opposed unions in this sector, in particular, in department stores, banks, and insurance companies (Kochan, Katz, and McKersie 1986; Lowe 1981; Schaefer 1988; and Sufrin 1982). It seems clear that to date these factors have been strong enough to prevent any major union growth in the private-service sector in both countries.

Developments in Canada and the United States

The major finding in this paper is that while union density is low in the private-service sector in both countries, the differences between the two countries are the same as in the other sectors. Canadian density rates exceed U.S. density rates by approximately three-quarters in both private services and for all other sectors. When these differences are combined with the larger public-sector component in Canada, overall differences become two to one.[10]

There has been much discussion of the sources of difference in union density between Canada and the United States (Adams 1989; Bruce 1989; Kumar 1987; Lipset 1986; Meltz 1989, 1985; Rose and Chaison 1985, 1987, 1991; Troy 1990; and Weiler 1983). The primary factors that have been identified are the more supportive labour legislation and its enforcement in Canada and the greater proportion of publicly funded employment. Supportive legislation and its enforcement would appear to both encourage union organization and discourage employer opposition (Bruce, in this volume). Since the legislation applies equally to the private-service sector and the private-goods sector, the differences in legislation between the two countries do not explain the reason for the very low (and proportionately similar) union densities in the private-service sector. The relatively low private-service-sector densities must be explained by factors that are common to the economies of both countries: (1) the characteristics of employment noted above (small establishments, part-time workers, young workers, higher turnover); (2) employee identification with management; (3) an antipathy toward or an uneasiness about trade unions; (4) vigorous employer opposition; and (5) inability of the labour movement to develop an organization structure and approach appropriate for the particular needs of these white-collar and service workers.

Even though the private-service-sector densities are low in both countries, the density in Canada is now three-quarters more than in the United States (10.7 percent vs. 6.2 percent). This difference, which is almost identical to that for all other sectors (52.0 percent vs. 29.1 percent) seems to be attributable to factors common to all industry sectors. As indicated above, I believe the largest component of these common factors is the more supportive labour legislation in Canada and its greater enforcement. The following discussion on a sector-by-sector basis indicates some recent developments in the private-service sector, particularly in Canada, that may be contributing to the widening union-density gap between the two countries.

Trade

The extent of organization in trade has fluctuated, but the trend seems to be a slight increase in Canada over time and a decrease in the United States. Supermarkets have tended to be the most highly organized area. Initially meatcutters were among the first to organize; as a skilled trade, meatcutters had characteristics similar to tradesmen in construction and manufacturing. Once the large supermarket chains had organized (including clerks), labour was effectively taken out of competition. In Canada, a move by one supermarket group (Dominion Stores) to get around unionization by franchising some of their less successful stores was thwarted by the Ontario Labour Relations Board (see below).

The most significant event in the trade industry in Canada in the last decade was the organization of workers in seven stores of the largest department store chain in Canada, the T. Eaton Company, by the Retail, Wholesale, and Department Store Union. Seven stores were organized in 1984, long after an earlier but unsuccessful organizing effort in 1948 (Sufrin 1982). After a bitter strike of almost six months[11] and major labour-movement and interest-group support, the union signed an agreement without a ratification vote. The agreement was deemed to provide so little for the employees that six of the seven stores were decertified at the end of the year when the contract expired. There was one lasting impact of the strike. The uncompromising attitude of Eaton's produced such a negative public reaction in the Province of Ontario that when the 1985 provincial election produced a minority government, the accord signed by the New Democratic Party with the Liberal party, which permitted the Liberals to govern for two years, contained an agreement by the Liberals to introduce first contract arbitration.

While the organizing drive at Eaton's did not produce long-term results, there was a more positive development at what was then the second largest department store chain, Simpson's, with five stores organized in 1985 by the Retail, Wholesale, and Department Store Union. Management at Simpson's did not vigorously oppose the union the way Eaton's had, and an agreement was reached without a strike. That agreement was renewed subsequently and continued when The Bay acquired Simpson's.

This mixed experience may be representative of the limited increase in union density in the trade sector in Canada.

Finance

Finance is the one private-service sector in the United States where there have been net increases in union density in the past two decades and only a fractional decline recently. In Canada the Labour Market Activity Survey puts union density in this sector at 3.5 times the U.S. rate.[12] As will be indicated, there was a burst of organizing activity in the late 1970s, but this has stopped.

In Canada, banks are chartered by the federal government and subject to federal labour legislation (the Canada Labour Code). There are only eleven chartered banks, of which six dominate the field with thousands of branches. Major efforts to organize the banks in the 1970s ran up against the requirement that a union organize a majority of all workers in a bank. The labour movement fought to be able to organize workers on a branch-by-branch basis, and in 1977 the Canada Labour Relations Board permitted certification of individual branches (Lowe 1980; Ponak and Moore 1981). A brief burst of organizing followed, but few long-term gains were achieved except in branches of banks in highly unionized areas. As Lowe (1980, 1981) documents, there was particularly strong employer opposition, and workers in certified branches got no more in wages and benefits (and sometimes less) than employees in nonunionized branches. Human-resource practices were also improved. The combination of high-turnover, part-time work, a high percentage of women in the large clerical sections, an uneasiness about identification with unions, the large number of small branches, and the improved human-resource policies (see Kochan, Katz, and McKersie 1986) made it difficult to sustain increased organizing in the banks.

A major exception was the organizing of the VISA centre workers of the Canadian Imperial Bank of Commerce (CIBC). The large concentration of approximately four hundred workers was organized in 1985 by the Union of Bank Employees and was on strike for seven and a half months. The Canadian Labour Congress (CLC) threw its support behind the union to the extent that strike pay was more than the employees were earning before the strike. There was also a large public relations campaign in favour of the union. After many allegations of unfair practices by CIBC, the Canada Labour Relations Board finally activated its first-contract arbitration provision and arbitrated a contract. A second contract was negotiated without a strike. Although the extent of organizing is not large, these examples indicate some of the forces at work in Canada in this sector.

Insurance Companies

The Canadian Labour Congress (CLC) launched a major organizing drive of insurance companies in 1974, establishing the Association of Commercial and Technical Employees (ACTE) as the vehicle to organize the workers. ACTE was to be a transitory organization that would either evolve into a trade union or enable members to transfer to existing unions. After a year-long public relations campaign and efforts to sign up workers, not one insurance company was organized. The problems in organizing included the "hothouse" nature of the union; ACTE was not a real union with roots. The image of unions in general was also a problem in that ACTE was unable to appeal to a white-collar group that had been part of a traditionally paternal relationship (Schaefer 1988). At the same time, this industry has long had a low-wage profile and there have been problems of lack of due process. The organizing drive did accomplish something: The insurance companies raised the wages of their employees and began to improve their personnel practices (Schaefer 1988).

Commercial Services

This large sector is made up of segments with widely different characteristics. It ranges from the highly paid professional services to business management, to the low paid personal services and accommodation and food services.

In total, there is a growing gap between the union densities in this sector in Canada and the United States. In both 1968 and 1976, union density in the commercial services was higher in the United States than in Canada (see Table 10-2). The major change occurred in the 1980s when union density in Canada remained close to 9.0 percent while it declined sharply in the United States.

Guttman (1988) discusses the problem of organizing workers in the commercial-service sector, where many employees work for contractors or "employee leasing agencies" in the janitorial, food services, and clerical industries, which "insulate themselves from the employment relationships through the use of subcontractors." Once the contractor becomes unionized, the facility owner can terminate the contact and thereby elimi- nate the union. This situation occurs in both Canada and the United States, but Guttman stresses the role of antiunion consultants and non- supportive labour legislation in the United States in raising the costs and reducing the probability of a union being certified. He also refers to a positive development in the 1987 case of Arcade Maintenance Inc., in the Pittsburgh Region of the National Labor Relations Board, where the question whether Mellon Bank should be held liable for firing a cleaning contractor because the contractor signed a union agreement was settled with all employees being reinstated to the full terms of the collective agreement with back pay and benefits totalling $750,000 (Guttman 1988, 26). Whether the case is a straw in the wind in the United States remains to be seen.

Related cases in Canada have been those of Beckers and Mr. Grocer. The Beckers case concerned franchise owners within a convenience store chain. The issue was whether they were really owners or employees. The arbitration board held that they were employees (*Labour Arbitration Cases* 1973, 337–348). In the Mr. Grocer case, a supermarket chain, Do- minion Stores, sold several of its stores for operation by independent operators under the name Mr. Grocer. The stores that were sold had been unionized. The Ontario Labour Relations Board held that the em- ployees of Mr. Grocer were still covered by the original contract (On- tario Labour Relations Board 1986). Both these decisions have implica- tions if franchise-operation employees are ever certified.

It would appear that management has been more aggressive in the United States in hiring consultants to prevent union organizing and that this has been facilitated by the less supportive labour legislation in the United States and the less rigorous prosecution of unfair labour prac- tices, especially in the late 1970s and the 1980s.

Issues for the Future

The characteristics of the private-service sector seem to combine all of the elements that produce the least unionization: high part-time employ- ment; high percentage of youths; high numbers of women; many small units; high turnover (at least in trade and parts of commercial service); tradition of identification with management and of hostility to unions; and strong management opposition to unions. While the legislation in

Canada has been deemed to be favourable to unionization (Adams 1989; Meltz 1985; Weiler 1983), it has not been sufficient to offset the combination of factors just cited.

Are there changes in the rules that government should consider to assist unions in organizing this sector? Are there changes the trade-union movement should undertake itself?

With respect to the issue of rules, it has been noted that legislation following an ultimately unsuccessful contract negotiation in retail trade led to the introduction of first contract arbitration in Ontario. (Four provinces as well as the federal government now have various forms of this legislation.) As well, Ontario Labour Relations Board rules have provided some potential assistance to franchise operators if they want to unionize. However, the question remains of the treatment of subcontractors' employees, who are now virtually unprotected if the subcontractor loses the contract with the primary employer. Perhaps it is time to consider what additions to labour legislation are necessary to prevent these employees being, in effect, deprived of basic protection under labour relations acts. One further issue that could relate to rules concerns the treatment of part-time workers. It has been traditional practice to establish separate bargaining units for part-time workers. Unions have not looked favourably on part-time workers, viewing them as competitors and as exerting downward pressure on wage rates and working conditions. Perhaps the time has come for both labour relations boards and unions to take a different approach to part-time workers by including part-timers in regular bargaining units and encouraging employers to prorate wages and benefits. Such a development could assist both the workers and union growth.[13]

A larger issue for unions relates to professional and quasi-managerial workers. It is certainly no accident that with the exception of the Teamsters, the only large unions that are outside the central labour federations are professional associations, particularly nurses and teachers. A major factor in the failure of ACTE was the inability of the CLC to appeal to insurance workers. They did not want to be associated with unions. This same issue seems relevant to the inability to organize bank workers. Perhaps it is time to consider the possibility of an alternative grouping within the labour movement, such as a central federation of professional and quasi-managerial workers and an organization of salaried employees as exist in Sweden. Such groupings might be better able to promote the organization of workers in the private-service sector than are present union configurations. Public-sector professional, quasi-managerial, and clerical workers have been organized, but not those in the private-service sector. With the expected continuation of the shift of employment to the private-service sector and the decline in union density in most other sectors, the labour movement faces a fundamental challenge but also an opportunity for growth in the 1990s.

Notes

1. An earlier version of this paper was prepared for the conference "North American Labour Movements into the 1990s: Similarities or Differences?" held at the Center for International Affairs, Harvard University, 3–5 February 1989. The author would like to acknowledge the suggestions of conference organizer Jane Jenson and the assistance received from Richard Veevers and Isabel Balon of Statistics Canada and the library and office staff of the Centre for Industrial Relations, University of Toronto. Peter Bruce, Virginia Diamond, Reuben Guttman, Leo Troy, and Paul Weiler provided helpful comments. Financial support for the research was provided by the Humanities and Social Sciences Committee of the University of Toronto and the Social Sciences and Humanities Research Council of Canada, through the Structural Change in Canadian Industrial Relations project at the Centre for Industrial Relations, University of Toronto.

2. While union membership has continued to increase in Canada, all sources of information show a recent decline in union density:

	1984	1985	1986	1987	1988
Union density as a percentage of nonagricultural paid workers					
Labour Canada (1988)	39.6	39.0	37.7	37.6	36.6
Statistics Canada's Labour Market Activity Survey (1984, 1986)	37.5		35.7		
Corporations and Labour Unions Returns Act (1988)	35.6	34.8	34.5		
Number of union members (thousands)					
Labour Canada (1988)	3651	3666	3730	3782	3841

3. The following table provides a list of the main subindustries within services:

Union Density and Share of Nonagricultural Employment within the
Private-Service Sector, Canada, 1984 and 1986

	Union Density		Percentage of Nonagricultural employment	
	1984	1986	1984	1986
Trade	12.5	12.9	17.4	17.9
Wholesale	12.7	13.7	4.2	4.6
Retail	12.4	12.6	13.3	13.3
Finance, insurance, real estate	9.2	9.2	5.6	6.0
Finance industries	6.0	7.1	3.0	3.3
Insurance carriers	14.3	14.8	1.2	1.1
Insurance agencies and real estate industries	11.5	9.6	1.4	1.6
Commercial services	11.5	9.6	1.4	1.6
Religious organizations	2.4	7.1	0.7	0.7
Amusement and recreation	12.8	10.4	0.9	1.2
Services to business management	6.2	6.9	3.9	4.2
Personal services	7.8	7.2	1.4	1.6
Accommodation and food	10.0	9.6	6.1	6.0
Misc. services	12.9	11.7	1.9	2.0

Sources: Statistics Canada, Labour Market Activity Survey, special tabulations; and Kumar 1988.
Note: Due to rounding, subsectors may not add to sector totals.

4. Due to classification differences between the two countries, the Canadian figure is only an approximation of the American approach. In the United States, government employment is defined as employment derived from direct or indirect government expenditures. To approach this definition I have removed education and health-care workers from the services sector in Canada and included them in public administration. For a comparison of public versus private-sector densities in the two countries, see Troy (1990). Troy estimates that in 1985, public-sector union density was 63.9 percent in Canada versus 32.5 percent in the United States. Comparable figures for the private sector in 1985 were 21.0 percent in Canada and 15.5 percent in the United States.

5. In the case of finance, insurance, and real estate, there is a large proportionate difference, 9.2 percent in Canada versus 2.6 percent in the United States. Data from the reports of the Corporations and Labour Unions Returns Act (CALURA) consistently show a much lower figure for finance, insurance, and real estate. CALURA shows 2.8 percent for 1986 vs. 9.2 percent from the labour force survey. The figures for 1984 are 2.7 percent vs. 9.2 percent, respectively. See Kumar (1988), CALURA (1988), and special tabulations from Statistics Canada of the 1986 Labour Market Activity Survey (LMAS). Using CALURA data and figures from the Economic Council of Canada, Troy (1990) has estimated that 8.5 percent of the trade-sector union membership and 50 percent of the finance, insurance, and real estate membership in 1985 was in the public sector. This reduces the private trade-sector union density by 6 percent and the private finance, insurance, and real estate density by 50 percent. I have chosen to rely more on the LMAS because of the comprehensiveness of the survey and the extent of the detailed information that is available. For an examination of the Canadian service sector using CALURA data, see Betcherman (1989).

6. The service sector in Canada includes education and health, which for the most part are included with public administration in the United States. To obtain comparable data for Canada for the years before 1984 would require reclassifying union members by industry. It was not possible to undertake this task for this chapter.

7. For example, the impact of the shift in employment in Canada between 1968 and 1986 was calculated by multiplying the change in the share of the private-service-sector employment, 6.7 percent, by total employment in 1968, 6,391,000. To the resulting figure of 428,197 was applied the other sector union density in 1968 (45.6 percent) as a reduction in membership and the private-service-sector density of 8.8 percent as an addition. The net reduction is 157,577 on a base of 6,391,000 or 2.5 percent.

8. For example, between 1968 and 1986 private-service-sector density rose by 1.9 percent on a base share of 39.4 percent, producing an increase of 0.7 percent, while the other sector's density rose by 6.4 percent on a base of 60.6 percent, producing an increase of 3.9 percent.

9. These and the immediately following data are for 1986 from Statistics Canada's Labour Market Activity Survey. The union density rates for the remaining age groups are: 45–54: 43.4 percent; 55–64: 43.2 percent; 65–69: 13.5 percent.

10. For a discussion of the impact of public employment on Canada's union density versus that in the United States, see Troy (1990).

11. The Ontario Labour Relations Act specifies that within six months from the commencement of a lawful strike employees can request reinstatement in their former employment.

12. As noted above in footnote 5, the CALURA data indicate a union-density rate for finance, insurance, and real estate of 2.8 percent in Canada in 1986, only a fraction above the U.S. rate of 2.6 percent.

13. In 1992 the proposed changes to the Ontario Labour Relations Act combined bargaining units of part-time and full-time employees and provided protection from subcontracting to prevent unionization.

References

Adams, Roy J. 1989. "North American Industrial Relations: Divergent Trends in Canada and the United States." *International Labour Review*, no. 1, 47–64.

Betcherman, Gordon. 1989. "Union Membership in a Service Economy." In the proceedings of the twenty-sixth annual meeting of the Canadian Industrial Relations Association, Quebec City.

Bruce, Peter. 1989. "Political Parties and Labor Legislation in Canada and the U.S." *Industrial Relations* (Berkeley) 28(2): 115–41.

Corporations and Labour Unions Returns Act (CALURA). Statistics Canada, Catalogue 71–2c2 Annual, Part II—Labour Unions, reports for selected years.

Freeman, Richard B. 1989. "What Does the Future Hold for U.S. Unionism?" *Relations Industrielles* 44(1): 25–46.

Guttman, Reuben A. 1988. "Representation Campaigns and the Future of Labor: A Legal and Theoretical Perspective." Paper prepared for delivery at the Midwest Political Science Association annual meeting, Chicago.

Kochan, Thomas A., Harry C. Katz, and Robert B. McKersie. 1986. *The Transformation of American Industrial Relations*. New York: Basic Books.

Kumar, Pradeep. 1987. "Organized Labour in Canada and the United States: Similarities and Differences." Paper presented at the thirty-sixth annual conference of the Association of Labor Relations Agencies, Albany, N.Y.

———. 1988. *Estimates of Unionism and Collective Bargaining Coverage in Canada*. Kingston, Ont.: School of Industrial Relations, Queen's University.

Labour Arbitration Cases. 1973. Second series, vol. 1. Agincourt, Ont.: Canada Law Book.

Labour Canada. 1988. *Directory of Labour Organizations in Canada*. Ottawa, Ont.: Ministry of Supply and Services Canada.

Labour Market Activity Survey (LMAS). Statistics Canada, Ottawa, special tabulations for 1984 and 1986.

Lipset, Seymour Martin. 1986. "North American Labor Movements: A Comparative Perspective." In S. M. Lipset, ed., *Unions in Transition: Entering the Second Century*, 421–51. San Francisco: ICS Press.

Lowe, Graham. 1980. *Bank Unionization in Canada: A Preliminary Analysis.* Toronto: Centre for Industrial Relations, University of Toronto.

————. 1981. "Causes of Unionization in Canadian Banks." *Relations Industrielles* 36(4): 865–93.

Meltz, Noah M. 1985. "Labor Movements in Canada and the United States." In Thomas A. Kochan, ed., *Challenges and Choices Facing American Labor*, 315–34. Cambridge, Mass.: MIT Press.

————. 1989. "Inter-state versus Inter-provincial Differences in Union Density." *Industrial Relations* (Berkeley) 28(2): 142–58.

Ontario Labour Relations Board Reports. 1986. Toronto: Ontario Labour Relations Board.

Ponak, Alan, and Larry Moore. 1981. "Canadian Bank Unionism: Perspectives and Issues." *Relations Industrielles* 36(1): 3–34.

Rose, Joseph B., and Gary N. Chaison. 1985. "The State of the Unions: United States and Canada." *Journal of Labor Research*, 97–112.

————. 1987. "The State of Unions Revisited: The United States and Canada." In *Proceedings of the 24th Annual Meeting of the Canadian Industrial Relations Association*, 576–94. Hamilton, Ont.: McMaster University.

————. 1988. "Continental Divide: The Direction and Fate of North American Unions." In Donna Sockell, David Lewin, and David Lipskky, eds., *Advances in Industrial and Labor Relations.* Greenwich, Conn.: JAI.

Schaefer, Mark. 1988. "Organizing in the Insurance Industry—Factors in White-collar Unionization." Paper prepared for Industrial Relations 2001F, Industrial Relations Theory, Centre for Industrial Relations, University of Toronto, December.

Statistics Canada. 1988. *The Labour Force, December 1987.* Catalogue 71–001 Monthly, January.

Sufrin, Eileen. 1982. *The Eaton Drive: The Campaign to Organize Canada's Largest Department Store 1948 to 1952.* Toronto: Fitzhenry and Whiteside.

Troy, Leo. 1990. "Is the U.S. Unique in the Decline of Private Sector Unionism?" *Journal of Labor Research* 9(2): 111–43.

Weiler, Paul. 1983. "Promises to Keep: Securing Workers' Rights to Self-organization under the NLRA." *Harvard Law Review* 96 (June): 1769–1827.

11   RUTH MILKMAN

Union Responses to Workforce Feminization in the United States

The rapid feminization of the U.S. labor force in the 1970s and 1980s, against the background of a popular feminist resurgence, generated unprecedented changes in the relationship of women workers to the organized labor movement.[1] Union membership became increasingly feminized, and issues of special concern to women workers gained new prominence on many unions' collective-bargaining and political agendas.

Yet rapid private-sector deunionization and related processes of economic restructuring, which occurred in precisely the same period that the social effects of workforce feminization became manifest, set limits on union responsiveness to the growth of the female workforce. The resilient historical traditions of male-centered unionism further constrained the capacities of many labor organizations to address the needs of their newly enlarged female constituencies. Indeed, the process of change has been uneven, with some unions responding lethargically and others quite creatively to feminization. In general, the unions that have most effectively met the challenge posed by the gender transformation of the labor market have been those few that have gained rather than lost members in recent years (typically, relatively young organizations recruiting primarily in the public sector). In these unions, a new kind of gender politics is emerging, combining demands for gender equality with a recognition of the special burdens imposed by socially constructed gender differences on women workers.

This chapter explores the historical and contemporary factors shaping recent union responses to workforce feminization in the United States, with particular attention to interunion variations and to changing labor-movement approaches to women workers. I argue that although women's recent advancement in the labor movement has been less extensive than gender transformations in the workforce and in the larger society might lead one to expect, the innovative gender politics emerging in those unions least constrained by the forces of deunionization or patriarchal traditions suggests some basis for optimism. In the event of a future revival of organized labor, when the conditions favoring change that now exist in only a few unions would become more widespread, women workers and gender politics will likely have a central place in the union movement.

The feminization of the labor force in the United States in recent decades is widely recognized as the single most important transformation in the workplace, if not in the larger society, during the postwar period. While the process of incorporating women workers into the waged labor force began in the early nineteenth century, only since World War II has a sustained attachment to paid work become typical for adult women. The overall female labor-force participation rate rose from 34 percent in 1950 to 43 percent in 1970, and then to 58 percent in 1990. The male participation rate, in comparison, was 77 percent in 1990, down from 86 percent in 1950. Women make up nearly half (45 percent) of the labor force today, compared to 29 percent in 1950 (U.S. Dept. of Labor 1983: 9, 11; U.S. Dept. of Labor 1991: 16).

The proportion of women among the country's union members has also grown dramatically in the postwar period, from 24 percent as recently as 1970 to 38 percent in 1990 (U.S. Dept. of Labor 1980: 62; U.S. Dept. of Labor 1991: 228). This feminization of union membership, however, has occurred in the context of an equally dramatic process of deunionization of the workforce as a whole. Among nonagricultural workers, union density was twice as high in 1956 as in 1986, falling from 36 percent to 18 percent in those three decades. The only major area of union growth in recent years has been in the public sector; private-sector union density fell to only 14 percent in 1986 (Freeman 1988: 63–65). The recent feminization of union membership is due largely to the extensive recruitment of women into public-sector unions, combined with large losses of male union membership in the private sector.

The general erosion of union density is one major constraint on labor-movement responses to workforce feminization. Another is the legacy of patriarchal union traditions. As many feminist commentators have noted, unions as institutions often have been indifferent or even hostile to women workers and have developed as male-dominated institutions that represent the sectional interests and cultural orientations of male workers (see Hartmann 1976; Cockburn 1983). Yet these accounts tend to overlook the fact that unions vary considerably in the degree to which they recruit women members, as well as in the extent to which women gain leadership roles within them, and in their level of engagement with issues of special concern to women workers. Indeed, union responses to the process of workforce feminization have been far from uniform.

Public-sector unionism, the site of the most extensive change in the relationship of women to the labor movement, is the most recent in a series of waves of worker organization that have shaped the labor movement in the twentieth century. Broadly speaking, organized labor today is the product of four such waves of unionization, each of which recruited in a distinct sector of the economy and had a different relationship to women workers: the craft unionism of the late nineteenth century, the "new unionism" of the 1910s, the industrial unionism of the 1930s and 1940s, and finally the public-sector unionism of the recent period.

The particular historical contexts in which each type of unionism arose shaped their varied approaches to women workers—approaches that later crystallized into institutional traditions that still survive intact today. Thus, to understand the contemporary relationship of labor unions to the growing population of women workers requires an appreciation of the diverse historical processes from which today's labor organizations originated.

Women and Unions in Historical Perspective

Throughout the twentieth century, as Table 11-1 shows, the feminization of the U.S. labor force has been accompanied by a parallel feminization of union membership, although with a definite lag.[2] The table reveals the extent to which women workers were recruited into unions during each historical wave of labor organization. It is evident that the craft unionism

TABLE II-I. Feminization of the U.S. Labor Force and of Union Membership, 1920–1988

Year	Number of Women in the Workforce	% of All Workers	Number of Women Union Members	% of All Union Members
1910[a]	7,789,000	20.9	76,750	3.6
1920[a]	8,430,000	20.4	397,000	7.9
1930[a]	10,679,000	22.0	260,000	7.7
1940[a]	13,015,000	24.4	800,000	9.4
1944[a]	19,110,000	34.7	3,000,000	21.8
1954[a]	19,678,000	31.1	2,950,000	16.6
1956[a]	21,495,000	32.2	3,400,000	18.6
1960[a]	23,240,000	33.4	3,304,000	18.3
1964[a]	25,412,000	34.8	3,413,000	19.1
1968[a]	29,204,000	37.1	3,940,000	19.5
1970[b]	31,543,000	38.1	5,398,000	23.9
1974[b]	36,211,000	39.4	6,038,000	25.0
1978[b]	42,631,000	41.6	6,857,000	28.1
1980[c]	45,487,000	42.5	7,191,000	31.9
1985[c]	51,050,000	44.2	6,910,000	35.6
1990[c]	56,554,000	45.3	7,327,000	38.4

Sources: 1910–1944 data: Dickason 1947: 70–71. 1956–1980 data: U.S. Dept. of Labor 1980: 62; U.S. Dept. of Labor 1983: 49. 1985–1990 data: U.S. Dept. of Labor 1986: 213; U.S. Dept. of Labor 1987: 219; U.S. Dept. of Labor 1991: 163, 228.
[a]Unions.
[b]Unions and employee associations.
[c]Represented by unions and employee associations (including nonmembers covered by contracts).

of the late nineteenth century and the first decade of the twentieth produced only minimal organization among women. Historically these unions, which banded together in the American Federation of Labor (AFL) in the 1880s, viewed women's labor as a threat to skill and wage levels, and most of them therefore excluded women (as well as blacks and many immigrant groups) from membership outright, until as late as the 1940s in some cases (Kessler-Harris 1975). This was male-centered unionism in its most extreme form, the source of deeply patriarchal labor-movement traditions that linger today. Indeed, the craft unions on the contemporary labor scene that originated in this period—such as the construction-trades "brotherhoods" and the machinists' union—are among those least receptive to women workers and their specific concerns, faithful to the legacy of their own past.

A second wave of unionism appeared in the 1910s, centered in the garment industry. This "new unionism," at once an outgrowth of craft unionism and a forerunner of the industrial unions of the 1930s, generated a fivefold increase in the number of women union members. The clothing-trades unions abandoned craft exclusionism in this period and recruited huge numbers of unskilled and semiskilled workers into their ranks, the vast majority of them young women. By 1920, almost half (43 percent) of all female union members were employed in the clothing trades (Wolman 1924).

Despite the feminization of their memberships, however, the leaders of these unions remained overwhelmingly male, and they tended to view their women members paternalistically—as weak workers in need of special protection, not as equal partners in the labor struggle. The garment unions today remain deeply marked by their historical origins, still with predominantly male leaders who maintain a paternalistic stance toward their overwhelmingly female (and now, Third World immigrant female) members.

The 1920s and early 1930s was an era of deunionization, when the absolute number of both female and male union members fell. But as early as 1940, the massive industrial organizing drives of the late 1930s brought the number of women union members to twice the 1920 level. By 1944, the peak of the wartime economic mobilization, there were three million women union members—nearly eight times the 1920 figure. But since these gains were paralleled by equally dramatic increases in union density among male workers, women's representation among union members lagged far behind their increased presence in the workforce.

While most of the Congress of Industrial Organizations (CIO) unions targeted predominantly male-employing industries and had an almost exclusively male leadership, their attitude toward women was different from that of both the craft unions and the "new unionism." Against the background of the suffrage victory and the growth of women's employment in the 1920s and 1930s, there was a shift in the larger political culture away from the traditional emphasis on the differences between women and men workers (implicit in both craft-union exclusionism and the paternalism of the "new unions") and toward a new, modern vision of gender equality. The CIO captured this new political thrust, explicitly opposing discrimination on the basis of sex, color, and creed, in a deliberate departure from craft-union tradition. This was a limited notion of gender equality, however, rooted in the broader principles of class solidarity and in opposition to employer efforts to divide the workforce through discriminatory policies.

The unions that emerged in this period have maintained a consistent commitment to the general principle of equality, and some of them were leading supporters of legislation against sex discrimination in the 1960s (Harrison 1988). With the exception of World War II, however, women remained peripheral to most of these unions, which were based in the heavily male basic manufacturing sector.

Finally, starting in the 1960s (precisely when overall union density in the United States began to fall) a fourth group of unions assumed prominence, mainly in the public sector but also in some private-sector service industries, such as health care. Only in this period, as Table 11-1 shows, did the gap between women's representation among union members and in the larger workforce begin to narrow significantly. Despite the fact that women were a rapidly expanding component of the overall workforce during these years, union density among them remained relatively stable, while for men it fell, at first gradually and later more sharply. In 1956, 31 percent of men and 16 percent of women workers were unionized; by 1990, the figure was 21 percent for men, while among the rapidly expanding pool of women workers, it held nearly steady at 15 percent (LeGrande 1978: 9; U.S. Dept. of Labor 1991: 228).[3] In this period, recruitment of women accounted for most of the growth in total union membership.

The unions most active in this recent wave of worker organization rarely set out to organize women "as women"; rather, the feminization of their memberships was an unintended consequence of recruiting heavily in fields where women workers are particularly well represented: at one point, teaching; later, health care; and most recently, public-sector clerical and service work. Ultimately, because this organizing occurred in a period of feminist resurgence and of broad changes in gender relations in the larger society, these unions not only recruited women as members but also (albeit to a much lesser extent) as leaders.

The unions that came of age in this period have been particularly active in reformulating traditional labor issues in order to better address the concerns of women workers. For example, the American Federation of State, County, and Municipal Employees (AFSCME) and the Service

Employees International Union (SEIU), the two largest unions in this category, led major campaigns for pay equity or "comparable worth" in the 1980s (Bell 1985). Indeed, partly as a result of these efforts, unionization has significantly narrowed the gender gap in earnings in the public sector (Freeman and Leonard 1987).

Within the labor movement today, then, many organizations are carrying on old traditions, be they inherited from nineteenth-century craft unionism, the "new unionism" of the 1910s, or 1930s industrial unionism. In contrast, the newer public and service-sector unions reflect more contemporary influences. The diverse responses of unions to workforce feminization reflect their varying historical roots, with the youngest and most dynamic unions tending to be most responsive to women workers and their special concerns. This pattern is reinforced by the characteristically greater openness of younger organizations to new ideas and modes of operation and the relative inflexibility of more "mature" unions with a more routinized existence and an entrenched bureaucracy that is loyal to established traditions.

The youngest unions are also those least hobbled by deunionization. In governmental agencies, especially at the state and local level, management opposition to unionism is far less formidable than in comparable private-sector workplaces, and unionization victories are thus considerably easier to achieve. Political pressure as well can often be exerted to advance unionism in the public sector (Freeman 1988). While organization remains minimal among the millions of women "pink-collar workers" in such deeply antiunion private industries as banking and insurance, some inroads have been made among clericals employed by manufacturing firms with unionized blue-collar workforces in the postwar period (Wagner 1979). More recently, clericals employed by private-sector universities (similar to public-sector institutions in that they are nonprofit operations with above-average vulnerability to political pressures) have also successfully unionized (Ladd-Taylor 1985; Gold 1988; Green 1988; Hurd 1989).

Patterns of Women's Union
Membership and Leadership

As a result of the rapid growth of unionism among pink- and white-collar women workers in recent years, the composition of the organized female labor force today looks quite different from the traditional image

TABLE 11-2. Women Members of Labor Organizations, Selected Industry Groups, 1991

| Industry Group | Number of Women Union Members (thousands) | Women Members as a Percentage of: | | Distribution of All Women Workers (%) |
		Organized Women in All Industries	All Women Employed in This Industry	
Public administration	594	9.7	24.9	4.9
Education	2,141	34.9	35.1	12.5
Services	1,150	18.7	7.1	33.1
Wholesale and retail trade	574	9.4	5.6	20.9
Transportation, communication, and public utilities	679	11.1	30.0	4.6
Finance, insurance, and real estate	92	1.5	2.1	8.9
Manufacturing	867	14.1	13.4	13.3
Mining and construction	35	0.6	6.1	1.2
Agriculture, forestry, and fishing	6	0.1	1.7	0.7
All industries	6,138	100.0	12.6	100.0

Source: Unpublished U.S. Current Population Survey data, provided by Barry Hirsch and Dave MacPherson, Department of Economics, Florida State University.

of the labor movement. As Table 11-2 shows, in 1991, the most recent year for which an industrial breakdown is available, nearly half (45 percent) of all women union members were employed either in education or public administration, even though these sectors account for only 17 percent of all women in the workforce. More than a quarter (28 percent) of the unionized female workforce were employed in either sales or services, reflecting (although still lagging behind) the enormous growth in employment in these sectors in recent decades. Only 14 percent of unionized women worked for manufacturing firms, labor's traditional stronghold. Indeed, while the manufacturing-based unions have suffered a sharp decline in recent years, unionism has grown rapidly in the public and service sectors, and this growth has been based on extensive recruitment of women.

While the industrial breakdown shown in Table 11-2 does not fully correspond to the historical waves of unionization identified above, the public-sector unions now dwarf all of their predecessors in female membership recruitment. The same basic pattern is also apparent from the data in Table 11-3, which shows female membership (and leadership) in the eleven individual unions that had 200,000 or more women members in 1985. Many of these organizations are based wholly or partly in the public sector, although in some cases their traditional jurisdictions (as suggested by their names) bear at best a remote relationship to the actual sources of their membership growth in recent years. The extreme case of this is the Teamsters' union, which now has half a million female members scattered through a wide range of occupations and industries. The Communication Workers of America (CWA) also recruits extensively outside its traditional jurisdiction, in both the public and private sectors. And virtually all of these unions listed have undertaken efforts to recruit white-collar workers outside their traditional base. For example, the Hotel and Restaurant Employees organized clerical workers at Yale University recently, and even the International Ladies' Garment Workers (ILGWU) now has a Professional and Clerical Employees division.

Recruitment of female members is only one aspect of the impact of workforce feminization on organized labor. As the case of the clothing unions earlier in this century illustrates, a large percentage of women in a union's membership may be a necessary precondition for a transformation in the gender composition of union leadership and for union attention to "women's issues," but it is by no means a sufficient condition for such a transformation. The large influx of female members into a range of different labor organizations in recent years has had a limited impact on the overall character of these unions or their institutional functioning, especially at the national level. Women's representation in top leadership posts, as Table 11-3 shows, is disproportionately small in relation to their representation in union membership in all eleven cases, and in most the disparity remains vast, despite some recent progress in incorporating women into leadership positions.

Although the data are much too fragmentary to warrant any definite conclusions on this point, it is suggestive that the two unions in this group with no women at all among their national officers and board members (the Electrical Workers and the Teamsters) are both old-line

TABLE 11-3. Female Membership and Leadership in Selected Labor
Organizations, 1978–1990

Organization	Year	Women Members (thousands)	Women as % of All Members	Women Officers and Board Members	Women as % of All Officers and Board Members
National Education	1978	1,240	75	5	55
Association	1985	1,000	60	3	33
	1990	na	na	6	67
International	1978	481	25	0	0
Brotherhood of	1985	485	26	0	0
Teamsters	1990	400	25	0	0
United Food and	1978	480	39	2	3
Commercial	1990	663	51	3	8
Workers					
American Federation	1978	408	40	1	3
of State, County	1985	450	45	4	14
and Municipal	1990	600	50	5	17
Employees					
Service Employees	1978	312	50	7	15
International	1985	435	50	9	18
Union	1990	420	45	13	34
American Federation	1978	300	60	8	25
of Teachers	1985	366	60	11	32
	1990	455	65	10	25
Communication	1978	259	51	0	0
Workers of	1985	338	52	1	6
America	1990	338	52	1	6
International	1978	304	30	0	0
Brotherhood of	1985	330	30	0	0
Electrical Workers	1990	240	30	0	0
Amalgamated	1978	331	66	6	15
Clothing and	1985	228	65	3	9
Textile Workers'	1990	160	61	5	20
Union					
International Ladies'	1978	279	80	2	7
Garment Workers'	1983	219	85	3	13
Union	1990	145	83	4	22
Hotel and Restaurant	1978	181	42	1	4
Employees	1985	200	50	2	8
	1990	143	48	1	4

Sources: 1978 data are from Coalition of Labor Union Women 1980: Tables 3 and 5;
1983–85 data are from Baden 1986: 236, 238; 1990 data are from Cobble, forthcoming.

AFL craft unions. In contrast, those organizations with the most extensive representation of women (the two teachers' unions, AFSCME and
SEIU) are public-sector (or in the case of SEIU, public- and service-
sector) unions that have grown rapidly in recent decades. Female leadership has also grown at the local and regional levels of the public-sector
unions. For example, 33 percent of AFSCME's local presidents and 45
percent of its local union officers were female in 1982 (Bell 1985: 288).
And in 1985, 319 of SEIU's 820 local officers were female, as were 9 of its
61 joint council officers (Baden 1986: 239). The increased representation
of women in such secondary leadership posts augurs well for the future,
since the next generation of top union leaders will come from this group.

As for the private-sector unions, it is difficult to see how women's
leadership could grow significantly in the near future without a revival of
membership recruitment, and even then the tradition of male leadership
would be a formidable obstacle to progress. At the same time, the feminization of union membership that has already occurred in the public
sector might also be a likely outcome in the private sector if unions were
able to overcome the conditions generating deunionization and resume
organizing successfully there.

The effects of radical economic restructuring in the 1970s and 1980s
have made such recruitment difficult. Yet the effects of restructuring on
women and men have been quite different. Factory closings and unemployment generally have affected male workers more severely than their
female counterparts, since men were far more concentrated in the manufacturing sector (Milkman 1987). Another type of restructuring, however,
has had a far greater impact on women, namely the erosion of traditional
patterns of full-time, permanent employment. Women are the vast majority of part-time workers, temporary workers, and homeworkers, and the
growth of such forms of "contingent work," loosening the traditional
bond between the firm and the worker, present special problems for
unions (Appelbaum 1987). It is remarkable that despite this additional
obstacle, recent organizing efforts have been more successful in recruiting women workers than men into unions, even in the private sector.

Gender and Union Organizing in the 1980s
Accumulating evidence suggests that unorganized women, far from being an obstacle to union growth or a factor contributing to the decline of
unionism (as is sometimes alleged), and contrary to the once-conven-

tional maxim that women are less "organizable" than men, have a *greater* propensity to unionize than unorganized men. In a 1977 survey, for example, 41 percent of female nonunion workers but only 27 percent of male nonunion workers responded "for" when asked, "If an election were held with secret ballots, would you vote for or against having a union or employees' association represent you?" (Freeman and Medoff 1984: 29). Other survey research has yielded similar findings (Kochan 1979: 25; Goldfield 1987: 137).

Women workers not only express pro-union attitudes more often than men but are also more inclined to support unionization in actual practice, on those rare occasions when they have the opportunity to do so, as voting data from recent National Labor Relations Board (NLRB) elections (which cover only private-sector workers) indicate. An analysis of 226 union organizing campaigns that culminated in NLRB elections held in 1982–83 found that unions won half of the campaigns in which women made up 75 percent or more of the workforce (mostly in health care) but only 39 percent of those where less than half the workers were women (mostly in manufacturing) (AFL-CIO 1984: Appendix, 18).

A similar analysis of 189 election campaigns from 1986–87 found an even more pronounced gender differential: Unions won 57 percent of the elections in units where women were 75 percent or more of the workforce but only 33 percent of those where the workforce was less than half female. This was the case despite the fact that nearly all the organizers leading the election campaigns in the sample (over 90 percent) were male. Interestingly, the win rate was higher (61 percent) for those few campaigns led by female organizers than for those led by males (41 percent) (AFL-CIO 1989: 6).[4]

Closer analysis of the data from the 1986–87 campaigns reveals a more complex relationship between the gender composition of the labor force and the likelihood of winning an election.[5] As Figures 11-1 and 11-2 show, in this sample, unions were most likely to win elections in units with overwhelmingly (95 percent or more) female workforces. For these units the win rate was a spectacular 90 percent (although the number of cases is small), double the rate for the sample as a whole (43 percent). Win rates consistently declined as the female percentage of the workforce fell, except for the units with an overwhelmingly male workforce, where the win rate was higher than for those with gender-mixed workforces (but still much lower than for the overwhelmingly female units).

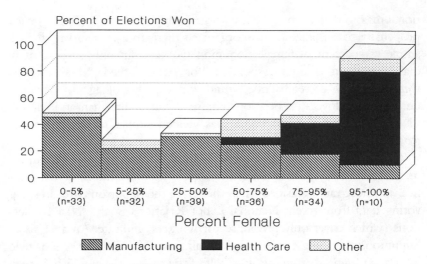

Figure 11-1. Election Wins by Percent Female and by Industry*

*Industry breakdown is for wins only.

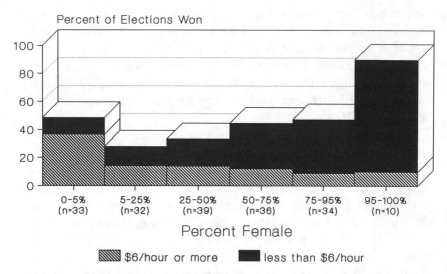

Figure 11-2. Election Wins by Percent Female and by Average Wage Rates*

*Wage rate breakdown is for wins only.

The units with high percentages of women tended to be health-care workplaces, and most had low average wages (under $6 per hour); those with high percentages of men were typically manufacturing units, and most had relatively high average wages ($6 or over). Independent of their gender composition, units in the sample with low average wages had significantly higher win rates (51 percent) than those with higher wages (34 percent). Units with a high proportion (over 75 percent) of minority workers (black, Hispanic, or Asian) also had significantly higher win rates (65 percent) than those with less than 75 percent minority workers (35 percent).[6] Manufacturing units had lower win rates (40 percent) than health-care units (55 percent), while units in other industries were in between (45 percent), although these differences are not statistically significant.

As Figures 11-1 and 11-2 also show, some of these variables are highly correlated: Units with a high percentage of women tend to have low average wages and to be in nonmanufacturing industries.[7] Thus a multivariate analysis is needed to determine whether each variable has independent significance in affecting win rates when the others are taken into account. Logistic regression analysis was conducted to estimate the simultaneous effects of four characteristics of the work unit (percent female, percent minority, average wage, and industrial sector—with the latter dummy coded as manufacturing vs. nonmanufacturing) on election outcomes (win vs. lose).

The results indicate that (as in the univariate analysis) percent female, percent minority, and average wage have significant effects on the probability of winning.[8] Percent female still has an independent and significant effect on winning, but once the other variables are controlled, what started as a J-curve becomes a more symmetrical U-curve. The main reason for this is that most of the work units with a very high percentage of women are also low-wage units, so that controlling for wages depresses the extreme right end of the curve.

Figure 11-3 shows the estimated effects of percent female on winning an election, holding percent minority, average wage, and industry constant at their means. Like Figures 11-1 and 11-2, this curve indicates that unions are most likely to win elections in work units that are gender-homogeneous, and least likely to win where the workforce is evenly mixed between men and women. For example, the odds of winning an election are more than twice as high (2.1 times greater) when the workforce is 95 percent female than when 45 percent of the workforce is fe-

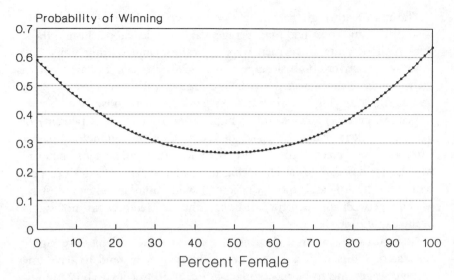

Figure 11-3. Estimated Probability of Winning by Percent Female*

*Evaluated at the means of average wage, manufacturing, and percent minority.

male, holding other factors constant. The odds of winning are nearly twice as high (1.9 times greater) when the workforce is 95 percent male than when it is 55 percent male, again holding other factors constant.

Figure 11-4 shows the combined effects of percent female, holding constant average wage and industry, on the probability of winning, disaggregating the data between manufacturing and nonmanufacturing and between cases where average wages are less than $6 per hour and those where average wages are $6 per hour or more. This graph reveals that, regardless of average wage and regardless of industry, the probability of winning is greatest at extreme values of percent female. In addition, regardless of percent female or industry, the probability of winning is greatest when average wages are low; and regardless of wages and percent female, the probability of winning is greater in nonmanufacturing than in manufacturing units.

Furthermore, Figure 11-4 suggests that wages are more salient than industry in differentiating the win rates of various work units across all possible levels of percentage female. More specifically, units where workers average less than $6 an hour are more than twice (2.2 times) as likely

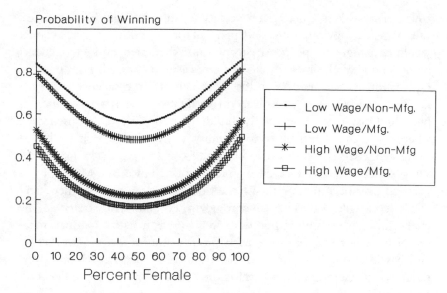

Figure 11-4. Probability of Winning by Percent Female, Wage Rates, and Industry

to vote to unionize as units where average wages are $6 an hour or more, holding other factors constant. By contrast, nonmanufacturing units are only slightly (1.2 times) more likely than manufacturing units to vote in favor of unionization. This pattern is not especially surprising, of course, since the effects of industry on winning were not statistically significant.

Overall, the probability of winning is greatest in work units with a low average wage and either a very high or very low percentage of women; conversely the probability of winning is smallest in units with high wages and a gender-mixed workforce. Specifically, units with a high percentage of females (95 percent) in nonmanufacturing workplaces with low average wages (the typical features of an overwhelmingly female unit) are almost five (4.8) times more likely to unionize than manufacturing units with a 45 percent female workforce and high average wages (the low point of the curve). In contrast, units with a high percentage of males (95 percent) that are in manufacturing workplaces and have high average wages (the typical characteristics of predominantly male units) are only about twice as likely to unionize as manufacturing units with high average wages and a 55 percent male workforce (the low point of the curve).

It is not especially surprising that low wages would, all else being equal, give workers a greater propensity to unionize than higher wages. But it is less obvious why, independent of their low wages, women would have a greater propensity to unionize than men, and why gender-homogenous work units would be more easily organized. One possible explanation is that gender-specific work cultures, the salience of which has been documented extensively in qualitative research by ethnographers and historians, facilitate the building of solidarity among workers, whereas it is more difficult to forge unity in a workforce that is divided along gender lines (see Westwood 1984; Costello 1985; Sacks 1988; Benson 1986; and Cobble 1988 on women's work culture; see Montgomery 1987 and Cockburn 1983 on men's; see Cooper 1987 on both women's and men's work cultures). The standard idiom of unionism, rooted in the craft- and industrial-union traditions, relies on a "macho," hardhat imagery of militancy that has long been problematic for women workers— and has increasingly become so for white-collar men, to whom adversarial, "cigar-chomping" unionism is often anathema (see Hecksher 1988: 62–70).

Traditional calls to militancy may be quite effective in building solidarity in all-male blue-collar work units, but not in gender-mixed settings. Similarly, while in organizing predominantly female work groups the labor movement has increasingly relied on appeals to gender-specific concerns and sometimes even on "pre-union" associations that exist entirely outside the established union structure (Seifer and Wertheimer 1979), such tactics may be less effective in galvanizing support for unionism in gender-mixed workforces.

Although this dilemma may be difficult to overcome, it is noteworthy that unions, especially in the public- and service-sectors, have been in the forefront of a new mode of advocacy on gender issues in the 1980s, best exemplified by the demand for government and business support for parental leave and child-care, and by the campaign for pay equity or comparable worth. In the past, organized labor was generally unreceptive to "women's issues" unless they were formulated in the class-based language of traditional unionism (as were, for example, protective legislation and, later, equal pay for equal work, which were both defined as policies that would prevent employers from taking advantage of women's special vulnerability and thus protect male wage standards). Yet in recent years, partly in response to the growth of female labor leadership, unions have come to recognize that they ignore the special interests of women at their peril, and have emerged as a key ally of the feminist movement.

Toward a New Gender Politics

The issues that have cemented this new alliance are rooted in important shifts in the composition of the female workforce that took place in the 1970s and 1980s. The most spectacular change was the increased workforce involvement of married women and mothers. Whereas before World War II the typical female wage worker was unmarried and few mothers of young children were employed outside the home, today wives and mothers are more likely to be in the labor force than not. In 1950 only 24 percent of married women (husband present) were in the labor force, and as recently as 1970 only 30 percent of married women with children under 6 years old were employed or seeking employment. By contrast, in 1987 married women (husband present) had a labor-force participation rate of 56 percent—equal to the rate for the overall female population in that year—and for married women with children under 6 the rate was 57 percent (U.S. Dept. of Labor 1988: 791, 805).

This historic shift has dramatically heightened the long-standing tension between women's family and work commitments. For most women, this conflict is still resolved at the individual level, perhaps most commonly through the "choice" of part-time work. Over one-fourth of women workers (26 percent, compared to only 11 percent of men) currently work part-time, and others, in increasing numbers, have "temporary jobs" or work at home (U.S. Dept. of Labor 1991: 26; Appelbaum 1987). In recent years, however, the issue of family-work conflict has become increasingly politicized, galvanizing new demands for both national and corporate policies on such matters as parental leave and child-care.

While pressing for national legislation guaranteeing parental leave to working parents (so far without success), unions have also won child-care and parental leave benefits for some of their members at the bargaining table. For example, the ILGWU established a child-care center in New York's Chinatown in 1983 and won parental leave benefits for 135,000 of its members in 1988. The following year the CWA and the IBEW (International Brotherhood of Electrical Workers) negotiated a contract with AT&T that provided $5 million for support of community child- and dependent-care services, as well as unpaid parental leave for up to a year, with guaranteed reinstatement. Many other unions have also successfully pursued family-work issues at the bargaining table (Chinatown 1988; Labor Letter 1988; Bennett and Trost 1989).

Another equally explosive issue is that, despite the dramatic growth of female labor-force participation, stark inequalities between female and male workers persist. While elite women have made substantial advances in professional and managerial occupations formerly monopolized by men, the vast majority of women workers remain concentrated in poorly paid, low-status, sex-segregated jobs (Beller 1984). In 1990, women's weekly earnings for full-time work averaged 72 percent of full-time male weekly earnings (U.S. Dept. of Labor 1991: 230). Employers continue to treat women as a source of cheap labor, different from and noninterchangeable with men, despite continuing pressure for equality and a quarter century of government policies that nominally endorse that goal. The recent growth of predominantly female part-time, temporary, and at-home employment has further reinforced gender inequalities, creating a new female ghetto of insecure, poorly paid, low-status, and highly sex-stereotyped work.

The most effective response to the persistence of the gender gap in pay in recent years has been the campaign for comparable worth or pay equity, which centers on the claim that jobs traditionally performed by women have been systematically undervalued in terms of wages and that equity requires a new, gender-neutral evaluation of the skills, responsibilities, and effort involved in various jobs, on which basis pay adjustments can be made (Treiman and Hartmann 1981). Unions have been the critical actors in this effort, bringing all of the major lawsuits, directly negotiating comparable-worth adjustments at the bargaining table, and in some cases even making pay equity a strike issue (Portman, Grune, and Johnson 1984). Particularly prominent in this area are AFSCME, SEIU, and the National Union of Hospital and Health Care Employees, District 1199 (Cook 1983: 16).

Drawing on the escalating tension between family and work, on the one hand, and the unmet demand for an end to sex discrimination at work, on the other, a new form of gender politics is emerging in which unions play a central role. Whereas historically advocates of equal treatment for women and men, irrespective of any socially or culturally constructed gender differences, have been in conflict with those who take gender differences as given and seek to protect traditionally female values and types of behavior, the new gender politics synthesizes the apparently contradictory strategic impulses of equality and difference. This new politics embraces the goal of equality for women but at the same time takes a positive view of gender differences and on this basis elaborates a critique, rooted in traditionally female values, of the basic structure of the world of work, with its highly individualistic and competitive male culture.

The pay equity issue is a good illustration of this new approach. While in practice comparable-worth reforms can be criticized for their limited, technocratic nature, they are rooted in an innovative and deeply radical critique of the gender ideology structuring the workplace (Evans and Nelson 1989). Supporters of pregnancy and parental leaves, while still divided on the legal details of special versus equal treatment (Vogel 1990), have also launched a critique, from a different angle, of the male values that shape workplace policies. Implicit in all of these specific reform movements is, as Alice Kessler-Harris puts it (1985: 157), "a belief that gender equality will be achieved only when the values of the home (which have previously been assumed to keep women out of the work place or to assign them to inferior places within it) are brought to the work place where they can transform work itself." Thus the new gender politics accepts difference as a strategic basis for making demands that will ultimately move toward equality. It is also the basis for a new model of unionism that moves women workers and their concerns from the margin to the center.

Recent developments, then, suggest a basis for optimism about the future for women in organized labor. Women not only have a greater propensity to unionize than men (especially in predominantly female work groups), but also unions are experimenting with a new political approach to gender issues that holds out the promise of taking account of specifically female concerns while also advancing toward equality. Although the changes that have occurred to date have been modest, this is largely due to deunionization and the continuing legacy of patriarchal traditions. The increased representation of women in positions of leadership and the emergence of gender issues as a central concern in the younger, most dynamic unions could be the precursor of a broader transformation in the labor movement if it ever overcomes its present crisis and begins to grow in size and influence once again.

Notes

1. My thanks to the members of Women and Unions Research Association, which discussed an earlier version of this essay at its October 1989 meeting

in New York City, for their valuable comments. Sue Cobble's written comments on the paper were extremely helpful, and she also generously provided me with the 1990 data presented in Table 11-3. Thanks as well to Jane Jenson for her useful editorial suggestions. I am grateful to Richard Freeman for telling me about the data used in the regression analysis, to Virginia Diamond and Alida Castillo-Freeman for granting me access to those data, and to Kate Bronfenbrenner for sharing her research on the characteristics of the sample as well as some of her own (as yet unpublished) research findings. Thanks also to Linda Ferguson for her help with the statistical analysis and to Don Treiman and Vilma Ortiz for their comments on an earlier version of the regression analysis.

2. Elsewhere (Milkman 1990) I have elaborated more fully on the typology sketched in this section.

3. The data for these years are not strictly comparable, due to changes in government enumeration methods, but the overall trend toward feminization of union membership in the context of general deunionization is unmistakable.

4. This difference is of marginal statistical significance ($p < .10$) using either a two-tailed t-test or a Fisher's exact test (two-tailed); this may be due to the very small number of cases ($n = 18$) where the organizers were female.

5. The AFL-CIO collected data (via retrospective interviews with lead organizers) on 189 single-union organizing campaigns in units of over 50 workers that took place during the period from July 1986 to April 1987. A total population of 981 NLRB single-union elections involving AFL-CIO affiliates with units of over 50 workers were held in the United States in this period. The sample was not random but shaped by differential access to various unions and their organizers, and in some respects the sample is not representative. Most important for present purposes, it underrepresents campaigns by unions that most often recruit women and minority workers. The Teamsters are not included in the sample at all, yet they petitioned for a third of the elections in this period. Also underrepresented in the sample are the Service Employees International Union, the Amalgamated Clothing and Textile Workers Union, and the Retail, Wholesale, and Department Store Workers' Union, all of which (like the Teamsters) organize women and minority low-wage workers to a greater than average degree.

The mean workplace in the sample had a nearly even mix of men and women (45 percent female), identical to the mix in the nation's workforce. Minorities (blacks, Hispanics, and Asians) made up 26 percent of the workforce, higher than in the national workforce. Wages averaged $6.55 per hour (the median wage, however, was $6.00) in the sample, lower than in the nation as a whole. Another respect in which the sample is quite different from the national workforce is that over two-thirds (68 percent) of the units were in the manufacturing sector.

Kate Bronfenbrenner (forthcoming) has conducted additional interviews to correct for these sampling problems. Her own analysis using the improved data confirms the basic findings presented here on the relationship of gender to organizing success. This suggests that the sampling problems, while noteworthy, are not fatal for present purposes.

6. Using one-tailed t-tests reveals that election outcomes differ significantly ($p < .05$) for percent female, percent minority, and average wage.

7. Pearson correlation coefficients are $-.48$ for percent female with average wage and $-.46$ for sector (manufacturing vs. nonmanufacturing) with average wage.

8. The following table shows the beta coefficients for each variable in the model. The model specifies a curvilinear function for percent female, as represented by the variables PFEM (percent female) and PFEM^2 (the square of percent female), because inspection of the data (as seen in Figures 11-1 and 11-2) revealed that a U- or J-shaped function best describes the association between win rates and the proportion of women in the workforce. The model specifies a logarithmic function for average wage (AVGWAGE and LOGWAGE) because inspection of the data (not shown here) revealed that while increases in wages were associated with a decrease in win rates, the effects of wages were not linear but were greatest at low wage levels and flatter at higher wage rates. Models that included interaction effects among the independent variables were also tested, but the coefficients for the interaction effects were not significant.

Variable	Beta	Partial R
INTERCEPT	6.55***	
PFEM	$-$ .057***	$-$ .162
PFEM^2	.001***	.159
AVGWAGE	.427	.021
LOGWAGE	-4.98**	.112
PMIN	.010*	.076
MFG	$-$ .314	.000

*Significant at .10 level, two-tailed.
**Significant at .05 level, two-tailed.
***Significant at .01 level, two-tailed.

References

Adams, Larry T. 1985: Changing Employment Patterns of Organized Workers. *Monthly Labor Review* 108 (2): 25–31.
AFL-CIO Department of Organization and Field Services. 1984: AFL-CIO Organizing Survey. Washington, D.C.: mimeo.

———. 1989: AFL-CIO Organizing Survey: 1986–87 NLRB Elections. Washington, D.C.: mimeo.

Appelbaum, Eileen. 1987: Restructuring Work: Temporary, Part-time, and At-home Employment. In Heidi I. Hartmann, ed., *Computer Chips and Paper Clips: Technology and Women's Employment*, vol. 2, 268–310. Washington, D.C.: National Academy Press.

Baden, Naomi. 1986: Developing an Agenda: Expanding the Role of Women in Unions. *Labor Studies Journal* 10 (3): 229–49.

Bell, Deborah E. 1985: Unionized Women in State and Local Government. In Ruth Milkman, ed., *Women, Work, and Protest: A Century of U.S. Women's Labor History*, 280–99. Boston: Routledge and Kegan Paul.

Beller, Andrea. 1984: Trends in Occupational Segregation by Sex and Race, 1960–1981. In Barbara F. Reskin, ed., *Sex Segregation in the Workplace: Trends, Explanations, Remedies*, 11–26. Washington, D.C.: National Academy Press.

Bennett, Amanda, and Cathy Trost. 1989: Benefit Package Set by AT&T, Unions Shows Power of Families in Workplace. *Wall Street Journal*, 31 May, A6.

Benson, Susan Porter. 1986: *Counter Cultures: Saleswomen, Managers, and Customers in American Department Stores, 1890–1940*. Urbana: University of Illinois Press.

Bronfenbrenner, Kate. Forthcoming: Seeds of Resurgence: Successful Union Strategies for Winning Certification Elections and First Contract Campaigns. Ph.D. dissertation, New York State School of Industrial and Labor Relations, Cornell University.

Chinatown Day Center. 1988: A Haven for 80, but 500 Must Wait. *New York Times*, 10 March, C6.

Coalition of Labor Union Women, Center for Education and Research. 1980: Absent from the Agenda: A Report on the Role of Women in American Unions. New York, mimeo.

Cobble, Dorothy Sue. 1988: "Practical Women": Waitress Unionists and the Controversies over Gender Roles in the Food Service Industry, 1900–1980. *Labor History* 29 (1): 5–31.

Cobble, Dorothy Sue. Forthcoming: Introduction. In Dorothy Sue Cobble, ed., *Women and Unions: Forging a Partnership*. Ithaca, N.Y.: Cornell ILR Press.

Cockburn, Cynthia. 1983: *Brothers: Male Dominance and Technological Change*. London: Pluto Press.

Cook, Alice. 1983: *Comparable Worth: The Problem and States' Approaches to Wage Equity*. Manoa: University of Hawaii, Industrial Relations Center.

Cooper, Patricia. 1987: *Once a Cigar Maker: Men, Women, and Work Culture in American Cigar Factories, 1900–1919*. Urbana: University of Illinois Press.

Costello, Cynthia. 1985: "WEA're Worth It!" Work Culture and Conflict at the Wisconsin Education Association Insurance Trust. *Feminist Studies* 11(3): 497–518.

Dickason, Gladys. 1947: Women in Labor Unions. *Annals of the American Academy of Political and Social Science* 251 (May): 70–78.

Evans, Sara, and Barbara Nelson. 1989: Comparable Worth: The Paradox of Technocratic Reform. *Feminist Studies* 15 (1): 171–90.

Freeman, Richard B. 1988: Contraction and Expansion: The Divergence of Private Sector and Public Sector Unionism in the United States. *Journal of Economic Perspectives* 2(2): 63–88.

Freeman, Richard B., and Jonathan S. Leonard. 1987: Union Maids: Unions and the Female Workforce. In Clair Brown and Joseph A. Pechman, eds., *Gender in the Workplace*, 189–216. Washington, D.C.: Brookings Institution.

Freeman, Richard B., and James Medoff. 1984: *What Do Unions Do?* New York: Basic Books.

Gold, Allan R. 1988: Union's Victory at Harvard Seen as Spur to Labor Drive. *New York Times*, 19 May, B11.

Goldfield, Michael. 1987: *The Decline of Organized Labor in the United States.* Chicago: University of Chicago Press.

Green, James. 1988. Union Victory: An Interview with Kristine Rondeau. *Democratic Left* (September–October): 4–6.

Harrison, Cynthia. 1988: *On Account of Sex: The Politics of Women's Issues, 1945–1968.* Berkeley and Los Angeles: University of California Press.

Hartmann, Heidi. 1976: Capitalism, Patriarchy, and Job Segregation by Sex. In Martha Blaxall and Barbara Reagan, eds., *Women and the Workplace: The Implications of Occupational Segregation*, 137–69. Chicago: University of Chicago Press.

Heckscher, Charles C. 1988: *The New Unionism: Employee Involvement in the Changing Corporation.* New York: Basic Books.

Hurd, Richard W. 1989. Learning from Clerical Unions: Two Cases of Organizing Success. *Labor Studies Journal* 14 (1): 30–51.

Kessler-Harris, Alice. 1975: Where Are the Organized Women Workers? *Feminist Studies* 3(1/2): 92–110.

———. 1985: The Debate over Equality for Women in the Work Place: Recognizing Differences. *Women and Work: An Annual Review* 1: 141–161.

Kochan, Thomas A. 1979: How American Workers View Labor Unions. *Monthly Labor Review* 102 (4): 22–31.

Labor Letter. 1988: *Wall Street Journal*, 19 July, 1.

Ladd-Taylor, Molly. 1985: Women Workers and the Yale Strike. *Feminist Studies* 11 (3): 465–89.

LeGrande, Linda H. 1978: Women in Labor Organizations: Their Ranks Are
    Increasing. *Monthly Labor Review* 101 (8): 8–14.
Milkman, Ruth. 1987: Women Workers and the Labor Movement in Hard
    Times: Comparing the 1930s with the 1970s and 1980s. In Lourdes Beneria
    and Catherine Stimpson, eds., *Women, Households, and the Economy*, 111–31.
    New Brunswick, N.J.: Rutgers University Press.
———. 1990: Gender and Trade Unionism in Historical Perspective. In Louise
    A. Tilly and Patricia Gurin, eds., *Women, Politics, and Change*, 87–107.
    New York: Russell Sage Foundation.
Montgomery, David. 1987. *The Fall of the House of Labor*. New York: Cam-
    bridge University Press.
Portman, Lisa, Joy Ann Grune, and Eve Johnson. 1984: The Role of Labor. In
    Helen Remick, ed., *Comparable Worth and Wage Discrimination: Technical
    Possibilities and Political Realities*, 219–37. Philadelphia: Temple University
    Press.
Sacks, Karen. 1988: *Caring by the Hour: Women, Work, and Organizing at Duke
    Medical Center*. Urbana: University of Illinois Press.
Seifer, Nancy, and Barbara Wertheimer. 1979: New Approaches to Collective
    Power: Four Working Women's Organizations. In Bernice Cummings and
    Victoria Schuck, eds., *Women Organizing: An Anthology*, 152–83.
    Metuchen, N.J : Scarecrow Press.
Treiman, Donald J., and Heidi I. Hartmann, eds. 1981: *Women, Work, and
    Wages: Equal Pay for Jobs of Equal Value*. Washington D.C.: National
    Academy Press.
U.S. Department of Labor, Bureau of Labor Statistics. 1980: *Directory of Na-
    tional Unions and Employee Associations, 1979*. Bulletin 2079.
———. 1985: *Employment and Earnings* 32 (1).
———. 1986: *Employment and Earnings* 33 (1).
———. 1987: *Employment and Earnings* 34 (1).
———. 1988: *Labor Force Statistics Derived from the Current Population Survey,
    1948–87*. Bulletin 2307.
———. 1991: *Employment and Earnings* 38 (1).
U.S. Department of Labor, Women's Bureau. 1983: *Time of Change: 1983 Hand-
    book on Women Workers*. Bulletin 298.
Vogel, Lise. 1990: Debating Difference: Feminism, Pregnancy, and the Work-
    place. *Feminist Studies* 16 (1): 9–32.
Wagner, David. 1979: Clerical Workers: How "Unorganizable" Are They? *Labor
    Center Review* (Amherst, Mass.) 2 (1): 20–50.
Westwood, Sallie. 1984: *All Day, Every Day: Factory and Family in the Making of
    Women's Lives*. Urbana: University of Illinois Press.
Wolman, Leo. 1924: *Growth of American Trade Unions, 1880–1923*. New York:
    National Bureau of Economic Research.

12   JULIE WHITE

One Union Responds: The Case of the
Canadian Union of Postal Workers

The literature on the role of unions in women's lives abounds with criticism of unions for their lack of recognition and support for women in paid work. One identified aspect of the response of unions to the entry of women into the labour force has been the attempt by unions to protect male members through policies of exclusion, whether in the form of protective legislation, the clear policy of abolition of women from the labour force, or the acceptance of women's segregation into limited job categories (Barrett 1980; Boston 1980; Frager 1983; Gannagé 1986). Such policies aimed either to exclude women from the workforce entirely or at least to confine them to specific occupations. The evidence suggests that unions have been most likely to respond with such policies during periods of technological change, in which the employer introduces unskilled and lower-paid women workers to carry out the newly created monotonous tasks that require little or no training (Cockburn 1983; Brenner and Ramas 1984). In protecting the positions, pay, and status of their male members against the inroads of cheap labour, unions have attempted to exclude women workers.

The Canadian Union of Postal Workers (CUPW) has witnessed a major entry of women into the once all-male occupation of sorting the mail, in combination with a deskilling of the work and massive technological change. The membership of the union has changed from 5.7 percent women in 1965 to 43.6 percent just fifteen years later (Statistics Canada 1965–80). Women were first introduced as low-paid part-time workers at the end of the 1950s and during the 1960s to sort mail on a simplified basis that required no training. Then in the 1970s the post office began a massive program of mechanization, and women were hired as full-time workers in a lower-paid job classification, called coders, to operate the new machinery. Despite the introduction of automation and the associated use of women as cheap labour, the CUPW did not long adhere to a policy of excluding the women but acted to protect them by bargaining equal pay and conditions. This paper examines why the CUPW did not follow exclusionary policies.

In the literature, little attention has been paid to the reasons for positive union response to women. Where such positive action has been explored, explanations have focussed almost entirely upon the activities of women themselves in forcing change within trade unions. Emphasis has been placed upon the growing proportion of women within unions (Baker and Robeson 1981), the development of women's committees and caucuses (David 1983; Field 1983; Langan 1976), alliances with the women's movement, and the actions of women as union activists (Briskin 1983: 270). While the actions of women in promoting their own interests are crucial to an understanding of change in unions, this argument alone is not sufficient explanation. For example, it cannot explain why unions that have a predominantly female membership (such as nurses unions) have not necessarily been in the forefront in obtaining improvements specific to women's concerns. Nor does it explain why some unions have made greater advances than others, despite a similar proportion of women members. The situation is not sufficiently homogeneous to allow for a one-factor explanation. In analyzing why the CUPW acted to protect women workers rather than exclude them, this chapter will consider a range of factors that may have contributed to that result. After describing the CUPW's response to the introduction of low-paid part-time workers and to the predominantly female coders during mechanization, the reasons for the CUPW's approach will be examined.

Equal Pay for Part-time Workers

Women part-time workers first appeared as inside postal workers in the late 1950s, to sort the mail on a simplified, alphabetical system instead of the "knowledge sort" by destination. The new system required no training, and the part-timers received lower rates of pay and almost no benefits. Initially, the union argued that part-time work should be abolished and refused to allow part-timers to join the union, positions not unrelated to the sex of the part-time workforce. At this time the full-time workforce was 95 percent male, while the part-timers were almost entirely women. For the purposes of this paper, the story begins once the part-time workers were accepted into the union in 1966 and the union's approach changed.

In 1966 the minimum hourly rate for full-time workers ranged from $2.07 to $2.59, while part-time workers were earning $1.55 an hour (CUPW 1966: 45). Thus, the part-time workers were earning 75 percent of the wages paid to the lowest paid full-time worker and only 69 percent of the pay of the full-time postal clerks, who like themselves, sorted the mail, but by destination. This does not, however, take into account the increments received by the full-time workers for years of service, for which the part-time workers were not eligible. A postal clerk would start at $2.25 an hour, but with seven increments could reach the highest pay of $2.76 an hour. Regardless of the number of years that they worked in the post office, the part-time workers received the same $1.55 an hour.

When organizing the part-time workers into the union in 1966, the CUPW promised to bargain equal pay for them. Initially, 60 percent of the part-timers were reclassified to the same positions and starting pay rate as the full-time workers, on the grounds that by this time many of them performed exactly the same tasks as the full-time workers. Then in 1970 the union negotiated a disproportionately large increase in pay for those part-timers called post helpers who had not been reclassified and remained in the lowest classification at level PO 1. Under this agreement the part-time postal helpers received an hourly rate of $2.83, 94 percent of the lowest full-time rate, a gap of $.18 instead of the previous $.32. Although still lagging behind the rates of the other part-time workers and the minimum full-time rates, under this agreement the postal helpers received a pay raise from $1.75 to $2.83, a 62 percent increase. It is hardly surprising that the part-time workers ratified their first collective agreement by "an overwhelming majority" (CUPW 1971: 26).

Following in the wake of the coder dispute, to be discussed below, the CUPW obtained the elimination of the PO 1 level classification in 1974, and the postal helper position was abolished. From that time all part-time workers had the same basic pay rates as the full-time workers. The final breakthrough in pay for the part-timers was accomplished in 1975, after a bitter forty-two-day strike. Since the union did not gain in wages from this strike, finally accepting the post office's prestrike wage offer, the press suggested that the strike had been unnecessary. Yet the CUPW had made other gains over those forty-two days. For part-time workers those gains included, for the first time, eligibility for pay increments and the same shift premiums as the full-time workers.

During the 1970s the CUPW was also bargaining for equal benefits for the part-timers, a process that continued into the 1980s. Looking at the contract today, the union has succeeded in entirely equalizing the benefits for full- and part-time workers. The one exception is pensions, which have been subject to legislative restriction.[1]

The Coder Dispute

Over the 1970s the post office underwent a massive program of automation. Finally, twenty-nine centres across the country were mechanized and a large proportion of the work changed from an essentially manual process to maintaining, feeding, and working on the new letter- and parcel-sorting machines. In the very first stage of technological change a major confrontation developed between the employer and the union, a confrontation that involved the use of women in the workforce. The first computerized letter-sorting machines were introduced into the Alta Vista Post Office in Ottawa in 1972 and the post office established a new classification of postal worker, with a new job description and a lower rate of pay, to operate the machines. When the first postal coders were hired in Ottawa, over 60 percent were women (Public Service Commission 1972).

The coder job was a full-time position and was classified by the post office as level PO 1, to be paid an hourly rate of $2.94. At this time, there was no level 1 position in the full-time contract, although the part-time workers called postal helpers were classified as PO 1 and were also paid $2.94 an hour. The postal clerks who sorted the mail manually were classified as level PO 4 and paid $3.44 an hour. Thus, the postal coder was classified at the bottom of the heap and paid $.50 an hour less than the workers who sorted the mail manually.

Management introduced the new coder classification suddenly and with almost no prior warning. At a union-management meeting in July 1972 the union was informed that workers on the machines would be called coders, had been classified at the PO 1 level, and would be paid $2.94 an hour. The post office management had already prepared the posters advertising this new position and intended to post them immediately. It was already decided that, should there be insufficient internal applicants, management would hold an external competition to hire from outside the post office. If postal clerks applied for the coder positions, they would be accepting a 15 percent cut in pay and would also lose all their seniority.

The employer attempted to allay the union's fears by giving reassurances that the existing workforce would not be directly affected. The post office minutes of the July meeting note: "Management confirmed that the start up in operating would not have any adverse effect on the job security of existing part-time or full-time employees in the Post Office" (Canada Post Office 1972a: 2). Three days after this meeting, postal workers in Ottawa walked off the job for a day in protest against the coder position. The regional general manager for Ontario wrote to explain the situation to all Ontario supervisors. Having expressed his regret at the mail disruption he noted the facts of the case, including: "Meetings have taken place between Management and the staff of the Ottawa Post Office at which time it was stated that no full-time or part-time regular employees will lose their jobs because of the LSM's [Letter Sorting Machines]. Nor will the classifications of any of these employees be affected by the LSM's" (Canada Post Office 1972b). In other words, if the union's present members were fully protected, there was no reason for concern for new workers in a new classification.

The union was not impressed by this point of view. At the July meeting, union representatives were appalled and vigorously protested the new classification. They called the pay rate "disgusting" and said that it represented a downgrading of jobs from PO 4 to PO 1. The union immediately perceived the issue as a crisis and moved to deal with it in three different ways: through further meetings and discussions with management, by informing and mobilizing the union membership, and through the legal mechanism of placing a complaint before the Public Service Staff Relations Board.

Further meetings with management ended with no resolution of the union's concerns, and management stated that it meant to proceed with hiring for the new coder jobs (Canada Post Office 1972c; CUPW 1972d). The closed competition for postal coder positions was posted in the Ottawa Post Office in July. No one applied. Consequently an open competition was held, and by 21 August the first coders had been hired from outside the post office, classified as PO 1, and paid $2.94 an hour.

Over the following weeks, the union issued information bulletins, front-page articles appeared in the CUPW newspaper, and the issue received considerable coverage by the national press. The coder issue became a central concern for the union's members. In August, demonstrations were held by postal workers across the country demanding that coders be reclassified to the PO 4 level. The union declared: "At this point we, the Postal Workers, have every reason to believe that we have been betrayed by our employer" (CUPW 1972a: 1). In September 1972 the union initiated a campaign to boycott the postal code, prompted by problems with mechanization in general but by the coder situation in particular. The purpose of this campaign was to bring some pressure to bear on the post office management by reducing the use of the postal code and thereby obstructing the effectiveness of the mechanization program. At another level the CUPW also signed up the coders, who already had many complaints about changing shift schedules, working most Sundays, erratic paychecks, and safety problems. The CUPW president noted: "The boss has angered them by his treatment. Consequently, we now have a new group of solid militant members" (CUPW 1972b: 1).

The union also applied to the Public Service Staff Relations Board, claiming that the employer had violated Section 51 of the Public Service Staff Relations Act. This section is meant to protect workers between the expiry of one collective agreement and the signing of another, by prohibiting the employer from making any changes in pay or working conditions during that period. The collective agreement had expired in March 1972 and contained the following article: "Where new classifications are created or existing classifications changed, the rates of pay for the new classifications shall be fixed by mutual agreement between the parties."[2] The union claimed that the employer had violated this provision by failing to consult the union over the introduction of the new classification and sought an order requiring the post office to refrain from proceeding with the new classification. Although the decision found that the employer had violated the law in not consulting with the union, management's right to establish a new classification with an interim pay rate was upheld.

Problems within the post office mounted as the workers became increasingly dissatisfied with the mechanization process. A new collective agreement was signed in February 1973 without resolving the coder issue, instead referring problems connected with the new technology to a manpower committee of union and management representatives. This committee spent ten months attempting to define its terms of reference and accomplished nothing. Coders continued to be hired and automation to progress with little input or control from the union. These tensions finally erupted in April 1974, when three hundred workers in Montreal were suspended for wearing T-shirts to work printed with the slogan "Boycott the Postal Code." This resulted in a national strike that was illegal because a collective agreement was in force. It lasted eight days, and the workers returned to work on the agreement that a special settlement committee would decide the coder issue.

The special committee avoided the contentious classification issue by simply increasing the pay of the coders to $3.88, a rate that was between the PO 2 and PO 3 levels but fitted into neither (the union called it the PO 2⅜ level). Further meetings were held with a mediator, and in December 1974 it was announced that agreement had been reached on questions of classification, including the question of the coder position (Taylor 1974). Under the new system the coders were reclassified to level PO 4 and the duties of the postal clerk and the coder were combined, as advocated by the CUPW for two and a half years.

The CUPW Approach to Pay Equality

The CUPW began with the traditional approach of calling for the abolition of part-time work, while excluding the women part-time workers from the union. Once the part-timers were accepted as union members, however, the union worked actively to ensure that they received equal pay and benefits and to insist that they not be confined to the lower-paid classification to which they were originally consigned by the employer. Likewise with the coder dispute, the union was not prepared to negotiate a lower classification and reduced rate of pay for the predominantly female operators of the new machines. Why?

Women's Activism

There is no evidence that either the struggles around part-time work or the coder dispute were regarded by the union or its members, male or female, as an issue of particular concern to women. In the case of part-time workers, once they became members of the union, references to their gender virtually ceased, and a clear effort to define them as union members, no different than the full-time workers, followed. Regarding the coder dispute, in the many union bulletins, articles, debates, submissions, and briefs on the subject, there is never any reference to the fact that the coders were predominantly women.

In 1966 when the union organized the part-time workers and immediately began negotiating improved pay and benefits, women composed just 6.1 percent of the union's membership. This figure rose dramatically as the part-time workers joined the union, but still, when the coder dispute began in 1972, women composed only 23.9 percent of the membership (Statistics Canada 1965–80). At this time there were no women on the national executive or any women in paid union positions within the union structure. There is no way of knowing how many women went as delegates to the national conventions, but at the 1968 convention, which lasted for five days, two women spoke, and at the next convention in 1971, women spoke on six occasions (CUPW 1968, 1971). It is clear that women did not have a strong voice within the union at this time. Women's committees and caucuses had not been developed at this point and were not even discussed at a national convention until 1977. It was not because of pressure from women within the CUPW that the union struggled for equality for part-time workers or turned the coder issue into a dispute.

That these issues had particular implications for women was not recognized by the union, in either a negative or positive way. On the one hand, the union did not draw strength from arguments concerning women's equality; the union never expressed concern that inequality for part-time workers was inequality for women or that the coder position would create a ghetto of low-paid women workers within the post office. On the other hand, the union did not deal with the issue differently because a high proportion of women were involved, nor did it influence the degree of protection provided to them as union members. It was not until the 1980s that the union began to recognize that it had been bargaining equality for women and to interpret its former actions from that perspective (CUPW 1983).

If participation and pressure from women was not the cause of the union's struggle to equalize pay rates and resist lower classification, other factors must be considered. The CUPW itself gave three reasons for its approach: the protection of existing members, simple justice, and the solidarity of its members.

Protection of Existing Members

The CUPW perceived itself as protecting the interests of its members, although taking a decidedly different approach from those unions that saw their members' interests best served by excluding or confining the women workers. The CUPW early understood that to permit the employer to create a lower standard within the bargaining unit would also damage the existing members in the long term, even though their wages would be protected in the short term. The damage could take two forms, the first being that a lower-paid job classification might depress the increases negotiated for all the classifications. Also, the union was shrewd enough to recognize that even if there were no lay-offs or pay reductions for existing workers, hiring patterns would change so that there would be fewer higher-paid workers and more lower-paid positions. This would have a broad impact upon the level of wages for work in the post office and in turn would adversely affect the ability of the union to bargain higher pay rates.

The union's fears proved to be well founded on both counts. The employer attempted to use the lower pay of the part-time postal helpers to reduce the wages of the full-time workers. Opposing the PO 1 classification of the coders, the union argued that the full-time contract included no PO 1 classification. The employer responded that there was a precedent for a PO 1 level for the postal helpers in the part-time contract, and the $2.94 rate of pay that management established for the full-time coders was the same as the rate for the part-time postal helpers. With regard to the longer-term impact, it was not until January 1974 that the post office released its staffing projections for the first fifteen locals to be automated, but it was then clear that the number of full-time workers at the PO 1 level—that is, the coders—was to expand, while the higher-paid PO 4 positions were to be decreased.

The CUPW recognized that protecting the members meant protecting all the members, certainly the predominantly male full-time workers, but also the part-time workers once they belonged to the union and the coders who were organized as soon as they entered the post office.

Simple Justice

Obtaining equal wages for the part-time workers and settling the coder dispute were part of the CUPW's approach of equalizing the situation of its members, an approach that was clearly expressed in its bargaining demands and policy statements. Since the 1974 national convention, the union's stated policy has been that all postal workers should be in one classification with one rate of pay. In the 1975 round of negotiations the CUPW was proposing that "there shall be only one classification for postal workers in the bargaining unit, that of a PO 5 or its equivalent" (CUPW 1975a: 2).

The union has worked toward this position not only by upgrading the wages of part-time workers and coders, but also by improving the pay of mail handlers, a small, predominantly male group, and by resisting the employer's attempts to introduce regional rates of pay. The CUPW has also always bargained for across-the-board rather than percentage increases, stating:

> The CUPW strongly prefers across-the-board increases stated in
> money terms rather than percentages. It is imperative that the gaps
> between lower and higher income Canadians be narrowed, an objec-
> tive incompatible with the common practice of percentage wage and
> salary increases. We support the concept of narrowing the income
> differentials between occupational groups both within our own
> Union and in society at large. (CUPW 1975b)

The CUPW did not merely express this opinion, it was decidedly successful in putting its philosophy into practice. This becomes clear from a comparison over time of the minimum hourly rates of pay for the lowest and highest paid inside postal workers, given in Table 12-1. The wage gap between the lowest and highest paid workers in the CUPW bargaining was narrowed from 34.9 percent to 2.4 percent over the twenty years from 1965 to 1985.

Equality and Solidarity

The third reason often cited by the union for its approach to bargaining was the necessity of maintaining solidarity among its members, in order to muster the strength to deal with the employer. Splits within the

TABLE 12-1. The Wage Gap between the Lowest and Highest Paid
Workers (Minimum Rates) in the CUPW Bargaining Unit, 1965 to 1985

	1965	1970	1975	1980	1985
Lowest pay rate ($)	1.55	2.83	5.02	8.66	13.12
Highest pay rate ($)	2.38	3.41	5.42	8.96	13.44
Wage gap (%)	34.9	17.1	7.4	3.3	2.4

Source: Canadian Postal Employees Association, *Postal Tribune* 33:8, August 1965,
pp. 14 and 63; collective agreements between the CUPW and the Treasury
Board and the Canada Post Corporation, 1970 to 1985.

union would detract energy from the union's main goal of obtaining
improved conditions from the employer. Having a group of lower-paid
workers within the bargaining unit was not likely to lead to solidarity but
to resentment and internal dispute. In a booklet called "Fighting for
Equality," the union defines equality broadly as covering sex, race, sexual
orientation, freedom from sexual harassment, equality for part-time
workers, seniority to determine access to jobs, and equality of pay and
benefits for all. Inequality among workers in any way is described as
useful to employers to weaken the bargaining unit and the collective
strength of workers:

> This Backgrounder deals with the importance of our fight for equal-
> ity. Discrimination creates artificial divisions that employers promote
> and use to undermine workers' collective strength. Equality, on the
> other hand, helps build unity among workers. Since our ability to
> fight for individual and collective rights depends upon our unity and
> solidarity, equality is central to all our struggles. (CUPW 1984: 2)

Thus, the CUPW insisted on protecting its members with some fore-
sight in recognizing how best to accomplish that goal, maintained a
strong philosophy of equalizing the situation of its members, and believed that equality would develop among the members the solidarity
necessary to deal with the employer. From this point of view workers
were workers, whether male or female, and the critical issue was not
gender but class solidarity. The question, however, remains, Why did the
CUPW develop this approach and why was it able to muster the strength
to resist the employer and put its policies into practice?

The Employer and Militancy

Another part of the explanation why the CUPW did not accept the employer's creation of low-paid classifications is that the union and its members did not trust much that the employer initiated. The labour relations atmosphere on the shop floor and at every other level had been remarkably bitter, and report after report lamented the inability to achieve peaceable negotiations in a situation of total distrust. The level of hostility was expressed by one delegate to the 1974 national convention: "We are in a stage of all-out war. I am dealing, day in and day out, with the most immoral, crooked, lying, two-faced management you ever saw in your life" (CUPW 1974: 540). Under these circumstances it was not likely that the union would come to any tacit understanding with the employer to permit a lower-paid job classification, even if the existing positions were protected. How had this situation within the post office been created?

Prior to 1967 the union did not have the legal right to negotiate or strike to improve pay and conditions. As conditions in the post office deteriorated during the late 1950s and early 1960s, postal workers found themselves powerless to influence events. Over the eight years between 1957 and 1965 inside postal workers received only two pay increases instead of the customary annual raise, and they watched their wages steadily fall behind those of other workers employed in public services, such as the police and fire fighters. When the government announced a pay raise in 1965 of just half what the union had been demanding, postal workers, led by the Montreal local, walked off the job. It was the first strike since 1924.

While pay was the major catalyst behind the dissatisfaction in the post office and the 1965 strike, many other grievances irritated the postal workers on a daily basis. These grievances were aired through the Montpetit Commission established by the government in September 1965 as a result of the strike. The grievances covered every aspect of the work, including health and safety, the hours of work, timing of paychecks and late payment of overtime, boot and clothing arrangements, vacations and other kinds of leave, examinations and promotions. The complaints were embittered by the perception of the workers that the department management did not treat the complaints seriously and made little effort to deal reasonably with the problems raised. To the Montpetit Commission the union stated that grievances were often ignored, or were channelled up the bureaucracy to become subject to endless delays, and that too often management made decisions without reference to the union or its concerns.

The atmosphere in the post offices was described as disciplinarian and intolerant. The Montpetit Report noted that "except in one or two districts, the attitude of some supervisors and postmasters towards their employees leaves much to be desired" and that as a result some union representatives "are rebelling to the point that they are alarmingly unwilling to compromise" (Canada 1966: 17). The military-style management, complete with a code of discipline and pay reductions for infractions, derived in part from the large number of veterans given preferential hiring in the post office after the war. In 1946, 79.5 percent of the total appointments to the post office were those receiving War Service Preference. Even in 1960 the figure was still 16.2 percent, only the Department of National Defense having a higher proportion (Canada 1966: 88).

In response to union pressure and growing dissatisfaction, the Public Service Staff Relations Act (PSSRA) was passed in 1967, giving federal public servants the right to negotiate collective agreements and the right to strike under certain conditions. Despite this new legislation, strikes recurred in the post office in 1968, 1970, 1971, 1974, 1975, and 1978. Needless to say, the legislation failed to resolve the problems experienced by postal workers.

The PSSRA is a restrictive piece of legislation. It prohibited the union from negotiating hiring, appraisal, promotion, demotion, transfers, layoffs, duty assignment, or classification. This meant that in the period of technological change in the 1970s, the union was legally prevented from bargaining many of the issues that were most critical for its members. Throughout the coder dispute, for example, the employer steadfastly maintained that the union had no legal right to involve itself in classification, which was a management prerogative under the act. Another problem was that the same items that could not be negotiated also could not be grieved through the usual grievance procedure, and therefore could not be sent to independent adjudication but were finally decided by management.

These legislative restrictions, combined with an autocratic and incompetent management style, inhibited the resolution of the many problems created by the reorganization of work in the process of technological change. The response from the postal workers was to change the union's name from the Canadian Postal Employees Association to the Canadian Union of Postal Workers, to elect a series of increasingly militant leaders through the 1960s, to draw up a new and democratic constitution for the structure of their union, to establish an extensive education program, to pass increasingly progressive policies with regard to their workplace situation, and to be prepared to strike to obtain improvements.

The conflict between the postal workers and their employer was deepened by the government's response to the economic decline of the mid-1970s. Postal workers were directly affected by the government's policies of spending restraint and wage controls. Deficits in the post office had begun to cause concern in the late 1960s, and even at that time, pressure was building to attain an efficient, that is, self-sufficient, operation. But the deficit increases of the 1960s were trivial compared to the early 1970s. The 1970 deficit was almost $53 million, but by 1973–74 it had reached $177 million, and at its height in 1976–77 it was $578 million (Canada Post Office 1970–1977). The post office came under increasing pressure to reduce the deficit, and given that 70 percent of the expenditures were labour costs, that meant holding the line on wages and reducing the cost of labour wherever possible. When the government introduced wage controls in 1975, post office management enthusiastically embraced the 6 percent limit. Meanwhile, the increasingly militant CUPW was determined not only to protect its members in the face of the mechanization of the post office but to obtain improvements based upon the increased productivity.

The progressive policies and militant action of the CUPW were then the result of several factors: an autocratic employer backed by restrictive labour relations legislation, the introduction of massive technological change by an employer reluctant to negotiate many of the implications with the union, and the increasing pressure to cut labour costs in response to rising deficits and wage controls. While the public was becoming exasperated by the series of postal strikes, the workers were drawing their own conclusions:

> Unions that are polite, restrained and non-aggressive invariably end
> up with the worst agreements. They may enjoy a good public image,
> but their members pay for it in paltry pay cheques and poor working
> conditions. The postal unions had a good public image until they be-

gan to resort to the strike weapon six years ago. Since then their image has gone down about as fast as their wages have gone up. (CUPW 1972c: 1)

The growing reputation of the CUPW for militancy was not just a reputation but the foundation upon which the union relied when consultation, discussion, mediation, conciliation, and negotiation failed. The importance of worker solidarity was stressed and reinforced by negotiations that weakened differences at the workplace. The union disregarded gender as a factor of importance and was sufficiently militant to insist that workers be treated equally. That the union's members were prepared to strike without legal sanction in 1974 obtained for them the settlement of the coder dispute. That they were able to sustain a long and bitter strike in 1975 obtained the final breakthrough in equal wages for the part-time workers.

In the development of research on women and unions, it has been necessary, as in other areas, to rewrite history from a women's perspective, given that earlier studies simply ignored women in their analyses (Logan 1948; Lipton 1967; Jamieson 1973). Consequently, there has been an emphasis upon the differences between men and women, why women were and are less unionized, the different responses of unions to women and to men, women's particular experiences of unions, and so on. The debate between the theoretical approaches of patriarchal ideology and capitalist competition has centred around the question, Why have unions responded negatively to women? There has been a concentration upon the conflicting interests between male and female workers, based either upon the sexism of male unionists or the competition wrought by capitalism. This has been a necessary approach where unions have not acted in the interests of women workers.

A different case, however, has been examined here, one where a union has acted to protect both its male and its female members. In this case, pressure from the employer, combined with other factors, created a solidarity of interest between men and women workers, who struggled together for interests of concern to both. In this instance a level of unity was achieved that overcame (perhaps sporadically, perhaps only temporarily) the divisions brought about both by patriarchal ideology and capitalist competition.

An analysis that takes this possibility into account must not simply assume workers' solidarity in resisting the employer. In the past this assumption has usually meant the exclusion of gender from the analysis. The intention must be to understand the dynamic relationship between gender differences and tensions on the one hand and the common interests of male and female workers on the other, and to recognize that unions have been neither homogeneous nor consistent in their response to women.

There is general agreement that the labour movement, or at least parts of it, is changing in its response to women workers. If we are to understand this process, without relying on the sole and insufficient explanation of the activity of women themselves, we must begin to explore not only why unions have resisted the involvement of women but also why they have sometimes supported women and their concerns.

Notes

1. The union was prohibited by law from negotiating superannuation until 1981, when the post office became a Crown corporation and the union subject to the Canada Labour Code. Since that time the collective agreement was extended, by law, for two years, and in the 1988 negotiations, the union was legislated back to work and a contract imposed. Consequently, there has been only one round of unrestricted negotiations (1984) in which the union might have bargained pensions for part-time workers. It was part of the union's demands at the time, but was not obtained.

2. Agreement between the Treasury Board and the Council of Postal Unions, Postal Operations Group (nonsupervisory), Code: 608/10/70, Expires: 26 March 1972, Article 32, p.65.

References

Baker, Maureen, and Mary-Anne Robeson. 1981. Trade Union Reactions to Women Workers and Their Concerns. In Katharine Lundy and Barbara Warme, eds., *Work in the Canadian Context: Continuity Despite Change*. Toronto: Butterworths.

Barrett, Michèle. 1980. *Women's Oppression Today*. London: Verso Editions and NLB.

Boston, Sarah. 1980. *Women Workers and the Trade Unions*. London: Davis-Poynter.

Brenner, Johanna, and Maria Ramas. 1984. Rethinking Women's Oppression. *New Left Review* 144.

Briskin, Linda. 1983. Women's Challenge to Organized Labour. In Linda Briskin and Lynda Yanz, eds., *Union Sisters: Women in the Labour Movement*. Toronto: Women's Press.

Canada. 1966. *Report of the Royal Commission of Inquiry into Working Conditions in the Post Office Department*. Ottawa.

Canada Post Office. 1970–1977. *Annual Report*. Ottawa.

———. 1972a. Minutes of a Meeting Held between the Post Office Department and the Council of Postal Unions. Ottawa, 20 June.

———. 1972b. Letter from J. C. Corkery, regional general manager, Ontario Postal Region, to all supervisors, Ontario Postal Region, Toronto, 29 June.

———. 1972c. Minutes of a Meeting Held between the Post Office Department and the Council of Postal Unions. Ottawa, June.

Canadian Union of Postal Workers (CUPW). 1966. *Postal Tribune* 34:12.

———. 1968. *National Convention Proceedings*. Montreal.

———. 1971. *National Convention Proceedings*. Calgary, Alta.

———. 1972a. *CUPW* 2:8.

———. 1972b. Letter from J. B. McCall, national president, to Arnold Gould, national director, Ontario Region, 5 October.

———. 1972c. *CUPW*, 2:10.

———. 1972d. Special Meeting. Ottawa, 23 and 26 June.

———. 1974. *National Convention Proceedings*. Quebec City.

———. 1975a. *CUPW* 5:1.

———. 1975b. CUPW brief to the Conciliation Board, Wage Proposal section. 18 August.

———. 1983. Address by Jean-Claude Parrot, national president, Canadian Union of Postal Workers. Annual conference on Equal Pay for Work of Equal Value, Organized Working Women, Toronto, 26 February.

———. 1984. Fighting for Equality. Backgrounder No. 3, April.

Cockburn, Cynthia. 1983. *Brothers: Male Dominance and Technological Change*. London: Pluto Press.

David, Françoise. 1983: Women's Committees: The Quebec Experience. In Linda Briskin and Lynda Yanz, eds., *Union Sisters: Women in the Labour Movement*. Toronto: Women's Press.

Field, Debbie. 1983. The Dilemma Facing Women's Committees. In Linda Briskin and Lynda Yanz, eds., *Union Sisters: Women in the Labour Movement*. Toronto: Women's Press.

Frager, Ruth. 1983. No Proper Deal: Women Workers and the Canadian Labour Movement, 1870–1940. In Linda Briskin and Lynda Yanz, eds., *Union Sisters: Women in the Labour Movement*. Toronto: Women's Press.

Gannagé, Charlene. 1986. *Double Day. Double Bind: Women Garment Workers*. Toronto: Women's Press.

Jamieson, Stuart. 1973. *Industrial Relations in Canada*. Toronto: Macmillan.

Langan, Joy. 1976. Trade Union Women's Committees. *Canadian Labour* 21:3.

Lipton, Charles. 1967. *The Trade Union Movement of Canada 1827–1959*. Montreal: Canadian Social Publications.

Logan, Harold A. 1948. *Trade Unions of Canada*. Toronto: Macmillan.

Public Service Commission. 1972. Eligible List No. 72-PO-CC-OTT-68, Postal Coders, Postal Operations Level 1, 8 August.

Statistics Canada. 1965–80. *Corporations and Labour Unions Returns Act*, Part II, Cat. 71-202. Ottawa.

Taylor, Eric. 1974. *Report*. Ottawa, 31 December.

13 CÉLINE SAINT–PIERRE

Recognizing the Working Mother: The Quebec Labour Movement and the Feminization of the Labour Force

The increase in the number of women in the labour market comes at a time when the labour movement is declining both as a social and as a political force in many industrialized countries. This phenomenon of decline is one of the central elements in the broader crisis of Fordism in that it involves a major alteration within one of the institutions that had played a central role in the regulation of Fordist social relations (Boyer 1981). Deunionization may, however, be reversible if labour legislation and union practices come to recognize new categories of workers.

When faced with a rigid form of work organization (Taylorism), the Canadian labour movement accommodated itself to the very strict rules and procedures that governed collective bargaining. In this way, it resembled the U.S. movement. Moreover, unions were concentrated in large industrial firms involved in mass production and employing a large number of workers, mainly male. Today the labour movement in its traditional strongholds is being forced to respond to the reorganization of the content of work and new forms of labour-management policy. It is also being challenged by the fact that most *new* job creation is taking place in

269

the expanding service sector. Workers in this sector—mainly young people and women—are very different from the typical Fordist worker.

This chapter focusses on the Quebec unions' response to the presence of this new configuration of workers. With little chance that workers in the secondary labour force will find jobs in the declining primary labour force, these "new" workers might well become the central actor of the post-Fordist era. In Quebec, labour force trends have generally moved in the same direction as in the United States and the rest of Canada. Yet, more than in other parts of Canada, the Quebec labour movement has confronted a challenge from other social movements, including the women's movement, which has played an important role in the definition of priorities related to the working conditions of women. The Quebec case thus offers an opportunity to examine the strategies that might help the unions survive the transition to post-Fordism and to renew their social and political roles.

The first part of the chapter presents data on the situation of women in the Quebec labour force (including comparisons with the situation in Canada as a whole) and outlines certain tendencies that are likely to shape the labour market in the near future. Next is an examination of unionization rates among men and women. These data underpin the analysis developed in the second part of the chapter, which examines the unions' responses to the increasing participation of women in the labour force and in the unions themselves. The relationship between the feminization of the labour market and the labour movement will be looked at in a dialectical way by asking: How have women's specific claims been addressed by unions and how have unions been pressed to transform not only their views and priorities but also their practices?

Women in the Quebec and Canadian Labour Force

In Quebec, women's participation in waged work has been rising since the beginning of the century, just as it has elsewhere (Conseil du statut de la femme 1984). Table 13-1 demonstrates that in Canada employment has increased more rapidly for women than for men, especially since the late 1970s. The percentage of Canadian women in the labour force rose from 29.7 percent in 1961 to 55.9 percent in 1986. The comparable Quebec statistics are 27.9 percent and 51.2 percent.[1] Whereas in 1971 women ac-

TABLE 13-1. Evolution of the Labour-Force Rate, Quebec and Canada, 1911–1986

Year	Women Quebec (%)	Men Quebec (%)	Total Quebec (%)	Feminization rate (Quebec)[a] (%)	Women Canada (%)
1911	16.2	87.3	52.3	15.3	16.2
1921	18.7	86.9	52.8	17.7	17.6
1931	21.9	87.1	54.8	19.8	19.6
1941	22.9	85.4	54.2	21.1	20.7
1951	25.0	85.0	54.6	23.2	24.1
1961	27.9	76.7	52.1	27.1	29.7
1971	33.9	70.4	51.8	33.3	39.9
1981	47.5	75.8	61.3	39.7	51.8
1986	51.2	75.1	62.8	41.6	55.9

Sources: Statistique Canada, Recensement du Canada 1971, Population active et revenu des particuliers, tableaux chronologiques, cat. 94–702, November 1974, Table 1. Statistique Canada, Recensement du Canada 1981, Activité, cat. 92–915, Table 1. Statistique Canada, Recensement du Canada 1986, Québec, Partie 2, vol. 1, September 1988, cat. 94–110, Table 1.
[a]The feminization rate is the proportion of the total labour force that is female.

counted for only 34.6 percent of the labour force in Canada and 33.6 percent in Quebec, by 1986 they had risen to 43 percent of the Canadian labour force and 42 percent of Quebec's.

Table 13-2 provides more detailed data on the changing labour-force participation rates of men and women of different age groups in Quebec. With the exception of very young women (15–19 years) and older women (65 and over), women's participation has been rising continually. Since 1951, women between 20 and 24 years have constituted the majority of working women, with a significant increase in their representation occurring between 1971 and 1981. The most important change, however, affects women between 25 and 34 years of age; their participation rate rose by 30 percent between 1971 and 1986. This trend also holds for those between 35 and 44. An examination of these patterns in Canada as a whole reveals similar trends. The only exception is that the participation rate for women between 15 and 19 is higher in Canada as a whole than in Quebec.

Men have not followed the same patterns, however. As Table 13-1 shows, employment increased more rapidly for women than men, espe-

TABLE 13-2. Labour-Force Participation Rates (%) according to Age and Sex, Quebec, 1961–1986

	Women				
	Years				
Age Groups	1961	1971	1976	1981	1986
15–19	37.9	32.5	37.8	42.2	41.0
20–24	51.3	61.4	67.5	77.3	78.9
25–34	27.0	39.9	50.8	61.9	70.4
35–44	24.8	34.4	45.9	57.4	65.3
45–54	26.7	33.8	40.4	47.6	52.9
55–64	20.3	26.4	26.8	28.8	27.6
65 and over	7.3	9.0	7.7	5.2	3.5
Average rate	28.2	35.0	41.2	47.7	50.7
	Men				
15–19	39.8	37.4	45.4	45.8	44.3
20–24	84.3	80.8	83.3	88.6	86.4
25–34	93.0	87.8	91.3	93.3	92.2
35–44	93.1	87.3	91.1	92.4	92.2
45–54	90.3	84.3	87.9	88.4	87.7
55–64	80.0	73.4	74.6	73.4	64.8
65 and over	27.5	21.5	17.1	13.8	10.8
Average rate	77.3	71.4	74.6	76.0	74.6

Sources: Statistique Canada, Recensement du Canada 1971, Population active et revenu des particuliers, tableaux chronologiques, cat. 94–702, November 1974, Table 2. Statistique Canada, Recensement du Canada 1976, Activité, cat. 94–804, September 1978, Table 9. Statistique Canada, Recensement du Canada 1986, Activité cat. 93–111, Table 1.

cially in the 1970s. Table 13-2 also makes it clear that the majority of men in the Quebec labour market are still between the ages of 25 and 55. There has, moreover, been a significant decline in the participation rate of men over 55. This is a sharper decline than that experienced by women in the same age group. There is also a slight decline in the labour-force participation rates of younger men (20–34).

TABLE 13-3. Labour-Force Participation Rates (%) according to Marital Status and Sex, Quebec, 1971–1986

Matrimonial Status	Women		
	1971	1981	1986
Single	52.2	58.8	59.5
Married	28.4	47.2	52.6
Widowed/divorced	20.8	25.8	26.8
Total	35.0	47.7	50.7
	Men		
Single	58.3	66.7	67.9
Married	80.2	82.3	79.7
Widowed/divorced	32.4	54.7	53.7
Total	71.4	76.0	74.6

Sources: Statistique Canada, Recensement du Canada 1971, Population active et revenu des particuliers, tableaux chronologiques, cat. 94–702, November 1974, Table 3. Statistique Canada, Recensement du Canada 1985, Activité, cat. 93–111.

Despite these aggregate trends, women and men still follow different career trajectories depending on marital status and child care responsibilities. The data in Table 13-3 show that before 1981 in Quebec an unmarried woman was more likely than a married woman to be in the labour force. Between 1971 and 1986, however, there was a marked rise in the participation rates of married women. For men, the situation was reversed. They were more likely to be in the labour force if they were married than if they were single. Women under 45 without children were also more likely to be in the labour force (84 percent) than those with children (50 percent). The pattern reversed for women over 45; 38 percent of female labour-force participants were mothers and only 21 percent had no children. While such statistics indicate that women are more likely to be in the labour force when their children are older, there is nevertheless a trend toward remaining in the labour force even when women have young children.

The data on labour-force participation rates of women and men in Canada as a whole generally follow the same pattern as Quebec. Married women, however, show a higher labour-force participation rate in Canada, and more single Canadian men have jobs.

Part-time work by Quebec women has increased recently. In 1975, 13.6 percent of working women were part-time workers. By 1987, the percent had risen to 22.8 percent. Although men are also involved in part-time work, it is usually only when they are young. In 1987, 64 percent of men working part-time were under 24. Women holding part-time jobs are in all age categories, although there is a concentration in the prime child-bearing age group; in 1987, 79.4 percent of female part-time workers were between 15 and 44. Women account for 70 percent of all part-time employees. Fully three-fifths of such part-time workers are in the service sector.

In Canada, too, part-time work has increased from 20.3 percent in 1975 to 33.7 percent in 1987. This figure is higher than in either Quebec or the United States, where the proportion (26.1 percent) is closer to Quebec's (McKie and Thompson 1990).

Rising labour-force participation rates have been accompanied by a rise in women's unemployment rate. In 1954, only 3.7 percent of Quebec women were unemployed, but that figure had ballooned to 14.1 percent in 1984 and dropped only to 10.6 percent in 1987. In other provinces, the rate has been lower, sticking around 8 percent. Unemployment is highest among young women and men: In 1988, 12.2 percent of Quebec women between the ages of 15 and 19 were unemployed, while unemployment for men of the same age cohort stood at 14.5 percent (Ministère de la Main-d'oeuvre et de la Sécurité du revenu 1989). The same pattern can be observed in Canada although the unemployment rates again were lower than Quebec's.

The data on wage distribution by sex show why pay equity has been one of the main issues faced by unions over the last few years (Conseil économique du Canada 1985). For Canada as a whole, in 1986 the average income of women working full-time was $19,995, 35 percent less than the average of $30,504 earned by full-time male workers. In Quebec the gap is slightly smaller. Nevertheless, it has taken over fifteen years to reduce the gap by 10 percent, from 59 percent (of the average male income) in 1971 to 69 percent in 1986 (Dumas and Mayer 1989).

The situation is better for unionized women. They earn 85 percent of the average male wage, a gap fully 10 percent smaller than that for non-unionized women. Unionization also means more to a woman worker than to a man. The wage differential between unionized and non-unionized women was 41 percent, as compared to 24 percent for men (Paquette 1989). In the whole of Canada the differential impact of unionization for women was somewhat less (a 34 percent difference), but nevertheless important (McKie and Thompson 1990).

The Quebec and Canadian labour markets remain segregated by sex, with women concentrated in certain sectors and occupations. Of a list of 500 possible occupations, fully 60 percent of working women in Quebec were in only 20 occupations. In 1986, the great majority of women worked in the service sector, especially finance, insurance, and real estate (60.3 percent) and in the social, commercial, industrial, and personal services (59.1 percent). In Canada, too, women are overrepresented in the growing service sector, making up 84 percent of its workers. Most women, moreover, are employed in small businesses rather than large corporations and in community, business, and personal services rather than in servicing industry.

The trends observed between 1975 and 1986 are likely to continue. Most new jobs will be created in the service sector and in areas where women are overrepresented. Labour-market forecasts suggest that the employment rate for men will remain the same or decrease, while the employment rate for women will continue to increase, but many of these jobs will be of a temporary, casual, or part-time character. In other words, there is little chance that many new jobs will conform to the Fordist norm of permanent, full-time positions occupied by unionized (male) workers who also enjoy the benefits of social security legislation. The exemplar of the post-Fordist economy has become a woman employed on a part-time or otherwise insecure basis in the expanding service sector (Saint-Pierre 1986, 1990).

Women in Unions

In the last decade the situation of women in unions in Quebec has begun to change. Under pressure from feminists both within and outside the labour movement, representation of women has altered in important ways, although much remains to be done.

For Canada as a whole, where 34 percent of all workers are unionized, unionization of women was only 28 percent in 1985, while the men's rate was 38 percent. Yet women do account for a rising share of the organized workforce: In 1962, they contributed only 16 percent of total union membership in Canada, but by 1984, this figure had climbed to 36 percent. Between 1975 and 1984, women accounted for fully 73 percent of the growth in union membership (Conseil du statut de la femme 1984).

In Quebec, 1964—the year that public-sector unions won collective-bargaining rights—marked the beginning of the climb of unionization of women. Between 1963 and 1986, the percentage of women in Quebec unions rose from 20 to 31 percent. Despite such increases, however, women are still less unionized than men, whose rate is 41 percent (CSN 1979, 1984).

In both Canada and Quebec, the majority of unionized women are found in the public sector, which reproduces the distribution of working women described above. Nevertheless, unionization has not kept pace with all the trends in labour-market growth. If the tertiary sector is expanding, unionization of the sector—especially private services—remains relatively low. And, of course, it is in this sector that so many women now work. Several factors hinder unionization of private services, notably union traditions and labour legislation that does little to overcome the problems of organizing small workplaces. Part-time workers also tend to fall outside the protection of union membership. It is only recently that part-time workers have been able to join unions, and this is mainly in the public and parapublic (e.g., health and education) sectors.

What position do women hold within the power structures of the unions? Data collected in 1981 and 1982 on the three main Quebec federations suggest the following:

1. In the Confédération des syndicats nationaux (CSN) women accounted for 44 percent of the membership but only 33 percent of congress delegates. They provided only 18 percent of the delegates to the Confederal Council that takes decisions for the CSN between congresses.

2. In the Fédération des travailleurs et des travailleuses du Québec (FTQ), then affiliated with the Canadian Labour Congress, one of every three union members was a woman, but women accounted for only one in ten of those holding union office.

3. Even in the Centrale de l'enseignement du Québec (CEQ), where women provided 70 percent of the membership, they held only

one-third of the positions of responsibility within the union hierarchy. Women held three seats of seven on the National Bureau, the main decision-making body. In 1988, however, the CEQ became the first of the main labour organizations in Quebec to elect a woman president.

Overall, then, the conclusion is that despite the steady rise in the unionization of women, they are still underrepresented in decision-making bodies. This holds true even at the local level.

In part to overcome this lack of representation and other barriers, women began to organize *within* unions in the 1970s. Women's committees came into being. These activist bodies were not set up by the all-male union leadership but were the result of initiatives taken by rank-and-file women, as well as women holding union office at the local level. The committees' main focus was training and information pertaining to the paid and unpaid work of women in the workplace and in the family. The committees also lobbied within the labour movement for support for demands of particular import to women as workers and as mothers. In 1982, there were over two hundred local committees (out of a total of three thousand locals). The number continues to increase at both the local and regional level, and more women are assuming union responsibilities (Paré 1983).

All three labour federations now have central bodies dealing with the situation of working women (comités de la condition féminine), each headed by a female vice-president in charge of the committee and of coordinating the work of lower-level women's committees. Such committees, at all levels, differ in important ways from pre-1970s women's commissions that tended to deal with "women's issues" in isolation from the general concerns of the labour movement. Now efforts are being made to overcome this separateness. While such a modification of analysis and strategy reflects a solid and growing representation of women and their interests within the labour movement, the situation remains precarious, especially in periods of recession.

Women's Claims and
Union Responses in the 1980s

The 1980s brought an important ideological reorientation of the Quebec labour movement with regard to understandings of women's place in the labour market and their working conditions. These changes were never easily achieved and followed from the determination of women inside and outside the labour movement. In fact, the history of the Quebec labour movement clearly indicates that improvements in the working conditions of women were due largely to the actions taken by women themselves in factories (textiles and clothing), in services (school teachers and nurses), and within the unions themselves (by elected women and female staff) (CSN and CEQ 1987).

Until the mid-1970s, however, the labour movement's emphasis on class as the basis for organization and recruitment left little room for thinking about gender differences. Any gains women made followed from demands designed to meet the needs of men. An emphasis on class tended to obscure the specific situation faced by women workers, and union priorities were set by and for the male majority. The central figure represented by the Fordist labour movement was a white male, head of a family, working in industry. His concerns dominated the unions' stance at the bargaining table. Thus, wage demands were calculated on the basis of the material needs of the male worker, not as an individual, but as the head of a family. Women's need for a "living wage" often disappeared in such calculations. If gender relations are understood as a form of political domination by men over women that cuts across class lines, the labour movement's ideological orientation in these years can only be described as patriarchal, reinforcing a traditional sexual division of labour in the workplace and the home.

The feminization of the labour force is challenging patriarchal ideology and practices. A "new" worker is now more often represented. The demands expressed by this new figure—the working mother—disrupt the traditional union discourse. This worker is often married, although she may be separated, divorced, or a single parent (see Table 13.3). She works in the service sector, mainly in public or parapublic institutions, in low-paid, subordinate jobs and is already a CSN or an FTQ member. If an FTQ member, she works in the private sector as a textile or a garment worker, in a cafeteria or as a cleaner (FTQ 1979, 1984, 1985).

An examination of the documents and statements of a variety of union committees over the last decade provides some insight into the emergence of this new figure. An awareness of the changes has been growing among rank-and-file members, due in no small part to the efforts of the women belonging to the committees. The time and energy required by women workers to integrate feminist ideology into their practices and to defend these before their male colleagues is enormous. Nevertheless, it is happening. One measure of the success is the transformation of the union centrals' definition of their priorities, reflected in the demands made in the 1989 public-sector negotiations (CSN 1988).

In the first round, the first set of demands directly expressed the needs of working mothers. They included calls for more day-care centers and for financial support for child-care from the state. This demand resembled that of the Canadian Labour Congress (CLC), which had already provided support for the Canadian Day Care Advocacy Association's call for a "universally accessible, publicly-funded, non-profit child care system" (CLC 1988). Paid maternity and parental leave were also important issues on the bargaining table. The second round of demands pertained to measures to secure women's equality in the labour market, including "equal pay for work of equal value" and affirmative action programs that would provide both equality of opportunity and access to jobs.

Other unions are also expressing similar concerns. They are concentrating on the working conditions of women and men employed in factories. Therefore, occupational health and safety, and education and training provide a central focus. Such matters can have a clear gendered dimension, however. Women factory workers are more prone to repetitive stress injury, a problem whose solution only recently has been made a priority. In addition, retraining programs for women clerical workers facing technological change are as important as programs for shop-floor workers. The campaign against sexual harassment, however, aims more directly at the transformation of working relationships between men and women in the factory or office.

Although the change in union demands reflects the successes of the women's movement in society and in the unions, the latter have still to overcome the problems involved in organizing many women workers. Small enterprises, banks, shops, custodial work—not to mention part-time, casual, and temporary jobs where women are found in growing numbers—are not easy areas to organize. What is needed here is union action to secure more proactive legislation at the provincial and federal level. More support for the accreditation of unions in very small units is necessary; stores, garment workshops, and businesses providing personal services are all workplaces with many women employees. Similarly, legislation to permit the unionization of casual and contractual workers would make even more women available for unionization. If this cause is not actively championed by the unions, many of the typical (women) workers of the post-Fordist economy will remain unorganized. Given the current trends in the labour market, this can only weaken the unions in the long run.

Union Democratization and
New Forms of Militancy

Labour legislation and union structures in Canada and the United States represent barriers to the unionization of workers in the growing secondary segment of the labour market (Gordon, Edwards, and Reich 1982). Trade unions face a choice. Either they can move defensively to protect the benefits already acquired by core workers, or they can make an offensive move. The latter could aim not only to secure benefits for workers who do not belong to the traditional working class—part-time workers, temporary workers, service-sector workers—but also to fight for the specific needs of women as women workers.

If they choose an offence rather than simply a defence, unions must take into account both the conditions of women who are already employed and the situation facing women who are not part of the labour force. This means that the labour movement has to extend its reach beyond traditional arenas like the negotiation of working conditions and wages. The difficult situation of women and the gender-segmented labour force relates not only to gender relations in the workplace, it is also affected by the division of labour in the home, where parental responsibilities are not equally shared and "caring" work is denied social and economic recognition.

A new awareness of work relationships between men and women has to be developed in the workplace and within the family in order to allow women access to better jobs at higher levels of responsibility. While union *ideology* now does reflect such an awareness, much remains to be done at the level of actual *practice*. If the current recession proves longer than the one with which the last decade opened, however, women's struggle for equality in the workplace, in the labour market, and in society in general may encounter a backlash as young and old, men and women, and immigrants and native-born compete for fewer jobs. Solidarity will be difficult to sustain as unions, too, compete for members, both old and new.

Pressure on the unions has also come from the growth of independent unions, that is, unions not affiliated with one of the three main federations. Working women who are sometimes unsatisfied with the response they get from the well-established unions are tempted to join or to form their own unions. Groups like nurses have led the way here.[2]

The unions are not, however, helpless. They can take steps to meet these challenges. A critical element here is the move to debureaucratization or democratization of union structures. Democratization could lead to more direct participation by unemployed union members as well as by rank-and-file members in defining the unions' priorities and strategies not only during negotiations but on a permanent basis. Such strategies would move beyond the defence of the specific interests of particular groups of workers to tackle all aspects of social and economic development. Over the last decade, the Quebec labour movement has taken steps in this direction.

Democratization in the 1990s signifies a lessening of not only the bureaucratic practices that govern internal union relations but also the administration of collective agreements. In many respects, North American unions bear a greater resemblance to insurance companies than they do to social movements. This bureaucratic way of functioning has discouraged many women from taking part in union activities. It also keeps in power those who are more proficient at maintaining routines than at initiating change.

Democratization also means a redefinition of what it means to participate and a redistribution of responsibility. Traditional forms of participation—evening meetings, weekend conferences, availability on a twenty-four-hour basis—are difficult for women with family responsibilities. Quebec unions are beginning to recognize the gender-specific consequences of these expectations and practices. Union women have insisted that union leaders and male workers begin to live up to their responsibilities as fathers and husbands. A redistribution of power and responsibility within the unions also requires redistribution of responsibility within the home. New opportunities that allow women to take on more important responsibilities at various levels of the unions' structures will then become possible, as will the potential for developing a new awareness of the need to build organizations in which women and men can truly be recognized as equals.

The question remains whether North American labour organizations will be able to meet this challenge at a time when they face tremendous pressures from the dissolution of the Fordist world to which they had grown accustomed. The emergent post-Fordist universe is a less welcoming one, where economic recessions succeed one another and where the new basis of accumulation depends on the exclusion of many categories of workers and the precarious situation of others. New labour-management policies tend to replace traditional labour relations, and the welfare state is withdrawing its support in many areas of social life.

As Quebec enters the 1990s, these challenges to the unions and the women's movement are made more complex by constitutional struggles. The movement for Quebec sovereignty has resurfaced, and the unions are very much part of it: Will Quebec's struggle for independence encourage the revival of social-movement unionism (Touraine 1984)? But constitutional matters are not the only challenge the unions face. Will the falling birth rate among francophones and anglophones in Quebec revive the spectre of a conservative "natalism"? It is precisely those women who are in their child-bearing years that constitute—now and in the future—the major group of part-time, low-paid, nonunionized workers who lack social security rights, and it is precisely these conditions that discourage them from planning to have more than one child. In this context, the unions have a specific role to play, bringing what is defined as "women's problems" to the public agenda.

North American unions are under tremendous pressure, but they will be more able to meet the challenge if they heed the demand of women both within and outside the labour movement. These demands bring to the fore the figure of the post-Fordist worker and foreshadow the new practices that need to be embraced if the unions are to survive and grow. Unions that take up the challenge at work, in society, and in political life are more likely to find a place in this new world than those which cling to practices now outdated.

Notes

1. In the same years, total employment increased by only 5.3 percent (McKie and Thompson 1990).

2. See Hébert in this volume on the growth of new forms of unionism outside the established structures.

References

Boyer, Robert. 1981: Les transformations du rapport salarial dans la crise: Une interprétation de ses aspects sociaux et économiques, *Critiques de l'économie politique*, Paris: Maspero, 15/16, 185–228.

Canadian Labour Congress (CLC). 1988: *The Equality Challenge: Taking Hold of Our Future*, Sixth Biennial National Women's Conference.

Confédération des syndicats nationaux (CSN). 1979: *Les travailleuses et l'accès à la syndicalisation*, Etats généraux des travailleuses salariées québécoises, Montréal.

———. 1984: *Dix ans de lutte—les femmes à la CSN continuent d'avancer*, 5e rapport du comité de la condition féminine de la CSN, Montréal.

———. 1986: *"On vit pas d'amour et d'eau fraîche" ou "Quelle est la valeur du travail des femmes?"* Rapport du comité de la condition féminine, 53e Congrès de la CSN.

———. 1988: *Pour un avenir à notre façon*, 7e Rapport du comité de la condition féminine, 54e Congrès de la CSN.

Confédération des syndicats nationaux (CSN) and Centrale de l'enseignement du Québec (CEQ). 1987: *The History of the Labour Movement in Quebec*, Montreal, New York: Black Rose Books. (Book written by B. Chiasson, M. Doré, H. David, L. Fournier, J. M. Montagne, H. Paré, S. B. Ryerson, C. Saint-Pierre.)

Conseil du statut de la femme. 1984: *Les femmes ça compte*, Québec: Direction générale des publications gouvernementales.

Conseil économique du Canada. 1985: *Pour un partage équitable*, Compte rendu du colloque sur la situation économique des femmes sur le marché du travail, Ministre des approvisionnements et services du Canada.

Dumas, Marie-Claire, and Francine Mayer, eds. 1989: *L'équité salariale, un pouvoir à gagner*, Montréal: Les éditions du remue-ménage.

Fédération des Travailleurs et des travailleuses du Québec (FTQ). 1979: *Une double exploitation—une seule lutte*, Colloque sur la situation des femmes au travail.

———. 1984: *L'égalité: source de changements*, Colloque sur l'accès à l'égalité en emploi pour les femmes, Montréal.

———. 1985: *Projet de réglementation concernant les programmes d'accès à l'égalité*, Mémoire de la FTQ.

Gordon, David, Richard Edwards, and Michael Reich. 1982: *Segmented Work, Divided Worker: The Historical Transformation of Labor in the United States*, Cambridge: Cambridge University Press.

McKie, Craig, and Keith Thompson, eds. 1990: *Canadian Social Trends*, Toronto: Thompson Educational Publishing.

Ministère de la Main-d'oeuvre et de la Sécurité du revenu. 1989: *La main-d'oeuvre et l'emploi au Québec et dans ses régions—Bilan 1988 et perspectives 1989–1990*, Québec: Gouvernement du Québec.

Paquette, Louise. 1989: *La situation socio-économique des femmes*. Faits et chiffres, Québec: Les Publications du Québec.

Paré, Hélène. 1983: *Les comités de condition féminine dans les syndicats du Québec*, Montréal: Secrétariat d'Etat, Programme de la promotion de la femme.

Saint-Pierre, Céline. 1986: Les femmes dans l'organisation du travail. In Centrale de l'enseignement du Québec, ed., *Mémoires d'un forum de femmes*. 158–63. Actes du colloque, Montréal: CEQ.

———. 1990: La place des femmes sur le marché du travail à moyen et à long terme. In Roger Tessier and Yvan Tellier, eds., *Historique et prospective du changement planifié*, vol. 1, 253–67, Québec: Presses de l'Université du Québec.

Touraine, Alain, Michel Wierworka, and François Dubet. 1984: *Le mouvement ouvrier*, Paris: Fayard.

Workplace Restructuring: Company Unionism or Industrial Democracy?

14 DONALD M. WELLS

Recent Innovations in Labour-Management Relations: The Risks and Prospects for Labour in Canada and the United States

In Canada, as in the United States, there is an emerging consensus about the need for increased labour cooperation with management productivity goals in response to heightened international competition.[1] The panoply of industrial relations innovations range from restructuring workers' attitudes to group problem solving, incentive-pay schemes linked to productivity, and a wide range of changes in job structures. Such changes in job structures range all the way from minor ones, such as job rotation and enlargement, to major alterations, such as job enrichment and semi-autonomous work groups. Programs associated with these innovations are becoming well known under such labels as employee involvement (EI), quality-of-work-life programs, sociotechnical systems (STS), team-work, and Japanese production management (JPM). Systems of pay such as profit sharing and productivity-gains sharing are often, although not necessarily, associated with these programs.

Those who champion these cultural and structural changes in the workplace typically present them as "win-win" opportunities in which managers gain greater productivity while workers gain increased job security, better jobs, and a say in decisions about work. The conflicting interests of employees and their employers are transformed by these innovations into a mutually beneficial collaboration.

In this chapter, I will provide a critique of these innovations from a labour perspective. Prior to doing this, I will assess the main differences between the Canadian and U.S. labour movements in their responses to these changes.

Labour-Management Cooperation in the United States and Canada Compared

A widespread view holds that the Canadian labour movement itself is a critique-in-practice of these innovations, that Canadian unions constitute a fundamental alternative to increased "cooperation" with management. Thus, a great many American union activists and pro-labour academics have taken inspiration from their vision of healthy, more adversarial unionism north of the border. Because the Canadian and U.S. labour movements face similar challenges, these American critics of labour cooperation see this vision as a desirable option for the U.S. labour movement: In essence, if the Canadians can do it, why can't we?

The Canadian industrial-relations system is more like the U.S. system than that of any other country in the world. The labour movements in both countries face openly hostile neo-liberal governments at the national level. Both exist in what is rapidly becoming a single continental economy. The two labour movements share many of the same unions, especially in the private sector, and both often face the same transnational employers, especially in the manufacturing and resource sectors, in which management has concentrated its attempts at concessions bargaining and innovations in "employee involvement." At an accelerating rate, Canadian and U.S. workplaces are being rationalized into continentwide and global organizations. This is occurring alongside increasing harmonization of monetary and fiscal policy by a postnational Canadian state that is anxious to fit into a U.S.-dominated continental politico-economic bloc. These pressures are undermining centralized union bargaining in favour of decentralized forms of labour-management relations at the level of the workplace and in favour of a form of enterprise unionism.

Canadian unions thus face many of the same economic and political forces now transforming labour-management relations in the United States. Indeed, in key respects labour unions in Canada are more vulnerable to these pressures. In part, this is because the Canadian economy is much smaller, more dependent on international trade, and more sensitive to international capital mobility. The Canadian labour movement has also faced more political pressure to participate in many of these industrial relations innovations. In contrast to the United States, where governments have played little if any role, Canadian governments have been determined promoters of participative management schemes.[2]

Despite these pressures, labour in Canada has been more successful at charting a robust and independent course than have the U.S. unions. Canadian unions have been better able to resist concessions bargaining and have maintained a level of unionization that is more than double the U.S. rate. While labour in the United States has often faced a Hobson's choice of embracing these innovations or facing decertification or a runaway firm, in Canada labour has generally sustained a more adversarial form of unionism. More than their U.S. counterparts, union leaders in Canada have viewed work flexibility and participative management as attempts to increase speedup, undermine worker solidarity, and bust unions (Kumar and Ryan 1988). Union centrals in the heavily unionized provinces of Ontario and British Columbia, for example, passed convention resolutions in the early 1980s that condemned quality-of-working-life programs and similar participative management schemes as antiunion. Recently, the Canadian Auto Workers (CAW) (1989) and the Canadian Paperworkers Union (1990) have produced position papers that are highly critical of such programs. The head of Canada's largest public-sector union, the Canadian Union of Public Employees (CUPE), has also criticized the "team" concept (Rose 1991). In this atmosphere, labour-management cooperation and contingent-pay systems have been slow to diffuse in unionized workplaces during the 1980s in Canada, while in the United States diffusion has been rapid (Verma 1990).

There are several major reasons for this difference. First, Canada has a stronger tradition of social unionism than the United States, where unions have typically been more narrowly concerned with bread-and-butter issues (Robinson, this volume). More skeptical views of participative management on the part of Canadian unions are consistent with this broader view of labour's role. Second, Canada has a social democratic party (the New Democratic Party) with much strength in several provinces, as well as some influence at the national level. Furthermore, while the Canadian state has been dominated by neo-liberal governments since the mid-1980s, the industrial heartland provinces of Ontario and Quebec have been controlled by more moderate parties, with the NDP in power in Ontario since September 1990. Because the provinces rather than the federal government have the primary responsibility for labour legislation in Canada, the political makeup of these governments is far from insignificant. In the United States, however, labour legislation is affected far more by the political complexion of Washington than by that of the state capitols. Third, since the Canadian labour movement is in a much stronger position than U.S. labour, employers have been less able to pursue the intimidating "dual" or "mixed" strategy of avoiding unions in some workplaces while demanding increased cooperation in their unionized sites (Verma and Kochan 1990). On the whole, Canadian managers are less strenuous in pressing new workplace changes than are their U.S. counterparts (Adams 1988a).

It is important, however, not to exaggerate these differences. There is growing evidence that the impact of international competition in particular and the overall shift of power in favour of management is tending to wear down Canadian union opposition to these innovations. Although major differences remain, the tendency to a more collaborative form of labour-management relations is operative on both sides of the border.

For several years the perception of the differences between the two labour movements in their basic levels of militancy and solidarity in response to human-resource-management innovations has been distorted. In part, this is because of a tendency to extrapolate the differences between the Canadian Auto Workers (CAW) and the United Auto Workers (UAW) to the rest of their respective labour movements. The CAW has done much to create an atmosphere in the Canadian labour movement that is quite different from that in the U.S. labour movement, which, along with the UAW, has frequently embraced these changes as calling forth a new era of harmony in labour-management relations.

The CAW, however, does not reflect the Canadian labour movement as a whole, but rather is the chief articulator of one tendency. Other influential unions in Canada, including the Steelworkers, the Communications Workers, the Energy and Chemical Workers, and the United Food and Commercial Workers, have taken a much more collaborative position in relation to the new industrial relations. A great many other unions in Canada have never articulated an official position on these issues. Many of them have consented to these innovations through silence.

In part, the difference between the CAW and other unions is a reflection of variations in economic fortune: The CAW has been less damaged than other industrial unions by the massive losses of manufacturing jobs. The CAW also has a united national leadership, a highly centralized bargaining structure, and a strong representation structure at the workplace level. These are advantages that many unions do not enjoy, making them more vulnerable to management pressure.

For these and other reasons, the official position of the CAW is not typical of much of the Canadian labour movement. Moreover, whereas the CAW's stance has often been interpreted as a militant "just say no" position akin to that of the New Directions faction in the UAW, in practice the CAW's position is more complex and subtle: It is a *negotiating* position. Locals of the CAW have made concessions in several areas, including the consolidation of job classifications, multiskilling, and team working, in exchange for such gains as better access to training and longer notice of technological changes affecting job content and job losses. Even before the current recession, there was a greater incidence of concessions in the Canadian auto industry than has been generally recognized (Katz and Meltz 1989). The CAW's most telling "strategic compromise," however, has been to accept the team concept at CAMI, a joint venture between General Motors and Suzuki, in exchange for uncontested union recognition in the plant (see below).

More broadly, although the CAW has been in the forefront of opposition to profit sharing, there is evidence of a large increase in gain sharing and profit sharing, particularly in larger firms in the Canadian steel and mining sectors.[3] A survey of over six hundred Canadian firms concludes that "broad based employee profit sharing has become quite widespread" (Long 1990).[4] Although comprehensive statistics concerning diffusion of labour-management cooperation programs are not yet available, knowledgeable observers are in broad agreement that these changes are spreading rapidly in the manufacturing sector and increasingly in the service sector, particularly in hospitals and government offices.[5]

This is not to say that the rate of diffusion of these innovations is not slower in Canada than in the United States. Rather, it is to suggest that the rate of diffusion is increasing in Canada and thus that the U.S. and Canadian labour movements are subject to the same tendencies. Aside from differences in the rate of diffusion, Kochan concludes that in contrast to the United States, changes occurring in Canadian unionized workplaces are being initiated much more through normal contract bargaining (1988: 45). This is to be expected, since in Canada the "non-union" option is less available to employers either as a source of pressure on unions or as an alternative locus of production. Joint labour-management participation schemes have proven highly difficult to sustain in the context of union opposition (Kochan and Cutcher-Gershenfeld 1988).

Finally, to a far greater extent than in the United States, in Canada there has been a remarkable expansion of labour-management consultation and information sharing at the sectoral and national levels, outside collective bargaining. Major examples include the Canadian Textile Labour Management Committee, the Canadian Steel Trade and Employment Congress, the Joint Human Resources Committee of the Canadian Electrical/Electronics Manufacturing Industry, the Western Wood Products Forum, as well as labour-management committees for automotive repair, dockworking, and the aerospace industry (Barrie 1987; Thompson 1990). The most significant labour-management cooperation nationally is the Canadian Labour Market and Productivity Centre, an ongoing forum on productivity issues. Backed by federal government funding, the centre brings together Canada's principal national union central, the Canadian Labour Congress, and the key national association of the largest employers, the Business Council on National Issues. The centre was closely involved in the negotiations that led to the establishment of the Canadian Labour Force Development Board, created to provide labour-management proposals on training.

Thus, unionized labour's responses to workplace innovations and pay systems in the two countries are much more complex than any simple pattern of divergence. While significantly less pervasive in Canada as yet, labour-management cooperation programs and contingent-pay innovations are being implemented in Canada at an accelerating rate.

Industrial Relations Innovations in Canada: The Dangers to Labour

Integrated Approaches: Sociotechnical Systems (STS)

It is often the most comprehensive, integrated innovations in the restructuring of workplace relations that highlight the implications for labour most clearly. Thus far, the most well developed of these innovations are rare, particularly in unionized workplaces. Sociotechnical systems (STS), attempts to integrate social and technical dimensions of the labour process, are among the most comprehensive. Classical STS design is built around "semiautonomous work groups" (teams of workers who have collective responsibility for a "natural" unit of work and much discretion in planning, executing, and monitoring their work). Although conventional exponents of STS argue that success depends on employee participation in the redesign of their jobs, there is no evidence to suggest that such participation has been a major factor at most of the sites in Canada employing the STS approach. Overall design has clearly been a management prerogative, and workers have made only limited, after-the-fact choices.

The *kind* of technology used is often a distinctive feature of STS sites in Canada. STS designs tend to be located where there is continuous process technology (e.g., chemical plants and refineries). STS sites also tend to have high capital-labour ratios. Together these two features encourage managers to place a premium on workers' abilities to avoid errors and to respond quickly to a variety of production situations. The intimate association of STS design with these technological and investment features suggests that managerial values have little to do with the change.

Management consultants have made STS design a minor growth industry, and a vast literature often portrays STS as an opportunity for unions to develop a more cooperative, "mature" relationship with management. A recent study published by the Economic Council of Canada suggests that the "fullest development of socio-technical systems theory might only be possible where union and management are . . . willing to work jointly towards fundamental change" (Mansell 1987: 13). Closer examination of the four cases cited by Mansell sheds a different light on the compatibility between STS and unions. Two STS experiments were used as prototypes to create nonunion STS sites elsewhere; in the third case, the union became a company union; and in the fourth, management claims to have no knowledge of STS ever having been implemented.[6]

One of the two unionized STS sites used to create a nonunion STS site is the Eldorado Resources uranium refinery in Port Hope, Ontario. The refinery workers are represented by the United Steelworkers of America. Managers used the Port Hope refinery as a prototype for an STS design at their new uranium refinery at Blind River, Ontario. The Blind River facility is a "union-free" site patterned after innovations that the Economic Council of Canada report considers "most impressive" because they were "implemented within the framework of an existing collective agreement" at the Port Hope site (Mansell 1987: 16).

According to Steelworkers organizers who have failed in their attempts to organize the new facility, the job structures introduced at Blind River that were based on the Port Hope refinery threaten the job security of the skilled trades workers. Eldorado has also used the Port Hope experience to create a special group of workers at Blind River who "act like stewards," voicing the concerns of their crews and departments to management and processing grievances according to a company procedure. The union organizers say that the managers manipulate this procedure by initially demanding much harsher discipline for infractions than they intend to execute, so that worker representatives can appear to succeed in bargaining for lesser penalties. In the eyes of the employees, this legitimates both these representatives and the company's procedure and makes union representation seem redundant.

Mansell's second example of a unionized STS plant is Royal Dutch Shell's chemical plant in Sarnia, Ontario. Managers at this $200 million chemical plant are extraordinarily dependent on the 130 employees who work there. The local union's chief steward says that a worker who makes a "wrong decision in the middle of the night could blow thousands and thousands of dollars. If we can put workers in a position where they can have so much impact by pushing a button, then the least we can do is to set up a system that allows them more control" (Mears 1986: 11). In fact the workers in this plant *already* have significant control through the technology. It is highly likely that the STS model is in large measure a reflection of that fact, not its cause. The study also neglects to mention that the Shell Sarnia plant has a sister plant in Alberta modelled on the same STS design. The Alberta plant, however, is not unionized.[7] So, contrary to the exemplifying compatibility with unionism, the union appears to be optional.

The third case is a Xerox assembly plant in Toronto, Ontario, where about 450 workers assemble photocopiers. These workers are represented by the Amalgamated Clothing and Textile Workers' Union. The site does not in fact qualify as an STS design, since no change has taken place in the jobs, most of which remain boring, repetitive, assembly-line jobs. Nor does the local union qualify as a genuine union. The employee relations manager at Xerox reports that the collective agreement is a mere thirty-seven pages in length because the company does not favour "a legalistic approach." In line with this goal, the first two steps in the grievance procedure are "informal dialogues" between workers and supervisors, and union representation during these dialogues is optional. The local union president reports that the week-long training in "Leadership through Quality" provided by the company encourages workers to take more responsibility for cost savings, imbuing them with the necessity to "meet the competition head on." The executive board of the local union meets monthly with management to discuss production objectives and to "give positive reinforcement" to the managers "to show them it's working," and local union leaders dine with managers every two or three months "just to rap."

The local union president finds that "more of the problems come from the shop floor" than from management, because "people forget the process. They forget to dialogue." He feels "hated" by the union members "who seem to be ungrateful." In one case, workers complained that management gave preferred jobs to younger workers with less seniority. The local union president "dialogued" with the supervisor and learned that the "younger workers [were] willing to move and older workers [were] more set in their ways." When he tried to explain this to the older workers, they remained dissatisfied and started a slowdown. He felt compelled to threaten them with "corrective action," telling them that he was "going to make a judgment that's right no matter if it's in the union's favour or management's favour." He clearly sees himself as a "go-between between management and the workers."[8] Local union leaders also appreciate the need to lay off workers when consumer demand drops and have agreed to the use of temporaries to give management the labour-force flexibility to meet these fluctuations in demand. The firm recently laid off forty-three of the temporary workers, but since they were not full-time workers, "nobody got hurt."

Inco Metals, the fourth unionized STS design mentioned in the study is a mystery: Inco's director of industrial relations states that he has never heard of such innovations at his firm.

Thus, none of the workplaces cited as examples of the application of STS in union settings proves, on closer investigation, to be altogether "union-friendly."

In addition to the council's examples, I have investigated the relationship between STS and unionism at three warehouses and a store, all of which were represented by the Retail, Wholesale, and Department Store Union. In the mid 1980s the union cooperated with management in setting up these sites. Two warehouses were "greenfield" sites (i.e., sites that were newly constructed). Before the greenfield sites were set up, the union entered into a voluntary agreement with management and took part in hiring interviews that were designed, according to a union official, to "weed out people who would cause aggravation."⁹ At one site, the union officials and managers selected forty out of over four thousand applicants in order to obtain what a union official called a "young, agile workforce."

There were no written, enforceable agreements pertaining to non-monetary issues. In hindsight, the union argues that this led management to violate oral agreements: Over time, management came to view the absence of contract language as carte blanche to restructure work relations. Union representatives complained that managers allowed workers to rotate on some jobs but not others; that the labour-management committee had little say: that seniority was ignored in assigning shifts; and that managers hired part-time workers to do the work of full-time workers. When union leaders requested that their informal union-management agreements be dissolved, the managers at one of the warehouses refused. The program was only withdrawn after a strike over the issue. Management has since shut down two of the other sites. The remaining two sites now have conventional union collective agreements.

Integrated Approaches:
Japanese Production Management (JPM)

Japanese production management (JPM), or "lean production," usually focussed on auto plants, also poses serious challenges to unions. Like STS, Japanese production management is rare in Canada, and, also like STS, it is centred around teams of workers. Team members are "cross-trained" in order to rotate between jobs. Members of the teams also take part in quality circles (groups of workers who meet to solve day-to-day production problems). The teams are loosely structured so that managers can have greater flexibility in moving workers from their "home teams" to other sections of the plant in response to changing needs. Such mobility reduces downtime and leads to the intensification of work. A looser team structure is also consistent with the role team members can play in monitoring each other against work inefficiencies. Since a premium is placed on the ability of managers to allocate labour flexibly, JPM plants have fewer, broader job classifications and more "multiskilled" workers than is typical of conventional assembly plants.

JPM's main goal is the constant elimination of production inefficiencies. This includes the elimination of as much indirect labour as possible. Thus, production teams perform quality inspection and housekeeping roles, machine repair, and so forth. JPM is intimately linked to the "just-in-time" delivery of parts used in production. Unlike conventional auto assembly, which allows workers to "bank ahead" by building a buffer of stock, just-in-time pressures workers (and parts suppliers) to meet production demands just as they arise. More generally, there is little reliance on inventories of either supplies or products. With little inventory to fall back on, quality defects can become a costly drag on production efficiency. This provides constant pressure on workers, a system Parker and Slaughter (1988) have dubbed "management by stress."

In Canada, this strategy has been implemented in its most developed form in four Japanese- and Korean-owned auto assembly plants.[10] Only one of these is unionized: the Suzuki–General Motors (CAMI) auto assembly plant, a greenfield site near a small town in rural Ontario. The price of union certification was the CAW's agreement—before any of the workers had been hired—that it would not oppose the introduction of Japanese work practices such as just-in-time, work teams, consolidated job classifications, and quality circles. The CAW signed a three-year contract in 1989, although by that time only about 225 workers had been hired. Thus, most of the 1700 production workers who work at CAMI neither voted to join the union nor voted on the collective agreement. The CAW's fear was that if it waited to organize the workers until the plant was fully operational, the organizing drive would fail.[11] In effect, CAMI was unionized only in a formal sense: The union had little place in the hearts and minds of the CAMI workers. Whether it will gain that place has yet to be determined.

The CAMI contract provides a normal steward structure and a conventional grievance-arbitration procedure. Japanese production management at CAMI, however, is clearly designed to reduce worker reliance on this kind of representation. After undergoing a rigorous, five-step, weeks-long interview and selection process, new workers, most of whom are young and lack factory experience, are trained in CAMI ideology through highly elaborate orientation programs. A group of academic and CAW researchers who have been studying the plant describe this orientation: "CAMI emphasizes that all employees, from the president to the production worker, are part of the same team, pulling together to produce 'world class' vehicles." This ideology is also seen in "the absence of exterior signs of rank, power and privilege. Workers are called production associates. There are no time clocks" (Robertson et al. 1991: 8–9).

CAMI has focussed much of its labour relations strategy on an effort to build up a cadre of team leaders. These workers are a layer of informal supervision and at the same time a core group of worker leadership inserted directly into the labour process. The company has been assiduous in cultivating their loyalty, even to the point of sending some of them on month-long trips to visit Suzuki plants in Japan. These team leaders are management's best hope for providing an alternative, company-oriented leadership cadre to compete with the union stewards and committee persons.

The union clearly recognizes that the team leaders' roles are contradictory. On one hand, they are like lead hands who assist workers as they work; on the other, they are like frontline supervisors, only they lack the authority to discipline their fellow workers. Bearing in mind that these team leaders are highly popular with the workers, the union is trying to win them over by highlighting the tension between these roles. In each team, the union is advising the team leader to be a "technical advisor" to workers but not to "manage people" (Robertson et al. 1991: 13). By promoting the leader's role of lead hand, the union is thus challenging CAMI's goal of eliminating excess labour, for according to JPM the lead hand's role of relieving overloaded workers is a form of excess labour. Thus, by making explicit the tension between supervision and production, the union is challenging CAMI's attempt to knit the two together. The union is also fighting to gain the workers' right to elect their own team leaders rather than have them appointed by management.[12]

It is too early to predict the outcome of this particular contest, but it is clear that JPM is spreading, especially in the North American automobile industry. Many managers in both countries have been impressed by the major productivity gains obtained at the NUMMI (New United Motors Manufacturing Inc.) auto assembly plant in Fremont, California (Krafcik 1988). Productivity increases at this General Motors–Toyota joint venture have been based on moderate levels of technological change and investment, making it less costly than comparable plants in North America.[13] Such performance and cost comparisons suggest that the Japanese model as it exists at NUMMI will enjoy wider application elsewhere in North America. Similar comparisons are being made between CAMI and other auto plants in Canada. Since CAMI is a joint venture with General Motors, the pressure to reproduce successful innovations from CAMI in other General Motors plants will be especially strong.

Even the CAW will find these innovations hard to oppose, especially if they occur in the context of nonunion sites or are a condition of new investment. The CAMI contract has already broken the General Motors bargaining pattern, and that precedent will be difficult to contain. The main difference between UAW and CAW approaches has not been whether or not to make concessions, but rather the degree to which concessions are made.[14] The difference between the Canadian and U.S. auto unions also concerns the *spirit* in which these concessions are made. The CAW never committed itself to a policy of "working together to create an organization promoting harmony, cooperation and understanding" the way the UAW did at Mazda (Fucini and Fucini 1990). Both in the plant and at its weekend classes on the team concept, the CAW has been careful not to sell JPM as any kind of solution, but rather as a necessary compromise that marks the beginning of a long struggle. That struggle will likely focus more on day-to-day issues centring on the labour process than on the kind of periodic collective bargaining that unions have come to see as normal. To do this, unions will need to develop a presence in the workplace that they have not had since the 1930s, when workers built industrial unions from the bottom up.

Partial Approaches

Integrated approaches like STS and JPM are the exception: The most typical kinds of recent workplace innovations involve partial approaches, the pursuit of a variety of *tactics* rather than a more integrated restructuring *strategy*. In these cases, the attention of managers is focussed on particular groups of workers or departments rather than on the labour process as a whole. At a particular site, management will form only some employees into problem-solving or consultation groups. Even the "leading edge" firms have made such piecemeal changes alongside uneven changes in technology and job structures (Robertson and Wareham 1987). Managers often unilaterally introduce most of the major changes in technology and job design, although some consultation with workers in regard to secondary details is not infrequent.[15]

Several Canadian studies point to a complex set of problems that this approach poses for unions. One concern is that the redivision of labour in line with new skill requirements creates a shift toward nonunion labour: Automation of blue-collar labour increases the proportion of largely nonunion white-collar labour in research, marketing, design, engineering, and other areas in the company (Robertson and Wareham 1988a, 1988b). A further concern has been management's use of technological change to redesign jobs in order to subcontract the work to nonunion workers (Robertson and Wareham 1989).

The restructuring of work around new skills has also created divisions among union members. In the context of new pressures to create multitiered workforces, significant divisions are emerging between the workers management has chosen to train and those who have been excluded. This often amounts to a generational split, where management considers older workers less worthy of retraining (Sobel and Meurer 1988). As management creates other layers of privilege among production workers, further tensions develop among union members.

Dissolution of traditional boundaries between job categories increases intraunion conflict among workers over the allocation of work. A major split has occurred, for example, within the United Steelworkers of America local at Stelco in Hamilton, Ontario, where management is using new technology as a partial basis for redefining both production and craft jobs. In some cases functions that were previously performed by skilled trades workers have been given to production workers. The union has tried to defend the skilled trades' job boundaries, but this has sometimes been at the expense of better jobs for production workers. Some have argued that the union should demand that skilled trades workers should be compensated with some of the functions now performed by plant engineers, but the union is not in a strong enough position to make this kind of gain. Job amalgamation for both production and skilled trades workers has resulted in work intensification, job elimination, and interference with promotion ladders (Sanger 1988; Adams 1988b).

Managers have also introduced new skill requirements in ways that increase their control over workers through favouritism in access to training and through training programs designed to socialize workers in corporate ideology.[16] For example, General Motors conducts training programs in which 70 percent of the content has been designed to create "cultural change" for what the programs term an "involved" workforce "equipped for our journey to world class" (Robertson and Wareham 1987: 47). General Motors also has a multi-million-dollar, week-long "Family Awareness Training" program, designed—as a local union leader has pointed out—to establish "a family atmosphere" between workers and managers (Kewley 1989). At the same time, such skills training is tied to the meritocratic ethos that lies at the heart of an ideological offensive against collective values.

Corporations have also been increasing their power through codifying employee skills in management manuals. This implies an undermining of the tacit "know-how" embedded in informal employee relations,[17] the kind of skills that form part of the basis of solidarity and informal worker control over work. Employers have also been attempting to introduce more credential-based promotion criteria that undercut union seniority provisions.

The Dangers to Workers and Unions

All of these innovations, both partial and integrated, carry with them a message: International competitiveness, technological changes, and a new, more progressive breed of manager are laying a new basis for cooperation between labour and management. This is a message that, while often vague, can be empirically evaluated. For instance, at the General Motors plant in Ste. Thérèse, Quebec, the CAW has agreed to the introduction of the "team concept," to a substantial reduction in the number of job classifications, and to flexible work rules, as the price for General Motors' commitment to keep the plant open. Despite this (and federal and provincial government subsidies and tax breaks totalling $330 million) the plant is still at risk of being permanently shut down. Since the introduction of the team concept, moreover, the 3,500 workers at the plant have experienced considerable work intensification: In the past three years the speed of the line has increased 25 percent, while the workforce has declined by 11 percent. The result has been an increase in the suicide rate in the plant to eight times the national average, a 15 percent increase in absenteeism, and higher levels of alcoholism and drug addiction. There has also been a large increase in off-the-job accident claims. These arguably reflect the pressures on workers to hide on-the-job injuries (in order to reduce workers' compensation claims) at a time when the increase in competition between workers has led to a faster pace of work and hence to increased injuries.

Local union leaders attribute the work intensification and these consequences to the team concept and to the plant's "continuous improvement processes."[18] This view is consistent with research on Japanese factories, which suggests an association between the pressures of just-in-time production and rates of suicide and accidents (Cusumano 1985: 305).

The role of the teams in constantly finding ways to increase efficiency, combined with their role in exerting peer pressure on workers to keep up with higher production standards, tends to make work especially difficult for older and unhealthy workers, for workers who openly criticize management, and for workers who used to have better, less strenuous jobs. Despite this, it is not at all clear that such work restructuring enhances job security by enhancing productivity. The intensity of work is only one of a host of factors contributing to productivity, and it is by no means among the most significant. Much depends on effective market demand for the firm's products or services. If demand is declining, jobs may be lost, regardless of productivity improvements. Everything else being equal, if demand is constant, productivity increases mean job losses. Even if consumer demand is increasing, productivity improvements can lead to job losses: Where productivity increases are translated into profits, management may invest the profits in other areas or in labour-displacing technology.

Another danger to unions that is often associated with such innovations is the direct co-optation of union leadership. There are several cases where management has preferred to co-opt union leaders rather than fight them. In the United States, some unions have accepted offers to sit on corporate boards of directors or on the boards of labour-management think tanks. In Canada, union leaders have more frequently accepted roles on labour-management committees at the industry rather than the corporate level. In the workplace, employers typically encourage local union leaders to become involved in "team" decision making, often about low-level production problems or cosmetic changes in working conditions. In some cases, this has led to circumvention of the grievance procedure and the contract, and local union stewards have become an informal adjunct of management (Wells 1987:85–87).

Many of these innovations focus on work groups and networks that generally constitute the heart of solidarity in the workplace. Within work groups, management frequently targets informal worker leaders who are the backbone of workplace militancy. Bringing this informal leadership onto their side can be critical to the process of turning peer pressure into group support for management goals. Thus, workers may take responsibility for supervising each other and may conduct productivity and quality competitions (voluntary work intensification) both within and between work groups. Unionists have been divided between individual "cooperators" and those who are less willing to go along. Union leadership has factionalized along similar lines, and the legitimacy of union leaders in the eyes of members has often suffered.[19]

The dangers to workers and their unions do not stop at the level of the plant. One of the major dangers to unions beyond the level of the enterprise has been "whipsawing," whereby the management plays off union locals against one another. Often out of fear of job losses, union locals compete against one another in making wage and work-rule concessions in exchange for management promises of greater job security (Clark 1989; Mann 1987; Yanarella and Green 1990).

Each of these aspects of work restructuring carries with it a challenge to the ability of unions to defend the interests of their members through traditional "job control" unionism based on narrow job classifications and a tight web of codified rules that regulate labour-management relations. These contractual defence mechanisms have traditionally defined the role of unions both in the workplace and in the collective-bargaining process. Such regulation of labour is now regarded by management as an impediment to increased productivity.

The challenge is not restricted to jobs. It extends to the very *collective basis* of unionism itself. In almost every case increased tension between union members follows from changes in their relation to the labour process. In some cases a redivision of labour creates gains for some at the expense of others. In other cases there is increased individual competition for access to training.

Until now, union contracts have regulated such competition between workers mainly on the basis of seniority provisions. This basis for maintaining a collectively legitimated method of distributing jobs, wages, fringe benefits, training, and the like among various age, skill, gender, ethnic, racial, and other categories of workers, as unequal as it may have been, is being eroded. This can lead to a horizontal and vertical frac-

turing of the basis of cohesion among unionists that has been a precondition of solidarity in the workplace. If management reconstitutes a sense
of collective consciousness by appeals to a corporate ideology of "cooperation," unions may find themselves without a legitimate role. In broad
terms, this is the potential threat to unions that such restructuring can
pose, even in the form of partial and unevenly diffused changes.

Union Responses

Less frequently now than in the past, union locals in Canada have refused to go along with innovations such as quality circles and employee
involvement. This refusal has been more likely when it has been supported by higher levels in the union, as has been the case in the Canadian
Union of Postal Workers, the CAW, the United Electrical Workers, and
a few others. Local unions have also been more likely to refuse to participate in these programs when the members have felt their jobs were secure whether or not they took part.

A policy of refusal has the merit of straightforwardness: A less clear-
cut position can increase confusion among union members who are already uncertain. As one worker at a General Motors plant put it, the
frequent lack of a straightforward policy has resulted in trade unions
"losing the battle on the shop floor because there is a total confusion as
to what is acceptable" (Rayner 1989).

Clear-cut refusal is especially fitting in cases where unions are weak
and where national leadership, willing and able to mobilize its members
around these issues, is lacking. Thus UAW members who oppose many
of these innovations often do not have the resources to negotiate their
own agenda. The New Directions Movement in the UAW is pushed
onto the defensive, refusing to participate. In some cases this kind of
recalcitrance has slowed down the implementation of programs such as
quality of work life (McSorley 1989), and there is little evidence that such
programs succeed where worker opposition is significant. In some cases,
it has been conjectured, workers may ally with disaffected sections of
"traditionalist" middle-level and front-line management. Certain supervisory jobs are clearly threatened, for example, by changes that call for
greater worker self-supervision. Such an alliance would, however, be unstable and for labour would likely prove wholly inadequate.[20]

Refusal may be preferable in the absence of union policy that addresses these issues, as is the case in many unions in both Canada and the United States. Outright refusal may not be appropriate, however, where unions are in a stronger position and have been able to define their own goals in the context of these programs.

Unlike the UAW, the CAW can bargain from a position of considerable internal unity: National leaders have broad support among the local-level leaders and much legitimacy among the members. The CAW leadership is sensitive to the fact that while the team concept is designed to increase management control, it also resonates with the needs and values of many workers. At a most fundamental level, teamwork appears to offer involvement in on-the-job decision making that has been absent from collective bargaining (Richards, Mauser, and Holmes 1988). Furthermore, group activity on the job can be a basis of solidarity, of informal leadership, of workers' abilities to improve their jobs and to resist speedups, and of much else that is valued by workers.

It is the degree of *perceived* correspondence between these needs, values, and group traditions, on the one hand, and changes such as teamwork, on the other, that often makes the latter so attractive to many workers and hence potentially powerful. Canadian and American workers are not alone in this. In West Germany, where teamwork is associated with higher wages, longer work cycles, opportunities for job rotation, and the inclusion of quality control and maintenance functions in production jobs, workers often favour these changes (Dankbaar 1988). Where workers have such attitudes because of such benefits, an outright rejection of such changes can easily be seen as contrary to their preferences and can allow management to portray unions as antagonistic to their members' interests.

Where unions are in a position to bargain about the team concept and related changes, they will need to specify what it is they want and what it is they do not want on an industrywide basis. Otherwise, unions risk reinforcing tendencies dividing one local from another by increasing variations between locals. Mobilization can focus on workers' involvement in determining these guidelines. This could become a basis for bringing union leaders and members together. This process can be used to strengthen ties between workers across the workplace, and since the guidelines would apply to all the workplaces affected, they could strengthen ties between the locals as well.

Guidelines can *reinforce* the value of participation and economic performance that is consistent with worker interests while opposing limits to participation that workers experience as they run up against the reality of hierarchy and the conflicts between their interest in better jobs and more pay and management's interest in speedup and profits. After ten years of the most advanced form of restructuring and the most optimal conditions for auto assembly work in the world, workers in the Volvo plant at Kalmar, Sweden, felt that their jobs gave them "too little room for the exercise of initiative and personal growth on the job" (Aguren et al. 1985).

Management innovations also need to be met with union restructuring, especially the connection between the members and stewards. The lowest level of union leadership is critical to union solidarity: It needs to emerge out of the solidarity of individual networks and work groups, to articulate and represent that solidarity, and to reinforce it through horizontal connections to other networks and groups. This is the traditional basis of the alternative to management's notion of "team building." The lowest level of union leadership is critical to the legitimacy of the union leadership as a whole: Most union members have some personal contact with their stewards but rarely with union leaders above that level.

It is critical that this level of leadership, whether stewards or informal group leaders, remain as autonomous as possible from management. Once they are induced into taking official or unofficial supervisory roles, they become a direct threat to the autonomy of the union and to the union's capacity to reinforce an awareness of the collective interests of workers.

The critical structural change for unions will be to diffuse union leadership by creating stewards (official or unofficial) who are elected by each team and strongly linked with the other team stewards. This will mean a major increase in the ratio of stewards to members. These stewards, themselves, will need to be *members* of the work teams, not just their representatives. This change would mean, then, reversing the postwar tendency toward full-time local leaders who are divorced from day-to-day working relations with their members. In the context of teamwork, the work groups that were once the basis of solidarity may well become the basis of identification with management. One option, discussed earlier in the CAMI case, is to ally the union to the team leaders, thus turning management cadres at the team level into union cadres. Otherwise, the teams are more likely to develop as an opposition force to the union (Mann 1987; Wells 1987: 39; Dankbaar 1988: 178).

Beyond this plant-level change, it will be important to find ways to reinforce the horizontal ties between locals so that management will be less able to play the locals off against each other. Otherwise the danger is that unions will drift into a form of microcorporatism: company-oriented unions at the level of the individual firm.

In the current economic circumstances, the main rationale for labour-management cooperation is how well these changes fit with the firm's competitive requirements. On this issue, unions are not without defences. Regarding claims that these forms of restructuring are necessary to ensure quality of production, for example, the CAW can point to the fact that the Big Three auto assembly plants in Canada have higher quality ratings *without* the team concept than U.S. plants achieve *with* the team concept. A recent survey of fifty-three auto plants in the United States concluded that "teams had either a negative effect or no effect on labor productivity and product quality" and that the number of job classifications did not have a statistically significant effect on the productivity of labour or the quality of production (Katz, Kochan, and Keefe 1987: 704).[21] A more recent study of twenty-one industries concludes that firms that have labour-management problem-solving committees are between 25 percent (the smaller firms) and 46 percent (the larger firms) less efficient than the firms that lack these committees (Harrison and Kelley 1991). These innovations, however, will probably continue as long as there are high-productivity examples such as NUMMI on which to focus management's attention.

Recognizing management's determination in implementing these changes, and aware of the dangers of passivity and refusal, more and more unions in Canada and the United States are now demanding that the innovations be integrated into the process of collective bargaining. This will increase the chances for unions to define and promote their own goals, but in many cases this is not going to be enough. The main weakness of unions is that they are not solidly entrenched among their own members while they are working on the job. The challenge of workplace restructuring is also a challenge to unions to restructure themselves. This means that collective bargaining needs to be integrated into the daily struggle between workers and employers. Unions need to bargain in an ongoing way on the shop floor and in the offices. One way to do this is to set up permanent bargaining committees of union members to supplement the periodic bargaining at contract times. Such committees could bargain around such issues as the changing role of team leaders, the composition and role of problem-solving committees, and the allocation of work between teams. In order to prevent these rank-and-file committees from contributing even further to the fragmentation of the members into competing teams, the committees would need to be coordinated across the entire workplace. In order to block tendencies toward "enterprise unionism" and to inhibit whipsawing, the committees would need to be linked up not only to the union leadership above the level of the local but also in a horizontal fashion to similar committees in other locals. The committees would provide an outlet for the members to take part in a more meaningful way in decisions about work through the union rather than under the aegis of management. They would also provide forums for workers to articulate their own needs, independent of the influence of corporate ideology in the joint committees with management. Finally, these rank-and-file committees could carry out an ongoing educational campaign to clarify workers' interests and needs in relation to restructuring in the workplace.

This kind of permanent worker mobilization in the workplace would have the goal of increasing workers' control over how they do their work. It would promote participation in the workplace on the basis of workers' own objectives. Where these kinds of reforms are possible, a revitalized rank-and-file labour movement centred in the workplace could build the solidarity and autonomy that workers require to build a more democratic workplace as the centrepiece of a more democratic society.

Notes

1. For their helpful advice in revising this essay, I am grateful to Dave Robertson, Jeff Wareham, Sam Gindin, Jane Jenson, Donald Swartz, and especially Ruth Frager. I am happy to acknowledge the financial support of the Social Sciences and Humanities Research Council of Canada.

2. Both the federal and the Ontario governments have been active promoters of "quality of work life" programs (Newton 1986).

3. Interview, Doug Olthius, Research Department, United Steelworkers of America, Toronto, 23 May 1991. See as well Benimadhu and Paris (1989).

4. Kochan (1988), too, cites a survey that reveals widespread profit sharing and gain sharing in Canada.

5. Kumar (1991), for example, notes a marked increase in "working together" strategies (e.g., employee problem solving, programs to improve la-

bour-management communication, and various other joint programs), especially in unionized workplaces.

6. Research on all the STS cases discussed here consists of my interviews with union and management representatives.

7. Leaders of the union (Energy and Chemical Workers) that represents the Shell Sarnia workers acknowledge the link between such innovations and union avoidance. One states: "I am involved in a number of quality of worklife programs. But wherever I have one that works, I have a dozen more that are simply designed to get rid of a union if it is there, or keep it out if it is not there" (Basken 1988: 21).

8. Two previous local presidents and one of the trustees, all of whom held union office after management introduced the "Leadership through Quality" program, have since taken management jobs. "This is one of the best plants in the company," the manager of employee relations says, because his relationship with the union is "more of a partnership" (personal interview).

9. As in previous instances of STS in union settings, this research also consists of interviews with management and the union. This and other quotations are from these interviews.

10. These are the Hyundai plant at Bromont, Quebec; Toyota, at Cambridge, Ontario; CAMI, at Ingersoll, Ontario; and Honda, at Alliston, Ontario.

11. This practice is similar to that of the UAW at the Japanese-model Saturn plant, where the union signed an agreement with General Motors to represent the plant without a membership vote (Downs 1989). Union fears about the difficulty of organizing such plants were reinforced by the UAW's defeat at the Nissan plant in Smyrna, Tennessee, in 1989.

12. This same battle has been fought at Mazda's auto assembly plant in Flat Rock, Michigan. In the last round of bargaining, the workers won the right to elect the team leaders. The plant is one of four unionized JPM plants in the United States (Parker 1991).

13. Comparisons have also been made between General Motors' Hamtramck plant in Detroit and Mazda's plant in Flat Rock, Michigan. According to Unterweger (1988) the latter is 25 percent less costly and more productive than the former.

14. The NUMMI agreement entailed more concessions than the CAW made to CAMI (Brown and Reich 1989).

15. With respect to technological change, a study for the Economic Council of Canada found a general absence of "real negotiation" between management and labour (Betcherman and McMullen 1987: 24).

16. Work restructuring at Pratt and Whitney Canada includes instilling commitment to productivity increases through training teams of workers in problem solving and group dynamics (Robertson and Wareham 1988b). North-

ern Telecom management created a "Team Excellence" program focussed on problem-solving groups in order to instil "company-centered" values for workers who are to join management in a "competitiveness coalition" (Robertson and Wareham 1988a).

17. Such codification is not without its potential contradictions: in work processes that require more wide-ranging, complex forms of worker cooperation, this practice contradicts the need to maintain a high level of this informal know-how.

18. *Toronto Globe and Mail*, 1 May 1989; *Financial Times of Canada*, 15 May 1989.

19. For an examination of these issues, see Grenier (1988), Rinehart (1984), Parker (1985), Parker and Slaughter (1988), and Wells (1987).

20. On the impact of industrial-relations innovations on managers, see Smith (1988).

21. A recent study of a General Motors plant was unable to confirm that Japanese-style innovations improved quality or productivity (Milkman and Pullman 1988).

References

Adams, Roy J. 1988a. *North American Industrial Relations: Divergent Trends in Canada and the United States*, McMaster University, Faculty of Business working paper no. 307.
———. 1988b. "The 'Old Industrial Relations' and Corporate Competitiveness: A Canadian Case," *Employee Relations* 10:2.
Aguren, Stefan, et al. 1985. *Volvo Kalmar Revisited: Ten Years of Experience*, Stockholm: Efficiency and Participation Development Council of SAF, LO, and PTK.
Barrie, Judy. 1987. "The Canadian Steel Trade Conference Inc.: A Constructive New Dialogue." In Roy Adams, ed., *Positive Industrial Relations: The Search Continues*, Montreal: McGill University Industrial Relations Centre.
Basken, R.J. 1988. "Foreign Issues and Applications-Discussant." In Alan Ponak, ed., *The Future of Alberta Labour Relations*, Calgary, Alta.: University of Calgary.
Benimadhu, Prem, and Helene Paris, eds. 1989. *Industrial Relations in 1989: Outlook and Issues*, Ottawa: Conference Board of Canada.
Betcherman, Gordon, and Kathryn McMullen. 1987. *Making Technology Work: Innovation and Jobs in Canada*, Ottawa: Economic Council of Canada.
Brown, Clair, and Michael Reich. 1989. "When Does Union-Management Co-operation Work? A Look at NUMMI and GM-Van Nuys," *California Management Review* 8.

Canadian Auto Workers. 1989. *Statement on the Organization of Work*, Toronto: CAW.

Canadian Paperworkers. 1990. *Team Concept and the Restructuring of the Workplace*, Montreal: Canadian Paperworkers Unions.

Clark, Gordon. 1989. *Unions and Communities under Siege*, Cambridge: Cambridge University Press.

Cusumano, Michael. 1985. *The Japanese Auto Industry: Technology and Management at Nissan and Toyota*, Cambridge, Mass.: Harvard University Press.

Dankbaar, Ben. 1988. "Teamwork in the West German Car Industry and the Quality of Work." In W. Buitelaar, ed., *Technology and Work: Labour Studies in England, Germany, and the Netherlands*, Avebury, U.K.: Aldershot.

Downs, Peter. 1989. "Union Blues," *The Progressive*, January.

Fucini, Joseph, and Suzy Fucini. 1990. *Working for the Japanese: Inside Mazda's American Auto Plant*, New York: Free Press.

Grenier, Guillermo. 1988. *Inhuman Relations: Quality Circles and Anti-Unionism in American Industry*, Philadelphia: Temple University Press.

Harrison, Bennett, and Maryellen Kelley. 1991. "Unions, Technology, and Labor-Management Cooperation." In Lawrence Mishal and Paula Voos, eds., *Unions and Economic Competitiveness*, Armonk, N.Y.: M. E. Sharpe.

Heckscher, Charles C. 1988. *The New Unionism: Employee Involvement in the Changing Corporation*, New York: Basic Books.

Katz, Harry, Thomas Kochan, and J. Keefe. 1987. "Industrial Relations and Productivity in the U.S. Auto Industry," *Brookings Papers on Economic Activity*, Washington, D.C.: Brookings.

Katz, Harry, and Noah Meltz. 1989. "Changing Work Practices and Productivity in the Auto Industry: A U.S.-Canada Comparison." In M. Grant, ed., *Industrial Relations Issues for the 1980s*, Quebec City: Laval University.

Kewley, Dan. 1989. "The Tools of Management Culture," *Oshaworker*, CAW Local 222, 19 January.

Kochan, Thomas A. 1988. *Looking to the Year 2000: Challenges for Industrial Relations and Human Resource Management*, Ottawa: Economic Council of Canada.

Kochan, Thomas A., and Joel Cutcher-Gershenfeld. 1988. *Institutionalizing and Diffusing Innovations in Industrial Relations*, Washington, D.C.: U.S. Department of Labor.

Krafcik, John. 1988. "Triumph of the Lean Production System," *Sloan School of Management Review*, Fall.

Kumar, Pradeep. 1991. *Industrial Relations in Canada and the United States: From Uniformity to Divergence*, Kingston, Ont.: Industrial Relations Centre, Queens University.

Kumar, Pradeep, and Dennis Ryan. 1988. *The Canadian Union Movement in the 1980s: Perspectives from Union Leaders*, Kingston, Ont.: Industrial Relations Centre, Queens University.

Lee, Bruce. 1988. "Worker Harmony Makes NUMMI Work," *New York Times* 25 December.

Long, R.J. 1990. "The Incidence and Predictors of Employee Profit Sharing and Ownership in Canada." In Alan Ponak, ed., *Teaching and Research in Industrial Relations*, Ottawa: Canadian Industrial Relations Association.

Mann, Eric. 1987. *Taking on General Motors: A Case Study of the UAW Campaign to Keep GM Van Nuys Open*, Los Angeles: Center for Labor Research and Education, University of California.

Mansell, Jacqui. 1987. *Workplace Innovation in Canada*, Ottawa: Economic Council of Canada.

McSorley, Randy. 1989. "How We Used Solidarity to Beat the Company's Quality of Work Life Scheme," *Labor Notes*, May.

Mears, Jan. 1986. "Workers Set the Pace," *Workplace Democracy* (Summer). Toronto: Quality of Work Life Centre.

Milkman, Ruth, and Cydney Pullman. 1988. *Technological Change in an Auto Assembly Plant: A Case Study of GM-Linden*, New York: Labor Institute.

Newton, Keith. 1986. "Quality of Work Life in Canada." In W. C. Ridell, ed., *Labour-Management Cooperation in Canada*, Toronto: University of Toronto Press.

Parker, Mike. 1985. *Inside the Circle: A Union Guide to QWL*, Boston: South End Press.

Parker, Mike. 1991. "New Mazda Contract Eases 'Management by Stress' System," *Labor Notes*, May.

Parker, Mike, and Jane Slaughter. 1988. *Choosing Sides: Unions and the Team Concept*, Boston: South End Press.

Rayner, Ivan. 1989. Article in *Oshaworker*, CAW Local 222, 19 January.

Richards, John, Gary Mauser, and Richard Holmes. 1988. "What Do Workers Want? Attitudes towards Collective Bargaining and Participation in Management," *Relations Industrielles*.

Rinehart, James. 1984. "Appropriating Workers' Knowledge: Quality Circles at a GM Plant," *Studies in Political Economy*, Spring.

Robertson, David, and Jeff Wareham. 1987. *Technological Change in the Auto Industry*, Toronto: CAW Technology Project.

———. 1988a. *Computer Automation and Technological Change: Northern Telecom*, Toronto: CAW Technology Project.

———. 1988b. *Pratt and Whitney Canada* (draft version), Toronto: CAW Technology Project.

———. 1989. *McDonnell Douglas Canada*, Toronto: CAW Technology Project.

Robertson, David, James Rinehart, Christopher Huxley, and the CAW Research Group on CAMI. 1991. *Team Concept: A Case Study of Japanese Production Management in a Unionized Canadian Auto Plant*, Toronto: CAW Technology Project.

Rose, Jeff. 1991. "The Team Concept," *The Facts* 13:1.

Sanger, Matt. 1988. *Transforming the Elements: The Reorganization of Work and Learning at Stelco's Hilton Works*, Masters thesis, University of Toronto.

Smith, Vicki. 1988. "Restructuring Management and Management Restructuring: The Role of Managers in Corporate Change," *Research in Politics and Society* 3.

Sobel, David, and Susan Meurer. 1988. *A Shameful Silence: Older Workers, New Technology, and Training*, Toronto: Metropolitan Toronto Labour Council.

Thompson, Mark. 1990. "Plus ça change: Canadian Industrial Relations in the 1980s," *Bulletin of Comparative Labour Relations* 20.

Unterweger, P. 1988. "The Human Factors in the Factory of the Future," Detroit Autofacts Conference, 12–14 November.

Verma, Awil. 1990. *Draft Report: The Prospects for Innovation in Canadian Industrial Relations in the 1990s*, Ottawa: Joint Committee of the Canadian Federation of Labour and World Trade Centres.

Verma, Awil, Thomas A. Kochan. 1990. "Two Paths to Innovation in Industrial Relations: The Case of Canada and the U.S.," Buffalo, N.Y.: Industrial Relations Research Association.

Wells, Donald M. 1987. *Empty Promises: Quality of Working Life Programs and the Labor Movement*, New York: Monthly Review Press.

Yanarella, Ernest, and William Green, eds. 1990. *The Politics of Industrial Recruitment*, New York: Greenwood Press.

15   STEPHEN HERZENBERG

Whither Social Unionism?
Labor and Restructuring in
the U.S. Auto Industry

Since 1979, the United Auto Workers International Union (UAW) has been faced with an unrelenting series of events symptomatic of the globalization of the motor vehicle and parts industry: the near collapse of Chrysler corporation in 1979; economic recession and rising Japanese market share from 1979 to 1983; the attempt by the U.S. Big Three (General Motors, Ford, and Chrysler) to transform their organizational practices and labor relations in response to Japanese imports; the construction of "transplants" in the United States by Japanese assemblers and suppliers; the increasing production of automobiles and parts in Mexico; and another recession and possible North American Free Trade Agreement.[1]

Among auto industry analysts, the UAW has received credit for recognizing early in the 1980s that the "world had changed" and that the adversarial labor relations, wage increases, and work rules that governed the U.S. auto industry from 1950 to 1980 could no longer be sustained. The national union's willingness to moderate wage demands and accept more flexible work organization has been rewarded by progressively stronger job and income guarantees for Big Three workers. These guarantees have provided Big Three UAW members with comprehensive protection from cyclical layoffs in the recession that began in 1990.

Despite the appearance of a fundamental reorientation of UAW policy in response to new international conditions, however, UAW strategy in the 1980s actually resembled that of the previous thirty years in several important respects.[2] First, UAW strategy remained focused on wage and benefit bargaining with the Big Three. Second, on the shop floor, UAW leaders continued to let local unions fend for themselves or supported management initiatives thought necessary to enable companies to pay pattern wages and benefits. Third, outside the Big Three, the increasingly nonunion and low-wage independent parts-supplier industry received little of the union's resources and attention. Fourth, in the political arena, union activity in an admittedly hostile climate remained focused on bureaucratic lobbying.

The process of national UAW strategy formation in the 1980s also resembled that of the previous three decades. The UAW's response to management demands took shape within the UAW's closed inner circle. It was modified little in response to rank-and-file arguments that flexible work organization would erode working conditions and compromise union independence. As in the past, UAW leaders marginalized their critics through their control over union resources, staff positions, and forums for internal debate more than by responding to opposition concerns. The process of internal union debate thus failed to confront the critical divisions within the membership and impeded the UAW's search for a more unifying response to industry globalization.

In sum, UAW strategy in the 1980s represented a limited break with traditional union practice. Given North American political and economic conditions, the UAW's reorientation failed to stem the move toward a highly segmented sectoral labor market in which the union represents only some workers in the core of the industry and plays a minimal role in regulating competition even within the core. Reestablishing a central role for the UAW in the industrywide labor market would require a more integrated multilevel union strategy. Such a strategy would integrate Big Three collective bargaining with a union vision of work reorganization, an attempt to spread this vision—and form of wage regulation—to the automotive parts sector, and the formation of coalitions with other groups to create regional, national, and continental policies that would support a more egalitarian, skill-based auto-sector pattern of development.

The rest of this chapter explores the restructuring of the U.S. auto industry in more detail. The second section describes the features of the postwar institutional system in the U.S. auto industry. The third and fourth sections analyze management restructuring strategies in the early 1980s and the union's response to management initiatives. The fifth and sixth sections outline how management strategy and the union response have reshaped in-plant labor relations and the UAW's position in the supplier sector.

Fordist Regulation in the U.S. Auto Industry

Institutional relations in the post–World War II auto industry exemplify the mode of regulation that prevailed throughout U.S. manufacturing during the heyday of mass production.[3] The postwar auto industrial-relations system contained four central features: (1) collectively bargained wage increases that kept real wages rising at roughly the national rate of productivity growth; (2) a "connective bargaining structure" that the UAW used to limit variation in wages, benefits, and working conditions at assembly companies and suppliers; (3) a broad managerial prerogative to run the shop, subject to specific restrictions embodied in seniority-based work rules and enforced in the grievance procedure and arbitration process; and (4) a centralized union structure dominated, after 1947, by a single intraunion political party (hereafter termed the "administration caucus").

In the technological, economic, and political context after 1950, the industrial relations institutions constructed in the 1940s provided benefits for employers, workers, and the UAW. For employers, work rules in highly Taylorized operations proved compatible with productivity growth that exceeded the national average and thus exceeded the wage increases paid by the Big Three. As productivity-based wage increases diffused throughout the whole economy, they generated demand for mass-produced vehicles. Work rules, the grievance procedure, and the union's obligation to help control wildcat strikes also reduced the frequency of work stoppages, which proved so expensive in mass-production operations. For UAW members, the postwar order provided steadily rising wages and benefits; limits on intraunion wage and work-rule competition; and protection against the poor working conditions and supervisory capriciousness that had fueled workers' organizing efforts in the first place. For the UAW and its leaders, the compromises of postwar collective bargaining provided institutional security.

Despite its multiconstituency benefits and formal institutional stability, some conflict remained within the postwar auto industrial-relations system. Workers resisted the shop-floor compromises negotiated by the UAW in two waves. In the 1950s, production workers at companies where decentralized management and collective action had earlier expanded worker autonomy challenged the imposition of the grievance system (Jefferys 1986; Herzenberg 1991). Beginning in the late 1960s—after the civil rights movement, and buoyed by tight labor markets—young, low-seniority workers in machine-paced jobs wildcatted to resist the work pace and to protest supervisory treatment and inadequate health and safety (Thompson 1985). Racial and generational division, better on-the-job conditions of more-senior, off-line workers, and the relative power of leaders and rank-and-file within the UAW prevented isolated wildcats from generalizing into a union campaign to fundamentally alter shop-floor relations.

When its compromises jeopardized their profits, employers also challenged the postwar industrial-relations structure. Most prominently, General Motors pursued a nonunion "Southern strategy" in the 1970s, partly in response to attendance and quality problems associated with shop-floor discontent among younger UAW members. The UAW put a stop to the Southern strategy in 1976, when it threatened to stage selective strikes unless the company agreed to remain neutral in representation campaigns at southern facilities. From around 1960 forward, the UAW had less success curtailing efforts by profit-squeezed independent parts supplier (IPS) firms to obtain wage concessions and avoid the union (Herzenberg 1991, ch. 5). This little-noticed decline in the fragile periphery of the auto connective-bargaining structure, however, left untouched the core of U.S. postwar auto industrial relations.

Management Strategy in the 1980s

Production-worker employment between December 1978 and November 1982 in the U.S. motor vehicles and equipment industry declined from 833,000 to 468,000. This decline resulted from the federal government's abandonment of the postwar commitment to full employment and from a rise in the Japanese share of the U.S. market to over 20 percent. Japanese imports symbolized the exposure of U.S. firms to global competition with a "nonadversarial" industrial-relations system that generated productivity and quality superior to the U.S. mass-production model.

Faced with declining sales, market share, and profits, assembly firms began to seek changes in the major collective-bargaining and shop-floor features of postwar labor relations. In the wage area, management sought to substitute lump-sum bonuses for annual base-wage increases. On the shop floor, the auto companies sought to replace narrow job classifications and work rules with broad classifications and teams. Management accompanied the adoption of broad job classifications and teamwork with new participation, quality, and training programs intended to overcome adversarial worker-supervisor relations and foster worker cooperation with performance-improvement efforts.

Many Big Three managers initially viewed work reorganization as a traditional recession-driven attempt to intensify work and cut labor costs. By the late 1980s, after the successful launch of several Japanese transplants and joint ventures, most managers saw reorganization as a way of adopting the "Toyota production system." By doing this, managers hoped to institutionalize both high work standards *and* worker cooperation with productivity- and quality-improvement efforts.

UAW Response to Management Strategies

In exchange for accepting work- and wage-rule changes, the UAW received advanced notification of company outsourcing decisions and, in the 1990 General Motors contract, the right to ask an arbitrator to reverse outsourcing unjustified on economic grounds. The union also won profit sharing and protection from layoffs resulting from company restructuring. Following past UAW practice, layoff protection improved incrementally over the course of the 1980s. Subject to a spending cap of $4.1 billion—an average of about three-months compensation per worker (excluding the government unemployment insurance contribution)—the 1990 General Motors agreement provided hourly employees with income guarantees of 95 to 100 percent of base wages.

The shop-floor changes and wage-rule modifications negotiated in the 1980s challenged the central compromises of the UAW's role under Fordism. The substitution of profit sharing and lump-sum payments for base-wage increases cost workers the annual improvements in income that they traditionally received in exchange for enduring auto production work. Profit sharing in national agreements and plant-by-plant modification of shop-floor relations weakened the system of connective bargaining through which the UAW sought to take wages and working conditions out of competition. The attempt to establish cooperative relations with union officials and shop-floor workers threatened the antagonism toward management that glued workers to one another and gave the union an unambiguous role as workers' advocate in the grievance system.

Three views on how the union should respond to management emerged in intraunion debate.[4] Within the administration caucus, Don Ephlin, head of the UAW's General Motors Department from 1983 to 1989, was the strongest supporter of union cooperation with management efforts to improve plant performance. Ephlin's negotiation of team agreements with the General Motors–Toyota joint venture in California (New United Motors Manufacturing Inc., or NUMMI) and with General Motors' new Saturn subsidiary helped accelerate the diffusion of teamwork to other General Motors locals. As part of their efforts to promote work reorganization at established plants, Ephlin and his staff allied themselves with pro-team factions within local unions (Turner 1988).

Ephlin supported cooperation with management partly because he believed that more militant responses, such as organizing, political mobilization, and attempts to forge alliances with foreign auto workers, were not realistic approaches to the defense of UAW jobs. Given this premise, Ephlin believed that failing to improve the competitiveness of UAW-organized employers would cost UAW jobs by increasing the market share of imports, nonunion transplants, and nonunion suppliers. Over the longer term, Ephlin argued, labor-management cooperation and job-security arrangements would encourage employers to think of labor as a "valuable resource rather than a fixed cost of production" (Ephlin 1986). In the process, cooperation would qualitatively improve workers' lives on the job.

Some of Ephlin's critics saw him as willing to agree to any management demands—including outsourcing to nonunion suppliers and Mexico, increases in work standards that eliminated jobs, and dilution of seniority—on the grounds that losing some jobs helped save the remaining ones. In some contexts, however, Ephlin and his staff did acknowledge the importance of restrictions on management in pushing management toward skill-intensive competitive strategies. At General Motors components operations, in particular, Ephlin's staff maintained that contractual job guarantees, UAW wage levels, outsourcing notification clauses, and UAW support for work reorganization had worked synergistically to create a cadre of managers who "look at the whole cost structure" in search of business strategies that do not depend on wage cutting or labor shedding.

The dominant, "traditionalist" wing of the UAW administration caucus included the union president since 1983, Owen Bieber, and, except for Ephlin, the heads of the union's other major departments. Traditionalists believed, like Ephlin, that moderating wage increases and negotiating workplace changes in exchange for job security would save thousands of UAW jobs (Lippert 1989; Friedman and Fisher 1988). They also perceived militant strategies in politics and bargaining as likely to backfire given public perception of the UAW as a "high-wage special interest."

Traditionalists differed from Ephlin because they acknowledged that work reorganization could, in some circumstances, erode working conditions and union independence. This position led traditionalists to let Ephlin play the role of teamwork advocate within the leadership (and to let him be the lightning rod for rank-and-file criticism of labor-management cooperation).

Following the example set by the UAW response to General Motors' Southern strategy, traditionalists also placed more importance than Ephlin on the continued use of strikes in Big Three bargaining. When Chrysler attempted to sell the eleven plants in its components division in 1988, union strike votes and threats to suspend cooperative programs led the company to retreat (Ruben 1988, 54). Chrysler agreed to keep seven plants open and place the two hundred workers at the other four locations in a job bank until they were placed in another plant. During negotiation of the 1990 General Motors contract, an authorized strike at an AC-Rochester General Motors parts facility, the only source of gas tanks for 55 percent of U.S.-built General Motors vehicles, sent General Motors an indication of the union's determination to win better income security (Patterson 1990).

Long-standing left-wing opponents of the administration caucus, and production workers organized under the "New Directions" banner, took the most critical view of national UAW policy.[5] New Directions emerged in UAW Region 5 in reaction to an unresponsive regional director, to the popularity of Assistant Director Jerry Tucker, and to Ephlin's attempts to encourage regional General Motors plants to accept teamwork.[6] The opposition argued that wage concessions and work-rule changes would not prevent jobs from leaking overseas, especially to low-wage countries. It also maintained that trying to save jobs on a plant-by-plant basis would facilitate corporate efforts to whipsaw local unions, raise work standards, and worsen working conditions. As more Japanese management approaches were introduced at NUMMI and elsewhere, the opposition charged that profit sharing, team structures, and joint labor-management committees represented a move toward enterprise unionism that would permanently subordinate worker concerns to the goal of raising profitability.

Like the Canadian UAW, the opposition called for resistance to wage- and work-rule concessions, more emphasis on organizing, and political mobilization. It also called for debate within the union so that the UAW could formulate its own workplace strategy.

Disagreement about how to respond to management strategy deeply divided the UAW for most of the 1980s. Division in the union was made deeper by the internal debate in which national union leaders relied heavily on their institutional power to marginalize their critics. In 1982, for example, when the union reopened the General Motors and Ford contracts to accept wage concessions, it did not hold its traditional, triennial unionwide collective-bargaining convention. At the 1986 constitutional convention, to which eighteen locals submitted an antiwhipsawing resolution in the wake of the announcement of the UAW–General Motors Saturn agreement, UAW President Owen Bieber told union delegates that the union's constitution already prohibited whipsawing (UAW 1986). Despite expressions of rank-and-file concern, however, the national union did not establish new means of enforcing the constitutional prohibition. In its 1986 effort to prevent Tucker from winning the directorship of Region 5, the union was found guilty of improper use of union funds and of improperly selecting delegates that voted for the administration caucus candidate.

One could argue that division within the union was inevitable given the scale of the changes negotiated in the 1980s. One could also read UAW leaders' reliance on institutional power as a considered judgment that this was the only way to ratify changes needed to save jobs. This reliance, however, is better understood as a continuation of historical union practice. Since the late 1940s, when a caucus led by Walter Reuther won a bitter factional fight, UAW internal debates have been carefully controlled by the leadership.[7] This top-down "management of discontent" prevented the reemergence of an opposition caucus, helped the UAW leadership to pursue its centralized-bargaining agenda, and contained rank-and-file pressure for more emphasis on shop-floor issues.

In the 1980s, by enabling the leadership to limit its response to the opposition, the union's internal structure impeded the UAW's search for a strategy that would reunite the membership and redefine a place for the union in industrywide labor-market regulation. The process of internal union debate also estranged union leaders from politicized activists critical to building ties with other progressive groups and with workers in other countries. A unifying UAW strategy might have united oppositionists and traditionalists by emphasizing their common skepticism regarding Ephlin's views on teamwork. It might have incorporated supporters of cooperation by emphasizing that an assertive in-plant role and limits on low-wage supplier and overseas competition would be necessary to expand significantly worker participation and to get U.S. firms to abandon their preoccupation with cost minimization. Such a unifying vision would have been reminiscent of Streeck's (1989) arguments about the institutional conditions necessary to incubate "diversified quality production."

A decade after the abandonment of the wage and work rules of postwar industrial relations in the U.S. auto industry, however, no clear national UAW vision of a union role within a cooperative North American system of labor relations has emerged. In the absence of such a vision, work reorganization has had a wide range of consequences for the integrity of the national UAW.

Plant-level Work Reorganization

Three distinct patterns of plant-level social relations could emerge from managerial attempts to adopt more flexible work organization in the auto industry: a "subordinate union," a "negotiation," and an "autocratic" alternative.[8] All three possibilities share formal institutional characteristics, such as teams, bargaining-unit team leaders, and shop-floor problem-solving groups. The three are distinguished by whether workers have a "militant" orientation—that is, perceive themselves as having interests distinct from those of management—and by whether workers that have a militant orientation express their militance collectively.

The *subordinate-union* alternative is the managerial vision of the Toyota production system. In contrast to the negotiation and autocratic alternatives, workers under subordinate unionism are "nonmilitant." Positions as team leaders and union administrators in joint union-management programs help secure the allegiance of union officials and a layer of hourly workers to company goals. Commitment of workers generally to managerial goals results from the understanding that income-security guarantees depend on plant profitability, and from work organization and operating practices.[9]

The key aspects of work organization and operating practice are "standardized work," "kaizen groups," just-in-time inventory, and the lack of absentee replacements in teams. Standardized work and kaizen groups formally incorporate workers and their ideas into the specification and improvement of the most efficient way to perform routinized jobs. Standardized work and the spread of machine pacing, in association with just-in-time inventory, raise the level of work effort. Just-in-time also raises the visibility of worker failure and the pressure to resolve problems quickly. The lack of absentee replacements in interdependent work teams creates peer pressure to attend work and to keep up on the job. In addition, the possibility of losing a job with high and secure income for failing to meet effort and attendance norms induces workers to attend work and keep up on the job.

In a subordinate-union model, managers gain workers' cooperation on the job *and* control of the purpose of shop-floor problem-solving and joint labor-management committees. In the two alternative possibilities, management gives up either worker cooperation or control. In the *negotiation* case, management faces militant workers who retain the willingness and capacity to defend their interests when they perceive them as different from management's. Perceiving workers' skills as critical to competitive success, managers concede significant control rather than risk losing worker cooperation. As with skilled workers and some self-paced work groups in the past, managers negotiate arrangements that allow them access to workers' knowledge but take account of workers' desire for autonomy, less stress, skill development, and career opportunities. In the negotiation case, as in the subordinate-union model, team leaders would be part of the union. A different set of structural and ideological pressures, however, would make team leaders more an upward extension of the work group than a downward extension of management. As well as company concerns and job security, labor-management committees in a negotiation pattern would deal with worker concerns such as ergonomics, training, and career paths.

In the *autocratic* model, management sacrifices workers' active cooperation rather than legitimate continuous "substantive negotiation" and workers' rights to participate in decisions that affect them. Despite a militant orientation, workers' resistance is confined to covert and individual acts in the face of unrestricted supervisory authority. Teamwork and the elimination of work rules thus represent a step back toward the supervisory favoritism and domination of pre-union days—although new technology and operating practices would give managers more control over the work pace than they had in the 1920s. Team leaders in an autocratic model become the analogue of "pushers" and lead men of the pre-union era. Supervisors selected pushers for their loyalty and willingness to work hard and placed them at bottleneck operations, where their work pace set the pace for the rest of the work gang (Lichtenstein 1988).

The development of a negotiation model is a necessary (although not sufficient) condition for the survival of an inclusive, sectorwide industrial union. In a subordinate-union model, workers do not conceive of organizing across plants to defend themselves against management. This paves the way for institutionalization of divisions between workers in different segments of the industry (assemblers/first-tier suppliers/lower-tier suppliers) and between permanent, contingent, and ancillary employees within the core. In an autocratic model, workers do not have sufficient solidarity and power to translate their opposition to management into organized sectoral or political activity.

Empirically, plant-level relations in the U.S. auto industry appear to contain elements of all three of the alternatives above, as well as of alternatives only incrementally different from traditional shop-floor relations. Recent case studies also point to underlying economic, historical, and structural factors that make each of the alternatives likely.

A number of economic and historical factors make subordinate-union forms of cooperation more likely than negotiated cooperation. Economically, UAW workers' willingness to cooperate on management's terms is heightened by the inadequacy of the U.S. social wage and the gap between UAW wages and wages of semiskilled workers generally. In 1990, hourly earnings in auto assembly plants equalled 1.59 times the U.S. manufacturing average wage (U.S. Department of Labor 1991). Excess capacity, now estimated to be at least two million units, also facilitates management attempts to whipsaw auto locals into accepting subordinate unionism. While whipsawing may have been alleviated by strengthening of UAW job security commitments, the spending cap on income security commitments and the need to renegotiate the commitments every three years keep alive the possibility of layoff.

The critical historical factor that makes a subordinate-union model more likely is the weakness of solidarity and union commitment left behind by the UAW's historic role on the shop floor (Herzenberg 1991). Under the grievance system, the illegality of work stoppages and the union's exclusion from management made it hard for the UAW to improve conditions for workers in general, especially machine-paced workers. This hindered the reproduction of a core of influential pro-union supporters and loosened ties between the local union and the informal social structure. By the 1980s, many workers saw the union's primary role as defending workers in danger of discharge for repeated absenteeism.

The union's historic shop-floor role also left behind identifiable groups of hourly workers and local union representatives ready to become team leaders and cooperative labor-union officials within subordinate unionism. Among hourly workers, the identifiable group consisted of "would-be craftspersons" (WBCs)—young workers with moderate to low seniority, higher-than-average education for production workers, and aspirations for more challenging production jobs.[10] WBCs tend to be critical of the union because it defends "poor performers" and because they feel that the seniority principle prevents them from obtaining promotions and job security that they have earned.

In the early 1980s, the moderate seniority of WBCs meant that many of them were laid off for periods of time during which their contractual and government unemployment benefits ran out. Trying to survive on savings or while working low-wage jobs left them deeply fearful of future job loss. As a result of their experience and worldview, many WBCs in the mid-1980s readily embraced the idea that labor cooperation with management was critical to keeping their plants open. They also saw work reorganization as likely to give them opportunities to get quality-related or team-leader positions that would satisfy their aspirations for more skilled jobs and might insulate them from future seniority-based layoffs.

Among local union officials, the union's fragile historical ties to the shop floor increased the number of officials with individualistic and careerist perceptions of their role and thus more likely to accept subordinate unionism as long as it contained a place for them as individuals. For such officials, appointed positions within joint union-management programs are particularly attractive because they offer off-line jobs partly insulated from local union politics. In addition, the training and skills provided to joint-program administrators make their positions better launchpads than traditional union jobs for personnel- or production-management careers. The 1990 UAW–General Motors contract establishes that each local shall have one joint-program representative for each 250 workers—that is, about as many joint representatives as elected shop committeepersons. The contract specifies that joint representatives will be appointed by the UAW vice-president in charge of the UAW–General Motors Department.

Any attempt to make team leaders and union joint representatives more accountable to rank-and-file workers is likely to provoke fierce resistance from individuals that expect to lose out as a result. At Mazda's plant in Flat Rock, Michigan, most team leaders forcefully opposed a 1991 contract clause giving teams the right once every six months to recall team leaders with a vote of two-thirds of team members.

For all the limitations of the union's historic role on the shop floor, many UAW members do have personal experience of and commitment to independent unionism. This plus two structural features of Japanese production methods could lead toward a negotiation model of teamwork that revitalizes the union's ties to shop-floor workers. The first structural feature is the physical demands of the Toyota production system. U.S. work reorganization based on this model has increased the fraction of each minute assembly workers require to perform their jobs; 54 seconds out of 60 at NUMMI (Feldman and Betzold 1988, 11); 48 seconds instead of 45, and still rising, at General Motors, Linden, New Jersey (Milkman and Pullman 1988, 41). This intensification, in turn, appears to have increased assembly-worker injury rates.[11] The integration of off-line classifications into assembly jobs and the introduction of standardized work also eliminate the enormous variation in work loads that used to divide high-seniority workers from workers on the toughest jobs. By exposing production workers generally to highly pressured conditions, the Toyota production system thus creates the material base for solidarity aimed at relieving this pressure.

The second structural factor is the limit on skill development and career opportunities within management-led work restructuring. Except for occasional participation in kaizen groups or special projects, most production workers within the Toyota production system have little near-term prospect of escaping high-pressure jobs. Realization of this is likely to produce the greatest resentment among precisely the would-be craftsmen initially attracted to teamwork. Given their predisposition toward cooperation, WBCs are probably concentrated at plants with significant numbers of heavily screened former UAW workers, most prominently Mazda, Flat Rock, and Saturn. Ironically, therefore, such plants could end up leading union efforts to modify the internal labor market and training systems in ways that better match workers' aspirations. As automation reduces the number of line jobs and as the current elderly cohort of skilled workers at Big Three plants retires, union demands for internal promotion to skilled jobs might significantly expand production-worker opportunities. Expanding production workers' skilled career opportunities would enable the UAW to gain more enduring ties to the rank and file than would simply reducing work intensity.

Concrete success alleviating pressured working conditions and expanding career opportunities at unionized Big Three and transplant operations would substantially increase UAW prospects of organizing the non-union Japanese transplants. To date, the UAW has gained recognition only at U.S. transplants that are joint vendors with U.S. firms or, in Mazda's case, produce cars for one of the Big Three. At nonunion U.S. transplants, the UAW withdrew a petition for a certification election at Honda in 1986, after a disappointing straw vote in a company captive-audience meeting (Ruben 1986). At Nissan in Tennessee, the UAW lost a certification election in July 1990 by 69 to 31 percent. At Nissan, the union campaigned on the issues of health and safety, line speed, and company failure to fulfill promises of participative management. Workers interviewed afterward nonetheless expressed the view that "the union didn't have anything to give me that I don't already have" (Brown 1989).

The UAW may well have been handicapped in its organizing efforts by its own ambivalence toward local union militance at UAW-organized team plants. As well as internal politics, this ambivalence appears to stem from UAW leaders' hope to organize transplants by persuading management that the union will be responsible and cooperative (Fucini and Fucini 1990). UAW conciliation toward management, however, makes the benefits of union representation ambiguous to transplant workers. A more assertive and independent role in organized team plants, however, might convince transplant workers of the union's ability to deliver on the campaign promises it made to Nissan workers. If the UAW cannot organize the transplants, this will create one more pressure toward subordinate unionism.

Uncoordinated local union efforts to transform subordinate unionism into a negotiation model could also lead management to retreat from cooperation in favor of an autocratic model of work reorganization. This outcome is also made likely by U.S. managers' historical emphasis on maintaining control and the intense competition in the industry. An autocratic model is most likely in suppliers that do not have the resources, employment stability, and long-term perspective necessary to institutionalize subordinate unionism.

Independent Parts Firms and Economic Integration with Mexico

The roles of the UAW and of wage competition in the auto industry depend not only on assembly companies but also on developments in the independent-supplier sector. Parts plants (including Big Three components plants) account for about three-quarters of auto industry employment.[12] In a range of products, domestic and foreign suppliers also compete directly with Big Three components plants.

Some have suggested that unions might protect workers in small and medium-sized suppliers by promoting worker-management, assembler-supplier, and supplier-supplier cooperation within high-wage, technically sophisticated industrial districts (Piore and Sabel 1984). In Michigan and some other north-central states in the 1980s, state planners attempted to catalyze the formation of industrial districts by providing industrial extension services and promoting contact among small and medium-sized manufacturers (Herzenberg 1991, ch. 12). The UAW, maintaining its traditional focus on the Big Three, played a secondary role in state-level efforts to create high-wage supplier networks.

In the absence of a sustained effort to prevent it, the UAW's position in the U.S. auto parts industry severely eroded during the 1980s. As established firms shifted investment to nonunion plants and new nonunion firms expanded, union coverage among IPS firms declined to less than one-third from over 50 percent in the mid-1970s (Herzenberg 1991; Ewing et al. 1990, 44). In bargaining in the 1980s, rising nonunion market share and a $10 billion jump in the U.S. auto parts trade deficit led to the abandonment of the notion that even large, organized parts plants should earn Big Three wages and benefits (Kertesz 1988). In IPS firms as a group (including nonunion ones), wages declined by over 10 percent in real terms from 1983 to 1989 and now equal around $9 per hour, less than 60 percent of assembly company wages (U.S. Department of Labor 1990). Since some UAW suppliers still earn $12 to $15 per hour, this average must include significant numbers of suppliers earning around $6, about one-third of Big Three levels. Competition with Mexican plants contributed to the pressure for wage concessions in U.S. suppliers. Employment in Mexican auto equipment plants serving the U.S. market reached around 100,000 by 1990.

In the last year, there have been isolated signs that the UAW would begin to focus more attention and resources in the supplier sector. In May 1991, the UAW organized its first major transplant supplier—Delta USA in Region 1A near Detroit. Significantly, the UAW kicked off the campaign at Delta, a seat-making subsidiary of Japan's Delta Kogyo Corporation, by having twenty-five activists of the Mazda local leaflet the Delta plant. If transplant suppliers produce parts on a "just-in-time" basis and if cooperation and skill development are perceived as more important by management than in U.S.-owned suppliers, first-tier transplant suppliers could be easier to organize than autocratic U.S. firms where engineers and managers monopolize engineering assistance provided to assemblers.

Region 1A of the UAW has also begun to promote cooperation among suppliers within a joint, regional UAW-supplier council. Based on the idea of a high-wage industrial network, the council intends to explore the possibility of establishing a training consortium and cooperative research and engineering efforts (Schippani 1990). This could lead to a joint effort by the UAW and unionized suppliers to pressure major assembly companies into sourcing preferentially from UAW parts firms.

If, however, a North American Free Trade Agreement (NAFTA) liberalizes Mexican restrictions on foreign ownership in auto parts firms, it could undermine fledgling efforts to institutionalize high-wage, high-productivity industrial districts in established U.S. auto regions. Depending on its provisions, and particularly in the medium term, a NAFTA that liberalizes trade and investment could also put U.S. assembler locals in competition with growing numbers of Mexican workers at plants where unions have a very limited shop-floor role (Shaiken 1990).

At the same time, proposed NAFTA negotiations in the context of a recession have generated an embryonic "post-Fordist" progressive coalition in U.S. politics, some of whose members are intent on articulating a more European model of North American economic integration. In the auto sector, such a model would presumably include continental limits on Japanese imports, measures to encourage wage growth in Mexico, and intracontinental protectionism until Mexican wages get closer to U.S. and Canadian levels (Herzenberg and Shaiken 1990). The ability of the UAW and other U.S. labor unions to take full advantage of the political opportunity created by NAFTA negotiations will depend on their willingness to help mobilize a grass-roots campaign that can enact a continental "social dimension" strong enough to root out commitment to low-wage strategies among employers. It will also depend on the UAW's ability to pool resources with dissident union militants that have worked most actively with the embryonic coalition and labor activists in Mexico.

Whither Social Unionism?

Extrapolating recent developments in the U.S. auto industry, one can discern the outlines of a highly segmented post-Fordist pattern of development. In this mode of regulation, autonomous, industrial unions would be succeeded by loosely associated plant- and company-level unions representing only permanent workers in some assembly firms.[13] Workers in subordinate assembly unions would see cooperation with management as the only way to protect their relatively privileged labor-market position. Beyond assembly firms, especially in lower tiers of the supplier sector, the absence of unions and intense competition would produce more crude and autocratic supervisory domination and favoritism. Outside high-tech "islands of automation" in the industry core, supplier firms would compete based more on low wages and high work effort than skill development and labor-management cooperation. The stunted development of labor-management and assembler-supplier cooperation in this structure could also translate into long-term reliance on Japan for engineering-intensive auto products.

To prevent the consolidation of a highly segmented pattern of development, the UAW must find a way of reaffirming among core workers a commitment to independent, industrial unionism. The key to doing this appears to be defining a union role that provides more than the economic security and restricted opportunities for skill development within subordinate unionism. By alleviating the stress of Japanese production methods and by structuring the internal labor market so that it provides career opportunities for production workers, the union might strengthen union ties to rank-and-file workers, establish a collective identity based partly on a "productivist" commitment to quality and skill development, and find itself able to organize transplants and suppliers. It might also gain a cadre of committed activists that could help it fight for regional development policies and continental trade, wage, and labor-market policies compatible with the evolution of agglomerations of integrated, high-wage auto production. Union promotion of regionally concentrated production and of the skill development and attention to quality that underlie the satisfaction of consumer demands might also strengthen community and wider public support for labor (Piore 1985).

Some of the leverage needed to move toward more-inclusive development is contained in management's need for worker cooperation and in employer vulnerability stemming from just-in-time inventory. In the 1980s, UAW leaders seemed wary of using this leverage except to prevent the Big Three from rapidly shrinking the industry core. The UAW's defensiveness was premised on the view that the union did not have the power to do more than provide economic security for its more-senior Big Three workers. This premise led the UAW to worry first about whether more-militant actions might accelerate job loss and to impede rather than encourage the development of the broad, independent perspective necessary to avoid subordinate unionism. In sum, while the building blocks of an alternative plant-level, organizing and political strategy exist within the union, UAW leaders' power to forestall worker mobilization and the strategic exercise of militance may prevent these building blocks cohering into an integrated vision of restructuring.

Were it not for the Great Depression, David Brody (1980) speculates, company unionism based on "the American Plan" might have consolidated and inoculated U.S. employers against industrial unionism. At this point in history, it may take a second depression to discredit economic deregulation, subordinate unionism, and the segmented pattern of continental development that would accompany them. Of course, a rupture that provokes collective anger by making it impossible for larger companies to honor employment-security commitments and long-term contracts with suppliers might simultaneously discredit the labor-management and assembler-supplier cooperation necessary to institutionalize a dynamic, progressive model of development.

Notes

1. The views expressed in this chapter are the author's own. They do not necessarily reflect the positions or opinions of the U.S. Department of Labor or the U.S. government.

2. On UAW strategy, see Lichtenstein (1985), Jefferys (1986), and Herzenberg (1991).

3. The body of this chapter relies primarily on Herzenberg (1991), which contains more extended versions of most of the arguments presented. This section also relies on Katz (1985) and Piore and Sabel (1984).

4. In addition to the secondary sources cited below, this section relies on interviews with over ten national UAW staff members, officials, and former officials, held between 1987 and 1989. See Herzenberg (1991: ch. 6) for more detail.

5. On the internal UAW opposition to the 1982 and 1984 General Motors and Ford contracts see Gardner, Kelly, and Weissman (1982), Milkman (1982), and Dyer, Salter, and Webber (1986). On New Directions, see New Directions Steering Committee (1986) and Mann (1987: 368–72).

6. Tucker's popularity stemmed partly from his role in successful efforts to resist concession demands at locals that feared strikes would lead to the use of replacement workers. Instead of strikes, the locals adopted in-plant "work-to-rule" strategies after contract expiration (Metzger 1985; Mann 1987). Reductions in output forced management to compromise at the bargaining table.

7. See Herzenberg (1991), Steiber (1962), Howe and Widdick (1948), Marquart (1975), and Jefferys (1986).

8. This hypothesis is based primarily on detailed case studies of two independent supplier plants of the Budd Company. For methodological and other details, see Herzenberg (1991: part 3).

9. For analyses of Japanese industrial relations that stress the same characteristics, see Dohse, Jurgens, and Malsch (1985) and Parker and Slaughter (1988).

10. The phrase "would-be craftsmen" is borrowed from Sabel (1982). For

more on the characteristics and perceptions of this group at the Budd-Detroit plant, see Herzenberg (1991: 485–86 and 515).

11. In 1988 Mazda had a rate of serious injury equal to 3.4 times the aggregate Big Three assembly-plant injury rate, according to state of Michigan statistics.

12. Probably as a result of their slower rate of productivity growth, parts plants also account for a rising share of employment. The ratio of production-worker employment in the auto parts industry to employment in assembly plants rose from 2.7 to 3.14 between 1987 and 1990 (U.S. Department of Commerce 1991). This took place despite the rapid deterioration in the U.S. auto parts trade balance.

13. Today the UAW represents about two-thirds of workers in the auto and auto parts industries, compared with perhaps 90 percent in the 1970s. With reasonable assumptions about organizing, transplant market share, and Big Three outsourcing as their workers retire, this is likely to be 50 percent by the year 2000. It could be a lot lower if any of the Big Three encounter serious financial trouble.

References

Brody, David. 1980. *Workers in Industrial America: Essays on the Twentieth Century Struggle.* New York: Oxford University Press.

Brown, Warren. 1989. UAW loses key battle at Nissan plant. *Washington Post,* 28 July.

Bureau of National Affairs. 1989. *Daily Labor Report* 212, A-8.

———. 1990. *Daily Labor Report* 142, A-15, and 226, A-7.

Dohse, Kent, Ulrich Jurgens, and Tomas Malsch. 1985. From "Fordism" to "Toyotaism"? The social organization of the labor process in the Japanese automobile industry. *Politics and Society* 14(2), 115–46.

Dyer, David, M. S. Salter, and A. W. Webber. 1986. *Changing Alliances.* Boston: Harvard Business School Press.

Edwards, P. K. 1986. *Conflict at Work: A Materialist Analysis of Workplace Relations.* Oxford: Basic Blackwell.

Ephlin, Donald. 1986. Saturn's strategic role in industrial relations. *Survey of Business,* Summer.

Ewing, Linda, Mark Grueber, Dan Luria, and Edith Wiarda. 1990. *The Michigan Foundation: A Study of the Modernization Process in Michigan's Small- and Medium-Sized Manufacturers.* Ann Arbor, Mich.: Industrial Technology Institute.

Feldman, R. S., and Michael Betzold, eds. 1988. *End of the Line: Autoworkers and the American Dream.* New York: Weidenfeld and Nicholson.

Friedman, Sheldon, and Lydia Fischer. 1988. Collective bargaining and employment security. *IRRA 41st Annual Proceedings.*

Fucini, Joseph, and Suzy Fucini. 1990. *Working for the Japanese: Inside Mazda's American Auto Plant.* New York: Free Press.

Gardner, Al, Pete Kelly, and Bob Weissman. 1982. "Analysis: Ford settlement" and "Analysis: General Motors settlement." Prepared for Locals Opposed to Concessions (UAW-LOC), Dearborn Heights, Michigan.

Herzenberg, Stephen. 1990. The uses of Japanese nationals at U.S. manufacturing plants. Unpublished mimeo, Bureau of International Labor Affairs, U.S. Department of Labor, June.

———. 1991. Towards a cooperative commonwealth? Labor and restructuring in the U.S. and Canadian auto industries. Ph.D. dissertation, MIT Department of Economics.

Herzenberg, Stephen, and Harley Shaiken. 1990. Labor market segmentation in the North American auto industry. Proceedings of the Canadian Industrial Relations Research Association.

Howe, Irving, and B. J. Widdick. 1948. *The UAW and Walter Reuther.* New York: Random House.

Jefferys, Stephen. 1986. *Management and Managed: Fifty Years of Crisis at Chrysler.* London: Cambridge University Press.

Katz Harry. 1985. *Shifting Gears: Changing Labor Relations in the U.S. Automobile Industry.* Cambridge, Mass.: MIT Press.

Kertesz, Louise. 1988. The view from the UAW: Odessa Komer says transplants take their toll on union jobs. *Automotive News,* 18 July.

Lichtenstein, Nelson. 1985. UAW bargaining strategy and shop-floor conflict: 1950–1970. *Industrial Relations* 24(3).

———. 1988. The union's early days: Shop stewards and seniority. In Mike Parker and Jane Slaughter, eds., *Choosing Sides: Unions and the Team Concept,* Boston: South End Press.

Lippert, John. 1989. Storm clouds over the UAW. *Detroit Free Press,* 11 June.

Mann, Eric. 1987. *Taking on General Motors: A Case Study of the UAW Campaign to Keep GM Van Nuys Open.* Los Angeles: Center for Labor Research and Education, Institute of Industrial Relations, University of California.

Marquart, Frank. 1975. *An Auto Worker's Journal: The UAW from Crusade to One Party Union.* State College: Pennsylvania State University Press.

Metzger, Jack. 1985. Running the plant backwards in UAW Region 5. *Labor Research Review* 7, Fall.

Milkman, Ruth. 1982. The anti-concessions movement in the UAW: interview with Douglas Stevens. *Socialist Review* 12(5), September–October.

Milkman, Ruth, and Sydney Pullman. 1988. *Technological Change in an Auto Assembly Plant: A Case Study of GM-Linden.* New York: Labor Institute.

New Directions Steering Commmittee. 1986. UAW Region 5 New Directions Movement report. September.

Parker, Mike. 1989. New technology, skilled trades, training, and the 1990s. Unpublished mimeo, 4 March.

Parker, Mike, and Jane Slaughter. 1988. *Choosing Sides: Unions and the Team Concept.* Boston: South End Press.

Patterson, Greg. 1990. GM and UAW reach accord to end strike. *Wall Street Journal,* 14 August, A-3.

Patterson, Greg, and Joseph White. 1990. GM-UAW pact allows company to cut payroll in return for worker buy-outs. *Wall Street Journal,* 19 August, A-3.

Piore, M. J. 1985. Thinking strategically for the industry: A new role for workers. Revised version of an oral presentation to the International Union of Bricklayers and Allied Craftsmen, Notre Dame University, March 28–30.

Piore, M. J., and C. F. Sabel. 1984. *The Second Industrial Divide.* New York: Basic.

Robertson, David, James Rinehart, and Christopher Huxley, and the CAW Research Group on CAMI. 1991. *Team Concept: A Case Study of Japanese Production Management in a Unionized Canadian Auto Plant.* Toronto: CAW Technology Project.

Ruben, George. 1986. Developments in industrial relations. *Monthly Labor Review,* May.

———. 1988. Developments in industrial relations. *Monthly Labor Review,* May.

Sabel, Charles F. 1982. *Work and Politics: the Division of Labor in Industry.* Cambridge: Cambridge University Press.

Schippani, Michael. 1990. Labor and industrial relations strategies in the state of Michigan. Paper presented at the Center for Labor-Management Policy Studies, City University of New York, 29 March.

Schlesinger, Jay, and Greg Patterson. 1989. UAW plays hardball with dissidents who say union is too close to firms. *Wall Street Journal,* 27 February.

Shaiken, Harley. 1990. *Mexico in the Global Economy: High Technology in Mexican Export Industry.* La Jolla, Calif.: Center for U.S.-Mexican Studies, University of California, San Diego, Monograph Series No. 33.

Steiber, Jack. 1962. *Governing the UAW.* New York: Wiley.

Streeck, Wolfgang. 1989. On the social and political conditions of diversified quality production. Unpublished paper, University of Wisconsin, Madison, July.

Thompson, H. A. 1985. Detroit: Wildcat 1973. Senior honors thesis, University of Michigan.

Turner, Lowell. 1988. Are labor-management partnerships for competitiveness possible in America? The U.S. auto industry examined. Berkeley: Berkeley

Roundtable on the International Economy, Working Paper No. 36, University of California, September.

United Auto Workers (UAW). 1986. *Proceedings: 28th Constitutional Convention*, Anaheim, Calif., 1–6 June.

U.S. Department of Labor. 1985. *Employment, Hours, and Earnings, United States, 1909–84, Volume 1.* Washington, D.C.: Bureau of Labor Statistics, March.

————. 1990. Industry wage survey: Motor vehicle parts, selected areas, August 1989. Washington, D.C.: Bureau of Labor Statistics, April.

————. 1991. *Employment and Earnings.* Washington, D.C.: Bureau of Labor Statistics, March.

16

CHARLOTTE A. B. YATES

Curtains or Encore: Possibilities for Restructuring in the Canadian Auto Industry

Since the 1980–82 recession, corporations have scrambled to restructure their operations in the hope of securing their position in a more intensely competitive world economy.[1] Such restructuring has called into question political and economic arrangements that served as the foundation for postwar prosperity. The shape of any future arrangements remains a mystery—one that will only be solved as the last scenes of the current economic drama are played out. Yet, as in all good plots, the ending to the current mystery of restructuring is not completely open-ended; it must be found in the players on stage, previous scenes, and the weapons at hand. Based on these elements, many political economists have laid out their own endings to the drama. Curiously, most of the endings have a common theme, the seeming inevitability of a lean production process modelled on the Japanese experience. Where they differ, however, is in their understanding of the impact of national historical factors on the interpretation and application of Japanization to various industries in different countries and in the desirability of the accompanying changes for workers, in particular.

This chapter does not purport to write yet another ending to the drama. Rather it simply adds a subplot to the mystery, based on the experience of restructuring in the Canadian auto industry. The story may read as if based on a best-seller formula; some characters are a little too familiar, as are key developments in the plot. This should come as no surprise. The Canadian auto industry is a branch-plant industry dominated by the Big Three North American automakers. Canada is not a Germany, a United States, or a Japan. The Canadian economy is not central to the restructuring process even though restructuring is central to the Canadian economy. Canada is one of the many countries dependent upon foreign investment and ownership whose governments and unions, nonetheless, have tried to shape corporate restructuring and ensure a continued place for themselves on centre stage.

This chapter tells the story of the restructuring of the Canadian auto industry by the major North American automakers. It examines the limitations and possibilities for this restructuring, given national economic conditions, government policy, and union resistance to many corporate initiatives. As with *Rosencrantz and Gildenstern Are Dead*, however, the curtain is drawn with no real ending to the drama, dependent as this ending is upon the playing out of the final scenes on a central stage elsewhere.

The Protagonist: Competition and the Japanese Example

Over the last decade the auto industry in Canada has undergone a massive transformation. In the postwar years, North American auto producers captured all but a small portion of the car market. The 1980s, however, have seen a staggering rise in the number of imported vehicles sold to Canadian consumers. In 1989, Japanese cars alone captured 22 percent of the market (*Ward's* 1990: 246). Auto production in Canada has also changed. No longer are the Big Three North American automakers (General Motors, Ford, Chrysler) the only firms building cars in Canada. Since the mid-1980s, Toyota, Honda, Hyundai, and Suzuki have erected their own plants in Canada or built joint ventures with North American producers, or both.

These changes are indicative of the decline of U.S. world dominance in automobile production, a decline that began in the late 1970s. At the root of the auto industry's declining competitiveness is its failure to meet the

Japanese challenge of more efficient utilization of resources and organization of production and its inability to meet shifts in consumer demand toward cheaper, more durable, fuel-efficient small cars. Early attempts by Ford and General Motors to compete with the Japanese were disastrous and merely underscored the need for some fundamental changes to North American practices.

Survival for North American auto producers requires an end to the erosion of market share and profitability. This means reducing costs while increasing efficiency and quality of production. In contrast to the 1960s, when a seemingly similar situation was met by minor tampering with existing structures and practices, the challenge to industry in the 1980s was fundamental. Fordist solutions to profitability and productivity appeared to have reached their limits and were identified, by many analysts, as the root of corporate problems. To meet the current economic challenges, well-established structures and practices will be transformed, a process herein referred to as restructuring.

The story of auto restructuring begins in the third quarter of 1979, when the auto industry first entered into serious decline. Developments from 1979 to the present can be understood as three acts in the play of corporate restructuring in which the main characters, the Big Three automakers, engage in three separate responses to the challenge of competition. Act one covers the period from the third quarter of 1979 to the end of 1981 and is best described as a period of crisis management. The second act begins in 1982 as the auto corporations embarked on massive experiments in restructuring. The third and final act, which will be part of the concluding section of the chapter, begins in 1987 and leads to the dramatic but unresolved climax as automakers scramble to deal with the issue of overcapacity.

From the end of 1979 to 1982, automobile and parts producers were crippled as a result of the economic downturn. Desperate to survive, the companies tended to rely on short-term cost-cutting strategies to keep themselves afloat. Popular wisdom at the time led automakers to believe that their major disadvantage vis-à-vis the Japanese was input costs, and, in particular, labour costs. Auto companies set the reduction of the wage bill as one of their major goals. Indefinite layoffs and plant closures became common occurrences throughout North America. In Canada, from 1980 to 1984, twenty-five auto and parts plants closed and approximately twenty thousand autoworkers were laid off (Van Ameringen 1985: 267). When increased production became necessary, overtime, instead of calling back laid-off workers, took up the slack. In this way corporations assured themselves greater flexibility in labour costs while limiting increases in employment (Ontario Ministry of Labour 1987). Further cost saving on labour inputs to production was achieved by negotiating wage and benefit concessions from the UAW, something that was less successful in Canada than the United States.

The auto companies also looked to government for help. Chrysler teetered on the brink of bankruptcy and, after much lobbying, was bailed out by loans from the U.S. and Canadian governments. These governments also responded to industry and union pressures for temporary relief from import competition by negotiating voluntary quotas on Japanese vehicle imports. Finally, as *Ward's Automotive Yearbook* reported in 1982, "the Reagan administration arrived in the nick of time with some deregulation and tax incentives" (11). Of particular importance for the American automakers was easing automobile-emissions regulations, which the companies claimed cost them $100 million per year (*Ward's* 1980: 16; *Ward's* 1981: 15, 18–19).

By the end of 1981, however, auto corporations began to realize that high labour costs were not their primary problem and that their profitability and market position would not be restored merely by forcing workers to accept wage cuts. North American producers once again looked to the Japanese for answers. This time they saw a more streamlined production process that improved quality, eliminated waste, and introduced flexibility so that companies could respond rapidly to changes in the market. These goals had to be achieved quickly to prevent the foreign automakers from permanently displacing North American producers. Thus, between 1982 and 1987, the Big Three automakers restructured production, management, and marketing.

While each corporation selected its own course of action, there was a common fascination with Japanese success. Toyota and Nissan were perceived to hold the secret to this success. When they examined Japanese firms, automakers found a streamlined and flexible production process that was capital and technology intensive. New information-based technology, such as computer numerical-control machines, gave some flexibility due to the ease with which specifications could be changed, improved job accuracy, the possibility for shorter product cycles, and greater integration of design and production. Further flexibility and market responsiveness was achieved by reorganizing and integrating automated assembly lines, the goal being to produce several vehicle models simultaneously on a single assembly line. Since 1982, the Big Three have introduced components of the new technology and reorganized their assembly operations accordingly (Womack 1990).

A second major innovation of Japanese auto production lay in the approach to quality control. Japanese carmakers had embraced and refined a concept of "total quality control," which focussed on defect prevention rather than inspection and involved workers from the design to assembly stages (Cusomano 1985: 326). Rather than inspect a small sample for defects—the North American approach—quality was built into each and every vehicle. Japanese success at producing high-quality cars forced North American producers to take seriously the issue of quality. Nevertheless, while the idea of total quality control seems to have taken hold, its implementation has been fraught with problems, not the least of which is North American automakers' resistance to completely abandoning their traditional and faulty methods of inspection.

Where the Big Three have moved most quickly on transforming the quality control process is in their relationship to suppliers. They have pressured parts suppliers to automate their production and checking systems to ensure that parts are built according to exact standards and high quality. In addition, independent suppliers are now expected to design as well as produce whole components for vehicles. Finally, corporations have moved to institute the Japanese system of KanBan or just-in-time (Holmes 1991).

Alongside such restructuring of production, the Big Three have entered into joint ventures with foreign automakers, especially Japanese ones. The auto companies have also tailored their management structures to the requirements of the new production techniques by reducing the size of the corporate bureaucracy and integrating management more closely with design and production (Keller 1989). Finally, automakers have experimented with new marketing strategies intended to improve their competitive position.

To maximize the productivity gains and efficiencies associated with their particular application of new technologies and to ensure a concomitant reduction in labour costs, automakers have undertaken an assault on the regulatory structures of collective bargaining dating from the postwar years. For example, automakers have proposed two-tier wage systems, profit sharing, and productivity-based lump-sum payments in lieu of regular hourly wage increases. In the parts sector there were pressures to keep wages below those in the assembly plants as independent parts suppliers attempted to pass on to workers some of the costs of restructuring. To enhance flexibility in the deployment of labour, automakers have demanded alterations to seniority arrangements, reductions in job classifications, and moves toward multiskilling of workers. These latter changes are coupled with corporate attempts to follow the Japanese model of teamwork and "consultation" with workers.

The goals of such demands are threefold. First, through reorganization of the labour process, better use can be made of workers' knowledge and labour time (Slaughter and Parker 1988). Second, by undoing arrangements such as seniority and job classifications, management gains greater flexibility and control in its use of labour as an input into production. Finally, these measures reduce labour costs by making wages and benefits the basis for competition between workers. The latter reverses the postwar arrangement under which master and pattern bargaining succeeded in taking wages out of competition.

Corporations have attempted to restructure using a combination of coercion and persuasion. Success in early demands for concessions from workers encouraged corporations to use this as the primary method for getting restructuring under way. In the early 1980s, following Chrysler's lead, the remaining automakers demanded deferments of wages and benefits and reductions in paid time off. Added to this were demands for fewer job classifications, for alterations in seniority arrangements, for inclusion of provisions for education, and for extension of management rights over short-term layoffs. Such concessions were most often accompanied by threats of plant closure or job loss (Yates 1988: ch. 8).

Decentralized collective bargaining, while initially an effect of concessions, also became part of the strategy pursued by corporations to gain flexibility and reduce wage costs. By ridding themselves of such structures as master and pattern bargaining, corporations could move to tie wages to productivity of the firm and to the performance of individual workers. Finally, the auto corporations have attempted to use ideology to mobilize workers and their unions in support of the corporate strategy of restructuring. A new management discourse of teamwork, joint decision making, and "equality of sacrifice" has accompanied corporate demands for concessions, heightened pressure for quality-of-work-life programs and the reorganization of production. Evidence of this ideological assault can be seen in the content of training programs intended to help workers adjust and learn about the new technology.[2]

These corporate strategies are, however, just that—strategies. They are based on North American *interpretations* of Japanese success and give little thought to alternative models for production. Many factors intervene either to limit the success of these strategies in Canada or to suggest possibilities for modification in their design. Three sets of factors will be examined in the following discussion. The first section discusses certain unique features of the Canadian market that have intervened to shape corporate strategy. The second section deals with government policy, and the third section with union resistance.

Setting the Stage: Production in Canada

As early as the 1920s, Canada's automotive industry consisted largely of branch plants of U.S. corporations. By the early 1930s, fully 83 percent of automotive products made in Canada were produced in such plants (Laxer 1989: 15–17). Only in parts production was there a strong Canadian presence. Given this domination of the industry by American multinationals, it is not surprising that Canada's auto industry is a truncated one that is almost exclusively oriented toward the assembly of motor vehicles and the production of certain automotive parts. Less of the workforce is involved in skilled labour than in the United States. Almost no research and development is undertaken in Canada and thus no design. Although all the major automakers maintain Canadian corporate headquarters, most important decisions are made south of the border.

These characteristics of the Canadian auto industry have an immediate impact on the ways in which its plants are integrated into and affected by the Big Three's restructuring initiatives. Canadian plants are only subject to those technological innovations that affect assembly and the closer integration of suppliers and producers. Thus, a tour of many Canadian plants will reveal the latest in welding robots, automated guided vehicles, and automated paint shops, but one would be hard-pressed to find any evidence of computer-aided design/manufacturing or the information technology necessary for concurrent engineering (the integration of engineering from design to manufacture). Moreover, the decisions to invest in these technologies, close old or open new plants, or shift production of a particular vehicle model to or from a Canadian plant rest outside the country. As corporations draft the plot for restructuring, governments and unions have limited opportunities for revising the script.

Canada has had a comparative advantage because of geographical proximity to the major plants in the United States (a must with just-in-time systems), its supply of literate labour, and the comparable productivity of Canadian workers vis-à-vis their American counterparts (Lavelle and White 1983: 53). Moreover, as of 1988, Canada's hourly compensation rate for workers involved in vehicle and equipment manufacturing was $16.61 (U.S.), compared to the American value of $21.84 (U.S.). Obviously Canada cannot compete with Mexican labour, which in 1987 was priced at $2.45 (U.S.), but its other advantages suggest that it will retain its part in North American production (*Ward's* 1990: 262).

The parts sector is the most fragile part of the Canadian industry. Pressure from the automakers on independent parts suppliers is coupled with automakers' determination to force these suppliers to absorb increasing responsibility and cost for restructuring. To remain competitive in the bidding wars for parts contracts, suppliers must now have the capacity to design the components as well as produce them. This requires heavy investment in research and development, which has been missing thus far. The costs of staying in business are becoming prohibitive.

Reactions to these problems have been twofold. Workers in the parts sector are likely to experience downward pressures on their wages due to intense competition for parts contracts, especially from firms located in low-wage countries, and attempts by suppliers to finance restructuring by lowering the wage bill. The alternative is relocation to countries such as Mexico.

Thus far corporate strategies have encountered numerous problems. The types of changes being undertaken by the automakers are massive and require a fundamental reorganization of production, management, and marketing. Moreover, all these changes have to come on stream quickly in order to restore the viability of the North American producers before competition destroys them. On the other hand, it is these corporate uncertainties that provide an opening for the Canadian and Ontario governments and the Canadian Auto Workers Union (CAW) to influence the restructuring process and ensure that Canada's auto industry remains a member of the industry's cast.

The Fifth Business: Government

Canadian governments, whether federal or provincial, have never committed themselves to a comprehensive industrial policy in the automotive sector. Nor have they shown much interest in using public policy to help build a domestically owned auto industry. Rather, they have been satisfied to concern themselves with the issue of domestic content, which government officials anticipated would translate into Canadian jobs and a certain level of investment. The boldest and most long-lasting Canadian policy initiative in this vein was the Autopact. Negotiated with the United States in 1965, the Autopact established free trade in auto parts and assembled vehicles in exchange for corporate guarantees of increased investment in the Canadian industry and certain levels of Canadian content (Beigie 1970: ch. 4). The increased integration of automotive production within North America and the accompanying rationalization of production that resulted from this policy encouraged spectacular growth within the industry. Between 1965 and 1976, vehicle and parts production grew almost 100 percent and 200 percent respectively. Employment grew by 30 percent (Van Ameringen 1985: 271).

Since 1979, however, the wisdom of tying Canadian auto production to the American auto industry has come into question. As the Big Three flailed in the face of import competition, Canadian auto and truck production declined by 14 percent and 19 percent respectively from 1978. These declines were in spite of the buoyant Canadian market for large, North American–built vehicles (*Ward's* 1980: 175). Hard times for the auto industry had begun, and Canadian corporate management had little influence over how they might be ridden out.

The Ontario provincial government, under the Conservative party until 1985, limited its role in the auto industry to crisis management, such as the introduction of severance-pay legislation intended to protect workers laid off due to plant closure. In addition, the province lent its support to Canadian autoworkers in their lobbies to have the federal government take action.

The 1980 federal election brought the Liberal party back to power on a nationalist policy platform articulated around a national energy program (Brodie and Jenson 1988: 314). This nationalism found its way into federal government auto policy. Over the next four years, until its defeat in 1984, the Liberal government, under intense pressure from the Canadian Region of the UAW, pursued an ad hoc policy of protection of the Canadian auto industry. When Chrysler sought a bailout loan in 1980, the Canadian government agreed on condition that Chrysler guarantee investment, maintain jobs, and not close plants without the prior approval of the minister of industry. These conditions contrasted with the loan

Chrysler obtained from the U.S. government, which was predicated on further concessions from workers.[3] Although hesitant to tamper with flows of Japanese imports, the Liberal government followed the American government's example of negotiating import quotas with the Japanese.[4]

As the auto industry began to rebound, the Liberal government looked to the industry's future. In 1983 it appointed a task force to examine the auto industry and propose policy alternatives for the future (Lavelle and White 1983). It joined the Ontario provincial government in investing in a new state-of-the-art assembly plant being built by American Motors Corporation. It also made grants to the troubled General Motors plant in Ste. Thérèse, Quebec, which was threatened with closure. Finally, the Liberals, consistent with their long-term policy of ambivalence to domestic ownership, actively encouraged Japanese auto producers to locate plants in Canada.

Just as the auto industry began to turn around, the Liberal government was defeated in the 1984 election. The Conservative party, led by Brian Mulroney, ushered in a new era of politics. Backed by big business, the new government promised a realignment in economic policy. In particular, the Tories argued that Canada's survival in the new international order of greater competition lay in a decentralized and deregulated economy. Economic revitalization must be driven by the private sector. Among other things, this meant an end to any policies that smacked of economic nationalism.

In 1985, after a few short months in office, it became clear that the centrepiece of the Conservative's economic realignment would be the Free Trade Agreement with the United States. Initially it was not clear what the free trade deal meant to the Autopact and the Canadian auto industry. After much debate and separate negotiations, Canadian content regulations for vehicles were reduced from 60 percent to 50 percent. According to some analysts, free trade has accelerated the pace of parts-plant closures as parts suppliers seek to rationalize their North American operations (*Ward's* 1990).

Consistent with its commitment to deregulation and market-driven economic recovery, and in contrast to the Liberals, the Conservatives have taken few initiatives to protect or help any industry, including auto, in adjusting to new market conditions. The one exception is grants to General Motors to keep the Ste. Thérèse plant afloat, a move that is clearly motivated by the electoral importance of Quebec to the Conservative party. Even in the area of training, the Conservative government has preferred private initiatives over government involvement (Mahon 1988: 11–12).

In taking this approach, the Conservative government has forfeited the opportunity to shape the development of the Canadian auto industry in favour of allowing the market to determine its future. To date, Canadian market conditions such as the lower cost of labour and the value of the dollar have favoured Canada, making it the beneficiary of large investments by both American and Japanese automakers. Nonetheless, as the 1990–91 recession has proven, the future holds no guarantees of continued prosperity. With the prospect of overcapacity now a reality, there has been another wave of plant closures and a suspension of new investments. Whatever is decided and whatever might be the potentially disastrous impact on the Canadian auto industry, corporate decisions will not face interference from the current federal government.

A Cast of Thousands: Autoworkers and Their Union

The Canadian Auto Workers Union (CAW), until 1985 the Canadian Region of the UAW, has understood the proposed changes to the labour process and the regime of labour-management relations as being aimed at tying workers' compensation interests to the competitive position of individual corporations. Such a linkage threatens the relationship between the union and its members. The union could find itself defending measures to ensure profitability at the expense of wages and protection of workers' rights. Furthermore, union locals could become tied to the interests of the corporation or their own plant in ways that would lead to competition among locals bidding to make their own plant or company the most productive and efficient. Such rivalry would pit union member against union member, thereby weakening the union organization itself. Proposed labour-management committees could result in a devolution of the union's role as protector of workers' interests.

In negotiating and "selling" concessionary agreements to its members, with no real guarantees of job security, the union could find itself the object of growing membership discontent. This would lead to divisions among the membership, thereby threatening the capacity of the union to mobilize membership support for a chosen course of collective action. The Canadian Region of the UAW has already had such a bitter experience. In 1979–80, the Canadian Region of the UAW negotiated concessions with Chrysler and a number of small auto parts and nonauto companies. Union members initially accepted concessions as the price of saving their jobs. Soon, however, these workers experienced economic hardship due to these giveaways and in many cases blamed the union for forcing concessions down their throats and failing to give leadership at a time of crisis (White 1985). Such conflict sapped the strength of the union and threatened to splinter it at the very moment when united action was essential.

Since the late 1940s, the UAW has relied upon institutionalized collective bargaining for its organizational strength. For instance, master and pattern bargaining have meant that wage and benefit packages were negotiated for entire corporations, rather than individual plants, and that the package won in one auto company served as a pattern for settlements in the other companies. This process secured the union leadership's centralized control over collective bargaining and, in combination with the union's monopolistic position as representative of autoworkers, tended to take wages out of competition and prevent companies from pitting one group of autoworkers against another. In this way, these bargaining structures were crucial to the organizational strength of the union. By accepting the reformulation of labour relations put forth by management, the UAW faced the possible erosion of membership support and of the union's established organizational position. This would be accompanied by a loss of power in the workplace and ultimately the political arena.

On the other hand, the CAW, like most unions, has also recognized that for the Big Three to survive, there must be increased productivity and technological innovation. If Canadian autoworkers do not accept concessions and changes to the work process, it is possible that corporations will either shift production to cheap labour zones or face possible bankruptcy. Further pressures to accept modifications in pay schedules and reorganization of work have come from the growing number of nonunionized plants established in Canada in the 1980s. Whereas in the postwar period the Canadian Region of the UAW relied upon its monopolistic position in the auto industry to reduce competition for wages and work standards, a growing nonunionized sector raises the possibility of whipsawing by corporations. Finally, as argued earlier, the political and economic climate in Canada since the election of the federal Conservative party has augured poorly for unions. In particular, autoworkers fear the loss of plants and jobs as a result of the Free Trade Agreement. These fears have been heightened by trilateral free trade talks.

Nonetheless, faced with the real possibility of membership disaffection from the union, the CAW chose to resist the most threatening management initiatives of concessions, plant closures, and decentralized bargaining. Through this resistance, the union secured its position with its members and strengthened itself. From this vantage point, the CAW has tried to shape the restructuring agenda rather than have it unilaterally imposed by the corporations.

The Canadian Auto Workers' struggles in 1980–83 were organized in response to plant closures and concessions. After lobbying failed to convince the government to intervene and protect workers from plant closures, the union resorted to plant sitdowns, the most famous of which occurred at the Houdaille plant in Oshawa in 1981. After twelve days of plant occupation and growing media and public outrage at company actions, a settlement was reached. Severance pay was increased almost six times the amount originally offered by the company, and pension benefits were improved and extended to include workers of fifty-five years of age. After workers at two other plants had sitdowns and met with similar successes, the Ontario government passed severance-pay legislation to protect workers faced with plant closures.[5]

The sitdowns proved to autoworkers that it was possible to fight corporations and win. Spurred on by this brush with victory, autoworkers prepared themselves to resist corporate demands for concessions. After earlier concessions caused autoworkers to blame their union for selling them out, the Canadian Region of the UAW determined that it would fight to win even modest gains at the bargaining table.[6] The first major test of the Canadian UAW's no-concessions stand came in the 1982 General Motors negotiations. Canadian Auto Workers successfully rejected the profit-sharing scheme and work-rule alterations accepted in the United States and instead negotiated a straight wage increase and continued cost-of-living allowance (COLA). This victory against concessions was quickly followed by an even more important one at Chrysler. The Canadian Region of the UAW forced Chrysler to back away from its demands for more concessions and to accept, instead, a move toward regaining parity for Canadian Chrysler workers via a $1.15 wage increase and other benefits.[7]

These successes led to other struggles against concessions in auto parts and nonauto plants. They also set the stage for Canadian autoworkers' rejection of a more fundamental restructuring of their collective bargaining relationship with the auto corporations. For example, in 1984 General Motors demanded that autoworkers accept a new agreement that contained lump-sum payments and a profit-sharing agreement to replace the traditional wage increase and COLA clause. Facing concerted opposition from both General Motors and the international, the Canadian Region of the UAW rejected this reformulation of collective bargaining. It retained the annual wage increase (although it equalled only 2.5 percent rather than the traditional 3 percent) and the COLA clause. The cost was high. Canadian autoworkers were forced to leave their international union and form their own independent union, the CAW.

In resisting plant closures and concession bargaining the Canadian Region of the UAW placed itself in a stronger position to effect restructuring. The reasons were twofold. First, the Canadian Region of the UAW protected the existing highly centralized form of collective bargaining. This hampered corporate attempts to force wages down and prevented local union variability and competition over wages, benefits, and work rules. The Canadian Region of the UAW therefore emerged from the worst of the economic crisis with the organizational strength to take concerted action. Second, Canadian autoworkers' militancy gave them media visibility and made their union the single most powerful one in Canada.

Evidence collected to date suggests that the CAW's attempts to use this newfound strength to negotiate the terms of restructuring have only been partly successful. The CAW has stalled unilateral North American management efforts to reduce job classifications, alter seniority arrangements, and introduce changes to pay structures such as two-tier wage systems. This, in turn, has reduced the capacity of the Big Three to impose the type of labour flexibility they initially intended. The terms of flexibility have become subject to negotiation. Although these successes are important, they are reactive and piecemeal. The union has not put forth a bold alternative vision to the lean production model offered by the corporations. Nor has it taken the initiative in long-range planning for the Canadian industry.

The CAW has willingly negotiated certain reductions in job classifications, which in many instances workers found as cumbersome as did management. Many job classifications, however, were initially introduced to provide easier jobs for disabled or older workers unable to continue the pace of regular jobs. In its determination to protect these workers, the CAW has resisted wholesale elimination of job classifications, opting instead to tailor classification changes to particular plants. This position, in turn, is linked to the union's rejection of management initiatives to radically alter seniority arrangements. Seniority curbs management's power to act in an arbitrary fashion in the workplace and use favouritism as a basis for assigning jobs to individual workers. Seniority and job classifications are therefore intrinsically linked and provide the union with a means of preventing discrimination by management against workers, which ultimately splinters the union membership on the basis of age (White 1987a: 8–9).

The CAW's determination to protect seniority and its gradual approach to reductions in job classifications have retarded, if not modified, the transition toward a more flexible deployment of labour by management. Nonetheless, in those plants where reductions in job classifications have been negotiated, the impact on the labour process has been dramatic. Additional tasks and responsibilities have been added to some jobs, lines have been blurred between skilled and unskilled workers, and certain jobs, such as absentee replacements and sweepers, are threatened with elimination (Robertson and Wareham 1987: 40–41). These changes have most often gone hand in hand with the introduction of teamwork.

Teamwork has perhaps been the source of greatest debate and possible divisiveness in the union. Almost impossible to define due to its varied forms, teamwork tends to refer to the reorganization of relations among workers and between workers and management on the shop floor. The workplace is divided into teams of anywhere from four to fifteen workers, who discuss workplace problems and learn each other's jobs, ideally with the objective of allowing workers to rotate jobs. Teamwork tends to accompany the introduction of new technology or, at least, new forms of labour relations.[8] For some autoworkers, teamwork is seen as a management device for speedups and eliminating seniority and transfer rights. For others, it holds the potential to improve the quality of work by reducing the monotony of the assembly line. Partly due to these internal divisions over teamwork, the CAW has developed no clear strategy on the issue. In some cases, such as the General Motors plant in Ste. Thérèse, the union has left the decision to negotiate teamwork to the union local itself. General Motors threatened to close the plant if such changes were not forthcoming. The local union, despite deep membership conflicts, opted in favour of teamwork rather than face the threat of no work at all (Gindin 1989). The CAW was involved in similar negotiations at the General Motors Oshawa Autoplex, where new technology resulted in the replacement of traditional assembly-line work with production islands consisting of small teams of workers. The bargaining strength of the CAW, combined with General Motors' determination to restructure work relations, has placed the union in a strong position to influence and negotiate the terms of teamwork at the Oshawa plant. The result has been the CAW's successful resistance to demands for elimination of sweepers, utility persons, and absentee replacements. This has prevented, perhaps temporarily, teamwork from becoming an alternate means for introducing speedups (Gindin 1987: 10). Nonetheless, the Oshawa union local has been most critical of the union's acceptance of teamwork.[9]

The major focus of the union's response to teamwork has been educational and ideological. The leadership's skepticism regarding the value of teamwork for truly improving the quality of work is reflected in the content of such education. Work by critics of teamwork such as Jane Slaughter and Mike Parker has been distributed to the membership and included in educational sessions (Gindin 1987: 7). Alongside these efforts, the CAW continues to bargain for input into and some control over the training that accompanies the introduction of new technology. Such union input and control is intended to counteract the strong emphasis on "cultural" training that is designed by management to encourage workers to identify with the corporation's competitive position (White 1987b: 226). Moreover, many autoworkers' experiences with training have led them to conclude that it has become the basis for discrimination in the workplace against older or more militant workers and central to political battles with corporations. Consequently, in attempting to gain some control over the training process, the CAW hopes to ensure training according to seniority and thus a reduction in favouritism (Robertson and Wareham 1987: 47–50). Again, these efforts have met with differential success, with the central union office having so far been unsuccessful in negotiating universal input into training.

More recently, the CAW seems to be embracing teamwork but trying to uncouple it from the lean production model. It is attempting to get corporations such as General Motors to experiment with more flexibility in job design to enrich workers' lives while simultaneously putting pressure on the company to desist from using this multiskilling as a means for eliminating jobs and speeding up the assembly line. Given corporate commitment to the lean production model, with its advantage of exercising increased control over workers, it remains unclear whether teamwork can be uncoupled from other transformations in the labour process.

Whereas the CAW has willingly negotiated some changes to the work process, it has been completely resistant to alterations in pay schedules. The union has so far rejected productivity bonuses, two-tier wage systems, and profit-sharing in lieu of regular wage increases (Gindin 1987:3). Moreover, the CAW has continued its struggle for wage parity, especially for workers in newly organized parts plants where downward pressure on wages has been most significant. This resistance has minimized membership fractures along company lines, whipsawing, and the devolution of collective bargaining to the local level.

Although the CAW has been relatively successful in protecting its collective-bargaining position and *negotiating* the terms of restructuring in the workplace, it has been unable to articulate and mobilize widespread support for an alternative solution to industry problems. While the CAW has been instrumental in lobbying government for many of the stopgap policy measures such as import quotas, its more comprehensive policy proposals have failed. In the early 1980s, the union promoted a trading policy that had the potential of forcing Japanese automakers to become part of the Autopact if they wanted to reduce tariff rates on their vehicles. This proposal died along with the Liberal government in 1984. Between 1985 and 1988, Robert White, president of the CAW, played a key role in the anti–free trade debate, arguing instead for a state-managed industrial policy that would protect jobs and encourage growth and research in Canada. With the reelection of the Conservative party in 1988, this alternative vision was defeated and the free trade deal put into place. Finally, the CAW has not publicly put forth an alternative model for the auto industry, seeming at times to accept as inevitable the introduction of lean and flexible production (Yates 1988: ch. 8; Lavelle and White 1983).

Changing the Scene: The Nineties
Bring Recession

Whereas the 1980–82 economic crisis pushed the auto corporations to restructure, the economic boom from 1984 to 1989 gave the companies time and money to act. With profits and sales at some of the highest levels in years, the Big Three and the CAW were cushioned during the transition toward a restructured industry. Not so in the 1990s. As 1989 drew to a close, the industry was confronted with a new recession. Over-capacity and soft consumer demand pitched North American automakers into a battle for survival. Parts plants were closed, long-term layoffs announced, and investment plans shelved.

Moreover, given the federal government's commitment to market-driven solutions, the opportunities for government to shape the path of auto-industry restructuring rest with the provincial government. Years of Conservative provincial government, followed by an interlude of Liberal party rule in Ontario, meant only short-term measures intended to help the auto industry while in immediate crisis. Nevertheless, the 1990 provincial election brought the New Democratic Party (NDP) to office in Ontario with a sizable majority.

The surprise of winning the election, combined with a difficult transition to power, has delayed many new NDP government initiatives. Consequently, it is premature to predict the course of action that this government will steer. A number of factors, however, will influence its auto-policy direction. The Canadian Auto Workers Union plays a strong and influential role within the NDP and the Ontario economy. Thus, it is obvious that the union will be closely involved in any new developments of auto policy. Second, the NDP has drawn into its fold economic and policy advisors whose vision of the restructured economy accepts as inevitable and even desirable the lean production model with its strong emphasis on new technology. While this is likely to make the government more proactive in areas such as training, it is also likely to blind them to the dangers for workers of streamlined production and Japanization. Finally, like most other Ontario governments, the NDP is sensitive to the central role played by the auto industry in the provincial economy. This combined with the government's avowed opposition to free trade should translate into some new auto-policy initiatives.

If election of the NDP is likely to enhance the CAW's ability to shape auto policy, the union's capacity to shape restructuring may be undercut by three other developments. First, the growing numbers of unorganized plants in Canada threaten to undermine the union's bargaining strength. The CAW has responded to this challenge by undertaking a massive organization drive. Ten new organizers were assigned to the CAW staff and succeeded between 1985 and 1987 in organizing one hundred new units (Gindin 1987: 4). Still unorganized, however, are most of the major plants established by offshore producers such as Toyota. Although the

CAW has launched organizing drives at the Honda and Toyota plants, it faces an uphill battle. Toyota, for instance, introduced a new worker bonus plan just as the CAW went public with its organizing drive. It has also been scrupulous in its use of the law to prevent any union distribution of leaflets at the plant gate.[10] Second, the 1990–91 recession forced workers to swallow some bitter pills. Third, the lack of an alternative to Japanization of the auto industry may leave the CAW incapable of seizing the moment to influence corporate responses to meet the challenge of the nineties.

The 1990s recession has limited the future options of the Canadian auto industry. Whether the Ontario government in combination with the CAW and North American automakers can prevent their assignation to the role of understudies in the world automotive industry remains to be seen.

Notes

1. The research for this paper was funded by the Social Sciences and Humanities Research Council of Canada.
2. In one instance of a training session at a General Motors truck plant in Canada, 70 percent of the training time was to be directed toward "cultural change training." (Robertson and Wareham 1987: 47)
3. *Globe and Mail* (Toronto), 1 May 1980; Canadian Regional UAW Director's Report to Canadian Council, 21 and 22 June 1980, 17–18.
4. Minutes to Canadian Council, 21 and 22 June 1980; Canadian Regional UAW Director's Report to Canadian Council, 14 and 15 September 1980, 1–4, 10; *Globe and Mail* (Toronto), 9 and 21 August 1980.
5. Minutes to Canadian Council, 21 and 22 June 1980; Canadian Regional UAW Director's Report to Canadian Council, 14 and 15 September 1980, 1–4, 10; *Globe and Mail* (Toronto), 9 and 21 August, 1980.
6. Canadian Regional UAW Director's Report to Canadian Council, 12 and 13 September 1981, 30 and 31 January 1982; Minutes to Canadian Council, 30 and 31 January 1982, 32; *Globe and Mail* (Toronto), 16 April 1982.
7. Canadian Regional UAW Director's Report to Canadian Council, 5 and 6 March 1983, 29.
8. For an excellent critical review of teamwork in the auto industry see Slaughter and Parker (1988).
9. Local 222 representatives. "The Wrong Direction for Labour." Statement distributed to Canadian Council meeting, 29 September 1989.

10. This information on Toyota is based on a tour taken by myself of the Toyota plant in Cambridge, Ont., 20 November 1990. Also see *Kitchener-Waterloo Record*, 22 November 1990.

References

Beigie, Carl. 1970: *The Canada-U.S. Automotive Agreement: An Evaluation*. Toronto: Canadian-American Committee.
Brodie, Janine, and Jane Jenson. 1988: *Crisis, Challenge, and Change: Party and Class in Canada Revisited*. Ottawa: Carleton University Press.
Cusamano, Michael. 1985: *The Japanese Automobile Industry*. Cambridge, Mass.: Cambridge University Press.
Gindin, Sam. 1987. Labour's Reaction to New Strategies in Human Resources Management: The Experience of the Canadian Autoworkers. Speech made in May.
Gindin, Sam. 1989: Interview, May.
Herzenberg, Stephen. 1991: The North American Auto Industry and Continental Free Trade Negotiations. Unpublished paper.
Holmes, John. 1991: The Globalization of Production and the Future of Canada's Mature Industries. In Daniel Drache and Marek Gertler, eds., *The New Era of Global Competition*. Kingston, Ont.: McGill–Queen's University Press.
Keller, Maryann. 1989: *Rude Awakening*. New York: William Morrow.
Lavelle, Pat, and Robert White. 1983: An Automotive Strategy for Canada. Report of Federal Task Force on Canadian Auto Industry. Ottawa: Government of Canada.
Laxer, Gordon. 1989: *Open for Business*. Toronto: Oxford University Press.
Mahon, Rianne. 1988: Toward a Highly Qualified Workforce: Improving the Terms of the Equity-Efficiency Trade-Off. Background paper for Study Team 2 of Vision 2000.
Ontario Ministry of Labour. 1987: *Working Times*. Report of the Ontario Task Force on Hours of Work and Overtime. Toronto: Government of Ontario.
Robertson, David, and Jeff Wareham. 1987: *Technological Change in the Auto Industry*. Toronto: CAW Technology Project.
Slaughter, Jane, and Mike Parker. 1985: *Choosing Sides: Unions and the Team Concept*. Detroit: Labor Notes.
Van Ameringen, Marc. 1985: The Restructuring of the Canadian Automobile Industry. In Duncan Cameron and François Houle, eds., *Le Canada et la nouvelle division internationale du travail*, Ottawa: Sciences Sociales.
Ward's Automotive Yearbook. 1978–1990.

White, Robert. 1985: Interview, December.

———. 1987a: A Perspective on Changing Labour Relations in the Auto Industry. Address to Twelfth Annual Automotive News World Congress, Detroit.

———. 1987b: The Old and the New: Workplace Organization and Labour Relations in the Auto Industry. In Gregg Olsen, ed., *Industrial Change and Labour Adjustment in Sweden and Canada*, Toronto: York University.

Womack, J. P., et al. 1990: *The Machine That Changed the World*. Toronto: Collier Macmillan.

Yates, Charlotte. 1988: From Plant to Politics: The Canadian UAW 1936–1984. Ph.D dissertation, Carleton University, Ottawa.

The Future: Strategic Continuity or Change?

17 RICHARD FREEMAN

What Does the Future Hold for
U.S. Unionism?

American trade unionism is slowly being limited in influence by changes which destroy the basis on which it is erected. . . . I see no reason to believe that American trade unionism will . . . become in the next decade a more potent social influence.
> —Presidential Address of Harold Barnett to the American
> Economic Association, 1932

Has the American community certain distinctive features among Western societies which may cause the American labor movement to reach a ceiling in the neighborhood of forty percent of total nonagricultural employees? . . . [Unions] have become increasingly accepted as a permanent part of the industrial scene . . . [but they] will be doing well, in the absence of a climactic period, to maintain their present relative proportion of nonagricultural employees in the period until 1975.
> —John T. Dunlop, 1958

It is impossible to bargain collectively with the government.
> —George Meany, 1962, cited in Kramer

As the above quotations indicate, predicting the future of unions in the United States is no easy task. Throughout American history unionism has developed along lines that contravene expert prognostications. Unions have grown when experts have seen no hope for unions, and declined when unions seemed to have become an established part of the economic order. The reason for this is that unionism in the United States develops in fits and spurts that are not predictable by standard marginal analysis or linear projections of past developments, while declining in intervening years. This latter characteristic differentiates the United States from many other countries.

As Dunlop (1958, 30) noted in his 1958 projections, which correctly forecast the downward drift in unionism in the 1960s but not the ensuing deunionization of the private sector, "the distinctive influence of these climactic periods is a major indeterminateness and error term in all projections." Nonlinear analysis can model the dynamics of spurts in union growth, but predicting the occurrence or amplitude of spurts lies beyond our tools and knowledge.[1]

How, then, can one address the question of the future of U.S. unions without hedging and equivocating?

My approach is to consider five "scenarios of change" that lay out a range of possible developments into the twenty-first century. I begin by reviewing briefly the state of unionism in the United States at the outset of the 1990s and then examine scenarios of continued rapid decline in union density; slow development of associational unionism and improved organizing efficiency; labor law reforms that increase unionism, possibly through plant-level works councils; and a new growth spurt among white-collar private-sector unions.

Being no less gutsy—or foolhardy—than other industrial relations/labor economics "experts," I speculate on each scenario's likelihood of occurrence. Given the track record of scholarly prognostications, I advise against betting your house or even old copies of *Industrial and Labor Relations Review* on my speculations, however.

The Decline of Unionism in the United States

The proportion of workers represented by unions in the United States has fallen at an accelerating rate in the past several decades, as several chapters in this book indicate. By 1990 only 16 percent of all workers were unionized and only 12 percent of private nonagricultural workers. The decline in the total density was due exclusively to the drop in the private sector, as traditionally unorganized public employees became extensively unionized in the 1970s and 1980s (Milkman, this volume). Within the private sector, moreover, density fell in virtually every industry, region of the country, and occupational category (see Table 17-1).

At the "margin" of new organization, the number of workers unionized through National Labor Relations Board (NLRB) representation

TABLE 17-1. Percentage of Wage and Salary Workers Who Are Members of Unions by Industry and Occupation, 1980–1990

	1980	1990	Change
Industry			
Mining	32	18	− 14
Construction	31	21	− 10
Manufacturing	32	21	− 11
Transportation and public utilities	48	32	− 16
Wholesale and retail trade	10	6	− 4
Services	9	6	− 3
Occupation[a]			
Executive, administrative, and managerial	8	6	− 2
Professional, technical, and kindred	23	20	− 3
Clerical	8	6	− 2
Sales	4	5	1
Craft and kindred	39	26	− 13
Operatives, except transport	40	27	− 13
Transport and equipment	45	29	− 16
Nonfarm laborers	33	23	− 10
Service, except protective service	13	10	− 3

Source: U.S. Bureau of Labor Statistics, *Employment and Earnings*, January 1981 and January 1991

[a]Occupations include persons working for the government, whereas industry excludes government workers. The occupation code changes between 1980 and 1990, and I report data on the 1980 code basis. I have made the following linkages to obtain the data: professional, technical, and kindred (1980) = professional + technical and related in 1990, weighted by employment; managers and administration (1980) = executive, administrators, and managers (1988); clerical (1980) = precision production, craft, and repair (1990); operatives, except transport (1980) = machine operators, assemblers, and inspectors (1990); transport equipment (1980) = transportation and material moving occupations (1990); nonfarm laborers (1980) = handlers, equipment cleaners, helpers, and laborers (1990).

elections plummeted to a bare 100,000 or so workers annually in the 1980s—a drop in the bucket in a labor force of more than 100 million. About one-third of union victories do not produce first contracts (McDonald 1983), and the gain in those unions covered by collective bargaining is insufficient to balance out the "natural" depreciation of density due to the death of older union plants and the growth of the workforce. The NLRB mode of determining union representation, which had served unions well for decades, failed them in the 1970s and 1980s.

What caused the NLRB election process to dry up as a source of organization? What underlies the precipitous fall in private-sector density? Among the factors that have been proposed as contributing to the fall are (1) structural shifts in the composition of employment among occupations, industries, demographic groups, and regions; (2) a worsened public image of unions; (3) government protective regulations that provide an alternative to unionism; (4) a decline in worker desire for unions; (5) virulent antiunion activity by management; and (6) sluggish union responses to new developments. Extant evidence, however, indicates that structural changes, public perception of unions, governmental regulations, and loss of worker desire for unions are not prime moving forces in the decline in unionization.[2]

The structural change hypothesis runs counter to three facts. First, the changes in the composition of the workforce have moved in the same direction across many countries as labor forces everywhere became more white-collar, female, and educated, and increasingly concentrated in service industries. Yet, falls in density such as those in the United States have not occurred everywhere. Second, density has declined in all private-sector industries and in all occupations in the United States (see Table 17-2). Third, the rise of unionization in the public sector shows the possibility of counteracting adverse compositional shifts by organizing traditionally nonunion workers. The drop in employment in steel, autos, and other centers of union strength devastated the union movement but does not explain the failure to branch out to new industries and groups of workers, a failure that differentiates the trend in density in the United States from that in Canada or many other developed countries.

The public-image hypothesis (Lipset 1986) cannot account for the decline in density during the 1970s and 1980s for several reasons. First, between 1972 and 1985, when density fell sharply, rather than worsen, public approval of unions remained roughly stable at 55 to 59 percent. Second, opinion polls show unionism enjoys as unfavorable a public image in some Western European countries as it does in the United States, but there is little comparable decline in density. Third, and most devastating for this argument, 1980s opinion polls for the United Kingdom show increases in favorable attitudes toward unionism while density fell![3]

TABLE 17-2. Changes in Union Density in Periods of Spurts and Other Periods, 1897–1987

	Density		Years When Density Grew		Years When Density Fell	
	Initial (%)	Final (%)	Years	Avg. % Change in Density	Years	Avg.% Change in Density
Spurts						
1897–1904	3.7	11.7	7	1.3		
1916–1921	10.7	19.2	5	1.7		
1934–1939	11.9	28.6	5	3.3		
1942–1945	25.7	35.5	3	3.2		
All			20	2.2		
Nonspurts						
1904–1916	11.7	10.7	6	0.6	6	−0.8
1921–1934	19.2	11.9	6	0.3	7	−1.3
1939–1942	28.6	25.9	1	1.0	2	−1.9
1945–1987	35.5	17.0	9	0.6	33	−0.7
1945–1970	35.5	27.3	7	0.8	18	−0.8
1970–1987	27.3	17.0	2	0.0	15	−0.7
All			22	0.6	48	−0.9

Source: Author's tabulation. The union density figures are based on Bureau of Labor Statistics estimates for the years 1900–1980 spliced with data from Leo Troy and Neil Sheflin, *Union Sourcebook*, and Bureau of Labor Statistics, *Employment and Earnings*, January editions. I applied annual percentage changes reported in Troy-Sheflin for 1897–1899 to get figures for those years for the BLS series, and applied the same procedure for the 1980s using Troy-Sheflin and CPS (Current Population Survey) numbers to fill in those years.

The argument that unionism is declining because governmental regulations substitute for union protection of workers at work places (Neumann and Rissman 1984) is inconsistent with the strength of unionism in Scandinavia, Germany, and other European countries with highly regulated markets. The decline of unionism when governmental protections loosened under Reagan in the United States and under Thatcher in the United Kingdom also speaks against this hypothesis, as does the desire for unions expressed by minority workers who enjoy legal protection under civil rights laws and who thus ought to be less interested in unionization than other workers. Finally, the need for union or unionlike agencies to monitor compliance with increased legal regulation at the shop floor suggests that something more is behind the trend.

Surveys of worker support for unions, conducted during the period when density fell especially rapidly, show no decline in the proportion wanting to be represented. In both the 1973 Quality of Employment Survey and the 1985 Harris Survey, approximately one-third of nonunion workers expressed a desire for union representation. In 1988 the Gallup Poll asked interviewees to respond to the following: "Even though there are advantages to having a union employee group, it would not be worth the cost or trouble to form such an organization." In this case 56 percent of non-self-employed members of the workforce disagreed with the statement, which implies that a majority favored union organization.[4] The fall in density in the private sector was, moreover, coincident with increased unionization of the public sector, a highly unlikely development if workers in general were turning away from unions.

My analysis and that of others (Farber 1987; Dickens and Leonard 1983; Goldfield 1987) suggest that the most important single cause for union decline is to be found on the other side of the ledger—in the behavior of management, which has conducted highly successful virulent campaigns against unions in organizing drives.

That management devoted considerable resources to defeating unions in the 1970s and 1980s is incontestable. Virtually every company faced with an NLRB election engaged in any of several actions to forestall unionization: aggressive lawful efforts to persuade/pressure workers to reject unions; unfair labor practices such as firing union activists to frighten workers into rejecting unions; and adoption of "positive labor relations" including company-created union work conditions such as seniority and grievance procedures to deter unionism. Indicative of the pervasiveness of the corporate antiunion campaign in 1983, 45 percent of the relatively progressive companies in the Conference Board's Personnel Policy Forum declared that their main labor goal was to operate "union-free"—a far cry from the 1950s and 1960s when large companies accepted unions at the workplace. Underlying the growth of management opposition is the presumption that unionism held increasingly adverse consequences for profitability in the 1970s, due to a higher union wage premium, growth of foreign competition, deregulation, and the like.[5]

Has management opposition been effective? With the exception of Getman, Goldberg, and Herman (1976)—whose results have been reversed in a reanalysis by Dickens (1983)—all studies with which I am familiar show that management opposition adversely affects the chance of a union victory in an NLRB election. Econometric estimates suggest, moreover, that management opposition as indexed by unfair labor practices is the single most important factor in the drop in new organization (Freeman 1986).

What about the union response to management antiunion activity? Union organizing activity has not kept pace with the growth of the workforce, as fewer NLRB election drives have been held per year in the 1980s than in the 1960s. Organization has concentrated on existing areas of union strength rather than on growing sectors of the economy (Voos 1983), and special AFL-CIO efforts to organize new workers, such as the 1980s Houston Project, have failed abysmally. With rare exceptions, moreover, union leaders have been slow to come to grips with the reality of decline, downplaying the fall in union density when absolute membership held steady and arguing that membership would expand when the economy began to boom. Not until the Committee on the Evolution of Work report—"The Changing Situation of Workers and Their Unions"— in 1985 did the top AFL-CIO leadership address seriously the moribund state of the union movement outside of the public sector.

The failure of union organizing to keep pace with the growth of the workforce should not, however, be viewed entirely, or even largely, as an independent cause of the decline in unionism. To an economist at least, it looks very much like rational optimizing behavior in response to the increased cost of winning an NLRB election: In many cases it does not pay to risk members' dues on drives in an environment where a vigorous antiunion management campaign can defeat the organizing effort.

In addition, as union density falls, the cost to each member of organizing a given fraction of the nonunion workforce rises. The inability of unions to develop successful innovations to counter the management offensive may, in addition, reveal something more about the "advantage" of employers in disputes (about which Adam Smith wrote in *Wealth of Nations*) than about any failure of union leadership (1937: 66). If Samuel Gompers and John L. Lewis were to return from the grave they might not do much better than the current AFL-CIO leadership. Gompers had his share of organizing failures, and Lewis was unable to arrest the decline of the United Mine Workers in the 1920s.

This reference to the past suggests that the decline in density in the past two decades is not qualitatively abnormal or peculiar for U.S. labor history, though it is exceptionally severe in magnitude and thus quantitatively abnormal. Analysis of estimates of union density from 1897 to 1987, based on Bureau of Labor Statistics data, shows the tendency for unionism to grow in the spurts noted at the outset, with sharp rises in density in four periods—1897–1904; 1916–1921; 1933–1939; and 1942–1945.[6] There are decreases in density in two-thirds of the other years, generally at a modest rate (see Table 17-2).[7] The average annual gain in spurt years was 2.2 percent, compared to an average loss in nonspurt years of 0.4 percent.

Additional analysis leads to the rejection of the hypothesis that increases in density have the same statistical properties as decreases. Increases in density are more concentrated in amplitude (the mean increase in years of rising density was 1.3 percent while the median increase was 0.8 percent) than decreases (a mean decrease of −0.9 percent compared to a median of −0.7 percent). Increases in density are more autocorrelated over time than decreases.[8] Note also, however, that the decline in density in nonspurt periods has been exceptionally long and substantial in the post-1945 period, accelerating in the 1970s and 1980s.

Is there any indication in the time series that another spurt is on the horizon? If one treats the recent growth of public-sector unionism as a successful spurt, even though it was insufficient to raise overall density, and treats 1942–45 as part of the 1934–39 spurt, there is a rough twenty-year period between spurts. While a stock-market chartist might predict a new burst of union activity in the 1990s to 2000s on the basis of this crude pattern, no one with knowledge of developments in labor relations would make such a mechanistic prognistication. All told, the most reasonable scientific assessment of the historical record is that if unions are to regain their share of the labor force, they will do so in a sudden hard-to-predict growth spurt.

While weak, this interpretation offers a more optimistic picture of the possible future for unionism in the U.S. than the developments of the past quarter century would indicate. It suggests that we ought not to be surprised at a sudden outburst of unionism, particularly among traditionally unorganized workers, in the next decades.

Scenarios for the Future

The first and easiest scenario to foresee is continued decline, as ongoing trends persist. Given the role of NLRB elections in organizing, the key parameters for projecting unionism in this case are the "natural rate of change" in membership due to changes in employment in organized establishments (r); the rate of growth of total employment (g); and the number of new members won in the elections less any loss due to decertification (NEW). The following equation relates the flow of new members to the stock of unionists (UNION) in any year t:

$$\text{UNION}_t = (1 - r)\text{UNION}_{t-1} + \text{NEW}_t$$

Dividing both sides by the number of employees in year t yields an equation between union density (UDENS) and the ratio of workers organized from t − 1 to t to the number of employees in year t − 1 (PCTNEW):

$$\text{UDENS}_t = (1/(1 + g)) \; [(1 - r)\text{UDENS}_{t-1} + \text{PCTNEW}_t]$$
$$- (1 - r - g)\text{UDENS}_{t-1} + (1 - g)\text{PCTNEW}_t$$

The steady state density implied by this equation is UDENS = PCTNEW/(r + g), which shows that long-run density changes when economic conditions cause union plants to contract or expand relative to the growth of total employment and when the rate of organizing changes. For example, if unions organize 1 percent of the workforce per annum, as in the 1950s, and suffer a net depreciation of density of 4 percent, the union share of employment would stabilize at 25 percent. If, alternatively, new organization falls to 0.7 percent of the workforce and r + g rises to 3.4 percent, as in the 1960s, the steady state density would drop to 21 percent of employment.

In the early 1980s the model was used to project private-sector union density for *What Do Unions Do?* (Freeman and Medoff 1984). Assuming, conservatively, an r + g of 3 percent and an organizing rate of 0.3 percent (the levels of the 1970s), a steady state density of 10 percent was projected, which was to be reached between 2000 and 2010. An increase in r + g to around 6 percent and a decline in organizing success through NLRB elections in the 1980s suggest that private-sector density will hit 10 percent more quickly, possibly by 1995. Indeed, the steady state density implied by 1980s parameters is just 3 percent—which would bring the United States to the "union-free" nirvana of the Committee for a Union-Free Environment and other rabid opponents of unionism.

Will organizing really be as unsuccessful and the depreciation of union density as high in the future as in the 1980s? The second scenario assumes that the answer to these questions is no—that spurred by declining density, by the "Workers and Their Unions" report, and by vigorous efforts to master the new environment, unions will develop innovative policies and organizing tactics to arrest the erosion of their strength. Among the innovations likely to impact the future are creation of new benefits and membership forms that encourage workers to join unions outside the collective-bargaining relation; more cooperative and concessionary collective-bargaining policies; strengthening of state-, local-, and community-based union organizations; and use of corporate campaigns and union pension funds in organizing drives.

New benefits and forms of membership, of the type recommended in the AFL-CIO report, are intended to give workers an incentive and opportunity to join unions when they are unable to establish contractual relations with employers.

By severing the link between membership and contracts at the workplace, these new forms of membership require major changes in the structure and operation of unions, including a significant backing away from exclusive representation, greater concern for occupational or professional work issues that enhance workers' independence on jobs as opposed to their seniority, and rules regulating managerial behavior. Although some unionists fear that the creation of "associate members" working without contracts will substitute for stronger union structures, the transformation of "company unions" in the 1930s and 1940s into collective-bargaining unions and the more recent history of employee associations in the public sector suggest the opposite: that associations are a stepping stone to collective bargaining (Ichniowski and Zax 1990).

Another potential union innovation that might help arrest the decline is development of community-based union organizations in which workers in a local labor market come together to deal with problems, ranging from provision of child-care to health and dental services. This requires strengthening of state and local union bodies at the expense of nationals, and continued reaching out from unions to other community organizations. It will further weaken the reliance of unions on exclusive representation at workplaces.

The cooperative-bargaining stance adopted by most unions in recent years and supported by the AFL-CIO report and the granting of wage concessions for job security are likely to have two effects on the future of unionization. In the short run, they should reduce the "depreciation" of density by preserving existing union jobs. In the long run, they should lessen employer opposition by lowering the costs of unionism to firms, making organizing easier. At the other end of the spectrum are new adversarial tactics: corporate campaigns and aggressive use of pension-fund moneys to pressure management toward neutrality in organizing drives. While using capital as an organizing tool would make Karl Marx and J. P. Morgan turn in their graves, such tactics make sense in a world where mobility of capital has weakened labor's power at workplaces, where pension funds own much of the nation's capital, and where takeover bids and mergers are a major component of financial life. More aggressive use of pension funds, however, may require reinterpretation of the fiduciary responsibility clauses of laws governing pension-fund investments, as well as changes in collective-bargaining contracts. It will also require unions to be imaginative in their investment strategies, investing in some cases in antiunion firms to influence their policies.

Are these innovations in union activity likely to arrest the decline in union density in the near term and bring about a revival of unionism? I think not. A major reason is the decentralized and democratic structure of the American labor movement, where dozens of independent nationals and thousands of local organizations, each with its own agenda and problems, make the key decisions, generally giving greater attention to the short-term interests of existing dues-payers than to the future of the labor movement broadly defined. Given this structure, it is not surprising that the "Workers and Their Unions" benefit scheme that has been most widely adopted—low interest credit cards for union members—has not become a standard inducement in organizing drives to attract and hold workers if the drive fails. As for adversarial tactics, while corporate campaigns and the like can be valuable tactical weapons, the democratic and political nature of unions will disadvantage them in battles against authoritarian management except in extraordinary circumstances.

These arguments do not, however, mean that the changes will have no impact on the future of unionism. Rather, they suggest that the changes will operate largely to reduce leakage in density primarily among blue-collar workers (those currently organized), stabilizing aggregate density at higher levels than those in the first scenario—perhaps at the 10 percent forecasted in *What Do Unions Do?*

The third scenario focuses on the possible impact of labor-law reform. In 1978 Congress came within a single vote of enacting a labor-law reform that would have strengthened NLRB enforcement of fair labor practices. While the 1978 law was too modest to limit substantially management's power to oppose unionism at workplaces, Congress could change the labor laws in ways that would substantially increase union organizing success.

Consider, for example, what might happen if the federal government required "quick elections" that limit the time management has to oppose organization; allowed the NLRB to certify a union as the legal representative of workers on the basis of card checks, as in some Canadian provinces; imposed major financial penalties for unfair labor practices: and strengthened the duty-to-bargain features of the law for first contracts, perhaps requiring binding arbitration to resolve first-contract disputes (Weiler 1983). Evidence suggests that changes of these types would have a substantial effect on organizing success. In the public sector, the passage of strong collective-bargaining laws appears to be the major cause of the 1970s spurt in collective bargaining (Freeman and Ichniowski 1988). In the private sector, right-to-work laws have been found to reduce union success in organizing workers through NLRB elections (Ellwood and Fine 1987). In Canada, unions have done better than in the United States, in part because Canadian laws limit management's ability to oppose unions. In the United Kingdom Thatcherist labor legislation has been associated with drops in density that reverse increases under the more favorable Labor legislation of the 1970s.

While significant changes in labor law can greatly enhance union organizing success, they are unlikely to do so by enough to raise union density. This is because current rates of organization are so low that even huge increases in the number organized through NLRB elections, say to the levels of the 1960s, would at most arrest the downward spiral in density. If, for example, the legal changes in the NLRA reduced management's role in representation elections to the extent that opposition indexed by unfair labor practices fell to the 1960 level, my largest estimate of the impact of unfair practices suggests that the proportion of workers organized would rise from 0.1 percent of the workforce to 0.3 percent, or some 300,000 workers per year. Assuming a rate of depreciation of 4.7 percent, as existed in the 1970s, density would drop to a bare 6 percent of the workforce.[9] Only if the legal changes were sufficiently strong to reduce the unfair practices/elections index of management opposition to the levels of 1950, raising the share of workers organized to some 0.7

percent of the workforce, would density rise, and then only modestly to 15 percent in the long run.[10]

Is there any possibility for such changes in the NLRA? I think not. The key determinant of the votes in the Senate on the mild 1978 reform was the percentage unionized in a state. Senators from high-density states favored the reform and those from low-union-density states opposed it (Freeman and Medoff 1984). The post-1978 decline in density suggests, all else being equal, that unions will have less political muscle to bring to bear for any new reform. This makes passage of legislation stronger than the 1978 bill a long shot. What is more likely to change in the future is the administration of the law, with future administrations, particularly Democratic ones, appointing members of the NLRB and adopting policies more favorable to unions than those of President Reagan. A more favorable board, of course, would ease the problems faced by unions in their organizing activity but could not possibly have a sufficiently large impact on the number of workers won to arrest the drop in density.

Are there any "radical" legal changes that might win conservative support, be enacted, and ultimately improve the standing of unions? I can conceive of three such changes.

The first, and in my opinion the least likely, is repeal of the NLRA, deregulating the representation process, and allowing labor-management conflict to determine union status as in pre–Wagner Act years. Given that NLRA restrictions on union economic weapons such as secondary boycotts have succeeded, while those on management practices have not, some union leaders favor this option. Conservatives favorable to deregulation and those who believe that union power depends on government intervention in markets should also favor repeal. Repeal would augment the power of some unions, such as the Teamsters, and probably lead to greater organization.

A related and more likely change would be to shift the locus of labor law to states, as in Canada, where provincial laws cover most workers. Letting states regulate union activity should appeal to conservatives and has the precedent of the right-to-work clause of Taft-Hartley. On the basis of the development of public-sector labor law, I would expect some states to enact and enforce laws more conducive to unionization than the NLRA as it operates today. As organizing cannot decline much furthur, even if other states enacted or enforced less favorable laws (exclusive of outlawing unions, which would not be permitted), union density would stand a good chance of increasing.

A third possible legal change would be to establish Western European–style works councils to give employees—nonunion as well as union—greater say at their workplace. Court and state legislative weakening of the employment-at-will doctrine and proposed federal plant-closing-notification legislation suggest that the nation is moving toward greater legal protection and job rights for workers in the absence of collective bargaining. As more U.S. workers find employment with foreign-owned firms, political pressure may grow for new arrangements that give workers greater job rights at the expense of foreign capital. To the extent that such arrangements buffer employers against court interventions in the employment relation, moreover, they might also be supportive. Nothing would give greater impetus to the associate membership and new union forms suggested in the "Workers and Their Unions" report than a works council–type law.

In sum, if changes in national labor law are to play a role in resuscitating U.S. unionism, I expect those changes to take the form of "radical" reforms that appeal to conservatives, that reduce the role of the federal government in regulating labor-management relations, and that enhance worker rights outside of collective bargaining.

What about any potential new spurt in unionism, my fourth scenario? Sidestepping the issue of whether a new spurt is likely to occur, can one offer any insights into the possible characteristics of a future spurt if it occurs? My reading of union history leads me to expect that any new spurt in unionism will involve organization of private-sector white-collar workers, particularly women, and the development of new union tactics, agendas, and modes of representation. This is likely to be associated with the formation of a new labor federation composed of the major public-sector and white-collar oriented AFL-CIO unions and professional and other employee associations.

Why look to a spurt among white-collar employees when there are sufficiently large numbers of unorganized blue-collar workers to fuel massive union growth?

One reason is historical. Spurts have generally involved "new unionism": new organizations with new tactics and goals representing traditionally nonunion workers rather than enhanced organization of groups with a history of unionism. Private-sector white-collar workers fit this historic pattern. A second reason is that the internationalization of the U.S. economy in terms of trade and capital flows and deregulation of product markets has weakened the economic power of traditionally organized blue-collar groups,[11] making it difficult for them to unionize in the face of management opposition. By contrast, even in a world marketplace, some groups of white-collar workers are likely to have the strategic position in the technological or market structure that Dunlop (*;948*) has cited as a key to organization. A third reason is that with the United States no longer being dominant in the world economy, a new spurt in unionism is likely to hinge on what unions do to improve working conditions, job flexibility, fringe benefits, workers' right to independent judgment, and fairness in promotions—these are the "collective voice" aspects of unionism discussed in *What Do Unions Do?*—and on their championing innovations, flexibility, and responsiveness that raise output, more than on their ability to win "monopoly wage gains" and contractual rules that limit management arbitrariness and abuse of power. White-collar unions should be better able to deliver on these fronts than traditional blue-collar-dominated unions, with of course some notable exceptions (vide union experiments with "quality of work life" at factories).

Why should the formation of a new federation contribute to a new spurt? One reason is that in the United States (and elsewhere) white-collar workers, rightly or wrongly, tend to prefer membership in employee organizations that are not part of the traditional blue-collar-based union movement. Given a choice between two otherwise equivalent organizations, one associated with the AFL-CIO and one associated with a new white-collar-oriented federation, many, if not most, white-collar workers would choose the latter. Even in highly unionized Scandinavia, blue-collar and white-collar workers have separate federations, suggesting that it is easier to organize the latter under a different banner.

A second reason is that a new federation, like a new business, can be expected to try out and adopt more rapidly than existing organizations the innovations in labor relations that will get unionism a new hearing from white-collar workers. These innovations might include the various forms of associational representation suggested in "Workers and Their Unions": endorsement of arbitration to resolve impasse even in the private sector, and stands on other issues that would reduce the fears of white-collar workers that unionism means confrontation, rigidity in workplaces, and the like. Past spurts in unionism have tended to involve major organizational changes in the union movement, with new structures and leaders offering "new unionism" to the traditionally unorganized. I see a new federation as the most likely such organizational change. I can think of no stronger signal that unions are no longer doing business as usual than the formation of a federation of unions with the greatest potential for organizing white-collar workers—including public-sector unions like the American Federation of State, County, and Municipal Employees, the Communications Workers, the Service Employees, the American Federation of Teachers, highly skilled groups like the Airline Pilots, the National Education Association, the American Nurses' Association—and related organizations like the American Association of University Professors, engineering societies, and fledgling doctors and interns unions.

Third, although American unionists view dual unionism with horror, labor history suggests that competition between federations and unions spurs organizing success. One of the catalysts of the 1930s–1940s spurt was the formation of the CIO. The 1970s spurt in public-sector unionism saw competition between the National Education Association and the American Federation of Teachers, between the Teamsters and various AFL-CIO unions, as well as among the Service Employees, American Federation of State, County, and Municipal Employees, and other unions within the federation. For all the ballyhoo about the advantages of a single federation, it may be no accident that union density began drifting down almost immediately after the 1955 merger.

By enlarging the choices to workers and, equally importantly, to management, which may end up favoring one union over another rather than go to war against any union at all, as is the current practice, competition can be a force for union growth. If the 1930s and 1940s are any guide, I would expect the AFL-CIO to respond with new tactics and organizing drives in response to a new federation, heralding an era of significant competition in unionism.

Are we likely to see a new spurt accompanied by the formation of a new union federation? This scenario is not very likely, if one measures with current indicators. First, there is nothing beyond occasional management skittishness to suggest that unions will make a breakthrough among white-collar workers in the private sector. Unions in the AFL-CIO are currently drawing closer together rather than furthur apart— circling the wagons, so to speak. While some unionists recognize that they might do better attracting workers outside the AFL-CIO, most view the federation as offering greater benefits than would accrue from independent operation. Second, as the "Workers and Their Unions" showed, the federation itself has taken the lead in trying to devise innovations to restore union strength. Third, the nation's largest union of professional workers, the National Education Association, which might be expected to play a key role in any new spurt in white-collar union growth, has shown some interest in organizing nonteaching employees in the education industry but not elsewhere.

Thus, for the near future at least, the fourth scenario looks highly implausible. Nevertheless, it does represent my best speculation about what might be involved in a new spurt of union growth, and in that vein I put it on the table for consideration.

Unionism in the United States is in grave trouble, and nothing short of massive dramatic changes on the labor scene is likely to bring about a significant renaissance of union strength. This chapter set out what might happen if such changes do not occur and speculated on the possibility and nature of the potential changes that might catalyze unionism. Twenty years from now readers will be able to assess whether I missed the boat by as much as "experts" in my discipline usually do when they peer into the future.

Notes

1. There is the possibility that, like the weather, spurts in union organization are virtually unpredictable, given dependence on slight changes in parameters or initial conditions.

2. This section summarizes arguments given in Freeman (1988).

3. Polls reported by Heckscher (1988: 258) show a 33 percent rate of confidence in unions in the United States compared to 26 percent in the United Kingdom, 32 percent in Italy, and 36 percent in France and Germany.

4. Because the figures on whether workers desire to be represented by a union are from separate surveys, they are not strictly comparable. Also, since the 1988 Gallup Poll had a different question, I would not interpret the responses as showing greater desire for unionization.

5. The growing literature showing that unionism reduces profits does not explore if the profit effect increased in the 1970s.

6. Because the Bureau of Labor Statistics (BLS) series is incomplete, I have spliced it with data from Troy and Sheflin (1985) and with CPS estimates

to bring the series back to 1897 and forward to 1987. The pattern of spurts shown in the BLS density figures differs from that given in Troy and Sheflin, for reasons I have not explored. Troy and Sheflin show a continuous rise in density from 1930 to 1947 due to the decline in employment in the Great Depression.

7. I have tested the statistical properties of the pattern of changes in density in several ways. First, with a simple nonparametric "clumping test" of whether changes are random over time or tend to clump together in chains (a chain consists of similarly signed changes). In the 90 years covered, there were 42 years of increased density, implying on the assumption of randomness 24.6 expected chains. The actual number is 19—statistically, significantly less at the 5 percent level.

The second method involves applying a similar test to large increases and decreases in density, where large is defined as a percentage point or more. With 20 years of large positive increases in density, the expected number of chains is 16; the actual number is 9. By contrast, in 16 years of large decreases, the expected number of chains is 13; the actual number is 13. Hence, it is the large positive changes in density that diverge from randomness, providing evidence for the spurt phenomenon.

The third method regresses changes in density on positive and negative lagged changes in density. Here I find a significant lagged effect only for positive lagged changes, implying greater autocorrelation of increases in density than decreases in density.

8. The discussion here parallels that in Freeman (1988), where I give the details of how I estimate depreciation rates.

9. I take the estimated .62 impact of ln unfair practice charges per election on ln workers won per employee (NEW) (Freeman 1986: table 2, column 2), assume that unfair practice charges per election decline from its 1984 value of 5.60 to its 1960 value of 1.16, and use the equation $D\ln NEW = .62\ D\ln (1.16/5.60)$ to evaluate the share of the workforce that would be union if unfair practices per election dropped to their 1960 value.

10. Here I use the .62 coefficient and assume that unfair practice charges per election fall to 0.78, its 1950 value, and apply the procedure in note 9.

11. By weakening economic power I mean reduced the demand for such labor and increased the elasticity of demand.

References

AFL-CIO, Committee on the Evolution of Work. 1985. "The Changing Situation of Workers and Their Unions," Pamphlet. Washington D.C.: AFL-CIO.

Bureau of National Affairs. Various years. *Directory of National Unions and Employee Associations*, Washington, D.C.

Davis, James. 1941. "The Theory of Union Growth," *Quarterly Journal of Economics* 55 (August): 611–37.

Dickens, William. 1983. "The Effect of Company Campaigns on Certification Elections," *Industrial and Labor Relations Review* 36(4): 560–75.

Dickens, William, and Jon Leonard. 1985. "Accounting for the Decline in Union Membership, 1950–1980," *Industrial and Labor Relations Review* 38(3): 323–34.

Dunlop, John. 1948. "The Development of Labor Organization: a Theoretical Framework." In Richard Lester and Joseph Shister, eds., *Insights into Labor Issues*, New York: Macmillan.

———. 1958. "The American Industrial Relations System in 1975." In Jack Steiber, ed., *U.S. Industrial Relations: The Next Twenty Years*, East Lansing: Michigan State Press.

Ellwood, David, and Glenn Fine. 1987. "The Impact of Right-to-Work Laws on Union Organizing," *Journal of Political Economy* 95(2): 250–74.

Farber, Henry. 1987. "The Decline of Unionization in the United States: What Can Be Learned from Recent Experience?" NBER Working Paper No. 2267, Cambridge, Mass. May.

Freeman, Richard. 1985. "Why Are Unions Faring Poorly in NLRB Representation Elections?" In Thomas Kochan, ed., *Challenges and Choices Facing American Labor*, Cambridge, Mass.: MIT Press, 45–64.

———. 1986. "The Effect of the Union Wage Differential on Management Opposition and Union Organizing Success," *American Economic Review*, May, 92–96.

———. 1988. "Contraction and Expansion: The Divergence of Private Sector and Public Sector Unionism in the U.S.," *Journal of Economic Perspectives*, Spring.

Freeman, Richard, and Casey Ichniowski, eds. 1988. *When Public Sector Workers Unionize*, Chicago: University Chicago Press.

Freeman, Richard, and James Medoff. 1984. *What Do Unions Do?* New York: Basic Books.

Getman, Julius, Stephen Goldberg, and Jeanne Herman. 1976. *Union Representation Elections: Law and Reality*, New York: Russell Sage.

Goldfield, Michael. 1987. *The Decline of Organized Labor in the United States*, Chicago: University of Chicago.

Hecksher, Charles. 1988. *The New Unionism: Employee Involvement in the Changing Corporation*, New York: Basic Books.

Ichniowski, Carl, and Jeffrey Zax. 1990. "Today's Associations, Tomorrow's Unions," *Industrial and Labor Relations Review* 43(2): 191–208.

Kramer, Leo. 1962. *Labor's Paradox—The American Federation of State, County, and Municipal Employees*. New York: Wiley.

Lipset, S. M. 1986. "Labor Unions in the Public Mind." In S. M. Lipset, ed., *Unions in Transition: Entering the Second Century*, San Francisco: ICS Press.

McDonald, Charles. 1983. "Memorandum to the National Organizing Committee," Washington, D.C.: AFL-CIO.

Neumann, George, and Ellen Rissman. 1984. "Where Have All the Union Members Gone?" *Journal of Labor Economics* 2(2): 175–92.

Smith, Adam. 1937. *Wealth of Nations*, New York: Modern Library.

Troy, Leo, and Neil Sheflin. 1985. *Union Sourcebook*, West Orange, N.J.: Industrial and Labor Relations Data and Information Services.

U.S. Bureau of Labor Statistics (BLS). Various years. *Directory of National Unions and Employee Associations*, Washington, D.C.

———. Various years. *Employment and Earnings*, Washington, D.C.

Voos, Paula. 1983. "Union Organizing: Costs and Benefits," *Industrial and Labor Relations Review*, 38(1): 52–63.

Weiler, Paul. 1983. "Promises to Keep: Securing Workers' Rights to Self-organization under the NLRA," *Harvard Law Review* 96(3): 1769–1827.

Capitalist Restructuring and the
Canadian Labour Movement

It is an understatement to note that the last decade has been a trying one for labour movements throughout the capitalist world.[1] The manifest restructuring of contemporary capitalism constitutes a profound challenge to their historic achievements and indeed to their very institutions. The central task of this chapter is to analyse the Canadian unions' response to this challenge. Much of the work on this subject has, explicitly or implicitly, contrasted the fortunes of Canadian unions with those of their American counterparts. It will be argued that although a comparison of the U.S. and Canadian labour movements can be useful, many such comparisons tend to exaggerate the Canadian unions' successes. When the unions' recent experience in Canada is examined in relation to the actual challenges confronting them, there is little to celebrate and much cause for concern. However, certain emergent tendencies within the Canadian labour movement suggest a more adequate response may be in the making.

The Nature of the Challenge

The conflicts rooted in the antagonism of interests inherent in capitalist relations of production, together with the competitive nature of the relations between units of capital, ensure that change is a constant feature of capitalist societies. Concentration and centralization of capital, changes in production technology, and the incessant search for new markets and products imply an ongoing restructuring of the composition and location of economic activity and the demand for labour. At times, however, further capital accumulation is constrained by the existing sociopolitical arrangements that frame it. Under these circumstances—properly understood as crises—restructuring does not only widen and deepen, but assumes a qualitatively different order, encompassing the sociopolitical framework itself. It is this type of restructuring that is occurring today.

The sociopolitical arrangement that framed the postwar economy was the Keynesian welfare state. In essence it embodied a class compromise: The working classes, or more accurately their political leadership, acquiesced to an economy based on the private ownership of the means of production, while capital agreed to political arrangements that would tendentially allow workers to achieve greater economic security and equity and to share in economic growth. These arrangements included a greater role for the state in sustaining "full" employment, public programs that socialized some of the costs of reproducing labour power, and, perhaps most importantly, state protection of workers' trade-union rights. The form of this compromise, of course, varied significantly from country to country, reflecting differences in the balance of class forces.

The long boom that attended the postwar settlement was generally seen as proof that capitalism had been fundamentally transformed and that the crises and conflicts to which it had been prone had been consigned to the dustbin of history by states expertly armed with Keynesian theory. This was not the first time that the end of capitalism "as Marx knew it" had been heralded. Nor was it any less premature than earlier such pronouncements.

The postwar boom reflected a particular historical conjuncture of forces, both domestic and international (Gough 1975), and by the early 1970s, these forces had largely dissipated. It is perhaps a measure of the fragility of this conjuncture that the announcement of its passing, in the form of President Nixon's decision to end the convertibility of the dollar, occurred just as trade, as a percentage of GDP in the advanced capitalist economies, returned to its 1913 level, the previous peak (Gordon 1988: 44).

The 1970s inaugurated a new era of global economic instability. Heightened international capitalist rivalry and competition coincided with a massive wave of industrial militancy as workers, buoyed by the freedom from fear of unemployment generated by the long boom, sought to buy into the affluent society. Profitability and growth declined sharply as capital found itself caught between the hamm.er of competition and the anvil of working-class militancy, for which Keynesian nostrums provided no solution. This impasse launched the restructuring process still in train today.

As growth ground to a halt, unemployment in Canada skyrocketed to double-digit figures. This was not just a matter of school leavers finding themselves members of the reserve army of labour rather than gainfully employed. The resurgence of international competition spawned plant closures and shutdowns as the weakest capitals were eliminated and stronger ones merged and rationalized their operations and shifted production, in part or whole, to selected Third World countries. Workers with long years of service in jobs allegedly secured by monopolistic employers and strong trade unions found themselves looking for work in unprecedented numbers. The steelworkers union, for example, saw its Canadian membership fall by 40,000, or some 25 percent, between 1979 and 1982 (Labour Canada 1988). This purge of capital values allowed for a renewal of economic growth in the mid-1980s, but the changed character of contemporary capitalism is unmistakable. The vast majority of jobs that have been created have been of the low-paid, part-time, and dead-end variety, and despite a period of continuous expansion of unprecedented length, unemployment remains near the level it reached in the trough of the previous business cycle.

The restructuring process has not been confined to capital and labour markets. The unfolding era of economic crisis has meant that, in the broadest sense, the old ways of doing business were increasingly incompatible with renewed capital accumulation, engendering changes in the way production is organized and in the relation between the state and civil society. Although these changes, too, reflect the operation of global market forces, they cannot be reduced to them. As Leo Panitch noted, "market forces never stand alone. They are enveloped in class struggles and class strategies" (1987: 135). This is not to suggest that capital has been pursuing some grand plan hatched in smoke-filled corporate boardrooms, but to acknowledge the emergence of a broad consensus among monopoly capital in Canada on an agenda for change (Langille 1987).

To respond to a constantly fluctuating environment, capital has sought a new flexibility through greater reliance on contracting out, just-in-time delivery systems, and part-time labour. Such flexibility has equally entailed efforts to enhance the interchangeability (and intensity of effort) of the workforce, to substitute flexible payment systems (i.e., bonuses, profit sharing) for fixed ones, and to de-emphasize industry and even companywide bargaining arrangements in favour of decentralized, workplace agreements. Underneath all these changes, as well as the growing interest in the "new human relations," lies a desire to loosen, if not to escape entirely, the grip of trade-union consciousness and solidarity on the workforce.[2] Under these circumstances, collective bargaining frequently has become a situation where what is being negotiated is not workers' demands for improvements but capital's demands for concessions, including at times the demand for an end to collective bargaining itself.

The changes in the relationship between the state and civil society that capital has pursued over the past decade, commonly referred to as business's neo-liberal agenda, have been equally, if not more, far-reaching. These changes, in broad relief, are scarcely less evident in Canada, notwithstanding popular reluctance to elect a government explicitly espousing neo-liberal ideology. This strategy is hardly about creating a smaller or weaker state; it is about restructuring the state so as to "free" capital from existing political constraints on its ability to pursue its own interests (Gamble 1979; Whitaker 1987). Canadian capital's (successful) campaign for a free trade pact with the United States is an integral part of this project, in that free trade is seen as a means of transcending the electoral constraints to this restructuring and of securing it against any attempt by some future government to subject production and investment decisions to democratic control.

At one level, restructuring has entailed far-reaching changes in state revenues and expenditures. Taxes have been shifted from capital and the highest income groups to wage and salary earners; aid to capital has mushroomed; and the social wage has contracted, enhancing workers' dependency on market forces.[3] But more fundamentally, it has entailed abandoning those state practices that have served to sustain working-class collectivism, above all, state support for the right of workers to organize trade unions, to bargain, and to engage in collective action. These changes have not entailed a withdrawal of the state from regulating class conflict, but rather a shift toward increased reliance on coercive measures

TABLE 18-1. Back-to-Work Legislation in Canada, 1960–1987

	Annual Average
1960–69	1.3
1970–79	4.1
1980–84	4.4
1985–87	7.0

Source: Panitch and Swartz (1988: 31, 119–20)

to secure the subordination of labour to the changing requirements of capital accumulation.

The scope of the Canadian state's escalating assault on trade-union rights over the last decade—an assault that has included transporting busloads of scabs through the picket lines of legally striking public-sector workers and the jailing of several national union leaders—has been well documented (Panitch and Swartz 1988). Table 18-1 illustrates this trend with respect to the use of back-to-work legislation (suspending the right to strike for workers engaged in legal strikes) by federal and provincial governments.

The federal government and most provincial governments have increasingly resorted not only to ad hoc temporary measures suppressing the right to strike for particular groups of workers for specific periods of time but also to new permanent restrictions on the collective rights of some or all workers in particular jurisdictions. Even policies of privatization and deregulation have been pursued less as economic measures than as means of weakening the state workers who provide the public infrastructure underlying private capital accumulation.

The increased frequency of such legislation is not the only change that has occurred over the period. The terms of settlement set out in the legislation have increasingly supported the employer's position, and, not surprisingly, the penalties specified for anyone presuming to defy such legislation have escalated dramatically. By 1987, the repressiveness had reached the point where the penalties for defiance by a union official included a five-year ban on holding any union office.

The object of this assault has not been to destroy unions and collective bargaining per se, but to empty these forms of their value for workers.

The new era in labour-state relations was legally consecrated in 1987 when the Supreme Court of Canada ruled (explicitly on the grounds that labour relations had to be adjusted to changing economic realities) that the freedom-of-association clause in the Canadian Charter of Rights and Freedoms only applied to the right to form unions and *not* to the right to bargain or to strike.[4]

Labour's Response: Canada and the United States

How then has the Canadian labour movement responded to restructuring? A good point of departure in addressing this question is the data on recent trends in union density in Canada and the United States (Kumar 1991: 10; Meltz, this volume, especially Table 10-2). These data show that between 1955 and 1965 union densities were comparable and stable in both countries (and essentially had been so since the late forties). In 1965, however, the trajectories start to diverge, with union density steadily declining in the United States and rising in Canada, at least until very recently.

These figures are by now well known, and there have been several explanations for them: the more favourable labour legislation in Canada, the growth of public-sector unions in Canada, and the existence of the New Democratic Party (NDP) as an electoral alternative to the two bourgeois parties. These explanations are not so much wrong as superficial (Calvert 1987). Explanations stressing differences in legislation beg the question of *why* they are different. Moreover, as Goldfield (1987) has shown, the decline in the rate of successful certification elections in the United States over the past two decades owes little to legislative changes and much to a shift in the stance of corporations toward the letter and the spirit of existing legislation.

Canadian private-sector unions, as well as public-sector ones, have fared better, numerically speaking, than their counterparts in the United States. Between 1976 and 1985, for example, the Canadian percentage of members of the Steelworkers (USWA) increased from 14 to 25 percent. Part of this shift certainly is the result of heavier membership losses due to plant closures and the like in the United States. Yet it is also due to the fact that the Canadian section has recently replaced some of its losses with new members, while the U.S. membership has continued to decline (Labour Canada 1988).

The two trajectories, above all, reflect the greater militancy and capacity for struggle of the Canadian labour movement, *relative* to its U.S. counterpart, over the period under examination. The reasons for this difference are inseparable from the different historical developments of the working classes, as well as the state, in the two countries.[5] It is possible here only to touch on some of these historical differences.

One of the most distinguishing aspects of working-class history in the United States is the relative absence of any significant experience of struggle for formal political rights by the "native born" white-male founders of the American labour movement. Virtually all these workers had the right to vote by 1830. This facilitated the integration of their unions into a system of patronage politics that both reinforced racial divisions within the working class and mitigated the impulse toward independent working-class political organization (Orloff 1988). In contrast, the struggle for the vote loomed much larger in the experience of early Canadian unionists, extending into the twentieth century. The heightened sensitivity to the value of democratic rights and the associated impulse toward independent working-class political activity that inevitably must accompany such struggle was further reinforced by the continuing influx of British skilled workers with a similar history who played such a central role both in organizing Canadian unions and promoting independent working-class political organization. Moreover, it should be noted that the initial formation of the modern Canadian labour movement largely occurred in the last two decades of the nineteenth century, in the midst of a massive upsurge in socialist ideas in the working class internationally and domestically, which inscribed a relatively radical character to their origins, compared to their counterparts in the United States.

The distinctive ways in which industrial unionism emerged in the two countries during the 1930s and 1940s were no less significant and reinforced existing differences. In the United States the failure of the renewed efforts at building industrial unions in the 1930s to secure any significant advance prior to the passing of the Wagner Act in 1935 meant that the Congress of Industrial Organizations (CIO) was in a certain sense the creation of the state, a linkage reinforced by the use of organizing slogans like "Uncle Sam Wants You in a Union" (Lichtenstein 1982).

The integration of the unions was furthered by their "No-Strike Pledge" after Pearl Harbor, when union leaders, confronted by the reluctance of many workers to pay dues to unions that would not defend their interests, sought "maintenance-of-membership" provisions from the state to bar them from leaving. This course of action could not be followed without a weakening of internal processes of democratic control. The United Auto Workers (UAW), for example, took steps to dismantle its nascent district councils, established to enable local leaders to exchange experiences and ideas and to enhance their control over their regional director.[6] Finally, the impact of these developments on the Communist party, whose members played such an important role in early CIO organizing, must be acknowledged. No group supported the No-Strike Pledge more. Even Roger Keeran (1980) reluctantly concedes that this stance distanced the Communists from the most militant tendencies within the CIO unions and furthered their exposure to the cruel winds of the Cold War.

In Canada by contrast, the state resisted demands for legislation protecting trade-union rights until 1944, and even then offered only temporary protection under the War Measures Act. Inspired, if not aided, by the advances of the CIO, workers began organizing without it, building from the bottom up to push the level of unionization from 17 percent of the nonagricultural workforce in 1940 to 24 percent in 1944 (Labour Canada 1975; Robinson, in this volume).

The Canadian state's intransigence earned it much enmity, precluding any significant support for a No-Strike Pledge and creating space for the Cooperative Commonwealth Federation (CCF) party to establish a link with the fledgling industrial unions. At the same time, members of the Communist party, whose contribution to this early organizing and to the massive postwar struggles that were crucial to securing permanent legislation far exceeded their numbers, retained their hard-won respect as defenders of working people. Although this did not save them from the Cold War purges of the late 1940s, which were aided and abetted by social democratic union leaders, it did spare them some of its worst excesses. The unions they led to a large extent at least survived expulsion from the Canadian Congress of Labour, and many individuals retained their positions in those unions that stayed, especially in the UAW (Abella 1973).

The final difference to be considered concerns the nature of public-sector unionism in Canada. Federal government employees, and most of their provincial counterparts, were excluded from the postwar labour legislation and remained so until the 1960s, when developments in Quebec finally led to a breakthrough (Lipsig-Mummé, in this volume). Until then, the profound conservatism of the Quebec state, despite substantial economic and demographic changes after 1945, repressive responses to a series of bitter strikes, and generally reactionary policies in the areas of education and social services, fostered a relatively radical working class and intelligentsia. In the 1960s, then, there was a political settlement with labour comparable to that of the 1940s, including the extension of substantial trade-union rights to public-sector workers in 1965.

The breakthrough in Quebec reverberated throughout the Canadian state.[7] If the fading bloom of the postwar settlement in the context of the 1960s ensured that Canada, too, would have a second wave of welfare state expansion, the developments in Quebec created the basis for the inclusion of reforms in labour legislation within it. Federal workers in Quebec were part of the politicization process and provided a powerful lead to their counterparts across the country in the struggle to secure similar rights.

The federal government hesitantly moved to respond, offering bargaining rights, but only over a narrow range of issues and even then withholding the right to strike. This strategy was shattered when postal workers, particularly in Quebec and British Columbia, launched a series of recognition strikes in the mid-1960s. This action persuaded the government that the prohibition of strikes would not necessarily prevent them, and the actual legislation, while still highly restrictive in terms of the permissible scope of bargaining, did include the right to strike.

As most provinces followed the federal lead, public-sector unionism emerged with a large militant segment that undertook numerous, often prolonged, and frequently highly successful struggles. As a result, their growth has not only had a quantitative impact on the Canadian labour movement greater than that in the United States but has also made a "qualitative difference as well, strengthening the elements of aggressiveness and competitiveness in the movement" (Huxley, Kettner, and Struthers 1986: 126).

With these long-standing differences, the labour movements in Canada and the United States began in the 1960s to move along trajectories quite different in character, just as the postwar boom was coming to an end.[8] Such divergences have not only distinguished the Canadian labour movement's response to the restructuring of the 1970s and 1980s from that of U.S. unions, they have also affected the process in Canada itself.

The greater militancy and capacity for struggle by Canadian unions is

evident throughout the period under discussion, not least at the end of
the 1960s, when the rate of inflation rose sharply. Both the U.S. and
Canadian governments sought voluntary wage restraint, but whereas the
U.S. unions agreed to cooperate, the Canadian ones did not (Panitch
1979; Maslove and Swimmer 1980). Indeed, wage demands escalated,
fuelling a dramatic increase in the incidence of strikes up to the
mid-1970s. Although the gains won brought Canadian unions many new
members, they also led the federal government to impose statutory wage
controls. The labour movement did not simply capitulate, however; it
struggled against the government, in the process calling an unprecedented, and in its own terms successful, one-day general strike. This
hardly secured repeal of the legislation. Yet the unions' opposition at
least meant that the government itself had to do most of the dirty work,
and some unions were able to demonstrate the continued relevance of
unions to members' well-being.

The response of Canadian unions to capital's demands for concessions
at the end of the decade again contrasts sharply with that in the United
States, where unions displayed little inclination to resist concessions. Indeed, some unions adopted the view that concessions were not even
losses—to be recaptured when circumstances allowed. Instead, they
sometimes defended contracts, incorporating them as good bargains, if
not breakthroughs, thereby propagating the view that workers' interests
would best be served by cooperating with their employers.

Many labour leaders in Canada rejected this as the wrong way for
unions to respond to capital's new offensive. With Canadian autoworkers
in the lead, the Canadian Labour Congress (CLC) formally rejected concession bargaining and pledged its support for struggles by unions resisting such demands. Concession bargaining was rejected, not just because
concessions were seen to be contrary to workers' immediate interests, but
because the unions perceived that selling defeats as victories, and cooperation with employers as the way to secure workers' interests, would undermine the very basis of unions as vehicles for collective struggle by
workers.

Such divergence over fundamental trade-union principles lies at the
heart of the growing tendency of Canadian workers in U.S.-based unions
to split from the internationals.[9] The significance of this divergence is
illustrated by the events surrounding two strikes against concessions in
the meat-packing industry in the mid-eighties—one in the United States
(Hormel in Minnesota) and one in Canada (Gainers in Alberta).[10] In the

case of the Hormel workers, their union literally disowned the strike, which ended in failure and threw the local into trusteeship. The same union represented the Gainers' workers, but a similar response by the United Food and Commercial Workers (UFCW) was precluded by the immediate support offered the local by the Alberta Federation of Labour in the context of the CLC's anticoncessions policy.

Daily clashes occurred as armoured busloads of scabs aided by the Edmonton riot squad crashed through the picket line of the workers and their supporters. Despite numerous injuries and mass arrests—over five hundred in the first month—the strike persisted, generating growing sympathy across the province and country. Over eight thousand people demonstrated in front of the provincial legislature in support of legislative reforms to strengthen workers' rights. While this support was not sufficient for the strikers to secure a clear victory, it did succeed in frustrating the company's attempt to break the union. This was not the sole result of the strike: Its broader legacy was the change it brought about in people's conception of the nature of Albertan society. It breathed some new life into its labour movement, and advanced the electoral fortunes of the NDP.

The sustained capacity for struggle, signified by the Gainers' strike, is what underlies the expansion of the Canadian labour movement over the past two decades. This combativeness is central to understanding why the state in the 1980s has continued and indeed escalated its attack on trade-union rights, an attack that has sought to undermine the effectiveness of unions as agencies for struggle while stopping short of challenging their actual existence.

It is the very persistence and success of this attack that cautions against any Panglossian celebration of the Canadian labour movement. Yes, compared to an American labour movement on its knees, the Canadian is bound to look tall. Yet when the actions of the Canadian labour movement are placed in the context of the offensive by capital and the state, its real weaknesses and limitations become more apparent.

Cause for Concern: The Scope of the Challenge

There has been a significant fall in union density in recent years, and recent legislative restrictions and the free trade pact with the United States will exacerbate this trend. Between 1981 and 1986, the increase in average weekly earnings fell from 4.3 percent to 2.8 percent. Real earnings have been falling for a decade or more, even while unemployment declined. Since 1983, union wage increases have actually trailed those of nonunion workers, a reflection of the fact that although the unions have opposed and even fought concessions, they have not escaped them (Gandall 1987; Industrial Relations Centre 1987). Not surprisingly, given such statistics, strike activity has also fallen sharply. The annual number of strikes has declined from over 1,000 between 1978 and 1981 to 645 in 1983, rising somewhat—to 825—by 1985. The number of workers involved has fallen almost continuously over the same period, from just over 400,000 to roughly 160,000 (Labour Canada 1985).

These figures do not suggest a return to the quiescent 1950s. Workers' will to struggle has *not* been quashed, as the Gainers' strike and other equally tenacious struggles across the country to secure or preserve union recognition and historic achievements suggest. At the same time, the labour movement has betrayed an inability to offer a meaningful, sustained, coordinated response industrially, politically, or ideologically to the current restructuring and the continuing state encroachments on fundamental freedoms that have been so integral to it.

The historic existence of international unions in Canada, with jurisdictions more appropriate to the larger U.S. economy, has contributed to a fragmented union movement in Canada with central labour bodies that are loose federations of highly autonomous affiliates. It is not uncommon to find several unions at the corporate level, not to mention in a given industry, each bargaining on its own. Despite the offensive by capital and the state, there have been very few mergers and little movement toward coordinated bargaining (Gindin 1988).

New organizing has been impeded by the same structure, especially in the service sector, where unions have lost members almost as fast as they have signed them up, since the workers organized have lacked bargaining power. National multiestablishment corporations dominate this sector, and no single union has the resources to organize on the scale necessary to take them on. At the same time, despite some encouragement from the CLC to behave differently, some unions inspired by a narrow corporate interest have refused to back organizing drives that fail to generate members and dues for themselves.[11] Instead, those that are able to do so have pursued new members wherever they can find them, including those in the jurisdictions, if not the ranks, of other unions, with all the divisive consequences that this implies.[12]

The response to corporate initiatives to reorganize work has not been any more coherent. The labour movement initially endorsed these schemes, at the end of the 1970s joining state-sponsored tripartite centres to promote them (Swartz 1981). Growing rank-and-file opposition to such an explicitly collaborative position has compelled some labour federations to reverse their position. The Ontario Federation of Labour, for example, withdrew from that province's Quality of Worklife Centre after a resolution to this effect was passed at its 1984 convention (Wells 1988a). Such opposition has stopped individual unions from openly endorsing these schemes, but very few have adopted an explicit policy of opposition to quality of work life, quality circles, and the like, nor have they attempted to turn the rhetoric of participation against capital by calling for democratic control of production and investment decisions. Most unions have opted for a passive position, largely leaving the task of coping with these management initiatives to individual locals.[13]

Nowhere are the limits of the labour movement's response to restructuring more apparent than in the core area—defence of trade-union freedoms.[14] The national one-day strike on 14 October 1976 against the Trudeau government's imposition of statutory wage controls marked not the beginning but the *end* of any real mobilization against controls, despite the strike's success. The CLC lacked any strategic direction and exhibited profound ideological confusion, advancing an illusionary call for a corporatist scheme of economic planning even while it used a liberal economist to make a free-market case against controls. Indeed, CLC president Dennis McDermott's attack on the postal workers for defying back-to-work legislation in 1978 suggested a lack of understanding of the issues at stake, as perhaps did the labour movement's singular failure to attempt to insert its rights into the constitutional debate that engulfed Canada in the early 1980s.

True, the 1982 CLC convention did overwhelmingly call for action—up to and including a general strike—in the event of further attacks on the right to strike. Yet the sound and fury of such convention rhetoric meant very little, begging as it did the question of how to secure a response to such a call. This attack came later that year, in the form of the federal government's "6 and 5" program, which, together with imitations thereof by several provinces, removed the right to strike for over one million public-sector workers by unilaterally extending existing collective agreements that contained a legal ban on strikes during their existence.

Only then did the CLC move, albeit hesitantly, to establish a committee to coordinate the response of the unions affected, none of whom proved able to mobilize their members.

To some extent, this failure reflected a lack of will to struggle on the part of certain leaders. This reluctance was frequently only symptomatic of deeper, more pervasive problems. One was the inability to mobilize members to pursue the coordinated, solidaristic, and political struggles required by the restructuring process—as opposed to the sectional, economistic struggles that had predominated since 1945. In part, the acuteness of this problem reflected the lingering effects of the Cold War on working-class consciousness and the unions. Nevertheless, it has been exacerbated by the highly restrictive and legalistic nature of the postwar labour legislation, which substituted certification votes in bargaining units defined by labour boards for recognition struggles and banned strikes during the life of collective agreements.

The debilitating effects of this kind of juridical and ideological structuring on the mobilizing capacity of the labour movement were inevitably severe. The legislation devalued the apparent need for militant struggle and the scope for solidaristic activity, while promoting a legalistic practice and consciousness among leaders and appointed staff, in which rights appeared as privileges bestowed by the state, rather than democratic freedoms won (and defended) by collective struggle.

Many unions, particularly those in the rapidly growing public sector, were little more than a collection of locals, neither made by nor staffed with solidaristic political struggle in mind.[15] It was, therefore, highly unlikely that the CLC, itself confused and constrained by the autonomy enjoyed by affiliates, could lead the kind of coordinated struggle required.

The problem of mobilizing members was not the only structural obstacle confronting the labour movement, as events in British Columbia—where, for historical reasons, there was the possibility of making credible the threat of a general strike—make clear. In July 1983 the provincial government introduced a wide-ranging package of reactionary measures. The scope and severity of these measures gave rise to Solidarity Coalition, which transcended the manifold divisions within the labour movement and between it and radical social and community activists.

Solidarity's campaign of demonstrations and escalating political strikes compelled the government to strike a deal with the unions, retreating on the measures most damaging to the unions, in exchange for a halt to the strikes. Made without consulting Solidarity as a whole, or even the union membership, the deal set aside the demands of striking education workers and the broader social and human rights issues that were an integral part of the struggle. Not surprisingly, it did not take long for the rain of coercive legislation to resume.

It was quite possible that the unions could have secured a further retreat from the July measures—and even could have forewarned governments against further such packages—had they been prepared to continue the strikes. Whatever the will of the membership here, it is clear that most of the union leaders had no stomach for further struggle, fearing that the inevitable charges of anarchy in the streets would harm the electoral prospects of the NDP. An overwhelmingly electoralist political perspective—born of their social democratic consciousness—led the union leadership to subordinate the extraparliamentary mobilization of the coalition to the electoral prospects of the NDP "next time."

This same political perspective, which sees the labour movement as but one interest group among many, has led the NDP to distance itself from such struggles rather than identify with them and try to clarify the class character of the issues involved. With very few exceptions, this has been the response of the party over the whole period, even in the 1984 federal election, when, in the wake of the "6 and 5" public-sector wage-controls package, over one million workers had their rights to bargain and strike removed. The NDP did not even raise the issue of trade-union rights in the electoral campaign, and its leader's only reference to "6 and 5" was perverse, citing it positively as an example of government "target setting."

Emergent Tendencies

The preceding paragraghs clearly imply that the labour movement needs to fashion a new response, in both the industrial and political arenas, to ongoing economic and political restructuring. This need will only become more acute as restructuring accelerates in the wake of the competitive pressures unleashed by the Free Trade Agreement. Does the labour movement understand the emerging contours of the Canadian and international political economy? Is there any basis for thinking that it has the capacity to generate an adequate response?

The past decade reveals little evidence for advancing affirmative answers to these questions. Nonetheless, here as elsewhere, historical trends
are complex and contradictory. The concern expressed by the labour
leadership over the free trade issue does suggest a new awareness of the
changes in train (Bernard, this volume). At the same time, recent changes
in the labour movement are suggestive of a growing basis for a more
adequate response and hence provide grounds for cautious optimism. In
this regard, three developments stand out.

First, challenges to the immobilizing ideology of legalism are increasingly visible. Strikes in defiance of laws prohibiting them, enjoying wide
backing, have become more frequent, indicating less deference to abstract
invocations of the "rule of law." This change is also reflected in a new
questioning by union leaders and members of how much they should
depend on legislation, as opposed to workplace mobilization, to secure
their demands in areas such as pay equity and health and safety.[16]

Such challenges are very much bound up with the growing impact of
the broad political and cultural changes of the past two decades on the
labour movement. The heightened concern with workplace health and
safety is related to the spread of environmental concerns in society as a
whole. This has been reinforced by the changes in union membership
that have accompanied its growth. In this regard, the most important
change is the increase in union members who are women. What makes
this so significant is that it has meant that feminism is no longer a movement external to the unions. A growing number of the unions' most
committed militants are feminists, and a growing number of women involved in feminist struggles are trade unionists. The extent to which the
unions have taken on issues like equal pay, day-care, abortion, and sexual
harassment has been in direct response to women organizing for them
(Saint-Pierre, this volume). In the process, women have challenged the
unions' traditional economism and extended their contacts with other
progressive social forces.

There has been a further, and no less significant, impact of feminism
on unions. Women's struggles have not only been about "issues," they
have entailed demands for structures, from women's committees to leadership positions, to enable women to clarify and press their concerns.
Demands for the creation of elected positions reserved for women have,
as Linda Briskin notes, created "a whole new level of debate around the
elections," and union leaders' resistance to women's demands to organize

separately, has raised the issue of their resistance to "rank and file organizing in general . . . to more democracy, to more rank and file input.
. . . It's been difficult for women to organize because it's been difficult
for most people to organize inside unions, and we have to see some of
the problems of women organizing within the unions as symptomatic of
larger problems" (1987: 13).

The 1988 Ontario Division Convention of the Canadian Union of Public Employees (CUPE) graphically illustrated this development. Delegates, angered by a back-room deal between the two leading contestants
for the presidency, defeated most of the official slate, choosing a relatively unknown local leader as president (Bickerton 1988).

Last, and of immense importance, are the recent splits by Canadian
sections from the international unions. The Canadian Auto Workers'
declaration of independence from the UAW is felt to be historic, but its
broad significance is not always recognized. The presence of U.S. unions
in Canada gave the Canadian labour movement a north-south orientation
that was the basis for its endorsement of Canada's neocolonial relationship with the United States. The deep opposition of the labour movement to the current free trade thrust of capital and the state is a reflection
of the break with this orientation. The growth of nationalist feelings
among Canadian workers has been accompanied, not only by a growing
opposition to U.S. imperialism (and Canadian complicity therein), but
also by a greater willingness to support struggles, domestic and especially
international, in which Socialists and Communists are visible participants.

The newly independent unions have necessarily looked horizontally,
not just toward mergers with other unions, but to developing links with
other progressive social forces as well, in the process pushing against
existing sectionalism and economism (Jenson and Mahon, this volume).
The struggle to separate has almost invariably brought to the fore the
issue of union democracy, which has been the basis of much of its appeal.
This has had implications not just for the practices of individual unions
but for the CLC (and to a lesser extent, provincial federations) as well.

One of the central functions of the CLC has been to referee jurisdictional disputes among its affiliates, with union democracy being seen as a
question of the internal affairs of autonomous affiliates. The struggles of
workers to split, challenging union jurisdictional rights in the name of
members' democratic rights, has raised calls for the CLC to strengthen

significantly the democratic standards required of its affiliates—the need for which is hardly confined to U.S.-based unions.[17]

However important these developments are, their limits in terms of ideology and structure cannot be ignored. The labour movement still largely understands the state as the government of the day rather than a constituent element of class domination. Struggles continue to be framed within the parameters of actually existing capitalism and the actually existing state.

This approach can be seen in the broadly based campaign against free trade that gathered around the labour movement. This campaign reflected the labour movement's new openness to popular social movements and a new understanding of the limits of continentalism, admirably framed in a language that posed the issue in terms of the "corporations versus the people." At the same time, the CLC's relationship with these social movements evinced a clear hierarchical character and a privileging of parliamentary over extraparliamentary activity.

Moreover, in this campaign and despite the sustained attack on workers' freedoms over the last decade and the persistence of massive social inequities, there was a clear tendency to glorify the decency and beneficence of the Canadian welfare state to which only Mulroney's abject tailing of Reaganism appeared as an exception. Against free trade, no alternative beyond a better managed capitalism—through a revitalized Keynesianism, trade diversification, and more Canadian ownership—was advanced, as if defeating the Mulroney government would itself ensure a secure future.

This limited perspective hardly applies to all activists or even all leaders, but almost all employ a discourse consistent with it. This partially reflects an understandable defensiveness in the face of capital's offensive—a desire to mobilize whatever collective resources are available. It also reflects an understanding of the difficulties in doing more.

Defensiveness, however, is no longer sufficient. Collective bargaining cannot achieve the gains it once did. Even an NDP government standing on its own cannot secure the needs, let alone the aspirations of working people in an era of international capitalist competition and restructuring. Going beyond defensiveness entails a struggle to change the political environment, the most significant aspect of which is the political consciousness of working people. Changing the political environment has to begin with and be sustained by a strong popular commitment to challenging the limits of actually existing capitalism and the actually existing state. The manifold tensions within the labour movement suggest the possibility of forging such a commitment, in which event the 1980s may yet be seen as having laid the basis for the advance of the Canadian working class.

Notes

1. I would like to express my thanks to Donald Wells for his thoughtful comments on the original draft. The financial assistance of the Social Sciences and Humanities Research Council in conducting the research for this paper is gratefully acknowledged.

2. Excellent contemporary discussions of management's new agenda can be found in Robertson and Wareham (1987) and Wells (1988b). See also Nichols (1975) and Swartz (1981).

3. A sense of the pattern of expenditure changes can be gained from examining recent issues of *How Ottawa Spends*, published annually by the School of Public Administration, Carleton University, Ottawa. Unemployment insurance has been a particular target throughout the 1980s. The most recent changes occurred in March 1989, when new restrictions on eligibility for unemployment insurance were introduced that will reduce expenditures by an estimated 10 percent (Maslove 1989).

4. The less than straightforward route to this ruling is explored in detail in Panitch and Swartz (1988).

5. Insightful surveys of Canada and the United States, respectively, are provided by Palmer (1983) and Davis (1986).

6. Provision for these councils, financed by a per capita levy, was first made in 1939. Basically, a council was established when a majority of locals in a region so voted, whereupon all locals had to join. At the 1943 convention, the majority report of the Constitutional Committee called for their abolition. This was defeated, but an amendment was passed establishing a method for terminating existing councils, something omitted from the original constitutional provision (UAW Constitutions and Official Convention Proceedings 1939–1943; the discussion at the 1943 convention can be found on pages 362ff. of the minutes).

7. The following discussion is based upon Panitch and Swartz (1988).

8. This difference is captured by Pradeep Kumar, a well-known industrial relations expert: "In the United States, unions have the attitude that they have to make themselves attractive to management, but in Canada unions believe they have to be attractive to workers" (*Globe and Mail*, 2 January 1989: 4).

9. This is not to deny the existence of other important determinants. For a fascinating account of the historical and conjunctural factors leading to the decision by Canadian autoworkers to leave the UAW—the most significant of such breakaways—see Gindin (1989).

10. This discussion is based on Selby (1986), Mills (1986), and Noël and Gardner (1990).

11. This is not the only problem the unions have had, as Warskett (1988) has shown. Nor am I suggesting that the labour movement has not supported such efforts. But this has generally been limited to supporting strikes to establish a "toehold" in this sector, instead of coordinating the organization needed to obtain a real "foothold."

12. For discussion of this activity in Quebec, see Hébert (this volume).

13. It is not strictly accurate to say that the CAW has left each local to its own devices. Interviews with CAW officials reveal that the union has monitored quality-of-work-life schemes and opposed those features of them that would weaken the union's presence on the shop floor. See also Wells and Yates (this volume).

14. The following discussion draws heavily on chapter 6 in Panitch and Swartz (1988).

15. The Canadian Union of Public Employees is a case in point, as Deverell (1982) has shown.

16. This is based on discussions with activists in a number of unions in both the public and private sector. For one of the few published discussions of this development, see Gonick (1987).

17. This was one of the central issues at the 1988 CLC convention as a result of the CAW offering a home to the rebellious east coast membership of the UFCW. To the workers involved, and the CAW, the issue was democracy (at the least, the UFCW was in violation of the CLC guidelines on autonomy), while to the UFCW leadership, the issue was raiding. The solution, in the form of a "compromise" constitutional amendment backed by both parties, clearly subordinated union democracy to jurisdictional protection, but this is hardly likely to be the last word (Bickerton 1988).

References

Abella, Irving. 1973. *Nationalism, Communism, and Canadian Labour: The CIO, the Communist Party and the Canadian Congress of Labour*. Toronto: University of Toronto Press.

Bickerton, Geoff. 1988. CLC Wilts, Ontario CUPE Erupts. *Canadian Dimension* 22(6): 22–23.

Briskin, Linda. 1987. Interview. *Athabaska University Magazine (Labour Supplement)* 10(5): 12–13.

Calvert, John. 1987. The Divergent Paths of the Canadian and American Labour Movements. *The Round Table* 303: 378–92.

Davis, Mike. 1986. *Prisoners of the American Dream: Politics and Economy in the History of the U.S. Working Class.* London: Verso.

Deverell, John. 1982. The Ontario Hospital Dispute, 1980–81. *Studies in Political Economy* 9: 179–90.

Gamble, Andrew. 1979. The Free Economy and the Strong State. *Socialist Register*, 1–25.

Gandall, Marvin. 1987. Labour in the Winter of '87. *Canadian Dimension* 21(1): 27–28.

Gindin, Sam. 1988. State of the Union: Raiding Democracy and the Role of the CLC. *Our Times* 7(3): 20–23.

———. 1989. Breaking Away: The Formation of the Canadian Auto Workers. *Studies in Political Economy* 29: 63–89.

Goldfield, Michael. 1987. *The Decline of the American Labor Movement.* Chicago: University of Chicago Press.

Gonick, Cy. 1987. FOS—Splitting the Manitoba Labour Movement. *Canadian Dimension* 21(6): 20–23.

Gordon, David. 1988. The Global Economy: New Edifice or Crumbling Foundations? *New Left Review* 168: 24–65.

Gough, Ian. 1975. State Expenditure in Advanced Capitalism. *New Left Review* 92: 53–92.

Huxley, Christopher, David Kettner, and Jim Struthers. 1986. Is Canada's Experience Especially Instructive? In S. M. Lipsett, ed., *Unions in Transition: Entering the Second Century*, 113–32. San Francisco: Institute for Contemporary Studies.

Industrial Relations Centre. 1987. *The Current Industrial Relations Scene.* Kingston, Ont.: Queens University Industrial Relations Centre.

Keeran, Roger. 1980. *The Communist Party and the Auto Workers' Union.* Bloomington: Indiana University Press.

Kumar, Pradeep. 1991. Industrial Relations in Canada and the United States: From Uniformity to Divergence. *Queen's Papers in Industrial Relations.* Kingston, Ont.: Industrial Relations Centre.

Labour Canada. 1975. *Directory of Labour Organizations in Canada.* Ottawa: Labour Canada.

———. 1985. *Strikes and Lockouts in Canada.* Ottawa: Labour Canada.

———. 1988. *Directory of Labour Organizations in Canada.* Ottawa: Labour Canada.

Langille, David. 1987. The Business Council on National Issues and the Canadian State. *Studies in Political Economy* 24: 41–86.

Lichtenstein, Nelson. 1982. *Labor's War at Home: The CIO in World War Two.* Cambridge: Cambridge University Press.

Maslove, Allan. 1989. *Tax Reform in Canada: The Process and Impact*. Halifax, N.S.: The Institute for Research on Public Policy.

Maslove, Allan, and Eugene Swimmer. 1980. *Wage Controls in Canada: 1975–1978*. Montreal: The Institute for Research on Public Policy.

Mills, Neal. 1986. Why Local P-9 Is Going It Alone. *The Nation*, 578.

Nichols, Theo. 1975. The "Socialism" of Management: Some Comments on the New "Human Relations." *Sociological Review* 23: 245–65.

Noël, Alain, and Keith Gardner. 1990. The Gainers Strike: Capitalist Offensive, Militancy, and the Politics of Industrial Relations in Canada. *Studies in Political Economy* 31, 31–72.

Orloff, Ann. 1988. The Political Origins of America's Belated Welfare State. In Margaret Weir, Ann Shola Orloff, and Theda Skocpol, eds., *The Politics of Social Policy in the United States*, 37–80. Princeton, N.J.: Princeton University Press.

Palmer, Bryan. 1983. *Working Class Experience: The Rise and Reconstruction of Canadian Labour*. Toronto: Butterworth.

Panitch, Leo. 1987. Capitalist Restructuring and Labour Strategies. *Studies in Political Economy* 24: 131–50.

————. 1979. Corporatism in Canada. *Studies in Political Economy* 1: 43–92.

Panitch, Leo, and Donald Swartz. 1988. *The Assault on Trade Union Freedoms*. Toronto: Garamond Press.

Robertson, David, and Jeff Wareham. 1987. *Technological Change in the Auto Industry*. North York, Ont.: CAW.

Selby, Jim. 1986. Pigs and Packinghouses: Peter Pocklington, the Police, and the Gainers Strike. *Canadian Dimension* 20(5): 4–6.

Swartz, Donald. 1981. New Forms of Worker Participation: A Critique of Quality of Working Life. *Studies in Political Economy* 5: 55–78.

Warskett, Rosemary. 1988. Bankworker Organizing and the Law. *Studies in Political Economy* 25, 41–74.

Wells, Donald. 1988a: Ontario's Quality of Worklife Centre Dies. *Canadian Dimension* 22(7): 26–27.

————. 1988b: Teamwork and the New Industrial Relations. *Canadian Dimension* 22(1): 33–36.

Whitaker, Reg. 1987. Neo-Conservatism and the State. *Socialist Register*, 1–31.

19   CARLA LIPSIG–MUMMÉ

Quebec Labour, Politics, and
the Economic Crisis:
Defensive Accommodation
Faces the Future

The decade stretching from the mid-1970s to the middle of the 1980s marked a watershed for union movements in most high-wage economies in the Northern Hemisphere.[1] Neither the Canadian nor the Quebec labour movements are exceptions in this regard. The convergence of long-range changes in the international and domestic division of labour, the series of short, sharp shocks that resulted from the "stagflation" of the 1970s, and the election of conservative governments combined to end the postwar deal that had defined the parameters of union growth and action for a generation. In the new harsher climate, few national union movements were able to reposition themselves rapidly enough to imprint a union agenda on the new political order taking shape.

Unions also came under fire at the point of production as capital became more aggressive in pursuit of its aims of restructuring employment and the work process. In many countries, the failure of industrial strategy revealed the weakness of political alliances. And in these countries, union movements found it increasingly difficult to protect working conditions and job security, harder to organize the fragmenting working class, and impossible to resist the erosion of the full-time job. They were becoming, in short, the defensive representatives of a shrinking labour aristocracy. Alternative social agendas were put on the back burner as the unions struggled simply to maintain the status quo.

How did union movements in developed countries face the failure of traditional strategies?[2] Across the very different national situations, by the mid-1980s three interpretations had crystallized.

First, in countries such as Austria, Australia, and the Scandinavian nations, union peak organizations sought to create or to intensify corporatist relationships in order to extend their influence over economic management. They chose to magnify the control of the political over the economic or to shift the resolution of private economic problems to the public arena.

Second, following political or economic defeat of national and symbolic significance, union peak organizations in countries such as the United States, Great Britain, or France retreated into fragmentation and depoliticization, leaving the task of strategic defence to their national affiliates or even to regional groupings. One result was the weakening of the peak council's organization and political authority. Another was the breakdown of coherent national policy toward the capital offensive, so that division and contradiction came to characterize union response.

There was also a third pattern. Some national union centres went through a period of strategic paralysis: They simply continued doing what they had always done, regardless of the fact that it no longer worked. Strategic paralysis, however, proved to be a transitional state, and was often superseded by a policy of defensive accommodation. In defensive accommodation, union peak councils, looking toward the U.S. union experience and fearing that internal division might result from firm opposition to capital's offensive, came to make their peace with the new employer strategies. These centrals took as their own, and proposed to members, programs that would not serve the movement's interests in the long run but that did, in the short run, stave off industrial confrontation (with presumed defeat) and the weakening of the union central's capacity for mobilization and the maintenance of internal cohesion. Despite its recent glamourous history of mass militancy, the Quebec labour movement falls into this third category.

In the 1960 and 1970s the Quebec labour movement articulated the boldest vision of unionism as a socially and individually emancipating force that North America had seen in a generation. Why did this movement fail so miserably to imbue its vision with a viable political strategy? Since that failure is a class, a societal, and, for many of us, a personal loss, I do not feel that I have final explanations. I will, however, argue that the roots of the Quebec union movement's failure to adapt, survive, and take a leading role in the resolution of the double crisis of the 1980s are to be traced to the ideological and structural history of the movement, including its heritage of union pluralism, historic failure to recognize the importance of politics, internal divisions, and divided loyalties. At many, if not most, critical historical junctures in Quebec life, national or Québécois identity has taken primacy over class identity, and at these same junctures the Quebec union movement has hesitated and then retreated from taking leadership in the nationalist movement (Leborgne 1976). That leadership might have permitted the unions to imbue nationalism, which has been Quebec's chief source of internal cohesion since the nineteenth century, with a working-class agenda.

In order to deal with these rather large questions, this chapter is divided into three parts. The first section looks at the historical roots of today's defensive accommodation. The second explores the manner in which the unions' approach to politics allowed other classes to determine the shape of social relations at three critical junctures: between 1972 and 1976 when the nationalist Parti Québécois (PQ) was emerging on the provincial scene; 1981–83, when the PQ, then the governing party of the province, sought a way out of the economic crisis at the expense of its public-sector workers; and finally in 1988, when the crucial national election focussed on the issue of the free trade deal with the United States. The final section sketches the several forms of defensive accommodation and their possible impact on future union action.

The Roots of Defensive Accommodation

Quebec, whose population is 82 percent francophone, sees itself and is seen as a separate society, distinguished from the rest of Canada by language, culture, and its status as an internal colony. The union movement is also assumed to be a separate entity, representing an isolated and doubly exploited francophone working class. The "apartness" of Quebec civil society is part reality, part illusion, and part conscious political choice. Its historical roots go back to the eighteenth century. Since then the sense of separateness has been reinforced, reinterpreted, and institutionalized by successive Quebec nationalist movements, by British colonial policy and the federal government's economic development strategies, by the Catholic church and the francophone bourgeoisie, by successive provincial governments, and by political and economic forces within the rest of Canada whose interest the continued internal colonization of Quebec has served. In contemporary terms, the decentralization of social and political life has also served to legitimate Quebec's apartness. Roughly 80 percent of Canadian jobs are regulated by the diverse provincial labour codes, while only 20 percent fall under federal jurisdiction. The Quebec provincial government also collects its own taxes and runs its own medical and education systems.

Francophone Quebec is webbed by a dense network of institutions, from trade unions through state-supported Catholic schools to the cooperative banks. This network was the historic creation of the Catholic church, whose alliances with conservative fractions of the English-Canadian bourgeoisie throughout the eighteenth and nineteenth centuries kept Catholic francophones distant from the centres of Canadian economic power and put the church in a position of unparalleled authority in defining the worldview and civil society of French-speaking Québécois. The church imbued the network of francophone institutions with a passivity toward politics and a nationalism whose content changed as the organization of Canadian capitalism evolved. In the years following World War I, the church used its pivotal role to marginalize all unions that were not created by it, that accepted non-Catholics as members on equal footing with Catholics, or that maintained links with the secular (international) unions of the day.[3] The separate Catholic labour movement that emerged as an important pole in the 1920s articulated an ideology of social corporatism (in the interwar European sense of the term) in explicit opposition to the craft-based business unionism of the international unions that had been established in Quebec since the 1890s. Although today the ideology of the formerly Catholic labour centrals, the Confédération des syndicats nationaux (CSN) and the Centrale de l'enseignement du Québec (CEQ), has changed fundamentally, that heritage of according a greater authenticity to unions created by the church (supposedly more purely Québécois) and thus legitimating union pluralism and rivalry remains an important factor in union action in the political arena.

Toward the end of the 1950s, a late-breaking wave of societywide modernization swept Quebec, dislodging the church and secularizing most areas of community life. In the heady years of rapid change that followed, a period known as the Quiet Revolution (1960–1966), the church withdrew from its overt role in most areas of civil society except education, leaving the newly reinforced provincial state as the new arbiter of social life. "Progressive statism" in combination with a moderate and diffuse nationalism defined the mainstream mode of modernization in the 1960s. It attracted wide social support until, in the radicalizing days following 1968, neo-nationalism split into two streams. Its dominant current—a welfare capitalism that was more concerned with cultural sovereignty for Quebec than with the difficult problems of external economic dependence on the United States—went on to take root in the Parti Québécois. Neo-nationalism's minority current was an eclectic mixture of Marxist theories of underdevelopment, national liberation, and a profound distrust of state power. This latter-day syndicalism took root in the community groups and in the union movement.

The social movement of the Quiet Revolution and of the more radical years that followed was composed of, and led by, that complex web of community groups and unions that had been created by the church in the interwar years. The church heritage, the impact of the latter's withdrawal, and the nature of the civil society that crystallized in its wake together left a lasting mark on the worldview and strategies of these community institutions in the 1960s and 1970s. Between the Quiet Revolution and the watershed years of 1972–76, four features marked the common elements that the diverse community movements retained from the past: the sense of social movement, or crusade; the tendency to seek leadership within the professional stratum of the francophone bourgeoisie, regardless of the class basis of those to be represented; the use of a now-radicalized nationalism as a powerful source of social cohesion; and an ongoing inability to engage in effective politics. The combination produced a syndicalism that permitted mass mobilization and a heady sense of confronting capitalism at its source during prosperous economic times, but became a dangerous dead hand when economic recession indicated the need to maximize and diversify influence in all the political and social arenas of power.

With the rise of inflation and unemployment in the 1970s, the continuing reality of Quebec's economic integration and economic dependence on both Canada and the United States reasserted itself as a central factor in Quebec political life, forcing all the community organizations, including the unions, to rethink their objectives, their opponents, and their modes of action. The unions and the community groups, which had shared a sense of movement and a *projet de société*, began to diverge.

From the mid-1970s on, the *groupes populaires* moved away from nationalism. More vulnerable than the unions, the *groupes populaires* came to see the government not as an abstract whole, or as an enemy, but as a terrain on which the canny and quick community organization could gain much-needed financial resources, technical know-how, and administrative support. In the difficult years since the mid-1970s, this strategy allowed many of these groups—in community housing, debt counselling, women's organizing, and consumer cooperatives—to survive. Only a tiny minority of the groups who continued to practise the maximalist syndicalism of the 1960s and early 1970s are still around to tell the tale.

In contrast, the Quebec labour movement was not as quick to adjust its mode of action to the deepening economic difficulties and the new political realities of the mid-1970s—a victim, perhaps, of the ongoing tension between the will to separateness and the reality of integration that is the manifestation of Quebec's troubled place within Canada. That tension has run like an unstable fault through the core of Quebec labour history in the twentieth century. Its record warrants a brief review.

In the years immediately following World War I, the tension between autonomy and integration in a rapidly industrializing, externally dependent Quebec led the young labour movement to divide into two competing union peak organizations, fragmented along religious lines. The Trades and Labour Congress (TLC) regrouped the Quebec unions affiliated to internationals that formed the American Federation of Labor. In Quebec, as in the United States and the rest of Canada, their ideology was that of Samuel Gompers, in which the only political action a solid union needed was occasional, defensive, nonpartisan lobbying. During the interwar years, TLC officials lobbied little in Quebec and played no organized role in elections. Instead, they restricted their activities to the purely economic domain, leading nearly all the strikes that occurred during that time. The economic militancy of the TLC, however relative, thus stood in contrast to its political dormancy.

The Confédération des travailleurs catholiques du Canada (CTCC) was created under the church's aegis in 1921 explicitly to counter the TLC influence and the "peril of bolshevism." The social corporatism of the

CTCC was part of a more comprehensive church strategy for confronting the danger that industrialization posed to traditional Catholic society. In union terms, this strategy meant holding the union to limited negotiations with employers in order to ensure that workers received "decent" family wages and that their working conditions recognized their dignity. Social corporatism also meant that unions were to be sectoral interest groups, charged with the protection of only one area of the worker's life. It meant recognizing the legitimacy of private profit and the hegemony of the employer, and it meant political passivity. But this political passivity was of a complex sort. From its inception, the CTCC had indulged in modest statism: It lobbied for the kind of legislation that would redress in the political domain the unions' extreme weakness in the economic. Its social corporatism was based on the principle that a union could petition the state for needed protection yet was not to organize collective pressure on the state to advance the union's own agenda. Indeed, the union might act as the state's conscience in economic matters, but it was not its role to articulate a political program. Much later, in the 1960s, this refusal to enter the electoral arena in any form lost its servile quality and was reinterpreted as syndicalism.

By the 1940s the two streams of corporatist and Gomperist unionism had been joined by a third, the social democratic unionism espoused by the CIO unions in the United States. These, in turn, came to organize in Quebec after their U.S. base was secured. Drawing their strength from heavy industry and textiles, by the mid-1950s the Quebec affiliates of the Canadian Congress of Labour had established a reputation for unparalleled militancy. In 1954–55 they advocated the founding of a social democratic party, thereby clearly drawing the lines between their orientation to politics and that of their two rivals, both of which, albeit for different reasons, abstained from electoral politics (Denis 1979: 179).

In 1955 Gomperism and social democratic unionism joined in the United States to form the AFL-CIO. In the new central the business unionism of the craft unions was then and remains today the preeminent orientation. In 1956 the merger forming the Canadian Labour Congress allowed the social democratic orientation associated with the big industrial unions to predominate in Canada (see Robinson, in this volume). One year later, the Quebec affiliates of the two streams merged to form the Fédération des travailleurs du Québec (FTQ). In the FTQ the social democratic tradition also came to dominate, but it did not surface as one of the two major modes for union political action until well into the 1970s.

The Quiet Revolution marked the beginning of the Quebec equivalent of the postwar deal. At this time, the Quebec economy was entering its second decade of unbroken growth. Investment from the United States, which had stimulated this growth, had two pertinent results. First, the Quebec state was given the financial margin of manoeuvre to accomplish the modernization that had been delayed and was now taking on all the allure of a national social project. Second, foreign investment remained so central to growth in all economic sectors that sooner or later any policy of modernization would have to come to terms with the problem of external dependence. The Liberal party, for decades in the wilderness of opposition, became the vehicle for this pragmatic ideology of modernization. Holding provincial office between 1960 and 1966, the Liberals presided over the impressive expansion of state employment, as the government took over medical and educational services formerly run by the church, created a social service network, professionalized the civil service, and multiplied the number of Crown corporations.

The growth of the state in turn triggered important shifts in the composition of the labour force. Between 1961 and 1969, direct and indirect public-sector employment grew by 35 percent (see Hébert in this volume). The rapid entry into the labour force of tertiary-sector workers had a significant impact on the unions. Roughly 175,000 new unionists from the public and parapublic sectors entered the ranks of organized labour between 1960 and 1970. By 1970, public employees had come to represent over one-third of all union members in the province. Their presence, however, was not evenly felt within the labour movement.

By the mid-1960s the Quebec union movement was divided among three peak organizations. The CTCC secularized and changed its name to the CSN. During the 1960s it enjoyed a close, unstructured alliance with the governing Liberal party and was perceived as the natural leader of the Québécois working class. Its membership rose from 80,075 in 1960 to 205,783 in 1970. By the latter date, the CSN had been transformed (in reality, if not in its own acceptance of that reality) into a service-sector peak organization (Gauthier 1972).

The FTQ fared less well during the Quiet Revolution, for it lacked the structural freedom, the financial resources, and the social identity as authentically Québécois that were necessary to operate as a central in its own right (Bernard 1969). It suffered from the preferential relationship between the CSN and the Liberals and from the conflicting nationalism that had come to characterize Quebec politics by the end of the 1960s. Its membership did not grow as rapidly as did the CSN's. Its share of the new public-sector employees was limited in the main to blue-collar workers in the subcentral levels of government. The FTQ remained the principal representative of blue-collar workers employed in sectors dominated by multinational capital. Given the comprehensive cultural and political leadership that the CSN exercised over the union movement during the 1960s, it would have been difficult to predict that the FTQ would soon articulate its own political strategy. In the 1960s the FTQ was clearly, though defensively, influenced by the CSN in the political arena.

It was the CEQ that benefited most dramatically from the Quiet Revolution. The rapid expansion of public education, coupled with a government-granted right to the obligatory membership of all teachers in the Catholic school system, pushed membership from 12,000 in 1959 to 60,000 in 1968 (Gauthier 1972). This 500 percent leap occasioned a transformation of power relations within the education sector, while the modernization of education triggered the evolution of the CEQ membership from a professional to a trade-union consciousness.

Thus, one may speak of a process of union modernization during the Quiet Revolution, effected within the context of an embracing national project. Yet the union centrals, particularly the CSN and CEQ, could not fail to recognize that the expansion of the state—in numbers, power, and arenas of intervention—made the politicization of union industrial policy unavoidable. When strike after strike pitted CEQ and CSN members against the Liberal government, the centrals found themselves torn between collaboration in the national project and rejection of its implications for the new working class. In a very real way, the national question paralysed the unions' capacity for political intervention during the Quiet Revolution. A progressive nationalist regime in power had found it easy to set the unions to competing among themselves for favours. The idea of autonomous union political action was not only difficult but somehow disloyal.

In 1966, however, the Liberals were defeated, and under the less than benign auspices of their conservative successors, the unions' interpretation of nationalism was radicalized, polarized, and took new form as syndicalism. In the late 1960s and early 1970s, that ideology was based on a certain number of postulates. First, the union movement came to see itself as the authentic and only representative of all the interests of the working class, an odd modernization of the sense of mission that had characterized Catholic labour ideology in its heyday. Second, the *groupes populaires* were meant to position themselves under the unions' wing. Third, the unions came to see themselves as a substitute for a revolutionary party, regrouping the broad coalition of community forces and challenging the power of the state through mass education, mass mobilization, and extraparliamentary confrontation. State power was to be challenged from outside, and unions were neither to compromise themselves by attempting to lobby within the system nor to corrupt their objectives of sweeping social transformation by consenting to share in the exercise of governance. There was, by definition, no political party that could be elected with which a union could ally itself without betraying its mission.

Strong dreams, these, and worthy of the maximalist days of post-1968. The problem was that although the union centrals were able to mobilize noteworthy street confrontations with the state between 1968 and 1972, mass mobilization neither produced concrete results in collective bargaining nor permitted the long-term implementation of the unions' own agenda for social change. At best, during their syndicalist phase, the unions were able to block or to modify offensive legislation or to up the ante sufficiently in private-sector industrial conflict so that the state had to step in. Yet the unions' own visions of an alternative society never came near to being implemented.

1972–1983: Critical Junctures
for Quebec Unions

There are times in the lives of trade unions when the decisions that need to be taken are particularly laden with consequence. These critical historical junctures make or break the union, determine its orientations for the middle distance, decide how much faith the members will continue to invest in it, and determine its future alliances and agenda. The period of 1972 to 1976 marked one such juncture for the Quebec union movement. Stagflation and the refinement of a flexible, effective government strategy for dealing with labour relations in the public sector came together to push the union movement to test the limits of what syndicalism could achieve.

By 1972, the Liberal party had split into two camps. The faction that retained the party name sought to continue the province's economic growth by intensifying its links with U.S. capital. It was reelected in 1970. The nationalist faction, which sought to continue the Quiet Revolution by enlarging the financial autonomy of the Quebec state from Ottawa, had quit the Liberal party in 1967 to form the Parti Québécois (PQ) one year later. Throughout the early 1970s the PQ's unclear but seductive relationship to the working class would expose labour's paralysing dilemma: to embark on or to eschew a labourist relationship with the PQ?

From 1967 onward, a succession of provincial governments had defined the public sector as the pivot of economic growth, and its wage settlements came to be the barometer by which the private sector measured what it would have to concede. At the same time, successive provincial governments refined a standardized wage policy for the public and parapublic sectors and erected an imposing network of bureaucratic structures to handle negotiations with the unions concerned. Given this context, it is not surprising that the public employees emerged as the largest and most internally cohesive bloc within the labour movement, present, but in unequal proportions, within all three centrals. In a very real way these workers symbolized the new working class, its anticapitalism, and the explosion of secular and individualistic aspirations unleashed by the Quiet Revolution. That solipsism would prove a dangerous illusion later in 1972 when private-sector workers rebelled against their marginalization in the articulation of union strategy (Ethier and Piotte 1975: 65–66).

The government's standardized wage policy had stimulated a parallel movement toward centralization within the unions. In 1971 they formed a Common Front, linking all three centrals, to bargain with the government. This bargaining apparatus created a de facto alternative structure to the union centrals themselves, pushing a wedge between private-sector and public-sector workers organized into the same central. In the FTQ, since only about 10 percent of the membership was involved, the link to public-sector unions in other centrals did not pose a serious organizational problem. Since all of the CEQ's membership was employed in the public sector, the problem did not arise there either. In the CSN, however, where approximately 40 percent of the members were employed in the public sector, the tension exploded between the (organizationally fragmented) interests of private-sector and public-sector workers linked into a Common Front structure that was absorbing more and more of the central's resources and attention. The catalyst was a strike.

In the spring of 1972, Common Front negotiations with the government broke down. The 210,000 members of the Common Front went on strike, ignoring court injunctions. The strike was seen as a general strike and was joined by a surprising array of private-sector and even federal employees. In its brief existence it included such actions as the capturing of radio stations in certain small cities and broadcasting union news, closing the roads to outlying communities, shutting down major parts of Quebec, and generally paralysing economic life. This spontaneous brush fire of worker rebellion stimulated unreal hopes: syndicalist dreams of the worker uprising that would topple the state in one convulsive heave. The strike, however, was broken by back-to-work legislation, supported by the PQ as well as by the traditional parties. Soon thereafter, the presidents of the three centrals were condemned for leading the "illegal" walkouts and sent to jail.

It would be difficult to overestimate the impact of the 1972 strike on subsequent union strategies. In light of its failure, the centrals drew two very different conclusions. Watching the supposedly pro-union PQ vote to break the strike, the CSN and the CEQ concluded that any alliance with a political party could only lead to the loss of union autonomy and radicalism. Syndicalism continued to dominate their strategies. The FTQ, however, drew a different lesson from 1972 and looked to closer partisan ties, notably with the PQ.

The CSN paid the highest price for its continued attachment to a strategy whose limits had been reached during the strike. Immediately following the breaking of the strike it suffered the secession of approximately 60,000 of its members, one-fourth of its total membership. Some 30,000 of these secessionists, grouped in the failing manufacturing industries such as textiles, footwear, and clothing, left in protest over what they saw as their "poor relation" status within the central and the Marxist orientation of the leadership.[4] The dissidents went on to form the Confédération des syndicats démocratiques (CSD), which continues to exist on the margins, a kind of pariah in the labour movement. The other 30,000 members seceded from the Civil Servants Federation of the CSN.[5] In the ten years following 1972, the CSN lost the majority of its white-collar and professional public-sector employees as well as almost all of its manufacturing sector. It became a peak organization representing blue-collar public employees, mainly in the health sector. The disquieting growth of independent unions in Quebec—now between 25 and 30 percent of the total—springs from this time and specifically from the hemorrhaging of the CSN.

For the FTQ, the strike, coupled with the damage that the CSN inflicted on it through raiding immediately thereafter,[6] revealed the dangers of interunion collaboration and the limits of romantic syndicalism. Links with the PQ seemed to offer the possibility of legislative protection against raiding and an opportunity for ameliorating labour legislation in other areas such as health and safety and minimum wages. Drawing from its dormant social-union tradition, the FTQ began to think in terms of "friendly" or "unfriendly" governments and preferred to do business with a friendly party in power, especially if that party were prepared to recognize some responsibility toward it.

The links that the FTQ developed with the PQ during the 1972–76 period were to prove crucial in orienting labour's political action for the next fifteen years. FTQ members (as, for that matter, CSN and CEQ members) voted massively for the PQ, staffed its political machine, and financed its campaigns. Yet the FTQ did not seek to transform the PQ into a labour party. It was content to play the role that the old CIO unions had chosen for themselves within the Democratic party in the United States, the role of one privileged interest group among many. It assumed that it could combine fervent participation in a nationalist party, whose objectives were defined by its bourgeois leadership, with the pursuit of social democratic goals. The FTQ gained much from that inside relationship during the PQ's nine years in office (see Tanguay, in this volume). It did not, however, gain political power. In the early eighties, it was to learn that the PQ entertained no sense of responsibility to the union movement and would, in a pinch, appeal to union members over the heads of their union organizations. The FTQ's nationalist and social democratic commitments had been set on a collision course.

Thus, when the economic recession hit with full force at the beginning of the 1980s, the Quebec union movement had separated into two streams. The CSN and the CEQ held on to their syndicalism long after this strategy had proved incapable of bringing them concrete gains. The FTQ returned to its social democratic heritage but thought it possible to combine social democracy with bourgeois nationalism without seeking control of the political party that was to be its vehicle.

In 1982, after losing a referendum to loosen Quebec's ties to Canada, the PQ awoke to the economic crisis. Its first reaction was neither to try to stem the loss of jobs in the manufacturing sector (which had been continuing apace since 1979) nor to halt the abrupt rise in unemployment (then at 14 percent), but rather to deal with the state's deficit.

The PQ government proposed to 350,000 public-sector employees that they voluntarily accept wage cuts of as much as 20 percent. When the Common Front refused, the government responded by playing the health sector off against education, the CSN against the CEQ. Late in 1982, the public sector lost the right to strike by a single legislative stroke. Early in 1983, the teachers went on strike in violation of the law but were ordered back to work in a bill that imposed the terms of "agreement." Bill 111 also proposed the loss of three years' seniority for every day on illegal strike, made it illegal to resign or to use any other pressure tactics until the collective agreement had expired three years hence, threatened decertification of rebel unions, and made it illegal for teachers to appeal to the Charter of Human Rights against this law. In Quebec's National Assembly, no one spoke for the unions. Out on a limb alone, unsupported by the CSN's health workers, who had concluded a separate agreement, and unable to stir the FTQ, which had few members in the public sector, the CEQ went back to work. Thus ended the Common Front and the dream of a radically transformative unionism.

It might be argued that syndicalism should have been abandoned after 1972, but what good had the FTQ's arrangement with the PQ done for its members? It might also be argued that when in the early 1970s the unions decided to allow the avowedly bourgeois nationalist PQ to take undisputed leadership of Quebec's national project, they were entering dangerous terrain. All three centrals allowed the PQ to enter into competition with them for the militant commitment of their members: nationalism, rather than working-class politics, became the touchstone. Both the party and the unions saw themselves as the sole respresentatives of the population. The one defined the population as the working class, the other as "the people," but the end result was the same. By failing to separate at least some part of their project from the PQ's program, by refusing to enter into competition with the PQ for the definition of nationalism, and by actively encouraging or passively allowing their members to commit themselves first to the party, the unions left themselves ill protected when the PQ turned against them.

It took the unequivocal defeat of 1983, with the destruction of interunion collaboration in the public sector, and the crushing of the culture of union militancy that had so distinguished the CSN and the CEQ from their North American counterparts to force these centrals to reexamine their strategies. The result has been defensive accommodation, a strategy that each of the centrals in its own way applied to the third critical juncture, the 1988 Canadian election, which focussed on the Free Trade Agreement with the United States.

Patterns of Defensive Accommodation

The years immediately following the destruction of the Common Front were terrible ones for the Quebec labour movement. They were years marked by impotence, bitterness, a turning against each other, and a turning inward. In retrospect, it is easy to argue that following the defeat, the centrals first needed to heal their wounds and regain self-confidence. Then they needed to give priority to finding new methods of collaboration, even if this meant subordinating the needs of a particular central or a sector to the good of the whole. Further, the Quebec centrals needed some symbolic victories, which meant good strategy and realizable goals. They also needed to forge a political voice, a party on which they could rely.

None of these things was done, with the partial exception of the FTQ, which, least damaged by the defeat, responded to the economic crisis rather than to the government. Its affiliated unions set in train bold schemes of new organizing and established the Solidarity Fund (an investment scheme financed by workers' contributions). Like the CSN and the CEQ, the FTQ could no longer enthusiastically support the PQ, but its faith in arms-length labourism did not diminish. It chose not to support the PQ in the 1985 provincial election and, with nationalism seemingly on the wane, sought another party to influence. When the 1988 Canadian federal election, which turned on the free trade deal with the United States, was announced, the FTQ announced that it would support the NDP. The NDP, long linked to the CLC in a weak, labourist alliance, saw the possibility of at long last gaining a foothold in Quebec (see Bernard, in this volume). Alone of all the major Canadian parties, the NDP had never elected a member from Quebec.

The CSN and the CEQ turned inward. When the next round of negotiations in the public sector occurred (1985), it was clear that there would be no more Common Fronts. Worse, legislative changes in the structure of public-sector negotiations weakened the centrals' ability to coordinate negotiations even for their own affiliates. As once governments had used centralized wage policy to push the unions on the defensive, now the PQ was prepared to use decentralization to destroy solidarity—where the unions had not already destroyed it themselves. Finally, militancy became a thing of the past. During the lead-up to the 1985 round, it was openly stated in the CEQ that the strike was *dépassé*, not a weapon anyone was prepared to use. Thus it is not surprising that the round of negotiations finished with a resounding union failure.

Nor was there much progress on the political front. Within the CSN and the CEQ, the Left continued to advocate union political autonomy. Even a one-time election campaign alliance with a friendly political party would be the kiss of death. Of course, negative politics could still be practised without jeopardizing organizational purity. Thus in the 1985 provincial elections, the CEQ and the CSN directed their members to vote against the PQ, contributing to the party's defeat. It was only after the 1985 round that the CSN and the CEQ—separately and in increasing rivalry—began to crystallize their respective strategies for the postcrisis social order.

For the CEQ, this was a three-pronged project: new organizing, substitution of professional identity for class identity, and a continued faith in electoral abstention. First, the CEQ sought to expand the central, to draw into it members from outside the education sector, and to transform it into a central for all public-sector workers. Here it scored some measure of success, growing at the rate of 13 and 11 percent respectively in 1986 and 1987. Second, it placed renewed emphasis on the role of teaching as a profession in order to counteract the bitter taste of defeat that the teachers, as trade unionists, had suffered in 1983. The professionalization of union values, however, fit awkwardly with its first strategy of encouraging the entry of thousands of nonprofessional public-sector workers into the CEQ. Finally, the CEQ continued to take its distance from party politics, this time not from syndicalist arrogance but from professional neutrality. This meant that in the 1988 Canadian election, when many CEQ members were becoming involved with the NDP to defeat the free trade deal, the central was only prepared to recommend negative voting.

The CSN, too, turned inward, but unevenly, as befits its more heterogeneous membership. In the private sector it supported involvement in quality circles, the development of Japanese-style consultative structures on the enterprise or plant level, and collaboration with employers over concessions. It looked at the draining away of its membership and sought to appropriate managerial strategies of union domestication before these were forced on it. Its approach, however, was uneven. It remained willing to support isolated strikes, often courageous ones where there was little chance of winning. As for the larger issues such as unemployment, inflation, and foreign takeover, the CSN's strategy consisted of the presentation of briefs to government and press conferences, the very stuff of pressure-group politics.

In the 1988 election, the CSN executive, like the CEQ's, recommended negative voting and went to considerable lengths to defeat the pro-NDP forces within its own ranks. Under these circumstances, it is not surprising that the NDP, despite three years of serious organizing in Quebec, proved again unable to elect a single member of Parliament.[7]

In Quebec, then, there are three separate patterns of defensive accommodation, three ways in which the peak organizations of Quebec labour, faced with the exhaustion of both syndicalism and the weakest of labourism, sought to move beyond a long period of paralysis and stagnation. Perhaps the best that can be said for these new strategies is that they are likely to stimulate new organizing and to ensure organizational survival. The worst is that they represent the absolute failure of labour's faith in the uses of politics. That failure, in turn, reveals the central, paralysing role that nationalism has played in labour ideology.

Quebec unions have historically been pivotal and particularly vulnerable actors in the shadow dance of separateness and dependence that defines the relationship of Quebec to Canada. The tension thus created has run like a fault line through Quebec labour history in the twentieth century. Between 1900 and World War II it led to the fragmentation of working-class organization into competing union peak organizations, divided along religious lines. Between 1921 and the present, it created a complex and unstable structure of interunion rivalry that has repeatedly hamstrung effective working-class influence over state policy. From the 1960s to the 1980s, the tension between separateness and dependence fused into an intense Québécois nationalism within the unions, but one that submitted itself, by omission and commission, to the leadership of a party that did not have a trade-union agenda in mind. It allowed for the forging of a dynamic rank-and-file militancy that transformed unions into social movements and their members into a temporarily self-aware working class. But it did not permit the fusion of nationalist and working-class agendas under a clear union leadership.

Notes

1. The original version of this chapter was presented to the Canadian-Australian Labour History Conference, Sydney, Australia, December 1988.

2. There is a substantial literature on this topic, but one of the most helpful collections is the two volumes that came out of the Harvard Center for European Studies. See Lange, Ross, and Vanicelli (1982) and Gourevitch et al. (1984).

3. Jacques Rouillard has written extensively on the Catholic labour movement in Quebec. In English, see Rouillard (1987).

4. The centrals all published orientation documents during 1971–72 that presented a Marxist analysis of dependence, class, and national domination to their members. *Ne comptons que sur nos propres moyens* (We Can Only Count on Ourselves), for example, was put out by the CSN and 100,000 copies were distributed to the membership. *L'Ecole au service de la classe dominante* was the CEQ's contribution, while the FTQ published *L'Etat rouage de notre exploitation*.

5. At the plenary of the CSN congress in Quebec in June 1972, the president of the Civil Servants Federation expressed his belief that its white-collar and professional members could get a better deal for themselves if they were not aligned to a central like the CSN.

6. After the defeat of the Common Front strike, the CSN sought to compensate for its losses by raiding the FTQ, particularly in the construction industry. Among other tactics, the CSN called for a government inquiry into corruption in the FTQ construction unions.

7. This gap was finally filled by a by-election victory in 1989. The NDP gained one seat in Quebec.

References

Bernard, Paul. 1969. *Structures et pouvoirs de la F.T.Q.*, Ottawa: Queens Printer.
Denis, Roch. 1979. *Luttes de classes et question nationale au Québec*, Montreal: Les Presses Socialistes Internationales.

Ethier, Diane, and Jean-Marc Piotte. 1975. *Les travailleurs contre l'Etat bourgeois*, Montreal: l'Aurore.

Gauthier, Henri. 1972. "La syndicalisation au Quebec," *Travail Québec*, Quebec: Government Printers.

Gourevitch, Peter, Andrew Martin, George Ross, Christopher Allen, Stephen Bornstein, and Andrei Markovits. 1984. *Unions and Economic Crisis: Britain, West Germany, and Sweden*, London: Allen and Unwin.

Lange, Peter, George Ross, and Maurizio Vanicelli. 1982. *Unions, Change, and Crisis: French and Italian Union Strategy and the Political Economy, 1945–1980*, London: Allen and Unwin.

Leborgne, Louis. 1976. *La C.S.N. et la question nationale*, Montreal: Editions Albert St-Martin.

Lipsig-Mummé, Carla. 1987. "The Web of Dependence: Quebec Unions in Politics before 1976." In Michael Biehels, *Quebec since 1945*, Toronto: Copp Clark.

Rouillard, Jacques. 1987. "Major Changes in the Confédération des travailleurs catholiques du Canada, 1940–1960." In Michael Biehels, *Quebec since 1945*, Toronto: Copp Clark.

About the Contributors

ELAINE BERNARD is executive director of the Trade Union Program at Harvard University and former director of the Labour Program at Simon Fraser University. Recent publications include "Labour and the Environment: A Look at BC's 'War in the Woods'"; "The Politics of Canada's Health Care System"; and "Labor and Politics in the U.S. and Canada." In addition to her academic work, for many years Bernard sat on the Executive of the British Columbia New Democratic Party.

PETER G. BRUCE is assistant professor of political science at the College of the Holy Cross, Worcester, Mass. Bruce has written on parties, state structures, and labor law in North America. His publications include the often-cited "Political Parties and Labor Legislation in Canada and the U.S.," *Industrial Relations* (1989).

RICHARD FREEMAN is Herbert Ascherman Professor of Economics at Harvard University and program director for labor studies at the National Bureau of Economic Research. He is author of numerous books and articles on unions and labor markets. In addition to the widely cited *What Do Unions Do?* (with J. Medoff), these include *Immigration and the Work Force: Economic Consequences for the United States and Source Areas* (edited with G. Borjas) and *Capitalism and Generosity*.

GÉRARD HÉBERT is professor of industrial relations at the Université de Montréal. He has published many books and articles on unions and collective bargaining in Canada and Quebec. Professor Hébert has been very active in his professional capacity, serving as a member of numerous policy-orientated research committees.

STEPHEN HERZENBERG is a labor economist at the Bureau of International Labor Affairs, U.S. Department of Labor. He has written on labor and adjustment in the North American auto industry, including "Automation and Global Production" (with H. Shaiken), and on the

broader issue of labor rights in the global economy. Herzenberg partici-
pated in the writing of the recent congressional study of U.S.-Mexican
economic integration.

JANE JENSON is professor of political science at Carleton University.
She is the author of numerous books and articles on Canadian politics as
well as historical-comparative work on the women's movement in Europe and North America. Recent coauthored volumes include *Crisis,
Challenge, and Change: Party and Class in Canada Revisited*; *Absent Mandate: Interpreting Change in Canadian Politics*; and *The Politics of Abortion*.

CARLA LIPSIG-MUMMÉ is professor of labour studies and director of
the Center for Research on Work and Society at York University. In
addition to the publication of numerous articles on Quebec unions, Lipsig-Mummé has long been committed to building links between union
and university researchers in Quebec, Canada, and Australia.

RIANNE MAHON is a professor at the School of Public Administration,
Carleton University. She is the author of *The Politics of Industrial Restruc-
turing: Canadian Textiles*. Recent articles include "From Solidaristic
Wages to Solidaristic Work: A Post-Fordist Historic Compromise for
Sweden?" and "Post-Fordism, Canada and the FTA: Some Issues for
Labour."

NOAH MELTZ is professor of economics and industrial relations and
principal of Woodsworth College at the University of Toronto. His recently published books include *Human Resource Management in Canada*
(with Thomas Stone), *The State of the Art in Industrial Relations* (with G.
Hébert and H. C. Jain), and *Unemployment: International Perspectives*
(with M. Gunderson and S. Ostry). He has also published numerous
articles on labor markets and industrial relations.

RUTH MILKMAN is associate professor of sociology and women's
studies at UCLA. She has written widely on labor and workplace issues.
Her publications include *Japan's California Factories: Labor Relations and
Economic Globalization* and *Gender at Work: The Dynamics of Job Segregation by Sex during World War II*, awarded the Joan Kelly Memorial Prize
in Women's History by the American Historical Association.

IAN ROBINSON completed his doctoral dissertation, "Organizing Labour: Explaining Canada-U.S. Union Density Divergence, 1963–1986," at Yale in 1990. In addition to his comparative work on unions in North America, he has written on Canadian constitutional questions, including *State, Society, and the Development of Canadian Federalism*, coauthored by R. Simeon. In 1991–92 he worked for the government of Ontario. Robinson is now on a postdoctoral fellowship to study the politics of continental integration in the European Community and North America.

JOEL ROGERS is professor of law, political science, and sociology at the University of Wisconsin, Madison. He has written widely on democratic theory and American politics and public policy. His books include *Right Turn: The Decline of the Democrats and the Future of American Politics* (with Thomas Ferguson) and *On Democracy* (with Joshua Cohen). Rogers serves as a consultant to the Labor and Human Resources Committee of the U.S. Senate.

CÉLINE SAINT-PIERRE is professor of sociology and academic vice-rector at the Université du Québec à Montréal. She has published numerous articles on women's work and the transformation of work in the service sector. Saint-Pierre is coauthor of *The History of the Labour Movement in Quebec* and coeditor of *Les Stratégies de reprise*.

DONALD SWARTZ is associate professor at the School of Public Administration, Carleton University. He is author of several articles on labor-related issues and is coauthor of *The Assault on Trade Union Freedoms: From Consent to Coercion Revisited*

A. BRIAN TANGUAY is assistant professor of political science at Wilfred Laurier University. He has coedited (with Alain-G. Gagnon) *Canadian Parties in Transition* and *Democracy with Justice: Essays in Honour of Khayyam Zev Paltiel*.

RICHARD VALELLY is associate professor of political science at the Massachusetts Institute of Technology and Swarthmore College. He is author of *Radicalism in the States: The Minnesota Farmer-Labor Party and the American Political Economy* and articles on voting behavior, parties, and social movements.

DONALD M. WELLS is assistant professor of political science and labour studies at McMaster University. In addition to journal articles on labor and on the political economy of military production, Wells has published *Empty Promises: Quality of Working Life Programs and the Labor Movement* and *Soft Sell: "Quality of Working Life" Programs and the Productivity Race.*

JULIE WHITE is an independent researcher based in Ottawa. Her most recent book is *Mail and Female: Women and the Canadian Union of Postal Workers.* She is currently working on a book on women and unions in Canada that will extend the analysis developed in earlier publications on women, work, and unions.

CHARLOTTE A. B. YATES is assistant professor of political science and labour studies at McMaster University. She has published several articles on the autoworkers in Canada and, more broadly, unions in politics. Recent publications include "Managing versus Mobilizing Discontent: American and Canadian Autoworkers' Response to Capitalist Restructuring and Membership Discontent," in *Bargaining for Change: Union Politics in Europe and North America,* and "Labour and Lobbying: A Political Economy Approach," in *Policy Communities and Public Policy in Canada.*